M000223312

MASTER OF THE AIR

MASTER OF THE AIR

William Tunner and the Success
of Military Airlift

ROBERT A. SLAYTON

THE UNIVERSITY OF ALABAMA PRESS
Tuscaloosa

Copyright © 2010
The University of Alabama Press
Tuscaloosa, Alabama 35487-0380
All rights reserved
Manufactured in the United States of America

Typeface: Garamond

Cover image: Americans celebrate the end of the airlift
(History Office, Air Mobility Command, Scott Air Force Base, Box 7, Folder 1)

∞

The paper on which this book is printed meets the minimum requirements of
American National Standard for Information Sciences-Permanence of Paper for
Printed Library Materials, ANSI Z39.48-1984.

Library of Congress Cataloging-in-Publication Data

Slayton, Robert A.
Master of the air : William Tunner and the success of military airlift /
Robert A. Slayton.
p.   cm.
Includes bibliographical references and index.
ISBN 978-0-8173-1692-1 (cloth : alk. paper) — ISBN 978-0-8173-8354-1
(electronic) 1. Tunner, William H. 2. Tunner, William H.—Military leadership.
3. Generals—United States—Biography. 4. United States. Air Force—
Officers—Biography. 5. United States. Air Force—Transport service—
History—20th century. 6. Airlift, Military—United States—History—20th
century. 7. Women Airforce Service Pilots (U.S.)—History. 8. World War,
1939–1945—Burma. 9. Berlin (Germany)—History—Blockade, 1948–1949.
10. United States—History, Military—20th century. I. Title.
UG626.2.T87S58 2010
358.40092—dc22
[B]
2009032190

For Mary Yasgur, true heroine

Contents

Illustrations

Acknowledgments

Any scholar—anyone who does serious work of any kind—knows how much one must depend on others, for assistance of all kinds, for help, for support. Friends count in this business.

So does money, and much of that came from my home institution, Chapman University. It provided me with a sabbatical, as well as one of the most remarkable awards in academe, the Wang-Fradkin. This unique stipend was created decades ago by someone who loved the academics at her school, and set up a fund to enable them to dream dreams. I have also benefited from holding the Henry Salvatori Professorship.

But Chapman provided much more, a wonderful history department in which to both teach and learn, study and do research. I am particularly grateful to successive chairs, Leland Estes and Jennifer Keene, and to my students, who identified Tunner early on as a fitting subject for a biography.

Historians are old school—or at least this one is—and we still travel to libraries to look at written records. That often means making sense of arcane catalogs and finding aids, moments when experienced librarians are as good as gold. I would like to extend my thanks to the following individuals for all their help in truly making this project possible: at Chapman University, Lorraine Attarian; at the Air Force Historical Research Agency, Joseph Caver and Dennis Case; at Air Mobility Command, Kathy Skipper and John Leland; at the National Archives, Ken Schlesinger and, in the Still Photos section, Kelly Moody.

There are also some individuals who have earned special mention. I have benefited for many years being part of the Southern California Social History Study Group, and as always they provided wise counsel. Steve Ross, my dear friend, came through with more good advice than I have any right to enjoy. And I am indebted to all those who consented to interviews for this project.

Two other individuals, whom I have never met in person, also provided remarkable assistance. Roger G. Miller and Donald Harrington, U.S. Air Force historians, agreed to look at the entire manuscript for this book, sight unseen, simply because they believe in collegiality. They returned the work loaded with suggestions, ranging from the kind of notation that only comes from close reading, to large innovative ideas that shaped some of the key arguments of this book. Mr. Miller, in particular, was a paradigm of generosity and patience, and I worry that I overstayed my welcome far too many times. To say I am grateful is to indulge in shameful understatement.

And in the end, there is always Rita, who makes it all worthwhile.

Introduction

In a new millennium, America stands alone as the preeminent military power on this planet. Across the globe, nations and individuals perceive the United States as a monolith of martial strength; no nation can realistically hope to cause much difficulty for its forces on a conventional battlefield.

This powerful reality, however, warps history. It fosters—far too easily—inevitability, the sense that since this is the current situation, it was foreordained to occur this way, that sooner or later we would achieve this unparalleled status. Nothing could be further from the truth.

Instead, the story of America's military includes examples of both triumphs and incompetence, of leaders with genius and determination pitted against political officers and embedded bureaucrats. The same service that is wildly innovative, can also at times be hidebound and convention ridden, especially during peacetime.

In particular, the triumphant image has no room for quirky individuals who pushed ahead an agenda of change in the face of entrenched institutions. These players—transformation agents—often found themselves in advance of conventional thinking, fighting to make the rest of the world—and especially the military—break out of standard thinking and accept, and fund, what was new and daring and risky. The armed services, on the other hand, have to make decisions, on how much to bend, how much to tolerate, from erratic geniuses, all of whom bucked tradition, but some of whom could also win wars as well.

William Tunner was one of these latter characters, an American military genius so innovative, so independent, and so cantankerous he made the feisty

George Patton look like a garden club's accountant. A man with a mission, early in his career he became involved in air transport, and discovered, almost by accident, his life's calling. Tunner became the father of military airlift, creating systems to make this the preeminent form of cargo carry for the modern armed services. Starting with work ferrying enormous numbers of planes across the country, and then turning the Burma Hump operation into a businesslike proposition capable of delivering unprecedented amounts of goods, he led the first great efforts at mass supply by air.

All of this culminated with the Berlin Airlift, which still remains, toward the end of the first decade of the twenty-first century, the largest airlift in human history. Most accounts give credit to Lucius Clay, commandant of U.S. forces in Germany, for this operation. No one should remove any laurels from that general and his determined leadership, but the grim reality was that not a single leader—from Clay himself to the most senior diplomats to the Pentagon generals to the press's most insightful commentators—believed that it was even remotely possible for airplanes to bring in enough to feed, heat, clothe, and provide for a city of over two million individuals. Everyone considered it a doomed plan, a stall for time that would soon run out of steam and hope, especially when it hit the wall of winter, a tough, demanding German season that frequently shut down air operations with suddenness and ferocity.

Everyone indeed, except General William Tunner. He knew airlift could work and actually sought out this terrific challenge to prove that his theories were viable. He became the architect of the airlift, the true victor of Berlin in those dark skies of 1948 and 1949. Supported by a cadre of devoted followers, these men figured out how to make airlift work at an unprecedented scale, so that by the time the Soviets called off the blockade, Tunner's planes were bringing in more supplies than had previously been transported by rail and truck, and rations to Berliners had actually increased.

This was an amazing reversal. Prior to World War II, air transport had been seen exclusively as a kind of specialty service, capable of carrying small, precious cargoes—like diphtheria serum—but nothing more substantial than that type of delicate item. Even during a global conflict, experiments of shipping mass goods by air had been tentative, with mixed results, and hardly accepted by higher command authorities. Tunner stood that notion on its ear and proved that airplanes could carry bulk goods sufficient to serve large cities—or armies in the field. The military would never be the same.

Thus, the notion that the Berlin Airlift was preordained to succeed does not square with the historical record. At the time, everyone predicted failure. Only when a determined, idiosyncratic expert took over the operation did it begin to deliver, eventually becoming a triumph that enabled the United States to start the cold war with a practical and moral victory. The story of the airlift, therefore, is not so simple or direct, but instead highlights the tensions and dilemmas that arise when the military must handle a visionary.

After Berlin, Tunner became the leading advocate of airlift in the world, fighting, politicking, working to see that an air service focused on warplanes like fighters and bombers brought in transport as an equal partner, a vital service that was indispensable if the United States was to fight and win wars on a global scale. Clad by then in the mantle of a visionary, he was at times both shrewd and indiscreet as he championed his cause. The air force now had to make choices about how to deal with his powerful ideas and intruding presence, how much to accept innovators who bucked tradition and military protocol.

Tunner won the battle to establish cargo as one of the core missions of the air force; the fact that much of military transport today is accomplished by cargo planes vast and small is testimony to that fact, as is the notion that almost all troops transit to a combat theater by air, rather than by sea. His most important accomplishment remains his role as birth father of military airlift, the individual who saw the future and convinced the air force to accept his ideas and incorporate them into their fundamental view of how a military fights and how it is equipped. But it was not an easy ride, nor a graceful transition. The story of William Tunner, therefore, is one of innovation, but also of how traditional institutions deal with agents of change, agents who challenge the very core of the institutions' beliefs and practices and force them to change for the better. Tunner proved that this could be done, but it was never easy to get new ideas adopted.

1 / Getting a Mission

The introduction gives no hint of what was to come, no indication of the prodigy. William Henry Tunner, an American military innovator, was born on Bastille Day, July 14, 1906, in Elizabeth, New Jersey. The fourth of five children of Austrian immigrants, Tunner was, according to his mother, "a completely average boy" as he grew up in the neighboring town of Roselle.[1]

The first note of excitement came via education. William's father had studied engineering in his homeland and believed all his offspring should attend college. A noble idea, but it cost money. One sister had just finished at teachers' college, and another two brothers were enrolled in a local academy. The idea of sending a fourth child to school meant considerable financial strain on the family.[2]

Then, one day in civics class, Tunner learned that he could get a free college education at West Point—if he qualified. Thanks to local congressman Ernest Ackerman, William discovered that all nominations to military academies were based on competitive examinations. The good news was that politics, status, and money would play no part.[3] The bad news was that it would not be easy.

In fact, that was no hardship. Tunner perked up, or as one reporter put it, "he got steamed up over the idea of going to West Point." The future pilot/general later wrote, in appropriate language, "I looked up from the page with a new hope. It was like coming out of the clouds to find a landing field right ahead." After that, "I crammed. I studied at home and used my scheduled study periods to attend extra classes." William actually took the test—a standard civil service exam—on two occasions, first in Elizabeth and then later in New Brunswick.

On his first attempt he scored the highest among all testers in the state and came in second on his next try. In 1924, at the age of seventeen, Tunner graduated high school in Roselle and entered the United States Military Academy at West Point.[4]

Tunner's life at the academy seemed reasonably pleasant, and he got good grades. He did not recall hazing as being particularly onerous, in later years remembering, "I felt it was just part of the game," adding, "A plebe doesn't have time to think, and so I was either too tired or too busy to consider the changes going on in my life."[5]

Records indicate, however, that at least by the time he became an upperclassman, William had become a most pleasant fellow, and often a ringleader in hijinks. Tunner remained, according to his brother-in-law, "the world's worst poker player and crap shooter," but had other sterling attributes, such as the time he befriended four of the ladies performing in George White's *Scandals,* and persuaded them to visit him and his classmates at West Point. Yearbook editors for Tunner's graduating class wrote in his entry, "Little did we think, back in the dim dark days of the summer of 1924 . . . that we had on our roster a man of so many diverse accomplishments and possibilities. He was playful, active, and an altogether normal plebe those days, but three years at the Academy have changed Will into an ardent promoter of all the new activities and devotee to all new sports." They cited him as "a loyal and generous friend . . . a man with an interest in everything from snaring mice to procuring delicious apples from unauthorized orchards." As a result of such escapades, "Even after three years with him, we never knew what to expect next. One week-end he brought into the barracks the full equipment for the production of fudge, and the next, he turned up with a huge and deadly double-barreled shotgun and calmly announced that he was going hunting." They also added, "Will's passions are golf, tennis, riding, fishing, cards—and his passions will not be denied."[6]

But more serious matters were also taking place, quietly in private conversations and more demonstratively in public acts. Like all students approaching graduation, William pondered his future. Before him lay the usual array of possibilities: infantry, cavalry, engineers, coast artillery, and others. Endless conversations ensued in the barracks as young men pondered their fate.

In his senior year, however, something intervened in the normal decision-making process. The army, making sure that cadets were exposed to all aspects of the service, sent all academy students for a week to Mitchel Field to learn about the U.S. Army Air Corps. Tunner rode in five different planes and was hooked. He never touched any controls, and the trips were pure vanilla—straight flying, no dips or turns, no stunts. But he had discovered the awesome truth, as he later wrote in italics, *"Man could fly."*[7]

The army agreed, with a caveat: the washout rate for officers choosing this path was extraordinary—70 percent. As a result, candidates usually chose another specialty and graduated with that on their record, the affiliation they would revert back to if they failed to make it through flight training. Accordingly, William Tunner graduated West Point on June 9, 1928, with a commission as second lieutenant in the Field Artillery.[8]

Tunner was part of a distinguished group of military flyers. Beating the odds, fifty-five of the seventy-five West Pointers who picked the Air Corps that year earned their wings. Tunner received his at Kelly Field, Texas, in 1929; the officer conducting his final check ride was a senior man by the name of Claire Chennault. The roster of his graduating class also included a flyer named Curtis LeMay.[9]

Tunner had learned much from his training; most important of all, as he put it, "I just plain loved flying." The young officer now worked through the usual appointments and promotions of a peacetime army. He started out at Rockwell Field, California, and soon served at Randolph Field, Texas; the Canal Zone in Panama; Fort Benning, Georgia; and Memphis, Tennessee, where he headed up a reserve detachment and worked to recruit young pilots into the military. In July 1934 he received promotion to first lieutenant, and in September 1935 he made captain.[10]

William Tunner never had a moment of destiny; his life changed because of a rather casual command and a downright unglamorous one to boot. In 1939 Tunner was running the Memphis operation when the chief of personnel came through for a routine visit. He liked what he saw and told the young officer to pack for Washington and the Military Personnel Division of the chief of the Air Corps.[11]

Neither the location nor the task interested Tunner. In later years he came down hard on the capitol, remarking, "I have always dreaded working in Washington," calling it "confining and frustrating." The work, furthermore, could not have been any less onerous: officers pursuing combat careers do not seek sidepaths into the field of personnel matters. This move, however, would have powerful consequences for the young man.[12]

While Tunner languished in Washington, the world burned. In September 1939, World War II officially began with the German invasion of Poland. A year later France, possessed of one of the world's preeminent land forces, had surrendered, and England stood alone, with the Battle of Britain filling its skies. The leading democracy still in the war needed equipment, and needed it fast, on an emergency basis. That meant massive orders placed in the United States, for every commodity from canned beef to large bombers.

When it came to the latter item, the British faced a problem: how to get the bombers to the battle front. Orders for planes made headlines, but without the logistical background these machines were worthless hulks sitting on the ground, awaiting transport over thousands of miles before they could confront the enemy. These were big weapons, furthermore; not many could fit in a freighter. In addition, the sea route was long and fraught with danger; in those days the U-boats were coming close to winning the war. Desperate, the British began flying bombers across the Atlantic, as the fastest means of delivery possible.

This was no mean feat. In 1940 Lindbergh's historic flight had occurred only thirteen years prior, and regular trans-Atlantic traffic was still a rare, elite event, flown only by four-engine flying boats, and only during the summer months. Pan-American, for example, assigned only eight planes to this task, each flying at the slow speed of 130 miles per hour, while TWA had five aircraft, albeit ones capable of 170 miles per hour. As the author of the leading book on Britain's Ferry Command put it, "on the eve of the Second World War the air connection between North America and Europe was on a very small scale." But war makes difficult choices possible, and a ferrying service began to bring multi-engined planes across the ocean.[13]

Pressed by necessity, the operation grew, but new challenges appeared. Before a plane could even attempt the Atlantic crossing, it had to be flown from the factory—often on the West Coast—to a departure point on the Atlantic seaboard, in either the United States or Canada. At first, Britain contracted with the companies to have civilian pilots handle this task as independent operators, but this proved to be a logistics and planning nightmare. There were relatively few pilots capable of flying multiengined craft, and the lack of organizational structure produced chaos, with pilots flying any route they chose, on any schedule, stopping overnight in any city they found friendly or intriguing. One alternative was to use British military pilots, but this was a rarity, or else the program would drain trained flyers from the Royal Air Force (RAF) at a time when it could hardly spare them.[14]

In an attempt to impose order on this situation, in late 1940 the British organized the Atlantic Ferrying Organization, or Atfero, and offered pilots the enormous sum of $1,500 a month. The American military, bound by several different Neutrality Acts, could do little to affect this situation.[15]

That changed completely on March 11, 1941, when President Franklin Roosevelt signed the Lend-Lease Act into law. Under its provisions, any country whose defense the president considered a vital interest of the United States could receive arms and equipment by sale, transfer, exchange, or lease. Industrial America, and the U.S. military establishment, could now begin to aid countries fighting the Nazi regime and its allies.

Shortly after the passage of Lend-Lease, Major General Henry H. "Hap" Arnold, chief of the Army Air Corps, journeyed to England to discuss issues of mutual interest with the British, and the matter came up again. Arnold liked the idea of using American airmen to ferry planes, not only because it would help an ally, but because it would provide flying experience for his own pilots. This time, upon his return, the general pressed the issue with President Roosevelt himself.

The result was a letter from the president to Secretary of War Henry Stimson, asking him to "take the full responsibility for delivering planes . . . that are to be flown to England." Roosevelt emphasized the point: "I am convinced that we can speed up the process of getting these bombers to England and I am anxious to cut through all of the formalities that are not legally prohibitive and help the British get this job done with dispatch."[16]

The date on that letter was May 28, 1941. It went from the White House to Stimson's office, was passed from there to the Chief of Staff, General George Marshall, and from there to Arnold. This process—the formal chain of command—seems long and bureaucratic, but this was almost wartime, so at 3 P.M. on May 29, only a day later, Arnold called in Major Robert Olds, an officer who would soon be serving in the Plans Division of the air staff. Hap Arnold informed him that the Air Corps had established a Ferry Command, that Olds was its commanding officer, and that he had better get about his business in a hurry.[17]

Olds was a tough guy and a character. A World War I fighter pilot, he had become an aide and disciple of Billy Mitchell, and later headed the Second Bombardment Group, which received the first B-17s to come off the production line. Olds promptly took his unit on a transcontinental flight and then broke the rules with another demonstration of air power. The army was under orders that they could not fly more than fifty miles off the coast; the sea space beyond that zone was the responsibility of the navy. Instead, Olds and his B-17s, with Curtis LeMay as his lead navigator and one plane filled with reporters, intercepted the liner *Rex* seven hundred miles offshore and buzzed the ship. Tunner remembered him as "a forceful and independent man; he'd speak up to officers of highest rank almost as quickly as he'd blister a subordinate. . . . He wanted action at all times." Despite the fact that he suffered from severe arthritis, Olds "had energy to burn, both on and off the job. He loved high living, and he loved women, too, for that matter; he'd been married four times" by the time he was given Ferrying Command. When he left Arnold's office, he turned to his secretary, Mrs. Jennie Smith, and announced, "Jennie, we've got a job to do." By the time the adjutant general actually posted the official order creating Ferrying Command on July 5, Olds had had the outfit up and running for some time, and the authorization had to be made retroactive.[18]

The first thing Olds had to do was assemble a staff. That afternoon, within hours, he brought in Major Edward Alexander as his executive officer. After that he needed a personnel officer, someone who could help him build the organization. Accordingly, the second man he picked for the team was a newly minted major by the name of William Tunner; Tunner's role would soon go way beyond that initial responsibility for staffing.[19]

The setting was not grand: Ferrying Command began in a large room in the basement of the Munitions Building, which featured bad ventilation and meager lighting; its one window opened over the space where the building's cafeteria left its garbage cans. Officers like Tunner, with no enlisted men available, manhandled file cabinets out of the way, got some lights and desks, and arranged at least for a glass partition to give their commanding officer some private space.[20]

This new outfit had two missions. First, to deliver planes—hundreds of planes, maybe even thousands of planes—from American factories to ports of embarkation in Canada, Bermuda, and other spots where pilots from Britain and other allies could take over; there was a general sense that the United States should completely take over this mission from the British and handle all deliveries within the United States. The other was to create an airline-type service for critical personnel and to meet any other needs as designated by the army. And although they had scant resources, their authority was potent: Olds had carte blanche—a letter from the president and a directive from the chief of Army Air Forces. On top of that, Olds had a memo from Major General E. S. Adams, the adjutant general of the entire U.S. Army (and not just the Air Corps) addressed to all flag rank officers, reading, "The chiefs of arms and services, commanding officers of posts, camps and stations and other agencies . . . are directed to give first priority to the activities of the Air Corps Ferrying Command when the assistance or cooperation is required." As Tunner noted, this meant—at least theoretically, that "if anybody was ferrying an aircraft across country and stopped in at an Army Air Corps base, all he had to do was wave this directive around and everybody on the base had to stop work and take care of that airplane."[21]

The operation had a lot to do in a short time. Many airplane factories were on the West Coast, with more plants popping up regularly as the nation armed itself. Few craft and fewer pilots could fly long distances, so Ferrying Command facilities had to be established at airports all over the United States, in locations as diverse as Love Field in Dallas, Wayne County Airport outside Detroit, and the facility in Presque Isle, Maine, where British pilots took over the controls of bombers and flew them across the Atlantic. The Foreign Division also grew, establishing airfields in South America and Africa. Having acquired a few B-24 bombers converted to passenger configuration, they flew special missions such as taking diplomat Averell Harriman on a secret mission to Moscow. No one even knew what air route to use on a flight like this in 1941, so Ferrying Command had to explore new flight paths, establish new bases. As General Olds's son, Robin, told the author, "It was a hell of a challenge in those days," and his father loved the work. It was also a great time to be a freewheeling, innovative young officer; everything was changing fast, and Tunner had a lot of leeway to shape the job as he saw fit, without having senior men scrutinize his every move.[22] In time, he would get used to this way of doing business, for better or worse.

Tunner's job was crucial: he was no paper pusher, but instead had to recruit pilots to fly all these planes around the nation and then the globe. Again, his armament was a blank check from the Air Corps, a directive stating that "any deficiency of pilots for ferrying crews will be made up . . . by the Army Air Corps, which includes all pilots of the Air Corps, including GHQ." Tunner started by drawing on the National Guard and Reserve, but soon had to raid line units, and then even civilian employees. On one occasion he went down to Miami, assembled all the local people involved in ferrying planes, whether they be pilots, radiomen, navigators, or whatever, and gave them a choice of joining the Air Corps or being drafted. Most made the discrete decision, according to Tunner.[23]

But this was just the start of his work. Tunner now had to set up training facilities for his new pilots, and establish a structure to monitor their progress and promote or eliminate men, depending on performance. Above all, he had to determine which pilots were qualified to fly which planes, and established the air force's first standardized qualification system, ranging from Level I for single-engine trainers to V for four-engine bombers and transports, with P for pursuit planes (fighters), and a special VI classification, a prized designation that meant a pilot was qualified to fly any type of craft. Tunner established high standards for each of these levels, and the system was later adopted by the air service as a whole. By the time of Pearl Harbor, Ferrying Command had moved fourteen hundred planes from scattered manufacturing facilities to transfer points on the East and Gulf Coasts. At the same time, Major Alexander had been sent to China and then got stuck there, so Tunner became the outfit's executive officer and began taking over wherever a new system became necessary, the indispensable man. By late 1941, when restructuring of the command divided it into Domestic and Foreign Divisions, Tunner officially took over the former, by far the larger, tasked with all ferrying operations in the United States.[24]

December 7, 1941, changed everything. While National Guard and Reserve pilots could remain in Ferrying Command, all regular military pilots were now desperately needed for combat, and orders went out that they were to report to their permanent units immediately. Tunner actually had twenty planes in the air piloted by these men; the situation shifted so quickly that they had to land immediately at the nearest field, abandon their planes for Ferrying Command to pick up later, and get back to their base for reassignment.[25]

Changes came fast. By January 1942 Tunner was running all domestic ferrying flights and had been promoted to lieutenant colonel. On June 20, Ferrying Command became Air Transport Command (ATC), with responsibility for all aerial transportation efforts in the U.S. military; as one air force publication explained, "The Air Transport Service maintains and operates the transport aircraft required to move the men and material of our Armed Forces wherever needed." This was not just an enlargement of an earlier operation, but a strategic shift concentrating all airlift under one command; the air force's official history explained, this made ATC "the agent not merely of the AAF [Army Air Forces] but of the whole War Department."[26] Tunner, by then a full colonel, logically became head of the Ferrying Division, the largest unit in ATC by far.[27]

He also had a new boss. Harold George had graduated from Princeton University's School of Military Aeronautics and had flown bombers in World War I. By 1925 he was chief of the Bombardment Section in the office of chief of the Air Corps, and then became chief instructor in bombing tactics at the

Air Corps Tactical School. In June 1941 he became the assistant chief of staff in charge of war plans and was instrumental in drawing up strategy for an air war against Germany.[28]

In March 1942, Hap Arnold, by then head of the Army Air Forces, called George to his office on a matter of some delicacy. Colonel Olds was ill and had been found unconscious at his desk. George would take over Ferrying Command, albeit on a temporary basis; George was a bomber leader and a planner and had expected an overseas command.[29]

The new man had spent a week sizing up the operation and managing it on an interim basis when Arnold called him back in with some brusque news: George was now the new permanent head of Ferrying Command, soon to be ATC. To soften the blow, in April he received his first star, a promotion to brigadier general.

Tunner took to George immediately. Olds had been flamboyant and a bit undisciplined, attacking staff constantly with brilliant but erratic notions. George was at least as smart—one writer called him "a planner par excellence"—and a diligent leader who worked from early in the morning to midnight if necessary. He immediately grasped some of the problems Tunner was facing and put an end to some of Olds's idiosyncratic methods that had caused the staff much wasted effort. He also ran a tight ship, and he frowned on hysteria or exaggeration; one memo to staff in 1942 warned them to avoid attaching terms like "urgent" or "priority" to messages without due cause, which could only be a wartime emergency "when lives or property are in *immediate* danger" (emphasis in original). Tunner referred to him as a "practical" leader, who made "good decisions . . . a very good man to work for" who trusted his men and gave them room to lead. He was the perfect boss for William Tunner: a supervisor who gave subordinates structure and guidelines instead of close scrutiny, allowing smart officers to develop their own ideas.[30]

With a new sense of mission, ATC became a giant. It officially opened for business on June 30, 1942, with approximately 11,000 officers and enlisted men. Within nine months, by late March 1943, it had expanded to 60,000 service personnel, and by war's end to over 200,000, with another 108,000 civilian employees. Starting with a handful of B-24s with bucket seats, the Foreign Division of ATC had, by the time hostilities ceased, 3,700 planes; in the single month of July 1945 the ATC flew 274,934 passengers and 124,637 tons of freight and mail. Each day, twenty-six regularly scheduled flights crossed the Atlantic along established routes, while another thirty-eight traversed the Pacific, many along routes that had not existed before then. At the heart of this overall operation, second only to General George as commanding officer, was William Tunner.[31]

Tunner's responsibilities were vast. To start with, he headed up the largest unit within ATC, Ferrying Division. In a 1943 memo, General George laid out the duties of that outfit, a list that included responsibility for ferrying all planes within the continental United States. This meant coordinating the tens of thousands of crews who flew these missions and had to be reassigned planes at dozens of spots all around the country, plus "the movement of tactical crews in tactical planes over routes operated by the ATC outside the United States" as directed by higher authorities. To give some idea of what that meant, before Pearl Harbor President Roosevelt pledged the nation to producing 50,000 planes a year, and Josef Goebbels, the Nazi propaganda head, scoffed at American hubris. In 1944, however, American factories turned out over 96,000 planes, and every one of these had to be delivered to a military unit. All of this under the command of someone the Associated Press referred to as "one of the . . . Air Force's youngest key men."[32]

Tunner began with steps that would become the hallmark of his later career, an emphasis on both efficiency and heightening his troops' morale. For the first time, he divided the country into sectors, with a Ferrying Group responsible for handling the products of all factories in that zone. Thus, the Second Ferrying Group out of New Castle Air Base in Wilmington, Delaware, moved medium and attack bombers—B-26s and A-30s—coming off the lines from Glenn Martin in Baltimore; light aircraft from the Piper factory in Lockhaven, Pennsylvania; and P-47 fighters from Republic Aviation on Long Island. At the same time, the Fifth Ferrying Group worked out of Love Field in Dallas, and moved B-17s and B-29s from the Boeing plant in Wichita, trainers from Beech Aircraft in that same city, and B-24 bombers off the grounds of the Consolidated operation in Fort Worth. Pilots for this massive operation had to be tested and assigned, using the structure Tunner had earlier designed, and then provided strict flight plans that took them exclusively to ATC fields with no dallying along the way. After each of the tens of thousands of planes was dropped off at its final destinations, the crew that got it there had to be directed to their next assignment, with minimal waste or unnecessary transit.[33]

Despite the organization and structure Tunner imposed on the outfit, he never forgot that men flew planes. In his memoirs, he noted that while the ferrying pilot "was not supposed to be a hero, but just to do his job," it became clear that "sometimes his job was not enough." While his crews never braved ack-ack or enemy fighters, they endured "long overwater flights of up to ten hours or more," flying "through all kinds of weather, through storms and . . . below-zero temperatures, with the gray-green, oily sea waiting below if they made the slightest mistake." Crews had to fly to "pinpoints on the globe," spots like Ascension Island, a dot in the South Atlantic "a thousand miles from anywhere," which ATC pilots commemorated with the jingle, "If I don't hit Ascension . . . My wife will get a pension," hardly a reassuring ditty. When needed, Tunner's men flew impossible hours; the airline standard was 100 hours a month, but ATC crews averaged 200 hours, and many hit 250 without blinking. One pilot flew 275 hours in five weeks and went out on the next flight because of a shortage of crews. At the same time, combat veterans declared that ATC stood for "Allergic to Combat" or "Army of Terrified Civilians."[34]

Among those who flew these missions was an up-and-coming movie star named Gene Autry. Like many performers, the singing cowboy took his place in the ranks after Pearl Harbor and wound up a flight officer in the Air Transport Command. He got to fly in everything from a Douglas SBD dive bomber to a P-51 Mustang to a C-47 cargo plane, but felt that "for the thrill that lasts a lifetime, nothing could beat a C-109," a B-24 bomber converted into a fuel carrier that had "this unfortunate characteristic. It would sometimes break in two." Autry liked the work, although he admitted, "ATC wasn't where the glamour was. You were in the cargo business. The fellows who flew the fighters and the bombers sometimes compared us to truck drivers. . . . But it was tough and important work, high risk and low profit, and it suited me fine."[35]

Tunner respected these men and knew success depended on them, so he took pains to look after all of his personnel, both those in the military and outside of it. As one example, to boost self-respect for civilian pilots working in a wartime culture, these flyers received a type of uniform, with wings over the left pocket carrying the letters "ATC." Indications of rank were illegal of course, but sleeve stripes appeared: three for captains, two for copilots, one for navigators, flight engineers, and radiomen. Many of the pilots received, as a result, unwarranted and unsought salutes from military personnel.[36]

But Tunner did something far more significant than provide snappy uniforms. He realized that the most important command decision he could make would be to increase safety for his crews, making sure they would return home; nothing would boost morale more than that. As a result, he took on a lifelong task that seemed contradictory: to achieve maximum efficiency and maximum safety at the same time.

Tunner began the Flying Safety Program, following talks with his brother

George, who worked for the Travelers Insurance Company. Just as insurance companies sent out experts to check on plants and equipment, Tunner created flying safety sections, each of which would cover one part of the widespread ATC operation. The officers assigned to this task had to review procedures and adjust them to achieve conditions of maximum safety. When that failed, they would inspect accidents and determine the cause, followed by recommendations to prevent another mishap from occurring. As a result of these measures, Ferrying Command began to have the lowest accident rate of any aerial unit in the armed services.[37]

Tunner got things done, and George began to press more work on his key man. On top of running Ferrying Command, Tunner had to establish a freight route from Miami to India that ran through Brazil and Central Africa. That meant having teams scout locations, determine routes, and establish bases on three continents besides North America; one of the pilots was Barry Goldwater, later a U.S. senator and presidential candidate. As soon as the North African theater stabilized, Tunner got the call to establish a service that ran from Washington, D.C., through Wilmington, Delaware, to Bermuda and then on to Africa, ending in Cairo. He also worked with the airline industry to create the Airlines War Training Institute to prepare civilian pilots for military aircraft and routines.[38]

Most important of all, Tunner delivered the planes America needed to fight a war; his record was as much a miracle as the production lines themselves. On May 29, 1941, he had a staff of two; in early July the first domestic planes arrived at transit points with ferrying crews aboard. Within a year, his outfit had made 13,595 domestic and 632 foreign deliveries, and the total for 1942 was 30,000. By 1944, its peak year, ATC delivered 108,000 planes, flying 9,000 missions a month. Over the course of the war, the totals stood at 291,525 domestic ferrying jobs and 21,092 planes shepherded to foreign locations.[39]

At the end of World War II, after later accomplishments, Tunner wrote a unique letter to a fellow officer, in which he reminisced about these early days. Now a brigadier general, Tunner wrote, "I am most proud of my old command and first love, the Ferrying Division," adding, "I feel that I have built it from its birth to its maturity." Tunner stopped here, recognizing the hubris, and explained himself: "I apologize if this appears to be bragging, but please accept this review as pardonable pride." He then went on to cite all that he had done, how the division had grown from a small office into a giant operation, developing an evacuation service for wounded that was "unparalleled," creating

1. General William Tunner in 1953. (History Office, Air Mobility Command, Scott Air Force Base, Box 7, Folder 5)

foreign air routes, while performing "a real training job." He concluded, "Each decision was part of me and obviously I loved it."[40]

Ferrying Command molded William Tunner, determining his career and focusing his personality. In his encounter with transport he had found his life's work and would go on to become the founder of military airlift in the world, as well as its foremost advocate.

There was no clear or good reason for this choice; life is sometimes like that. Tunner never sought out this mission—it just arrived amid the mix of wartime tasks. But Tunner was a Type A, driven personality, and once this landed in his lap, he would take it on and master it, devote himself to it. If instead, he had been assigned fighter command, he would have led the first Mustangs over Berlin; or if detailed to draw up water supply, we would be using his designs for pipelines to this day.

Once Tunner became invested in airlift, once he had a cause, the real power of this man's mind began to appear. Not content with merely managing this new concept of military air transportation, he began to develop a theory to support his future work.

Most important of all, Tunner fought all his life for the notion that airlift was a strategic task, as important to winning a war as dropping bombs or flying fighters. Tunner came to believe that airlift could perform any operation, that it would eventually even replace seaborne commerce. In 1945, when only a decade and a half prior biplanes had still dominated the air routes, this seemed beyond visionary, indeed, foolish. The fact that twenty years later, during the Vietnam War, almost all U.S. ground troops arrived by air, only confirms both the man's insight, as well as his dedication to an ideal.

This notion of airlift dominance had enormous consequences, however, ones that would also earn Tunner, its leading advocate in the military, a roster of enemies. First, if airlift was that important, it must have a central, independent structure, an idea stemming from his experience with Ferrying Command. The standard Army Air Forces organization at this time was the numbered air force. The ATC did not fit within this system, and instead reported directly to the chief of the AAF, outside of the usual chain of command. It had developed, in other words, into one of the first true global commands in the United States military.[41]

Tunner built on this concept and eventually became the foremost advocate of an independent airlift structure. In later years he would become the father of the Military Airlift Command (MAC), pressuring the Pentagon to ensure that it was the equivalent of such heavyweights as the Strategic Air Command (SAC) and Tactical Air Command (TAC), answerable to the National Command Authority and the Chiefs of Staff. Tunner wanted airlift to be at the same level, to have the same centralized command structure, and to enjoy the same political and bureaucratic support as the combat arms. At times, however, the fighting branches would resent the intrusion, the notion that cargo haulers should receive the same status held by fighting pilots.

Next, and another issue Tunner pushed till he died, was the idea that airlift was a professional task, and that professional training and insights were needed to do it well, just as in any other branch of the military. Thus, infantry, no matter how tough or courageous, could not do the job of engineers; they simply did not have the necessary knowledge and skills. Similarly, generals from bomber wings should not expect to order around an airlift operation and have it succeed.

This had vast ramifications for personnel and budgets and for the general's career as well. Tunner was saying that airlift must be led and staffed by professionals in the field, not by people assigned from other departments. Over and over, on every occasion possible, in presentation after presentation, Tunner declared that, with all proper respect for his colleagues, they did not have the knowledge to run airlift, that only individuals trained and dedicated to that mission could do this job. This also meant a new budget line, one that would draw funding from the rest of the military, and especially from the other parts of the air service, in the zero-sum game of Pentagon and congressional politics.

All these ideas were guaranteed to irritate important people both inside the military and beyond. In any service, generals commanding the war fighters—the "tip of the spear"—consider themselves a breed apart and see the other specialties as services, and secondary, supporting elements. Tunner wanted to sit at the same table, with an equal seat, an insulting notion to them, and he also made clear that they could not do his job.

Even worse, he wanted to cut their funding. That was not deliberate, of course; no offense was intended. But if airlift got more money, someone else got less. It was that simple. No one appreciated a new kid on the budget block.

Army and air force officers in the field would object as well. Because he believed in a centralized transportation command making strategic decisions, Tunner fought for the principle that any airlift plane had to report exclusively to him, and not to a local commander, or even a theater commander. This was bound to cause problems: an officer is engaged in life-and-death struggle, a battle closely fought, and an asset he needs desperately drops in from out of the sky, literally. That plane could save lives, win battles. How dare some fool back behind the lines with no combat responsibilities tell him to keep his hands off? Tunner was sympathetic and would be a pioneer in supporting front-line soldiers, especially during the Korean War. He knew, however, that if he let loose the reins, the local situation would bleed him dry and destroy his strategic capability to wield airlift in pursuit of large missions.

Civilian leaders also would mount a challenge to Tunner's revolutionary ideas. They could never dream of operating fighting aircraft, but many airline presidents felt that carrying goods was their unique responsibility, not to mention the profits that came from lucrative government contracts. Tunner argued that military airlift was a different bird altogether from civilian hauling, in terms of cargo, routes, dangers, and logistics, and must be handled by a large and formidable military command. This would not go unopposed.

Despite the roster of opponents, Tunner never hesitated in becoming the leading champion of military airlift in the world (no other country but America had this capability on any scale for several decades). As he reflected, "We learned early that there was a particular and definite *expertise* required in delivering planes over long distances, an *expertise* requiring techniques and training over and above those necessary for the flying of combat missions." Elsewhere, he wrote, "air transport is a science in itself; to be carried out at maximum efficiency air transport must be run by men who know the techniques of air transport and are dedicated to air transport—*professionals!*" (all emphasis in the original). Tunner believed that airlift was a unique field of expertise and could only be run by people with advanced knowledge of transport systems, with specific management skills, and a dedication to solving the problems this kind of mission created—issues like what kind of tie-down straps worked best, rather than the general concerns of an air service. When the Pentagon assigned just any officer to head an airlift operation, Tunner always objected; such a move belittled everything he stood for, and minimized both the importance and complexity of mass transport by air.[42]

As one example of his vision, by late 1942 his Ferrying Division was telling anyone who listened that planes flown across the Atlantic suffered only 3.7 percent losses, as opposed to one-third of all those carried by ships getting destroyed and going to the bottom. The implication was clear: airlift should be given that task instead of the merchant marine or commercial suppliers.[43]

Tunner also began to develop a personality that would suit a pioneer but that would create problems in the highly formalized culture of the military. He was starting to take on the traits of an entrepreneurial innovator in private business.

During his work with ATC, Tunner had a great many opportunities to come in contact with airline entrepreneurs, some at very close quarters, and they had a big impact on him. When Harold George got the news he was to take over ATC, he protested to Hap Arnold, "I know nothing about the problems of creating a worldwide system of air transport." Arnold replied that, "There are some exceptionally broad-visioned people in our airlines who could make substantial contributions," and then brought up the name of C. R. Smith.

C. R. Smith was a legendary president of American Airlines, serving in that post from 1934 to 1968. The day after George's conversation with his chief, he met with Smith in a hotel suite and discussed the challenges facing his new command. Heading the list was the need for top administrators fluent with the issues surrounding air travel and air transportation. Smith pulled out pencil and paper and compiled a list of roughly twenty names; when George asked who they were, the airlines boss informed him, "They are the best in our airlines." Smith then suggested, "Let's send a telegram to each airline president stating that these people are essential in the military service in the conflict for survival facing the nation," and proceeded to compose a message on this basis.

George later recalled that the proposed telegram was "exceptional," but one issue remained: Who should sign it? The military man felt, "There's only one man who can sign that kind of a message—and have it mean anything to the recipients—and that's General Hap Arnold," chief of the Army Air Forces. C. R. Smith agreed completely, but then declared, "Let's sign his name and put it on the wires." When George demurred, on the reasonable grounds that he had no such authority, Smith argued, "He can't shoot you for doing it—why not give it a try?" and the telegrams went out, despite the violation of military protocol.

Several days later George informed his boss of what he had done, and Arnold was unflappable. Recognizing that the two men had shown they could work together, he told George to bring C. R. Smith into the service and make him a colonel on the spot. George did so, and appointed Smith his deputy commander, a position the new man held for the duration.[44]

Smith joined ATC, but continued his idiosyncratic ways, even though he was in uniform. As one writer described it, "If C. R. Smith 'flew a desk,' . . . he flew it like no one else in the U.S. Army Air Corps." He hated red tape and bureaucratic procedure, and in the true idiosyncratic fashion of an industrial pioneer, wrote all his memos himself, without any copies, whatsoever. One of the few items he brought over from American Airlines was a favorite manual typewriter, and Smith would knock out brief, powerful notes to subordinates, just as he did when running the corporation; there were no carbons, either. Finally, he sent out a critical order to ATC in Casablanca without keeping any record, and when this got misplaced, higher-ups called him on the carpet. The army dutifully installed a new typing machine with a roller designed to hold six carbons, along with a clerk to run the gadget.

Besides these individual quirks, Smith frowned on other basic military formalities. He hated being saluted and rejected the idea of rank, believing it blocked mobility and perpetuated incompetence. He complained to an associate, "In business, if you're smarter than the other guy, you'll get ahead. In the military, if you're smarter than some other general, you'd better watch your step or you'll wind up in some place like Samoa." Tunner adopted the man's business style, but did not heed this bit of advice.[45]

Smith was hardly the only business character drawn into the ATC. Bruce Gimbel of the department store family came aboard as a pilot, despite a crippled arm. Fred Atkinson, head of personnel at Macy's, followed his competitor's lead and joined the outfit. The deputy commander in North Africa was a Braniff vice president, Robert Smith (no relation to C. R.). Also from the airlines came men like Otis Bryan of TWA, who mapped many of the overseas routes Tunner would use and later became FDR's personal pilot.[46]

Tunner was aware of these men and others, mentioning them in any extended recollection of his work at Ferrying Command. But there is no evidence that he had a lot to do with any of them, although C. R. Smith's senior position—deputy to General George—must have guaranteed considerable contact.

Far more important, they created a culture that shaped the young officer's development as a leader, that molded his style and personality. Initiative was valued above all else, and one should not wait for orders. Your only real boss was yourself, and when you knew something had to get done, pay attention to the job and ignore the higher-ups. Above all, run your own show whenever you could, and accomplish the mission.

Tunner also encountered entrepreneurs in the burgeoning aeronautics industry and was deeply influenced by their freewheeling approach to leadership. He knew Donald Douglas, the founder of Douglas Aircraft, quite well, for example, and the overlap between their approaches to management was striking. Douglas, as one observer put it, "would have to be his own boss to pursue his own designs"; Tunner would always want to run his own show and always make sure it demonstrated how important the fundamental mission—the importance of airlift—really was. Both believed in tackling big projects and not turning back, as Douglas had done with the creation of the DC-3, the world's first successful commercial airliner, and Tunner would do with the Berlin Airlift. Douglas believed that one of the keys to success was the loyalty of his leading men; one of his top engineers remarked, "We didn't work for the Douglas Company . . . we worked for Doug." Tunner, too, would form his cadre of aides, Tunner's men, who traveled with him to hotspots all over the globe for decades, devised solutions to the great dilemmas of air transport, and received, in turn, Tunner's total allegiance, often extending far beyond their time in military service.[47]

These traits combined with his personal energy to create a unique figure, the entrepreneur industrialist as military leader. Tunner, like men such as Donald

Douglas and Henry Ford, had a new concept that he wanted to champion with drive, persistence, vision, and brainpower. Driven by that vision, he was also an independent, someone who did not accept orders easily unless they facilitated his assignment.

In time this codified into what may be termed the Tunner Approach. First, he was a visionary. Tunner could see things others did not and always kept an advanced objective as his true goal.

Next, he had a strong will, was persistent, and overcame obstacles as quickly as possible, even when stiffing supervisors damaged his career. William Tunner never accepted the idea of inevitability.

Part of this derived from his own work habits. He toiled extremely long hours and drove those around him to do the same; getting the work done was far more important than sleep or recreation. One officer complained that "Will's great fault is his impatience. That business of wanting something yesterday, but not today, is a little hard to take."[48]

He was also an independent. Tunner wanted to get the job done, not follow traditional rules or structures.

One of the keys to getting that job done was efficiency. A *Time* reporter, with great insight, observed that "Tunner is far more akin in outlook and operation to the Detroit executive, the industrial leader who makes mass production tick," and noted, "he is preoccupied with costs and time-study." Tunner had no place for cowboys or renegades, preferring subordinates who could solve problems and increase output. Although Tunner never sacrificed his men's well-being and spent considerable effort on safety and morale, he was a true disciple of Frederick Taylor, the founder of industrial engineering and time-motion studies.

Not surprisingly, his main goal became production. This would prove that the great idea really worked, could really deliver.

Finally, alongside the independence, was a fight for recognition—not for himself, but for his ideas. Tunner would always challenge the established order in his quest to make airlift a player in military circles, and he never backed down, a trait which simultaneously won strong victories and made significant enemies.

A typical early example came up with the creation of the Air Transport Command. To understand what happened, the reader must be familiar with certain military definitions. The term "division" usually refers to the central unit of the army, a combat outfit that combines all the basic arms and has roughly ten to fifteen thousand soldiers. It can also designate, however, a major unit within a larger command structure, such as the Intelligence Division. In either case, it is one of the most significant components in the military and is headed by a senior officer, most often, in the case of the large ground formation mentioned above, a two-star major general.

In the army, the designation below this is a "brigade," usually two or three brigades to a division. This is a smaller unit in size and status as well, commanded by a one-star brigadier general. The equivalent to this formation in the Air Force is a "wing."

When ATC began, there were six Foreign Wings, covering the many parts of the globe the unit would operate in, such as the Caribbean or Africa–Middle East. Ferrying was also a wing under this structure, but as one author dryly observed, "Command Headquarters reckoned without Colonel Tunner." Tunner felt—accurately—that ferrying was by far the preeminent activity within ATC, with the largest mission, the greatest responsibility, and the most personnel. He protested, vigorously, what he considered a "reduction in echelon," and accordingly, the unit he commanded became, from the start, the Ferrying Division in recognition of its higher status.[49]

Thus, the career of William Tunner poses an important question: How does the military—that most disciplined and ranked of American institutions—respond to this kind of intense talent and willful independence? Tunner had genius, but when necessary, he was prone to following his own course and not the traditional route. At times the air force would have a hard time accommodating this, with mixed results for both Tunner and the service.

One other comparison underlines this issue. Although Tunner most resembled civilian business leaders, there is also a relation to one military figure, Brigadier General Billy Mitchell. Although the comparison is limited, and thus can be stretched too far, there were still similarities. Mitchell saw that a particular branch of the service had capabilities far beyond what anyone envisioned for it, in this case airpower. He believed fervently that it could do things that were vitally important, despite the fact that few of the leaders of his era shared this insight. In addition, he wanted to raise the Air Corps's status by creating a unique service, run by air professionals only; as the U.S. Air Force historian Roger G. Miller explained, after the First World War, Mitchell developed "a deep commitment to the belief that the nation needed an 'air force,' not an 'air service.'" He would pursue these goals using whatever means of publicity were available to him and would not be bound by the usual rules of protocol or by generals who he felt were ignorant obstructionists. In the same vein, Tunner sought to place airlift within the pantheon of key air force commands and would fight to get it there over all opposition.[50]

William Tunner was poised to take on big projects. He had the vision, the talent, the drive. First, however, he would become involved in an issue that would also make him a pioneer in social justice, although—as always—for his own reasons.

2 / Tunner's Women Pilots

The standard account of the United States in World War II is one of glorious triumph, an unimpeded march to victory; it was no accident that Studs Terkel, one of the most sensitive chroniclers of American life, titled his volume on that era, *The Good War.*

Reality, however, is rarely that simple, and a closer view of the events from 1941 to 1945 displays a more nuanced story.

Success, for example, was hardly guaranteed. By mid-1942, months after the United States had entered the conflict, Bataan, Corregidor, and Burma had just fallen, and there was no indication of a U.S. counteroffensive. All of Western Europe had succumbed to Nazism, and in the east, a massive German thrust was advancing on Stalingrad with nothing in its way. In North Africa, meanwhile, Rommel was pulverizing the British with relatively little loss to his Afrika Korps. At home, Britain could still do little more than suffer bombings and respond with an air offensive. As the authors of one of the best single volumes on World War II described it, "German victories in summer 1942 represented the last moment when the Wehrmacht's skill and force structure were still sufficient to gain and hold the initiative."[1]

Thus, the notion that the Allies were destined to win was hardly in the air at this point, while a sense of desperation, a notion that extreme measures and extreme sacrifices would be needed to win this, was a far more typical viewpoint. In the face of such a dire threat, the usual assumption is that the nation came together as one to provide a comprehensive war effort.

Not exactly. While it is accurate to state that the vast majority of Americans supported the war, what is astonishing is how unwilling they were to forgo a myriad of prejudices, thus blocking many groups from participating in this struggle. The idea that the country brought together every segment in a patriotic surge is simply not correct; instead, at a time when every citizen was needed, blatant discrimination severely limited the notion of any kind of full mobilization of resources.

By now, the notion that racism still existed during World War II is a well-documented one, led by efforts to popularize the struggle of the Tuskegee airmen to gain a right to fly and fight. During the war the Red Cross segregated blood supplies, to appease fears of southerners that they would acquire unwanted characteristics if treated with negro blood. Factories placed orders for "whites only," denying themselves the skills and passions of blacks, and race riots broke out in Beaumont, Texas, and in Detroit, Michigan, after both cities experienced an influx of African American workers. In the former example, the rumor that a black man had raped a white women led to an episode that caused three deaths and hundreds of lesser casualties. The result was that twenty-five hundred black employees in local factories left the city temporarily, creating a loss of 210,000 hours of work in various defense plants. Detroit was even worse, where during a riot twenty-five African-Americans and nine whites were killed and eight hundred were injured; the War Production Board estimated two million hours of work lost in the first two days of the riot alone. During the summer of 1943, there were 242 major race fights in forty-seven cities across the United States.[2]

Color, however, was not the only barrier to full participation in the war effort. There was still, for example, considerable anti-Semitism in the United States Army, a belief held by officers such as George Patton. The last American military attaché in Berlin, for example, Colonel Truman Smith, opposed the melting-pot concept, compared the Germans to "the average white inhabitant of Alabama or Georgia, but with a racial feeling towards the Jew . . . rather than the Negro," and noted that, "The international tendencies of Communism appeared to cover exactly with the international tendencies of Jewry." Munich, he hoped, would permit Hitler "to liquidate the Jewish problem once and for all."[3]

Smith was not alone. E. R. Warner McCabe, eventually to head the army's G-2 Intelligence Section, was a defender of white supremacy and told superiors he thought it was "difficult to distinguish between the various Slavic races." Throughout the late 1930s, standard speakers at the Army War College were

Lothrop Stoddard and Henry Fairchild, two of the most extreme intellectual racists America had produced in the twentieth century.

Both within the military and the civilian law enforcement sectors, intelligence agencies generally held the view that Jewish immigrants were generically of suspect loyalty; authorities branded one Jewish female applying for a visa a "German agent" on the grounds that she had "ample funds" that must have been intended for subversive activities. In another case, a German refugee with impeccable scholarly credentials—he was sponsored by the Librarian of Congress and the Rockefeller Foundation—was initially denied admittance. When that decision was overturned on appeal, the FBI and the Military Intelligence Division protested strongly, bringing up such salient evidence of radicalism as the fact that his other sponsor had been the New School for Social Research. General George Strong, head of G-2 from 1942 to 1944, actually ran a security check on Albert Einstein, and then sent forth word that, "This office would not recommend the employment of Dr. Einstein on matters of a secret nature, since he was 'an extreme radical' . . . [who] has been sponsoring the principal Communist causes in the United States," noting, furthermore, that Einstein had been "ousted from Germany as a Communist."

These trends continued within the military itself. One paper presented as late as 1940 at the Army War College questioned the idea of admitting naturalized Americans to the service (at a time when there would soon be a massive manpower shortage) on the grounds that the army had to "exercise great care in the selection and of recruits in that we do not accept those who are agents of foreign governments." One lieutenant wrote a senior officer that a new unit to which he had been assigned was the first one in his experience "that didn't have a bunch of Jewish officers in it. . . . Thank God for it." The situation got so bad that, as one critic noted, "many a Jewish GI settled the problem . . . with his fists."

Women were less likely to strike their malefactors, although it was not because they were welcomed in the services. Despite the fact that 350,000 American women enlisted in the uniformed branches during the war and performed exemplary service, neither their entrance nor their subsequent terms in the military were smooth sailing. Despite the strong support of General George Marshall, the army chief of staff, Congress initially refused to create a female group within the army; their chief lobbyist reported, "In my time I have got some one hundred bills through the Congress, but this was more difficult than the rest of them combined." Some of the senior admirals in the navy would have preferred "dogs or ducks or monkeys" to females, if it were possible for those animals to perform the same chores. As late as March 1944—only three months before D-Day—the office of WAC (Women's Army Corps) director was still so emasculated, still so blocked by institutional and personal barriers, that Marshall had to order a reorganization so that it would report directly to him. Women in the army also faced a glass ceiling, holding them down to the lowest rank; at a time when only 24.3 percent of all males in the enlisted ranks were privates, the equivalent figure for women was 38.5 percent.[4]

Attitudes changed slowly. One SPAR (women's Coast Guard) officer claimed that "reception by the men ranged from enthusiasm through amused condescension to open hostility." A woman Marine observed that during training, drill instructors seemed to resent these ladies "more than a battalion of Japanese troops." By 1943 a slanderous whispering campaign on women soldiers' morals had become so extreme—one rumor claimed that 90 percent of their ranks sold sex for cash and that 40 percent had become pregnant from "servicing" their male counterparts—that the FBI investigated whether it was actually a plot by Nazi propagandists. Finding no such evidence, the services could only agree with a study of army recruiting, which concluded that the problem was not with women, but with blatant prejudice from the American male, who despite the increasingly pressing needs of total war, still "absolutely forbids his wife, sweetheart or sister to join a military organization."[5]

There is no question that this attitude was widespread throughout American society, limiting American women's ability to contribute to a war effort that through 1942 seemed in genuine jeopardy. The National Catholic Women's Union branded the Women's Army Auxiliary Corps (WAACs) "a serious menace to the home and foundation of a true Christian and democratic country," while America First, an isolationist organization, labeled the corps as "unnatural." One father complained, "If my daughter is a member of an organized uniformed group of whores . . . I want to know and get her out of the WAAC," while a soldier concluded, "Join the WAVES [Women Accepted for Volunteer Emergency Services] or WAC and you are automatically a prostitute in my opinion."[6]

Worst off of all were black women in the services; in the army their officers could not issue commands to any white servicemen, while an official report noted that "some post commanders are at a loss" to figure out what to do with these troopers, "other than in laundries, mess units, or salvage and reclamation shops." In some cases the solution was simple: black members of the WAACs bused tables in the Officers' Clubs and served as maids in their quarters.[7]

Evidence abounds, therefore, that during World War II, the United States resisted full mobilization when it went against any of a myriad of engrained and powerful prejudices. It would take a strong figure to overcome this kind of resistance, even if his motives were less than progressive.

William Tunner's involvement with women's issues stemmed from a simple notion: he needed pilots. The brute fact was that as head of ferrying activities within the Army Air Forces, and literally thousands of planes coming off the assembly lines that had to be delivered to active units around the globe, he had far too few pilots for what was perceived as a low-priority mission. Complicating matters even further, many planes had to be ferried three or four or more times before they reached the front lines, as they bounced from factory to factory and received supplemental equipment such as radios or weapons. As Ann Hamilton Tunner, who served as a pilot for the ATC and later became the general's second wife, described the situation, "you build an airplane but it has to get off the parking lot, you know, and . . . we didn't have a lot of pilots. It was his assignment to get planes from factories off to little strips around the country; little airstrips were popping up all over the place to train pilots. . . . They had to get the planes, and we didn't have a lot of pilots."[8]

One answer came from a remarkable woman named Nancy Harkness Love. Born into the finest of Philadelphia families, Nancy Harkness attended Milton Academy and Vassar. At sixteen, however, she broke the mold and learned to fly, discovering one of her great loves in life. In college, she earned money—and flying time—by taking her classmates for a spin using planes rented from a local airport. On one occasion she descended so low over campus that she practically reached treetop level, and the campus officials, hardly amused, suspended her for two weeks and forced her to stop flying for the whole semester, as a condition of reinstatement. In 1936 she married Robert Love, an Air Corps Reserve officer and businessman, in a wedding that featured headlines such as, "Beautiful Aviatrix Weds Dashing Air Corps Officer." The two started a small firm based in Boston called Intercity Airlines, and Nancy Love also flew for the Bureau of Air Commerce, testing new landing gear and performing navigational duties for local townships.[9]

As early as 1940, Love was engaged in ferrying planes for the British on a private contracting basis, taking them from factories to locations where agents of the Commonwealth took over. As she later described her work, "I landed at an airport right at the boundary of the United States. I taxied the plane to the border, cut the switch, and climbed out. Then some Canadians pulled and

2. Nancy Love. (Library of Congress photo, courtesy Texas Woman's University Archives)

shoved the plane across the border. I turned around and brought back another one." At this time she was the only woman engaged in this kind of work in the United States.[10]

She was not the only female pilot in the country, however. As early as 1929, when Fay Gillis started the first club for women aviators in the country, there were 117 female licensed pilots. In 1940 the availability of lady aviators sparked an idea in Nancy Love; after all, her husband, since recalled to service, was now deputy chief of staff at Ferrying Command. On May 21, 1940, Love wrote to Colonel Robert Olds, who worked in the Plans Division in the Office of the Chief of the Air Corps, to propose something novel: that women join up to help ferry planes. In her letter, she noted how, "I've been able to find forty-nine [qualified women pilots] I can rate as excellent material. . . . There are probably at least fifteen more of these. . . . I really think this list is up to handling pretty complicated stuff. Most of them have in the neighborhood of a thousand hours or more—mostly more, and have flown a great many types of ships."[11] Olds endorsed the plan and sent it on, but Hap Arnold, head of the Air Corps, was not ready for such a revolutionary notion, and turned it down. The furthest he would go in terms of accepting women pilots was to recommend that they fly as copilots on commercial planes, thus freeing up men for the military.

Nancy Love, however, had established a basic principle that would cause problems as the Air Corps reformed and that still is the subject of debate. In her early proposal, and in every plan that she set up after that, Love sought a small number of pioneers who were previously trained and capable of doing the same work at levels equivalent to those of men, if not higher. She suggested, in other words, that women be recruited on the basis of their ability to do the job already, nothing more and nothing less, and thus should be allowed to work equally—nothing more and nothing less. This is now referred to as equality feminism, and it is not the only way to approach issues of gender.

By 1942 much had changed since the time Love had submitted her first proposal. The United States was in the war, and Arnold had already accepted another plan to get women pilots into Ferrying Command, as we shall see, although it had not reached fulfillment yet. Nancy Love was now working for Ferrying Command as a civilian in the Operations Office of the Northeast Sector, Domestic Wing of Ferrying Command in Baltimore, gaining local knowledge as well as administrative experience on top of that she had acquired as co-owner of an airline.

The sequence of events is not clear, but in 1942 Love raised her idea of using qualified women pilots again. According to Tunner's autobiography, the first move came at the water cooler in ATC headquarters. He was sharing a sip with Colonel Love, when the junior officer, talking to himself, mentioned that he hoped his wife got to work okay that morning. The couple lived in Washington, but she commuted to Baltimore by plane.[12]

According to Tunner, this was electrifying knowledge—in his own work he italicized the words "by plane." The general blurted out, "Good Lord. . . . I'm combing the woods for pilots, and here's one right under my nose. Are there many more women like your wife?" Love replied. "Why don't you ask her?" and arranged a meeting, "right then and there."

Tunner and Love must have had partnership at first sight. She was his kind of personality, with his kind of interests: she loved flying, and she approached things from a businesslike standpoint. In his writings, Tunner cited the fact that she had 1,200 hours of flying time, "but was also experienced in organization and administration." Nancy Love was beautiful, a head turner, but for Tunner the important fact was that "she proved that a woman could be both attractive and efficiently dependable at the same time." The officer was impressed.[13]

William Tunner, in other words, was about to get involved in pioneering social reform, not out of liberal instincts, but because he refused to observe customs that got in the way of doing his job. Later in his career that would lead to difficulties, but in 1942 his motivation was clear. As he later wrote, "By this . . . time we needed pilots, any pilots, badly."[14]

Tunner and Love began to meet and to draw up strict guidelines for recruitment. Besides being between twenty-one and thirty-five years of age, candidates had to be U.S. citizens, high school graduates, and have two letters of recommendation. They also had to be highly qualified aviators, with 500 hours flying time, at least some of which was in planes with over 200 horsepower, which meant that they had flown something other than small private aircraft. There was a considerable pool to draw from: by mid-1941 there were 2,733 licensed female pilots in the country, and 154 held commercial licenses as well. On June 18, Tunner sent a memo to General George, ATC commanding officer, proposing that women be accepted as full-time ferrying pilots, and that they form the 1st WAAF (Women's Auxiliary Air Force) Ferrying Squadron.[15]

As usual, Tunner moved fast, and the plans started to come together. The same day the memo went out he was exploring locations for a new base where women could train and live, and found facilities in Wilmington that would be vacant within a week. By June 22 he was writing George again with this information, proposing that a group be activated right away, on July 15, and that Mrs. Love be named a first lieutenant and serve as operations officer. Tunner, in other words, treated Love as an equal; if she did the job, she got the credit, and the commission as an officer.[16]

By then, General Arnold was a supporter of women pilots, but with qualifications. On July 13 he wrote Congressman W. R. Poage (D-TX) how, "It gives me great pleasure to inform you that the Air Transport Command . . . is giving consideration to the use of women fliers as ferrying pilots." However, there were "certain technical difficulties . . . due to the deficiencies of the existing legislation" authorizing women in the Army Air Forces. In particular, there was no provision, "no authority for the commissioning of flying officers in the Women's Auxiliary Army Corps, nor is there any authority for flying pay."[17]

As a result, the proposal changed: twenty-five women pilots would be organized in a civilian squadron and initially fly only certain kinds of planes; interviewed decades later, Tunner called the lack of commissions "a sad thing . . . they did the same job that the men did." He soon demonstrated that the fifty women pilots could be adequately but separately housed at Newcastle Army Air Base in Delaware, while they ate at the same mess hall as the men. They were asked to apply in person, carrying proof of their accomplishments. After checking the documents, Ferrying Division gave a flight check, then sent the women to school for thirty to forty days to learn military procedures and routes, as well as about the planes they would be flying. They would be paid $250 a month ($50 less than men) and $6 per diem when in the field (the same as men).[18]

On September 10, 1942, Secretary of War Henry Stimson officially announced that women pilots would be recruited for ferrying work, in a unit called the Women's Auxiliary Ferrying Squadron (WAFS). Within one week, Nancy Love had accepted seven women; by December 19 the full roster of twenty-five slots had been filled.[19]

As planned, these were exceptional individuals, fully qualified to compete with men on equal terms and match or beat them. The first pilot Love accepted was Fay Gillis, founder of the premier women's flying club, and along with personalities like Amelia Earhart (who died in 1937), one of the most famous women flyers in the country. She had fourteen years flying experience with 1,400 hours in the air, and she was accepted on September 12, only two days after the official announcement.[20]

Love and Gillis were in good company. Of the twenty-five founding members of WAFS, twenty-one were not only pilots but also instructors in flying; the average experience for the entire cadre was 1,162 hours of flight time per member, far above the 500 hours called for in the initial qualifications. Barbara Towne of San Rafael, California, for example, had started flying lessons with money saved from her allowance, but when her father discovered her commitment to the air, he paid for her tuition at the Ryan School of Aeronautics in San Diego. There she worked as a mechanic and learned everything about planes from the ground up; her dad also bought her a plane so she could continue to fly. Another charter member, Barbara Erickson of Seattle, started flying while a sophomore at the University of Washington, and had mastered seaplanes as well as landplanes. She was teaching school when Love's telegram of acceptance arrived and, seeing the news, simply stopped the class and took off for Wilmington. Still another, Dorothy Fulton, had 2,500 hours flying time, and actually ran her own airport in New Jersey, while Evelyn Sharp of Ord, Nebraska, started flying when a barnstormer could not pay a bill owed her father, so gave the daughter lessons instead. She worked at odd, hard jobs to pay for more lessons, becoming a barnstormer and a flying instructor. By the time she got the call, Sharp had 2,950 hours in the air. Many of these women had families and children, and some were well educated; Adela Scharr had an M.S. in psychology and taught this in St. Louis, flying on the weekends.

By 1942, however, these pilots were not alone. Another group of women had been formed, with a different founder, and a different philosophy.

Jacqueline Cochran was another one of those women who made aviation history. In a story more suitable to pulp women's fiction than military history, Cochran began life in extreme poverty amid the lumber and textile factories of

rural Florida; she never knew her birth date, her parents, or even her real sur-
name (she picked the name *Cochran* out of a phone book). As she described
those times, "Food at best consisted of the barest essentials—sometimes nothing except what I foraged for myself in the woods of the . . . sawmill towns my
foster family called home. . . . We were always a little hungry." With only two
years of schooling, she talked her way into a factory job while still a child, and
by age ten had become the inspection room supervisor, with fifteen workers reporting to her. Seeking something more, she taught herself beauty culture—as
one friend put it, "Her threshold for boredom was very low indeed"—and operated salons in Montgomery and other cities. Eventually, these towns became
too small for her, and she invaded New York City, wangling a job at the exclu-
sive Antoine's salon in Saks Fifth Avenue's flagship store. In 1934 she started
her own cosmetics firm, which soon became one of the largest in the United
States.[21]

In 1932 Jackie—as she was usually known—took some flying lessons at
Roosevelt Field on Long Island, during a vacation; she was hooked. Moving on
to schools in San Diego, it took her only three weeks to qualify for her pilot's li-
cense. In 1935 she became the first woman to enter the Bendix Transcontinental Race from Los Angeles to Cleveland, and in 1937 she took first place in the
women's competition and came in third among all contestants, including the
men. That year she also became the first woman in American history to make a
blind landing, outside of Pittsburgh. The next year she took the laurels at the
Bendix against all comers and received the General William Mitchell Memorial
Award for "contributing to the progress of aviation in the U.S." In 1939, with
war approaching Europe, she set a new altitude record for women by flying to
over 30,000 feet, and established world speed records over 1,000 and 2,000 kilometer distances. After the war, Cochran became the first woman to break the
sound barrier, and in 1964 flew an F-104 at 1,429 mph, smashing many of the
standards she had established earlier. When she died in 1980, Jackie Cochran
had held over eighty records for speed, altitude, and distance, more than any
other pilot—male or female—has ever achieved in the history of aviation. Her
contemporary, Chuck Yeager, described Jackie Cochran by noting, "She didn't
have the word *consequences* in her makeup. She had no fear at all. . . . She was a
remarkable person and a real competitor."[22]

By 1939 Jackie Cochran was urging the White House to let women get
involved in the burgeoning war effort. In a prescient note to Eleanor Roosevelt,
Cochran insightfully recognized what would later be Tunner's great concern:
"In the field of aviation the real 'bottle neck' . . . is likely to be trained pilots."

Women pilots could free up men for combat duties if women were assigned to "all sorts of helpful back of the lines work." By 1941 her thinking had advanced considerably; that year she penned an article for *Flying* that would lay out the essence of her large concept. The government should utilize not just accredited women pilots, but train a new flying corps with starting membership of at least one thousand, to be used for every air task except combat. Thus, Cochran was advocating a women's role even before Nancy Love, but with a wildly different concept, that women should be trained for new roles that they could not previously fill.[23]

Later that year, Cochran was at a luncheon at the White House, celebrating aviation leaders, when Clayton Knight approached her. Knight was in charge of American recruiting efforts for the British Ferry Command, and he proposed that Cochran fly a multiengined plane to London as a publicity device. Jackie loved the idea; as usual, being the first woman to fly a major plane got her involved, fast. In a short while she qualified on her new craft and passed all physicals. Male pilots objected, but by then Jackie was married to Floyd Odlum, a Wall Street heavyweight with clout in very high places. Odlum contacted Lord Beaverbrook, British minister of procurement, who brokered a compromise wherein Jackie would fly the plane while a male copilot handled takeoff and landing. On July 17, 1941, she flew a two-engined Lockheed Hudson bomber from Montreal to Prestwick, a Scottish air base.[24]

But something else came out of that meeting with the Roosevelts. Eleanor had shown interest in Cochran's ideas of a women's pilot corps, and the president provided a letter of introduction to the assistant secretary of war. In a short while Jackie wound up in conversation first with General Arnold and then Colonel Robert Olds of Ferrying Command, the same individual who played a key role in Nancy Love's plans.[25]

Cochran began implementing her ideas on her own. Olds had brought her onboard as a volunteer "tactical consultant," but provided no support. Instead, Cochran moved seven top secretarial employees from her cosmetics firm to Washington and proceeded to go through the entire bank of three hundred thousand Civil Aviation Authority (CAA) pilot forms, from which they extracted the names of three thousand women. The problem was that of this select list, only three hundred had more than the bare minimum of two hundred flying hours, only thirty had more than one thousand.[26]

Cochran now codified her ideas. She would attempt a grand social experiment, not just to bring qualified women pilots into the Army Air Forces, but to change the status quo by training thousands of females for new responsibilities that had previously been the purview of males only. In one memo to Colonel Olds, she criticized him for "thinking in terms of present movement of equipment," whereas she was "thinking of shaping up a women's pilot organization for its future usefulness in time of war with . . . ferrying as an initial . . . incident."[27]

As noted earlier, General Arnold turned down the idea of women pilots, and Cochran turned her attention to recruiting for the British. When the formation of WAFS hit the news, she was furious and determined to fight back; one of her future trainees noted that "If Jackie Cochran were threatened, she'd respond like a tigress." She promptly called for a meeting again with Arnold, who by then, in Cochran's own words, "knows me well enough to know how much I enjoy a good battle." Dean Jaros, author of a study of American airwomen, highlighted the moment by noting "Arnold was fully aware of Cochran's aggressiveness, to say nothing of her and her husband's Washington connections." At a meeting on September 15, 1942, which included the Army Air Forces' director of individual training, members of the chief's staff, and Jacqueline Cochran, the service agreed to create the Women's Flying Training Detachment (WFTD), with Cochran as director.[28]

Under Cochran's powerful leadership, the WFTD soon became both active and substantial. Training began in Texas, with the major facility at Avenger Field in Sweetwater. Among those who joined up was Ann Hamilton, later married to William Tunner. An Oklahoman, she had learned to fly in a civilian pilot training course in Tulsa. By 1942 she owned a Piper Cub, and, according to her oral history, "I heard that Jacqueline Cochran planned on taking women pilots and training them to fly military airplanes. . . . I flew my little plane down to Fort Worth to see Jacqueline Cochran, and everything happened fast." Within ten days she was part of the second class. In time, the program, under various names, would receive 25,000 applications from American women, of whom 1,830 were approved for training, and 1,074 graduated. Applications came in from not just Americans, but Canadian, British, and even Brazilian women as well. One resident of the U.S.'s northern neighbor beseeched Cochran, "Because we are fighting on the same side in this war . . . and because one more flyer (be he Canuck or Yank) means one less German, I would like to ask you on bended knee if there would be any chance of accepting me . . . I am physically fit; have a college degree; can sing the Star Spangled Banner; have never been a nazi spy; and would gladly take out U.S. papers." The four-month course included 180 hours of classes on the ground and 135 hours in the air.[29]

For all the women who went into either of the two programs, Love's or Cochran's, there were some common experiences. One was a problem with being taken seriously. In an initial newsreel on women pilots in the air service, the announcer concluded with the line, "What will they think of next?" *Life* magazine, in one story, found it relevant to include Nancy Love in a list of six well-known women with gorgeous legs. General Tunner, in an oral history interview, remembered how, "When a female voice would come out of the clear calling the tower, why, they immediately stopped traffic. . . . But the women, I noticed, weren't met by contingents of men waiting to carry their bag and their parachute . . . there was resentment." On one occasion, at a time when the women still wore rough clothes on missions, a group of ferryiers landed in a strange town and, according to one account, "were taken for some new kind of disreputable women and put through a painful experience with the local police."[30]

Even though these flyers eventually acquired a uniform, it did not help. Bystanders asked if they were WACs, WAVES, airline hostesses, Red Cross workers, leaders of the Girl Scouts, and even part of the Mexican Army. A typical conversation would start with someone inquiring what the uniform represented, with the pilot explaining that she ferried planes for the Army Air Forces. The stunned reply was usually something like, "All by yourself?" Though the answer came as an affirmative, many Americans in and out of the service still had to ask, "Who pilots the plane?"[31]

The commanding official was the Director of Women Pilots, and Jackie Cochran received this post. Nancy Love was made head of the WASP (Women Airforce Service Pilots) flyers in the Ferrying Division, an appointment that may have been most amenable both to her and to General Tunner.[32]

That consolidation ended the bureaucratic duplication, but it did nothing to still the issue that Tunner had wound up in the middle of. Modern scholars discuss the ongoing difference between equality feminists and difference feminists, the former arguing that women must be treated as equals, the latter that women are unique and must be treated as such, especially through innovative reform projects. Nancy Love clearly saw herself in the former camp, asking that women be taken on under the same rules and standards that applied to men. She sought a small group of women who already possessed skills equivalent to, if not surpassing those of their male counterparts, and fought to gain them an equal place in the war effort. Her view is best expressed in the official ATC history of all these programs, which stated, "there is no important difference between male and female civilian pilots." Cochran, on the other hand, wanted something entirely different. Her goal was not just to help the military, but to use it to change the existing social structure. She sought not just to give women equality, but also to change the cohort of women who qualified for traditional male employment. Thus, she pursued a grand experiment, not just a fight for equal rights. The military saw this conflict as well and did not paper it over; General George's memo to General Arnold in September 1942, endorsing a women's training school, started by acknowledging how, "It is obvious that there are two, and differing conceptions of the program to be undertaken in connection with the training and subsequent utilization of women by Army Air Forces."[33]

There is no question that General William Tunner played a major role in these developments, and while he clearly favored one side of the discussion, his views were never dogmatic or unyielding.

Tunner definitely leaned toward Nancy Love and the WAFS and was not inclined toward Cochran or her organization. General George's letter, cited just above, went on to declare, "The Air Transport Command has no extensive facilities for the training of women pilots . . . Present program . . . is to employ women with more than five hundred hours of flight time and commercial licenses," only, and "No extension of the program beyond the utilization of women with these qualifications is planned . . . at this time." If that wasn't enough, he concluded, "ATC had no plan for the establishment of an extensive school plant, designed for the purpose of giving either primary or intermediate instruction to women pilots." An early work on military airlift in the United States reported, "The Ferrying Division was not happy at having the older designation . . . established nearly a year and already famous, taken away from it." Quietly, ATC kept the original WAFS signs up on many bases and over the women's barracks, much to the displeasure of Jackie Cochran. In the official history cited above—which Tunner must have seen—it dismissed the merger under WASP with faint praise by remarking, "To a mild degree this coordinating and planning agency . . . brought [the two earlier agencies] closer together." Finally, Tunner was notoriously independent—the entrepreneur as officer, who operated as he saw fit; while Jackie Cochran was a hard-driving pioneer determined to be her own boss and run her own program without interference. There is no record of Tunner condemning Cochran, but he could not have appreciated her style, nor her goal of training women that he felt unqualified for the mission.[34]

Beneath that dispute, however, Tunner led the way in standing up for women's rights in the Army Air Forces. The "Group Manual" for ferrying personnel is striking in how it lays out requirements for civilian pilots in cold, formal language, without any reference to gender disparity. He backed this up in person, as well; at a staff meeting on April 28, 1943, for example, Tunner told his crew that from then on women would no longer be restricted to ferrying small planes and trainers, but instead would be allowed to fly on any plane they qualified for, including the heaviest four-engine bombers and the hottest pursuit planes. This idea met with sufficient resistance at all levels that Tunner repeated it at a subsequent meeting on May 11. Late in June, officers raised the issue of whether or not women would be permitted to handle the hottest fighter in the air force, the P-51 Mustang, and Tunner replied, according to the official record, that women "would fly anything they were capable of flying."[35]

Tunner felt so strongly about this issue that he tried to stage a major publicity stunt that would have gotten nationwide coverage, a harbinger of his efforts in later campaigns on behalf of airlift. In 1943 he organized a scheme wherein Nancy Love and Betty Gillies would fly a B-17, one of the nation's premier bombers, all the way to England. There seemed no risk—both women were qualified on four-engine planes and had in fact flown a B-17 to Labrador already—but it would be a powerful demonstration of what women were capable of, an important bit of advocacy for giving them equal rights in the air as long as they were qualified.[36]

Tunner had cleared this verbally with the Office of the Chief of the Air Staff, and on September 4 the mission began, with the first two jumps taking them to Goose Bay in Labrador. The ATC sent formal notice ahead that the plane and its pilots were about to depart, a message that went to the head of its European Wing, who just happened, at that precise moment, to be having dinner with none other than Hap Arnold.[37]

Arnold had never been directly informed of Tunner's idea, a typical oversight, and he did not take kindly to it; he believed, in all honesty, that there would be a huge outcry if women were shot down in a dangerous, experimental mission. The chief felt strongly about this, to put it mildly, moving with all possible speed to stop the B-17 from taking off. Radio commands filled the airways, and fifteen minutes before the plane was to begin taxiing, the base commanding officer came tearing onto the runway to tell Love and Gillies that they had to abort the mission, leave the bomber there, and return home by transport. A photographer snapped the two disappointed pilots, gamely trying to smile. Jackie Cochran later commented that individual accomplishments of exceptional women should not be fostered, that new opportunities should only be sought for the group as a whole. Tunner's recollection of the event was that "they [Love and Gillies] were heartbroken! So was I."[38]

Another gambit Tunner used—again a harbinger of things to come—was to get pilots to compete in order to raise productivity, in this case pitting women against men. Male pilots were experiencing problems with the Bell P-39 Cobra, an unusually designed plane and something of a clunker, with a high accident rate. Tunner agreed that "it had the glide angle of a brick," but also maintained that "it was perfectly safe if it was flown according to specifications." Male pilots were having the problem, while, "Our women . . . read the characteristics and specifications of the plane they were to fly before they flew it." To the general, "the solution of the P-39 problem was a natural one." He assigned a group of female pilots to the P-39 detail, who performed flawlessly. In Tunner's words, "They had no trouble at all, none at all. And I had no more complaints from the men." His main goal, of course, was to make sure P-39s were delivered safely and efficiently, but along the way he also proved a point about women's flying capabilities.[39]

Tunner also fought another ridiculous idea that the army tried to enforce, namely that women pilots should not be allowed to fly during their menstrual cycle, based on rules in the existing CAA manual. The ATC Surgeon rejected this notion, writing the Air Surgeon that this should be handled as a private matter by the local WAFS supervisor and if necessary, a flight surgeon. The Army Air Forces' top medical officer agreed that this was a local issue, in part, as the official WASP account so delicately put it, "it would have been difficult to enforce the . . . rule . . . since, without the rather intimate cooperation of the women pilots concerned, it is difficult to understand just how the Group commanders and operations officers could tell when a WAF was in a period."[40]

Most ATC officers got the point, until the Third Ferrying Group at Romulus, Michigan, tried to enforce a rule that women could only fly light trainers during their menstrual cycle. Love hit the roof and marched in to see Tunner. Naively, he told her he "assumed that each girl would have to stand down for 3 or 4 days each month." Love "immediately informed me that was not the case." The language, however, must have been a tad more emphatic, as Tunner also noted that she "straightened me out."[41]

Having been duly enlightened, Tunner acted. A letter went out from the ATC chief of staff notifying personnel that flight limitations were being imposed on women pilots that disregarded their professional qualifications. The missive listed specific restrictions that would need to be changed, and concluded bluntly: "It is the desire of this Command that all pilots, regardless of sex, be privileged to advance to the extent of their ability in keeping with the progress of aircraft development."

There is no question that Tunner also showed the same interest in his women pilots that he rendered to their male counterparts. Ann Tunner, a WASP, recalled how she met him one time in Cincinnati as part of a group flight: "He had a lot of questions to ask about what we were flying and what we were doing." She knew that he was getting a daily report, but still felt he wanted to know everything about their particular mission and how it was going.[42]

Tunner even embraced Cochran's flyers in a fair and even-handed manner. As was true throughout this episode, his goal was more important than his prejudices or societal custom. In October 1943, he cited seventeen trainees who he felt were still not qualified to ferry planes, but then listed fifty-three more who were qualified for the highest level of skill, piloting fast pursuit planes (Tunner called any pilot with this rating, "the best there was"). These women came from all the branches of the Army Air Forces' programs for women.[43]

Tunner's connection to the WASP was controversial, but unlike later troubles, this was not primarily his fault. He wound up in the middle of a dispute that still occurs, whether or not equality should be sought solely for qualified women, or if this goal should be extended to a larger social experiment, to raise large groups of females into that category. William Tunner sat within the former camp, but he was there firmly and of his own free will, and that alone made him something of a progressive.

He had not come by this from conviction, but rather from single-minded dedication to excel at his mission, a classic Tunner characteristic. Ann Tunner told how "He was desperate. He had a job to move airplanes. He had to move 'em. . . . He needed pilots—he wasn't going to put a gender on them." William Tunner was a doer at all costs, and custom be damned.[44]

Tunner, however, also learned and changed, based on experience; his views soon went way beyond the simple motivation of getting a job done. Later in life, an interviewer asked the general how the women's "record stack[ed] up against the men? Were they about equal?" Tunner vigorously replied, "No, they were better." He cited the fact that both their accident rate and even their delivery rate was superior. At least as important to someone like Tunner, who had an industrial engineer's regard for small details, women were more likely to "take the regulations and technical orders home and study them, and they knew them by heart. We never had any trouble with the women when we asked them about parts of the airplane that they were to fly, and how to handle them." Male pilots, on the contrary, "were not as good. They were not as well trained. They were not as knowledgeable as the women pilots." He then took it even further, in 1976 criticizing the then-current military command structure by saying, "why the Air Force has forgotten all this, I can't explain," adding, "we have got to make use of all our resources to win, and all of our resources means we have got to use every human that we have."[45]

Love and Cochran—and Tunner—had much to be proud of. WASP was unique among the various female auxiliaries, because it was the only one where women served exclusively in professional, male-dominated jobs—in this case as pilots. The number of women in Ferrying Division reached a high of 303 in April 1944. In July 1943, before the formation of WASP, only 88 female pilots worked with the division, but each of them flew planes an average of 4,000 miles that month. By the end of that year, women were in the cockpit of almost every important American warplane, from cargo planes like the C-47 and C-46; to bombers like the A-20, the B-25, B-17, and the B-24; to top pursuits like the P-38, P-39, P-40, P-47, and the P-51, a total of 77 different craft altogether. Nancy Love alone was qualified on at least seventeen different planes. In the case of the P-47 Thunderbolt, by spring of 1944 literally all deliveries from the factories were being flown by women pilots, and in the fall three-quarters of all domestic ferrying of fighters were accomplished by females. Their record, collectively, up to October 1944 was a total of 500,000 hours in the air, and by the end of the war they had traveled 60 million miles. William Tunner had a right to be as pleased with their accomplishments as anyone. But by then, he was working on another project, one that would take him to the top of the world.

3 / The Hump

To understand the Burma Hump, one must first recognize the role China played in World War II. When most Americans think of the Pacific theater, they remember great island campaigns like Iwo Jima and Okinawa, or magnificent naval battles like Midway or the Philippine Sea. For the Japanese, however, China was one of its leading concerns, second only to the threat from U.S. forces. Throughout the war, notwithstanding the pressure from the U.S. Navy, Army, and Marine Corps, Japan always maintained a force of roughly one million troops in China, a land that would cost them four hundred thousand dead by the time they surrendered in August 1945. By means of comparison, total U.S. war dead in World War II, in both Europe and the Pacific, was roughly three hundred thousand.[1]

Early on, President Franklin Roosevelt recognized the critical importance of China, how it kept a potential adversary pinned down, and thus must be maintained in its war effort. In March 1941 he told the nation, "China expresses the magnificent will of millions of plain people to resist the dismemberment of their nation. China . . . asks our help. America has said that she shall have our help."[2]

China most definitely needed that help, having little capacity to forge the materials of modern warfare on its own. In 1936 that nation produced only 870,000 tons of pig iron, a figure that was less than half of what the United States made in 1870, as it was just beginning to ramp up to industrialization. Oil came out of Chinese refineries at the rate of only a few hundred barrels a day. There was capacity for making small arms, but no ability to make advanced weapons systems such as tanks or planes or artillery. As the writer William Koenig put it, "China's ability to maintain any kind of a war effort became almost entirely a question of supply."[3]

The route to supply China ran through Burma, the key link between the British colony in India and Chiang Kai-shek's armies; in December 1938 the Burma Road opened, a 700-mile gravel path that went from Lashio in Burma, south of the Himalayas, to Chunking. This was the primary system used to funnel supplies to China, but on January 15, 1942, the Japanese, at the peak of their strength and with momentum from an unparalleled string of victories, advanced into Burma with 35,000 men and hundreds of planes. Facing them were two weak British and Indian divisions with almost no air support. As Commonwealth troops retreated, on April 3 the last British planes left for safe haven in India, and on April 29 the Japanese Army cut the Burma Road, isolating China.[4]

Roosevelt declared, "it is obviously of the utmost urgency . . . that the pathway to China be kept open," adding, "The Japanese may have cut the Burma Road but . . . no matter what advances the Japanese may make, ways will be found to deliver . . . munitions to the armies of China." On March 21 the president ordered the military to open a ferrying route to China; General Hap Arnold wrote back that airport facilities along these routes were woefully insufficient, to send in airplanes without these facilities would be "very wasteful and perhaps disastrous." Instead, he suggested that an air route be opened between bases in India and the Chinese forces. His original plan involved use of a private contractor, the China National Aviation Corporation (CNAC), a joint venture between Pan American Airways and the Chinese government. There was no way this organization could muster the resources for a task of this magnitude, and in a short time, the U.S. Tenth Air Force, based in India, took over the mission; Colonel Robert Olds made the first military flight over the Hump on April 8, 1942. Their orders included a goal of 2,500 tons a month by February, with 5,000 tons after that. Soon this would be upped to 7,500 and then 10,000 tons each thirty-day period, as China, plagued with problems of corruption and incompetence, grimly tried to hold on.[5]

At first, those figures were fanciful; not much followed Colonel Olds's pioneering flight. In April and May the army managed a scant 196 tons, and by November 1942 the figure was up to 819 tons. On October 21 the Army Air Forces ordered the Air Transport Command to take over the operation, which became effective on December 1; it was now in charge of a force of only forty-four planes, of which 80 percent were two-engined craft. By February 1943 the

ATC experts got the figure up to 2,871 tons, beating the quota, but with little chance of going much further, let alone filling the giant hole that was China's quest for military aid.[6]

The problem, however, was that the route, at the end of the longest supply chain of World War II, ended in the worst flight path imaginable. The "Hump" referred to a pathway that was unique, covering roughly 500 miles from Assam in India to Chunking in China; pilots had to, simply put, fly over the Himalayas. In an age when some early model P-51 Mustangs had a ceiling of only 30,000 feet, trying to traverse the world's tallest mountain range in a lumbering transport was not only daunting, but often fatal.

As a result of this topography, flying and living conditions were horrendous. Pilots had to climb to 16,000 to 18,000 feet to make it over the Hump in the best of weather, which was rare; often they had to go up to 20,000 feet in an attempt to reach clear airspace. Planes barely made it across peaks traveling at 95 mph, with so much ice on the wings that by the time they landed these appendages had warped and bent.

It would have been difficult to fly over heights like that in good conditions, but few Hump pilots ever saw such weather. The region was a meeting place for three major Eurasian air currents, a zone where they came together and created enormous winds. Adding to this were the vast peaks and valleys, which together, created some of the most monstrous up-and-down drafts on the planet, with winds sometime reaching 250 miles an hour (by way of comparison, a Force 5 hurricane, at the top of the scale, is defined as having 155 mph winds or higher). Planes caught in these ferocious blasts could drop 5,000 to 8,000 feet in a minute, and if they did not have enough clearance, smash into a mountain peak with tremendous force. In some cases aircraft would shoot up to 28,000 feet, then get slammed down to 6,000 feet, all within two minutes. At first, before the crews learned to rig the loads better, cargo would literally rip itself out of the belly of the plane when subjected to that kind of force. One pilot claimed, "Flying a P-47 in combat was not as dangerous as flying a C-47 across the Hump."[7]

What the winds did not destroy, rainfall took care of. On May 24, 1943, for example, one of the American air bases got hammered by five inches of water within one hour, three feet over the course of the day.[8]

Everything—planes, pilots, supplies—became soaked, as operations ceased under the downpour and men became sick with fever and dysentery, while supplies of food, medicines, and spare parts all dwindled. Sanitation was often a cold shower and as one veteran put it, "an eight-holer toilet . . . about a hundred yards from the tents." When a request went out for desperately needed replenishment of toilet paper, authorities sent back the following: "Quartermaster aware of toilet paper shortage. A large quantity coming by water." Instead, during mail call, after hometown newspapers and magazines got handed out, the standard catcall was, "read 'em and wipe." Edwin White, who served on the Hump, described how for an entire month the daily ration for everyone—officers and enlisted alike—was two slices of Spam, six tablespoons of okra, bread, and coffee, with each unit deciding locally how to divide this largesse between breakfast, lunch, and dinner. As White put it, "We were sent over here to a life of chronic shortages. We were without regulations, without tables of organization, and all the other items dear to the heart of a bureaucrat and which are essential if you are going to get a request filled by higher headquarters. We had airplanes without spare parts or spare engines." One estimate had it that within a year of being assigned to this theater, personnel were operating at only 60 percent efficiency, a figure that dropped to 30 percent if they endured another six months.[9]

Numerous participants, in various capacities, testified to the rigors of the Burma Hump. The journalist Theodore White flew this route and dubbed the Himalayas the "knuckled fingers of death," ample testimony to his mental state as he made the flight. Colonel Edward Alexander, at one time leader of this effort, sent back a message that began with an understatement. "The weather here has been awful," he penned. "The icing starts at 12,000 feet. Today a C-87 (the cargo version of the B-24 bomber) went to 29,000 feet on instruments, was unable to climb higher, and could not get on top. It has rained 7 ½ inches in the past 5 days. All aircraft are grounded." Singing cowboy Gene Autry described the cliffs as "looming in front of them like a solid wall. . . . They had the biggest mountain range in the world, a clumsy ship with a lot of weight, and each flight was a suspense story." Autry did not persevere in this work, with good reason; as he put it, "I only flew the Hump once, to see what it was like. But if you worked it right, once was enough."[10]

The first officer assigned to master this mess was Colonel Edward Alexander; he had everything working against him. Taking over at the start of an operation like this meant getting the worst end of the stick. It was his job to build all the initial infrastructure—the airbases, hangers, supply depots, mess tents—while explaining why the tonnage carried was not high enough yet. In May 1943, for example, at the Anglo-American Trident Conference in Washington, U.S. and British representatives committed themselves to a second front in Europe, but as a gesture to Chiang Kai-shek, also promised to increase the tonnage flown to China. This led to the quota of 5,000 tons by July, 10,000 tons by September. As commanding officer, Alexander dubbed it "the July–September Objective," but as one air force historian noted, "Overworked airmen assigned to the Hump operation had less kindly names for it."[11]

As if this were not bad enough, ATC, as usual, got no respect from other branches of their service. Early on, when the Tenth Air Force learned the cargo men were taking over, they merged all local supplies into their own stockpiles, thus cutting off ATC until new material arrived. Their commanding general also appropriated six planes for the use of his forces, a decision not reversed till Hap Arnold issued a direct order. Even at the local level, pilots found nothing but contempt. On one occasion a transport was coming in to Luichow, an ATC base, with some P-51 fighters also in the area. Expecting priority at their own facility, they called in that, "Since we are already in the pattern, request you hold fighters till we land." The tower replied, "No problem," but only because the fighters were coming in first, "but will be on the ground and off the runway before you make your final turn." Irate, the colonel in charge of the lead transport announced his rank and demanded, "Luichow is an ATC base, we are an ATC ship. I insist you let us land first." Instead of being respected, that order received nothing but scorn. Fighter jock Charlie Vest announced to the airways, "Nyah, nyah, nyah, Colonel. I'd rather have a sister in a whorehouse than a brother in the ATC." The unnamed colonel was now beside himself, and yelled, "Who is the stupid pilot that made that remark? Give me your name, rank and organization." Vest calmly asked, "Colonel, don't you know the name of that stupid pilot?" and when the colonel barked, "No! Give me your name immediately. That's an order!" Vest calmly replied, "Colonel, this 'stupid' pilot ain't that stupid!"[12]

Alexander fought back, building bases and playing an important role in developing the Hump route. But the problems were immense. In a special report, he wrote, "Health is good," but "virtually all personnel suffer from chronic dysenteries," 20 percent of the entire complement would soon have malaria, and "the supply of fresh vegetables and fresh meat is scarce and growing scarcer." Most dangerous of all, "morale is good," yet there was a time bomb ticking that Tunner would later have to defuse, "a widespread feeling . . . that . . . they will be sent home or to another Theatre after one year's service in this area," even though "such a plan is wholly impractical."[13]

Given the sheer variety of pressing problems, safety remained a key issue yet to be tackled. C. R. Smith, former president of American Airlines and now a senior officer in ATC, studied what was happening in Asia both under the Tenth

Air Force and his own people and came to a melancholy conclusion, that they were paying for tonnage in "men and airplanes." He explained how, "The kids here are flying over their head . . . and they bust the [planes] up for reasons that sometimes seem silly. They are not silly, however, for we are asking boys to do what would be most difficult for men to accomplish." Smith concluded, "with the experience level here, we are going to pay dearly for the tonnage moved over the Hump. . . . With the men available, there is nothing else to do." Safety would become one of Tunner's chief concerns.[14]

Something had to give. Alexander, worn out and sick from the strain, was officially relieved of command on October 15, 1943, although by September he was effectively out. Brigadier General Earl Hoag became head of the India-China Wing of ATC, but the real leader to the men was his executive, Colonel Thomas Hardin, transferred from the Central Africa routes.

Hardin, a former airlines executive, was a hard charger. He started by issuing two general commands. First was the dictate that "Effective immediately, there will be no more weather over the hump," or in other words, pilots had to fly regardless of weather conditions. Second, and in the same vein, flights would not be canceled because of reports of enemy aerial activity. A month later, he instituted night flights over the Hump, on the basis of "crews have to sleep but the planes don't." General C. R. Smith summarized things in one memo by noting, "Hardin is steaming like an old fire engine. . . . I have never seen a man work harder. . . . He works in the office in the morning and spends the afternoon going from one field to the other. He has broken most of the Air Force rules about operations."[15]

The results were predictable. On October 13 ATC lost six planes, but set a new single day record of 200 tons. On October 23 five more went down, but the load carried reached 300 tons. During the month of November the flyers suffered thirty-eight major accidents, twenty-eight in December. In January 1944 every 1,000 tons cost 2.94 lives, or roughly one American died for every 340 tons brought in. But during the Christmas month they busted the 10,000 goal open, bringing in 12,590 tons to China; by June 1944 this figure was up to 18,000 tons. On January 31, 1944, Hardin got promoted to a one-star, and took official command as Hoag moved up and out. The unit also got recognition, going from a Wing to the India-China Division of ATC.[16]

Pilots were flying planes that were remarkable, but never designed to handle this kind of punishment. The most famous plane on the Hump, and one of the greatest airplanes of all time, was the Douglas C-47 Skytrain, the military version of the DC-3. This was the first true airliner ever built, the plane that moved passenger carrying from an era where one donned goggles and took the second seat in a biplane, to a world of luxury and comfort similar to the amenities of a Pullman car. As Ann Tunner exclaimed, "When the DC-3 came along there was just nothing else like it, there wasn't anything to compare it to."[17]

The grace of the plane was not its appearance. When this author flew in one in 2002, he jotted down, "Plane is kind of stubby . . . Its proportions are right, but it's no greyhound, no race horse like a P-51." It "taxis quickly on the runway, moves surprisingly fast. Just skedaddle down the runway. In flight, however, it is slow; [the ground] just glides beneath it, gradually unfolding."

Several qualities made this plane one of the most beloved of all time, even to the hard-pressed Hump pilots. First, it was a delight to fly, gentle, forgiving. Ann Tunner said it flew like a Piper Cub, "just like a big Cub," that she "was crazy about the C-47" because it "just responded so beautifully." Pilot J. B. McLaughlin loved the bird because, "We got away with youthful stupidities that would have killed us in any other airplane."[18]

Next, the C-47 could carry far more than anyone ever imagined. Whatever the job, it did it, even when all the books said it was impossible, that aerodynamically the plane could not have taken off.

The C-47 was supposed to have a peak load of three tons—6,000 pounds—or twenty-eight passengers. On one occasion, an ATC pilot named Harold Donahue had to evacuate children just in advance of Japanese units. Faced with a 1,800-foot runway with a mountain at the end, he watched as sixty-one children and eleven adults boarded; with him and his copilot that made seventy-four. But the plane took off and got them to safety. In another instance years later, the manifest read "PAP" for Pierced Aluminum Planking, the boards used to shore up runways. The plane responded sluggishly to controls, however, so at the end of the voyage, the crew went back to check their load. Instead of PAP, they found PSP, or Pierced *Steel* Planking, a much heavier material; they had been carrying 13,500 pounds. One pilot had so much weight on board a C-47 he could not get off the ground as the end of the runway approached. Desperate, he just raised the landing gear with the wheels still on the ground. The C-47 wobbled, and made it into the air. As one flyer put it, the nickname for the plane was Gooney Bird, because "these planes were just stupid. . . . They didn't know they could do the things they could do."[19]

But most of all, pilots loved the plane because it was the greatest survivor ever put into the air. The C-47 flew no matter what happened to it. One of these aircraft got hit broadside by another plane in a horrendous midair collision, the impact carving out a hole in the fuselage four feet wide by five feet high, but it got home safely. In another accident, a C-47 lost its entire left wing all the way back to the engine cowling; as one aviation writer put it, "No one knows what kept [it] in the air. By all the principles of aerodynamics it should have spiraled steeply to the ground." On another occasion, a C-47 lost its wing to strafing; when a replacement arrived, it was for an earlier model; this wing was five feet shorter than the original, but the crew bolted it to the plane, and amazingly it flew off on its mission.[20]

Hump commanders needed more output, so they supplemented the C-47 with the C-46. It was a difficult plane to fly, unlovable and unforgiving, and a firetrap to boot; pilots called it "Dumbo" and a "Plumber's Nightmare." But it could hold 12,000 pounds—legally—and flew faster and especially, much higher than the C-47, so hundreds got sent to the Hump route.

The combination of these planes, the dangerous flights, and the poor conditions meant that morale had plummeted by 1944, with a dose of fatalism thrown in. One veteran wrote that flying the Hump had become akin to "Playing black-jack against a professional dealer; do it long enough and you lose." Maintenance and supply had gotten so bad that when fuses blew they had to "wrap up burned out ones with the foil from cigarette packages and use them or go out of business." Typical of the rations by then was tinned butter, "guaranteed not to melt in the tropic heat. It did not; neither would it melt on your pancakes, or toast, or in your mouth. It was like soft candle wax."[21]

The situation was reaching crisis point. China was being battered by Japanese armies and became more and more vulnerable, with modern weapons seemingly the only answer. In the summer of 1944 ATC sent several review teams to the theater, all of whom concluded that the forces there must be augmented or else the mission had to be turned over to someone else. New airfields had to open, more planes must arrive. One of these reviews estimated that if done right, the airlift could be bringing in 20,500 tons by October, 31,000 tons by December, figures far above what was then possible. The authors of that optimistic report were Colonel James Douglas Jr., ATC deputy chief of staff, and Major General William Tunner, head of the Ferrying Division. Almost immediately, General George, head of ATC, took Tunner at his word, and assigned him in September 1944 to head the India-China Division.[22]

The idea of sending Tunner over was not a new one, but he did not want the job and had fought the move. Back in May 1944, C. R. Smith called him in to discuss the transfer; Tunner "didn't particularly like the idea because anybody who goofed in the Ferrying Division was on the roster to go to India." At another time, he wrote, "Pilots generally hated it and men who were sent there figured that they had had it." By then Tunner considered himself a leader, and did not feel he should be sent to a backwater. As the general put it in a 1962 letter, "The Hump Command did not have the savory reputation that I felt my own command had earned."[23]

Thus there was a good deal of ego involved here. India was, to his mind, "a small division." He was moving there from a much larger organization, one that he had built from scratch into a force of 10,000 pilots and 60–70,000 enlisted men, with airports all over the country. Thus, Tunner tried to engineer a more prestigious command by suggesting that the India Division be merged with the Central Africa Division. He would take over the new, enlarged outfit, one fitting his stature, and with headquarters, possibly, in a more civilized place like North Africa. Smith fell for none of this, and commanded, "Nothing doing. You're going to India."[24]

Tunner's instructions from headquarters were two-fold. First, and most critical, he had to raise the tonnage being flown to China. And second, he had to lower the accident rate. Tunner would succeed in both missions and was one of the few individuals who saw them as linked, and not in opposition.[25]

He began by doing his homework, taking a quick trip over to check things out before he moved in fully. The soon-to-be commander flew a C-46 over the Hump, so that he could understand what his men went through. Once he landed, Tunner dismissed his staff and walked around the enlisted men's area alone.

What he found confirmed his worst stereotypes. Scraggly beards indicated that men did not shave or even maintain neatly trimmed facial hair. Uniforms "were worn out," and as Tunner politely put it, "showed the lack of laundry." Faces were "expressionless," and absolutely no one saluted, despite the presence of a flag rank officer. Finally, he corraled one group and inquired, "Weren't you trained to stand up when your boss comes around to see you"; at least in Tunner's mind, "I wasn't being nasty or even sarcastic. I really wanted to know." The reply was a grudging grunt of agreement, a shrug more than anything else, but Tunner persevered and asked, "Well, why don't you do it here?" To this, they could only answer, "Nobody told us to."[26]

Tunner's first step was really his most important, the simple declaration that weather, in fact, did matter, that it was, as he recalled in his memoirs, "a factor which every Operations Officer would consider in dispatching aircraft." Tunner wrote, "I knew that I had to send men out to fly under these conditions, and that frequently I would have to fly the route myself. But I did not believe that it was my duty to send men out into conditions known to be far more dangerous than usual." If a pilot flew into a particularly vicious storm, he "had my orders to turn around and come back," while the ground crews would "hold up all flights . . . in hopes the storm would abate." The results were delayed planes and angry higher-ups, but "fewer pilots flew themselves and their planes into mountains."[27]

His next decision was not nearly as popular. For the men on the Hump, the main goal was not to deliver supplies, but to get the hell out as soon as possible. That meant flying 650 hours; after that a pilot was rotated back home.[28]

The problem was that pilots flew far too much, in order to accumulate the magic number as soon as possible. When Tunner took over, some crews were doing 165 hours a month; this was downright dangerous, as the fatigue it induced led to accidents. Colonel E. D. Abbey, the flight surgeon, told Tunner during one of their first meetings, that 50 percent of the flying staff were "bordering on a frank operational fatigue."

Tunner's solution won him no friends. He increased the amount of hours needed to transfer out to 750 and imposed a minimum tour of one year. Pilots groused, but this forced them to moderate their flying time and live longer.

In addition, although it was much less well known, Tunner made sure the rotation system worked for non-flying personnel in a fair, efficient manner. Previously, rotation was often ignored, not out of necessity, but from sheer inefficiency.

Tunner first came across this during one of his early walk-arounds, similar to the one he had done on his initial visit. He would stroll up to groups and say, "Hello. I'm General Tunner." Most of the time, he got a similar diffident reaction to what he received previously, but one soul stood out, "the worst-looking sad sack of them all, a shaggy specimen who seemed to be in a kind of stupor." Tunner turned to the airman and asked him how long he had been in India, and the reply was, "since the spring of 1942." That meant he had been there for 2.5 years, an eternity. Tunner now questioned the man, almost facetiously: "Why haven't you been rotated? Do you like it here?" The simple answer came, "No, I don't like it here, but I can't get anybody to listen to me." Tunner posed the simplest of questions, "What do you want to do?" and got the most direct of answers, "Sir, I want to go home." The commanding general of the entire Hump operation now issued an order: "All right, you can go home. Go pack your bag and get ready." But the man had truly been there too long. He still stood, motionless, as Tunner went on to the next hut. Finally, the commanding officer had to go back, and gruffly asked, "What's the matter? Can't you get your bag packed? Do you want me to help you with it?" but the man just stared at him. Finally, in slow plain tones, Tunner made it clear: "Listen, there's an airplane leaving here in thirty minutes for the States. I want you on the plane, understand? *You're going home!*" (emphasis in the original).

This was more than just simple human decency; as every commander knows, getting rid of a soldier like that would help morale, because it removed a negative influence from the men's quarters. Even more, the man was a mechanic, and as Tunner pointed out, "Who would want to fly over mountain peaks, dense jungles, and head-hunting tribes in an airplane he had been working on?"

The matter did not rest there. Tunner went through the rolls of the entire division, slowly and methodically, rooting out fellows who had earned the right to head home, but who had been overlooked by sloppy bookkeeping. The time in theater may have been extended, but for the first time, the rotation policy began to work efficiently and effectively.

But that was only the start of Tunner's efforts to improve safety, and then later, overall morale. Tunner believed in efficiency, believed that it could not only increase productivity, but save lives. He took his right hand man and chief pilot, Colonel Red Foreman, and assigned him a crucial task. From then on, each unit, from the division on down, would have a flying safety committee that reported to Foreman. This outfit would investigate every accident and submit a full account. From this, statistical analysis would emerge, as Tunner discovered answers to questions such as what field had the most accidents? What time of day produced the most accidents, what type of aircraft? What conditions caused all the different types of mishaps, the separate categories of landing, takeoff, taxiing, inflight accidents and so many more? Were there any common maintenance issues involved? Any common weather patterns? The safety committee had to check not only the pilot's activities, but also anyone who had come in contact with the plane for the two days prior to the accident, from the base's operations officer to the lowliest mechanic who cleaned windshields.[29]

Tunner compared this to what corporations like insurance companies did; the corporate model guided him throughout. But armed with this data, the first ever in the theater, he could now effect reforms that would change flying conditions and save lives. New flight rules went into effect, that changed the Hump operation into a corporate machine.[30]

While his predecessors had really built up the Hump airlift, adding airfields and planes, Tunner introduced a high level of structure. His staff reviewed the files of every pilot, discovered what they knew and what they did not know. Often men were flying planes they could not handle and should never have been assigned to and were doing tasks way beyond their capabilities. To rectify this, command put into place a comprehensive training operation, so that every crew was the master of their aircraft in all conditions. New flight rules appeared to curb individual excesses. Pilots had occasionally flown at tree-top heights through mountain passes, but now headquarters dictated flight levels and enforced them. The flight safety staff investigated a number of accidents where a plane was on a perfect flight path to land, but failed to pull up and plowed into the tarmac. It turned out that some pilots believed that they did not need to use oxygen masks, and developed anoxia as they climbed the Himalayas, a condition which affected vision and mental judgment. New rules now dictated that all pilots had to wear their masks, with no exceptions. They now made regular radio reports whether they wanted to or not, while takeoff and landing procedures all became standardized. Even meals became the subject of regulation, as better diet meant healthier men and less sickness meant increased production. Doctors eliminated foods that caused gassiness, a dangerous condition in unpressurized cabins at those heights.[31]

Throughout these changes, one philosophy guided Tunner, that of industrial efficiency worthy of a business pioneer. In words that would have made sense to Frederic Taylor or Andrew Carnegie, Tunner declared that his "controls . . . enabled us to get a firm grasp on the business of flying . . . the Hump. We were a big business, and to run a big business successfully we had to know what was going on. I wanted to know just exactly what every airplane on every base was doing every minute of the day." What made this quest unique, however, was that it was not directed toward profits. Instead, William Tunner applied this to a particular vision: if you adopted this kind of corporate efficiency, airlift could not only save China, it could do anything. It would move mountains, become a force unto itself, and would have to be recognized as a major branch of any air service. It could even feed cities, although Tunner never dreamed in those terms back in 1944 and 1945.[32]

Tunner did not stop there. While his main objective was to stop men from crashing, he also improved techniques for finding them in the jungle if they did crash despite his best efforts.

Part of this was sheer humanitarian instinct, part of it was an efficiency drive to keep all pilots operational, but part of it was to boost morale. Tunner knew the stories of what bodies found in the jungle looked like, and what such knowledge did to his men. In one case, for example, a young radio operator bailed out of a C-46 that was going down in the jungle. His parachute lodged in the trees about five feet above the ground, and all efforts to extract himself led only to the man winding up upside down with his leg stuck in the harness, his head and shoulders on the ground, with no help in sight.[33]

That was bad enough, but horror followed. Red ants attacked him and started to literally eat him alive. Alone, untrained, he ignored the log within easy reach that would have enabled him to gain leverage to free himself, and tried to shoot through the strap in a panic. When that failed, the ants became too much to bear, and the last bullet went into his temple.

There had been a search-and-rescue team before Tunner, of course, but he worked hard to improve it. The general was a firm believer that key men made the difference, so he appointed Major Donald Pricer, a hard charger, and gave him free rein to pick the best crew available. The size of the rescue operation doubled, and Tunner even took planes off the line and put them to work saving downed pilots. To start with, six craft went over to this outfit, including four B-25 twin-engined bombers. Every one of them got painted over, the military colors giving way to a mix of air force blue and bright shades of yellow and orange so that stranded men could see them at a distance. In addition, Tunner somehow got hold of some of the first helicopters, had them assigned to his command, and used them for search and rescue in the jungles.[34]

Finally, Tunner inaugurated a survival school, because, as he explained, pilots were petrified of local conditions and making dumb mistakes; "The only way I could . . . dispel this fear was to strip the jungle of its secrets." Every base now had to create a jungle training camp out in the middle of the forest, with every air crewman assigned to an indoctrination program there that would prepare them for conditions on the ground in a most hostile environment.[35]

All this made sense, and it also worked. Documents compiled by the India-China Division show that the accident rate at most bases in both countries between July and October 1944, as Tunner took over, was between 1.3 and 1.8 accidents per thousand miles flown. The figure dropped by December, then shot up in February, the worst month for weather. After that, they plummeted through to August; by that date the rate was less than one accident for every *4,000* miles flown, a reduction of roughly 600 percent.[36]

The wisdom of this trend was not always appreciated by higher-ups, and Tunner had to deal with this dissatisfaction. While General George thoroughly supported the quest for safe flying conditions, General Albert Wedemeyer, by then supreme commander of the U.S. effort in China, wrote to George and complained that the local ATC had "given flying safety first priority over tonnage production," and objected to the "insistence that the number of accidents be reduced even at the expense of essential tonnage." In particular, he urged ATC to accept accident rates similar to those of combat units, which were much higher. Tunner, knowing both that his superior would back him and that he was right, simply ignored the demands, and got away with it, but came across only as a rebel, willing to ruffle feathers and not respond to authority. Wedemeyer, however, gained respect for this young logistician and would later play a key role in Tunner's career at a crucial moment.[37]

Tunner's single-mindedness also made waves among the troops. In order to turn the India-China Divisions into a military outfit, with high morale, he felt he had to break the men out of their lethargy by enforcing official discipline. His public statement was brusque and bold: he had "been sent to this command to direct American soldiers, and while I was their commander, by God, they were going to live like Americans and be proud they were Americans." Tunner felt he had sensed something in his men, that they "were wanting . . . to be proud of the Army, proud of the Air Corps. They wanted to be proud of their job" and even the officers were "resenting being in such a horrible place."[38]

To accomplish this, he ordered that filthy huts be cleaned out, with a full dress inspection every other day, every week in the officers' quarters as well. Men had to get haircuts, shave beards, wear clean clothes. Every base had to schedule a formal parade on Saturday, attended by everyone not in the air, the first ever put on in that theater.[39]

This did not go over well at first. Even Ann Tunner admitted that in that region "the weather is not conducive to looking good and clean and shaving every day." But Tunner was resolute. He told an interviewer, "I didn't listen to any opposition, and said I didn't want to hear any. I just told them to put out the orders." After that, Tunner believed that "when it came to bitching . . . I'd take second place to no one." But morale went up.[40]

Tunner also made sure his rules were fair. Officers had to change even more than enlisted men, as Tunner recognized their greater responsibility as leaders. Not only did they have to follow the new dress code and go to parades, there was now a mandatory staff meeting at 8 A.M., every day, seven days a week. When asked how the staff reacted, he replied without qualm, "Very well, because 8 o'clock was the time to go to work." The frequency was not an issue either, because "there was always enough business to carry on," what with all the problems of running the Hump. Everyone present could voice any problems as they worked out solutions, and there was no time limit, either maximum or minimum. If they finished up in ten minutes, as sometimes happened, the meeting was over. If it took hours to get everything squared away, that was how long they stayed in the meeting.[41]

Tunner backed this effort to transform morale with real measures to improve conditions. He used B-25 bombers, stripped down for the mission, as sprayers to kill mosquitoes and thus cut down on malaria; combined with Tunner's usual rigid enforcement of rules on mosquito nets and taking atabrine, the outfit developed the lowest malarial rate of any unit in China or India.

Little things helped. Every base now had to set up a twenty-four-hour cafeteria for flight crews, and trucks brought food out to the flight line. New quarters got built, and quiet zones established so that exhausted men could sleep without being disturbed, even by their own buddies.[42]

Tunner also had the instinct of a public relations executive, and he began trying out a number of tactics he would perfect during the later Berlin Airlift. Headquarters began to publish a newspaper, the *Hump Express,* to let the men know what they doing was newsworthy, that it was something they could be proud of. The paper was filled with the usual items on personnel, plus cheesecake pinups and humorous feature stories. But over and over, in every issue, airmen read of the accomplishments they had pulled off. In the January 18, 1945, issue, for example, the first page contained a banner headline, "ICD [India-China Division] Shatters Mark in Banner Year," while the column one story was "Longest Flight on Record Made By ATC Glider." On page 3 the paper reported that "Monthly Hump Tonnage By End of '44 25-Times That of First Month of Operation, Dec. '42."[43]

Tunner also started up one of his best tricks for increasing productivity, a competition to see which outfit could deliver the most, with the Army Air Forces always the winner. He delighted in pitting one unit against the other to gain the laurels of the top hauler. In Berlin this would become a masterpiece in the art of stimulating employees to work better and harder, but it began during the Hump with headlines like, "It's Banner Day at the 1328th; Break Fifteen Records." The article, datelined Assam, began, "Selecting Dec. 24 as a banner day, this base broke just about every record in the book for one day's Hump operations. Fifteen division records are known to have been shattered." To everyone in the theater, the message was clear; if you did not like that other unit's notoriety, you had better out-fly them.

There was one other tool William Tunner used to win over his men, and that was humor. Despite his hard-boiled decrees, the commanding officer always had a delicate sense that men needed to laugh at their situation, and even him if need be, if things were going to get better. He agreed to publish a collection of cartoons, "Skootering," which included one where a man walks into the flight surgeon's office with his arm bent in multiple places at radical angles, while the medical officer observes, "Frankly, Lieutenant, I think you are trying to get out of flying." One cartoon showed a man plummeting out a plane sans parachute, exclaiming, "Gad! That wasn't the washroom after all."[44]

Even though he had done a good job on this problem—Tunner's wife remarked that "He was very, very pleased that he cleaned up the morale in India"—the general knew that the task of making the Hump successful would need machines as well as men.[45]

By then, of course, Tunner had built up a host of contacts in the Pentagon and was a hallway diplomat and infighter. Back when he had first been assigned to the Hump and flew over for a preliminary visit, Tunner had been approached by Colonel Jim Douglas, who worked on planning for this operation within ATC, and wanted to get a look for himself. The new commanding officer was no fool and saw opportunity when it threatened to break down his door; Douglas was C. R. Smith's deputy (and a future secretary of the air force), so Tunner was "Delighted with this," and with good reason: "Jim was a man of real stature and if there were things that the Hump needed, and I knew that the list would be unending, why he was the man in Headquarters who would and could follow up and get the necessary action." Douglas got the grand tour of the China-Burma-India (CBI) theater.[46]

Indeed, Tunner did have a little list, and at the top were advanced transport planes. Tunner's predecessors had led the way, arranging for a vast buildup in the Hump air fleet. Now, Tunner would build on this, arranging to get his hands on the best in the fleet, four-engined craft with power to fly heavier loads faster and with greater safety. Thus, the CBI now got C-54s (the four-engine successor to the C-47) and C-87s, the hauler version of the B-24 bomber. By December 1944 Tunner had already built up the operation to 249 planes and 17,032 men, but by January this had scooted up to 287 planes and 19,025 personnel, an increase of 15 percent in planes and 12 percent in men in just one month, evidence of Tunner's skills at bureaucratic battles. That was not all the commanding officer had in mind. Using Douglas, the deputy chief of staff at ATC as his conduit, he arranged to open three new airbases, and had the rest of the Army Air Forces release 1,500 trained mechanics to his command. As the war closed down in July 1945, this had gone up to 332 planes, 23,359 military personnel, and 47,000 civilian employees.[47]

Tunner now turned to what was clearly one of his great loves, efficiency. In many ways a disciple of Frederick Taylor, the general set out to rationalize his operation and make it work by the clock, not by whim or personal fancy. His biggest target and greatest success was in the area of maintenance. Though this seems like the epitome of mundane functions, in fact it involved his most controversial decision in the CBI, because it dissolved one of the most sacred relationships in the U.S. Air Force.

To understand what Tunner did, it is crucial that one understand how planes were repaired and serviced at that point in every military air fleet in the world. Each pilot and plane had a maintenance crew assigned to them, and for good reason. The system created incredible loyalty, as exhausted crewmen, working with minimal tools and few replacement parts, strove to do the impossible not for a faceless war machine, but for a flesh-and-blood pilot whose life literally depended on them and their skills each and every day. In return, pilots worshiped a good crew and its chief, and would do anything for mechanics who kept them flying without fear that the plane would fail them. This kinship was a bond of blood, spiritual and intimate.

Tunner had another idea. For all the benefits of this approach, it was slow and individualized, like making custom goods. And he wanted mass production.

The innovator behind this was another one of Tunner's bright young men, Lieutenant Colonel Robert White. White had been an executive working for Standard Oil in China before the war, and then wound up in Training Command. He wanted to get out of that hum-drum operation, he wanted to go back to China, and he wanted to experiment with a new idea he had developed. Tunner would support all three goals and named White his Division Aircraft Maintenance Officer.

White's idea was something he called production line maintenance, or PLM. Instead of spending time on planes as they came in, the emphasis would be on the regularly scheduled maintenance overhauls, at 50, 100, 200 hours or whatever. But these would not be done by mechanics who personally knew the pilot and plane, but by men assigned to specific stations, points on an assembly line, where they serviced whichever plane was next in the queue. Each station would have a specific task, and the men on that platform would do that job, and do it well, over and over again, at a much faster rate than they would have accomplished otherwise. Station 1, for example, performed general inspection and engine run-up and diagnosis; the crew at Station 2 cleaned planes, Station 3 handled carburetion and communications, while Station 4 worked on the power plant. Overall there were seven stations, and a C-54 could get a major overhaul within twenty-two hours and be back on the Hump, producing tonnage.[48]

There were other benefits as well. Before PLM, there was no standardization of procedures or facilities. On some bases, expert mechanics handled specific tasks only, while on others the crew chiefs managed all work. Tools varied, as did repair methods. After the reforms, headquarters trained all mechanics to an equivalent skill level, and reassigned personnel to make sure every field had the necessary personnel. In time, Tunner's staff took the idea to its logical conclusion, assigning each base one type of aircraft. That base would then handle all the maintenance needs of this model for the entire theater; planes from all over got sent to fields where the pilots knew no one, but had to trust staff whose knowledge of that specific craft was unparalleled. Mechanics now did the same work the same way, on one type of plane, only they did it much faster; operational rates went up by 85 percent while time lost to inspection dropped by 25 percent. In addition, there was an economy of scale for parts and supply.[49]

This was not an easy or popular step to take. As Tunner observed, under his system, "No one [mechanic] had his own airplane from then on." The official air force history of the Hump claimed that "Many pilots were distrustful of the quality of PLM maintenance and strongly preferred the old way of doing things, in which each airplane was the direct responsibility of a given crew." Tunner admitted that "they didn't like it," but added, "It worked! We had better airplanes out of it, better-maintained airplanes, and we were able to jump our production. Our production steadily rose."[50]

Tunner also broke tradition in one other way regarding maintenance. He looked at human beings as a resource to help him accomplish the mission, and social custom be damned. As he noted in his memoirs, it became obvious that "each base was set down in the midst of innumerable native villages and towns teeming with men who seemed both idle and hungry." Why not put them to work doing the menial tasks, like cleaning the planes? Why not indeed?[51]

What started with modest goals soon became an elaborate social experiment, just as Tunner had done with women pilots. Indians learned mechanical skills from Americans, and eventually, of the 225 men on the line at Tezgaon—the base that serviced C-54s, the pride of the fleet—85 were locals. This included the entire group that removed spark plugs on every inspection from routine to total overhaul.

Though the standard accounts do not touch on the danger involved here, this was, in fact a bold social move. First, there was the matter of pride and nationalism; someone else was working on an American plane and doing a good job. In addition, there was the matter of race, a hot-button issue, conceivably, for a country that still enforced legal segregation in many states.

There is no evidence that any of this resentment surfaced. Otha Spencer, a Hump veteran, told how one afternoon in their hut, his copilot was working on a calculus problem for a correspondence course. The Indian housekeeper they employed hovered nearby then reached over and, pointing to a set of figures, announced, "Your error is there." After that the Indian and the American officer worked as a team on math quizzes, while the housework diminished a tad in quality. Part of the rationale for this acceptance might lie in Spencer's observation that "The British educational system in India was efficient. The Indians were intelligent, well educated, and spoke beautiful soft English."[52] Nevertheless, Tunner had taken a chance, and he would find even more static when he tried it later in Germany, despite the absence of the racial issue.

As the last year of the war beckoned, Tunner's work started to pay off. By September 1944 his pilots had carried 22,314 tons of supplies to China, but in December this shot up to 31,935, and in January 1945 the figure was 44,098. For the first time, the figures were not just exceeding the quotas set in Washington, but surpassing them by wide margins. He was also winning over the men; in December, pilots at the Misamari base decided to give their commander a Christmas present. On that day, instead of enjoying turkey or ham dinners, they flew more missions than ever before, a total of eighty-one flights instead of their daily average of thirty. In June the division managed to transport 74,969 tons, a far cry from the early months when they had to strive to reach figures of 5,000 or 10,000 tons.[53]

Tunner now came up with an unprecedented idea, one that changed the entire culture of the Burma Hump airlift. Henceforth, there would be no more quotas to meet or beat. The men of ATC could bust any new standards wide open, so the only goal they had left was sheer tonnage. From then on, the purpose of the airlift was to figure out how to get the maximum amount of goods to China, with any figure one could dream up becoming a possibility. Claire Chennault, founder of the Flying Tigers, wrote in his memoirs that "Tunner recognized no limit to the tons that could be provided by air," and because of that, he "pushed the tonnage up to incredible figures."[54]

The tour de force came in August. In July, Tunner had received a routine bureaucratic memo to the effect that Army Air Forces Day was coming up on August 1, and there should be some kind of celebration.

Tunner saw an idea there. He decided that, instead of holding a parade, his men would honor their service by showing what they could do. He proposed a one-day effort that would be unprecedented, that would rally the men to their best effort and boost morale as everyone got in on trying to beat the other unit. As Tunner dryly noted, his was a "unique form of observance."[55]

This took plenty of planning, from having more tonnage on hand, to making sure every plane was ready to fly, to creating new flying schedules. Every member of the command staff, every officer was expected to head out to a base and pitch in for the entire day, including Tunner. For that twenty-four-hour period, nobody would sleep.

It worked. Men stuck in the doldrums got excited by the idea, and put out an effort that had never been seen before. Notwithstanding the peaks they had to fly over, the crews of the India-China Division made 1,118 trips over the Hump in that one day, carrying 5,327 tons; Tunner flew three round-trip missions himself. An ATC transport transversed the route every minute and twelve seconds, and unloaded goods at the rate of one ton every fifteen seconds. There was not one single accident all day, either. After it was over, Tunner sent the command a special message, telling them of his "great pride," explaining, "You did not turn in this remarkable performance, unprecedented in air transport history, because you had good planes, good weather, and good luck. You did achieve it because each of you, every officer and enlisted man on every base involved, knew his job and gave it all he had." This was, therefore, "everybody's day and everybody's record."

The totals for what was done on the Burma Hump reflect far more than the work of William Tunner, of course. Overall, aircraft flew roughly 650,000 tons into China, a figure that included not just weapons and food and gasoline, but men and mules, and even a shipment of beer (General George received a protest on that last item, but replied that local commanders should decide what would help win the war). This was the equivalent of the cargoes of seventy Liberty ships, or 6,500 of the standard freight cars used in the United States. Half of this was delivered in 1945, after Tunner had taken command. But the price was high; from 1942 to 1945 over a thousand American crewmen died in the effort to deliver the necessities of war to China.[56]

The Hump airlift got lost in the folds of history for some time, a process that started immediately following the end of the war and continued for decades to come. Families and returning soldiers of all nations wanted to forget, and only a few great victories, a few famous generals, became enshrined in the popular imagination. Americans thus remembered D-Day and the Battle of the Bulge, Eisenhower and Patton, while the Brits honored Montgomery of El Alemein, and the Russians looked to Stalingrad and Zhukov. In the Pacific the great moments were sea battles like Midway, and extraordinary island campaigns like Iwo Jima and Okinawa. The Hump had none of this glamour, none of the drama associated with these epic struggles, representing instead a slow, steady grinding effort to help win the war.

Complicating matters even further, the CBI became a victim of politics. In 1949 China became Communist, and the issue of why Harry Truman "lost China" became a Republican battle cry. The notion that instead, during the war, the United States went to extraordinary efforts to aid China would have undercut that charge, leading one supporter of airlift to declare, "Ignorant persons . . . have recently attacked the then administration for failing to give full support to Chiang Kai-shek *during the war.* To one who followed these efforts day by day, he received more than might reasonably have been expected" (emphasis in original). Despite such efforts, the McCarthy period was soon upon the land, and the Hump may have been pushed aside as a distraction from the senator's effort to save America.[57]

Questions such as how much the Hump operation contributed to winning the Second World War, or its place in the subsequent cold war conflict, are still open to debate and discussion. But there is no doubt of the importance it played in the history of airlift or in the life of William Tunner.

First, in this quiet, forgotten backwater of a global conflict, airlift had reached maturity. The Strategic Bombing Survey, famous for analyzing raids in Europe, concluded, "The major significance, for the future, of all air operations in CBI . . . was the development of air transport operations," that "air transport had expanded beyond the wildest predictions of 1942." The official U.S. Army Air Forces history of their service's war record echoed this conclusion, observing how, "From a primitive barnstorming enterprise the air service from India to China had burgeoned into a large-scale operation, far beyond the wildest dreams of the men who assisted at its beginnings." But, "Most important in the long run . . . the Air Transport Command's crowded airways to China were the proving ground, if not the birthplace, of mass strategic airlift." In 1947, Major General Robert Webster, the head of Military Air Transport Services (MATS), lectured a class at the National War College that instead of just fighters and bombers, "we have come out of that war with an additional type, the transport plane, and that we should think in terms of fighter-bomber-transport—since they are all equally important."[58]

The Hump not only changed airlift, it transformed William Tunner. His lifetime mission, which had been evolving through his work at Ferrying Command, now crystallized amid the peaks of the Himalayas. He became a visionary, not from a philosophical stance, but because of the logic of the situation he had been put into. Tunner was always the kind who set out to do a job completely; in a later interview, he simply said, "My job was to get the maximum tonnage to China and reduce accidents as much as possible. That was my mission, generally." Taking that charge to the nth degree, however, meant he started to see things, see possibilities no one else did, not just in his local command, but in the entire world of aviation.[59]

Tunner now became the herald of airlift, not only its greatest practitioner, but its foremost advocate as well. This role, this sense of destiny, never left him and would persevere over time. In 1950 he told a *Time* reporter, "We who worked the Hump always knew that what was done there could be picked up bodily, carried to any part of the world and started up again." Much later, in his memoirs, he resorted to clichés, writing, "After the Hump, those of us who had developed an *expertise* in air transportation knew that we could fly anything anywhere anytime" (emphasis in original) but the ideas were the same. His wife added, in an interview conducted in a new century, that "the operation of the Hump proved a lot of things. He just accomplished such . . . things on the Hump there was very little in the air that couldn't be conquered after that."[60]

Tunner began to argue positions that flew in the face of all conventional wisdom, but usually—though not always—with plenty of facts to support him. Most planners and leaders, both civilian and military, saw airlift as something that would supplement basic ground transportation for small items needed in a hurry, such as delicate spare parts. Tunner told them that this was nonsense, that airplanes could replace roadways and rail lines for hauling everything, including even bulk commodities, a claim no one else thought feasible in 1945. He railed at the foolishness of reopening the Burma Road, pointing out how much that effort had cost, and how airlift could have done the job better and cheaper than ground transport if the military just saw things as clearly as he did. "Too many of our people," he argued, "were obsessed with the rebuilding of the Burma Road." How could they justify the "thousands and thousands of US engineers, engineer troops, working on the Burma Road when they would have been better used working on airports in India?"[61]

He was right, of course, and his figures made the alternative land route look like a fool's errand. When the Burma Road reopened in 1945, after a terrific effort employing massive resources, it could barely carry more than 5,000 tons a month, at a time when airlift was hitting figures ten times that. But there was also the tone of the acolyte, who could not see other views, and might alienate many others with his extreme comments; later Tunner would declare that airlift could have accomplished everything the fleet did at Normandy, hardly a line designed to win friends.[62]

It was not just Tunner's vision that matured in Burma, it was his approach. By the time he finished there, he had truly become a business executive in a military uniform. Every account of the Burma operation uses the same language, that what had been a haphazard program had become as efficient as an assembly line. The term used in several works, both official government documents and the memoirs of veterans, was that when Tunner arrived, "the age of big business" came to the Hump. One of the first writers to do a history on this part of the war used that term, but added another telling remark, delineating Tunner's true position, as well as his approach to airlift: "It remained for an executive like Tunner to harness it for unlimited growth and productivity and thus bring the airlift to its final achievement." Most telling of all is the official report of the India-China Division of ATC, a promotional document instigated by Tunner and reviewed by him, and thus a fair indication of his viewpoint and priorities; on the first page, the second major heading, underlined, was *"ICD (India-China Division) is a huge business, organized and operated as such."* Only the unit's mission statement came before that.[63]

While this approach would provide Tunner with the tools for making mass airlift work, it would also get him into trouble. Like all great entrepreneurs, he became a lone operator. That worked in a backwater like India, where he was his own boss, at least on the local scene, but would eventually be a problem when he had to handle intruding superiors. By then he was growing contemptuous of top officers who were not up to his standards for vision and command, and believed he could do the impossible. In 1960 Catherine Gibson, his longtime secretary and one of his closest confidantes, replied to a request from the general who was seeking memories and stories for the memoir he was working on. "Miss Katey" or "Miss G," the names by which she was generally known (she signed her letter with the latter appellation), provided many warm anecdotes, but also added one other story she thought was funny. Tunner went to negotiate with the British about getting another airfield for the Hump. The setting was formal, with Tunner and his staff on one side, facing what Miss G referred to as "an impressive line of not-too-cooperative Britishers." Put another way, they were getting in the way of what Tunner saw as a necessity if the Hump was going to work at his remarkable level. The Brits tried to deter Tunner by pointing out that the only field available had short runways and a river blocking expansion; surely he did not want this facility. One of Tunner's aides whispered a comment to the general, and he nodded, then used that idea as the basis for his reply. As Miss G described it, "you blandly announced that you would accept the airfield and *change* the course of the river!" She did not record the reply of the British officers.[64]

In 2002, the author asked Ann Tunner what her husband was proudest of, after a long career that involved him in some of the crucial events of the period 1940 to 1960. She calmly explained that she did not know the answer to that, that he had never spoken in those terms, but that he had always felt "like the greatest step forward in air transportation was the Hump." A year later, his son expressed the same thought, that this "was the role model." In his memoirs, the general summed up what had now become a new approach to the entire concept of military logistics and more. He wrote, "From the Hump on, airlift was an important factor in war, in industry, in life."[65]

Thus, by 1945, Tunner had transformed air transport, but few noticed and fewer cared. He was not just far away from the glories of the European Theater, from the Eighth Air Force and the D-Day invasion, he was in the most forgotten zone of the war. Recognition, both of the man and the concept, would have to wait.

4 / Tunner's Men

By the time he had finished in Burma, Tunner had developed one other asset that would help him exercise leadership, a strong and loyal staff. Tunner's team was noteworthy, not only for the quality of the men, but even more, for their relationship with the boss.

Tunner had been assembling this crew even before his days in Ferrying Division, so that by the time he finished in Burma, most of the team had been assembled that would forge the Berlin Airlift. This was never a conscious search, but simply the product of a unique relationship that bound men to their leader. Tunner demanded astounding levels of work from his key men and rewarded them with devout loyalty in return.

Being a member of the Tunner team was no joy ride. T. Ross Milton, his chief of staff during the Berlin episode, described his boss as being "very demanding and sometimes just impossible," a belief shared by other veterans of Tunner's campaigns as well as members of his family. Sybil Sims, the widow of Hal Sims, one of the stalwarts of this crew, remembered, "Men worked, they worked hard," and that the workload was "very demanding." Her daughter, Suzanne Sims Baker, shared this sentiment, stating that the men on this staff had "hard work day and night." Ray Towne, another member of the inner circle, wrote that every staff meeting had to focus on the mission, or as he recalled it, Tunner would bark, "Don't tell me what you've got—tell me what you're here for." James Breedlove, who served as Tunner's aide for several months, called him a "strict person. He didn't take any unnecessary hems or haws or guff from his officers. . . . If we performed there was no problem, but . . . if you failed to perform you knew about it." Even Dr. William Tunner, the general's son, thought of his dad as a perfectionist, someone who was very demanding: "If you didn't do it right," he told the author, "you heard about it."[1]

Despite the accuracy of these accumulated comments, they carry only one side of a complicated story; every one of the individuals quoted above also held Tunner in the highest esteem, if not devotion. And these emotions were based on an equally unassailable set of experiences.

If Tunner demanded hard work, he also, in Milton's words, "set an enormous store on loyalty." He would do anything for these men, and even for the regular pilots and crew under his command. If they poured out their hearts and sweat for him, Tunner, the independent innovator, would take every opportunity to support them, even if it meant ruffling feathers among the brass.

Tunner's son recalled that the father was always the "champion of the men who worked for him," while Dorothy Towne, Ray's wife, observed, "You couldn't flatter General Tunner"; instead he deflected the accolades to his command. As Dee Towne (as she was universally known) explained, "He would consider all the team, all the guys."[2]

Evidence of various types supports these claims. During the Hump, Tunner fought for better conditions for his men, starting with an upgraded PX and leading to improved quarters. On most bases, for example, the accommodations for all flyers passing through was one big, open hut. Tunner ordered that the room be divided, so that men with the same schedules slept in the same sections and did not disturb others. Quiet signs also went up so that their sleep was not disturbed.

Later, when he was running the entire operation that fed the city of Berlin by air, *Life* magazine decided it wanted to put Tunner's picture on the cover. This was arguably the most important periodical in the United States at that time, but Tunner refused, writing a public relations officer at U.S. Air Forces in Europe that, "while I deeply appreciate the importance which they attached to this effort, I would greatly prefer not to have my picture on the cover of LIFE magazine. I suggest . . . if they want the Airlift on the cover, one of the pilots or someone else directly connected with the physical carrying of the coal to Berlin." At the same time, he also had a second point to make, that in some of the pictures *Life*'s photographers took of him, the wings on his uniform were out of line, and he preferred that these shots not be used. "It would not be good for the Air Force to show the pictures of me in improper uniform," he explained, "and I would greatly appreciate it, if they decide to use any of the pictures, if they select the ones which show me in proper uniform." Dorothy

Towne observed that "he had great personal discipline," that he was "always well groomed. . . . I imagine even when he lived in a tent in India he was very well groomed."[3]

If these emotions held toward the men under his command, they were far stronger when they involved his immediate staff. In an interview late in his life, Tunner maintained that one of his main jobs was simply "to energize my staff with the importance of what they were doing. If I got them concerned about the job, they would take it from there." The general always seemed to know what motivated these men, and spent a lot of time getting the best from them. Tunner's son said the general "could read people," that he "paid attention to people's personality and their traits," while Ann Tunner, his widow, exclaimed that he "was a terrific judge of men. . . . I never knew how he could just tell."[4]

Again, there was the pattern of directing benefits to these men. When Tunner arrived in India to take command, he automatically was expected to join the Saturday Club, an elite setting for members only; one had to have rank to achieve that status. Instead, Tunner pointed out to management that he had other ideas. Writing the secretary of the club as both a brigadier general and the commanding officer of the U.S. Air Forces' Hump operation, he explained that he had brought key staff with him from the states, but, "Due to the restriction of . . . members not being able to bring guests, I am unable to use the club as much as I would like. . . . It is frequently desirable that I gather with my staff . . . after work and I would like them to be able to join me for dinner." As a result, "anything that you can do to expedite their membership into the Club will be appreciated."[5]

One of the best descriptions of Tunner's unique relationships with his officers, of what was delivered by both parties, came from Russell Waldron, who served with Tunner in the 1950s. Tunner was a three-star general in command of the Military Air Transport Service by then, and Waldron ran the western division. At first things did not go so well; Waldron's boss demanded results, so "every day he'd call me and raise hell, and I'd hold the phone out about a foot from my ear, and when the noise had stopped, I'd bring it up to my ear and say, 'yes sir' or 'no sir.'" Soon, however, Waldron began to produce. He took to the skies and personally checked on as many bases as possible, calling back to Tunner as to "what I'd found out and what corrective action I had taken." Waldron was doing his job, and doing it extremely well, so the calls from Tunner stopped.

But William Tunner did not forget first-rate and loyal service. A few years later, when both men were leaving the air force at roughly the same time,

Waldron received a call out of the blue. Once again, Tunner was at the other end, with a surprise announcement. Strictly on his own, he had made arrangements, and now told Waldron, "I've got a job for you." This was news to the junior man, big news, totally unexpected news. He asked what kind of job, and Tunner calmly replied, "Vice President for Operations at American Airlines," a remarkable opportunity. Thus, on Waldron's last efficiency report, Tunner wrote, "Of ten commanders reporting to me, I considered General Waldron to be the strongest and to have the greatest potential. I considered him to be the most knowledgeable commander on the subject of airlift that I ever knew. He had quiet confidence, very intelligent, and quickly secured my respect for him."[6]

The result was a group known throughout the air service as "Tunner's Men." The author of one of the first books on military airlift in the United States felt that "the men of his [Ferrying] Division held themselves to be somewhat apart from and above the rest of the Command; even after he [Tunner] had been transferred to India and many of them were scattered into other parts of the organization, they remained Tunner's men. He defended them against all comers." Reporters for *Time* discovered the same thing, that "even when removed from his command they remained 'Tunner's men.'" T. Ross Milton described how things were with a story that took place in the late 1940s. The Military Air Transport Service (MATS) had just been set up within the air force and was headed by General Lawrence Kuter. Tunner was Kuter's deputy, and Milton was top staff to Tunner. Around that time, the vice chief of staff of the U.S. Air Force, a four-star general, called in Milton and exclaimed, "Look, you tell your boss—and I mean your real boss, not Kuter . . . ." In everybody's eyes, Milton was Tunner's man first and foremost.[7]

The founding member of this club was Robert Foreman, known universally as "Red." Born in Fort Worth, Texas, he grew up in Memphis, and fell in love with flying at a very early age; as his widow, Betty Foreman Churchman, put it, "Red put together his first airplane from his mother's bed sheets." As soon as he could, he learned to fly the real things, and even wound up flying for Lucky Luciano for a year as his pilot. Red was a local boy, and he did not even know who the mobster was till the FBI questioned him. To someone like this, the only thing that had mattered was that Luciano had a beautiful plane and he let Red fly it, and even paid him for that pleasure. As Betty Foreman put it, when it came to flying, "That was his life."[8]

Back in the thirties, Tunner had headed up a reserve detachment in Memphis, and Forman was, according to Ross Milton, "a local boy who had learned how to fly." Though Foreman had been a barnstormer and a crop duster, at that time he was running a skating rink and a swimming pool, while squeezing in flying whenever he could on the weekends. But Tunner recognized something else about this young man, that he was quite obviously "a gifted flyer . . . a gifted pilot."[9]

By the time the Tunner circle had formed, everyone knew what Foreman's strengths were. Milton recalled that Foreman "was not a very good staff officer; he didn't know how to do things in a staff way. But he was a practical man, and he had good judgment on operational matters." Above all, he "knew a lot about airplanes." In his memoirs, Tunner referred to Foreman as "one of the finest pilots I ever knew," and generally used him as his chief pilot, the officer "who was over-all supervisor of every pilot." During the Hump, it was Red Foreman who helped devise the flying standards, and then checked out everyone who flew in the operation.[10]

Foreman had one other attribute, and that was a most amenable personality. Everyone recognized what a swell guy he was, with Tunner's son recalling him as a "great affable guy." Ann Tunner claimed, "He would just get along with absolutely everyone, not by a wish or an effort, he just plain did. Everyone loved Red." This was even true for General Tunner, who described Red as "the most popular officer who ever served with me," adding, "I don't know of any man who spent fifteen minutes with Red Foreman who didn't come away with the belief that he had found a lifelong friend."[11]

That was, in all likelihood, true for most people, but it was a clear fact that the description "lifelong friend" applied most powerfully to Tunner and Foreman. Simply, they were best friends, with Ann Tunner commenting that Foreman was "very close and loyal" and that "they had great devotion for one another."[12]

Red Foreman became Tunner's right-hand man, the first person he contacted for any big mission; on both the Hump and in Berlin, it was Foreman who flew Tunner's plane when the general arrived to take command. Milton described how this easygoing southerner was "very close to Tunner. I guess Tunner trusted Red more than anybody else, anywhere." As a result of this unique relationship, Foreman also began to serve one other unique function for the staff, to explain and interpret the commanding officer's orders. Milton said that while "everybody knew he was the old man's friend, confidant," no one saw him as either a flunky or as a spy. Foreman "was very loyal and straightforward . . . very honest." He would never back away from an order, but would help his fellow officers understand what was expected of them and how to get the job done.[13]

Red Foreman was clearly Tunner's closest associate, so the story of Hal Sims, an officer who was part of the Tunner Club but nowhere near as close as Foreman, serves as a better indication of how the community worked and what the general would do for those who served with him.

Hal Sims was an artist who grew up in Georgiana, Alabama. He had wanted to go to art school, but when the Depression hit the family could not dream of a step like that, and he wound up in a Civilian Conservation Corps (CCC) camp. Seeking a profession, he turned to the air, and became a navigator for Pan American Airlines, then joined the Army Air Forces in December 1942. Assigned to Ferrying Command, he came to the attention of William Tunner, who took him under his wing. Sims became his chief navigator, but in addition, the general recognized this officer's skill with paint and pen and ink, putting him in charge of chart making and presentation displays; Milton recalled him as "quite artistic," capable of making "great charts," which were crucial to getting staff to understand any situation. Tunner had recognized Sims's skill, as his daughter put it, "the importance and effectiveness of his ability to translate an idea into a visual graphic illustration."[14]

There is no question that Sims and Tunner were close; again, he was one of the first people Tunner took to Berlin with him when he assumed command. Particularly telling, Suzanne Sims Baker, the navigator's daughter, recalled that Sims held Tunner in the highest regard, that "it was considered an honor any time our family was invited to be guests of the Tunner family," and that her father "may have regarded him as a father figure and role model." This was a significant remark, given that Sims's own father had died when he was eighteen, an event that shattered the young man's life forever. It was that tragedy, in the midst of the Depression, that had forced Sims to give up his dream of art school and led him to government relief and an alternative career, although he never lost his passion for graphic illustrations and art. Baker mentioned that when she grew up, there was "never a bad word" about the commanding officer in their household, that instead her father "really looked up to General Tunner," believing him to be "*professional* and unwavering in his dedication to his duty and position," and as a result, her father had "unquestionable respect for his judgment, his choices."[15]

That did not mean that Tunner cut Sims any slack—quite the contrary. Being one of Tunner's men meant you had to work harder than anyone else. During the Berlin Airlift, for example, Sims had the enormous responsibility, as chief navigator, of figuring out flight routes and helping Red Foreman devise air patterns to keep the stream of planes orderly and constant. In addition, he had to come up with all the charts for the ever-increasing volume of data, plus graphic illustrations. Yet, despite that prodigious load, he still had to fly cargo missions just like anyone else, putting in fifty-seven hours of flight time in October 1948 and sixty-three hours in November, or roughly fifteen hours of flying each week on top of his other work.[16]

In return for this dedication and service, Tunner stood by Sims in a variety of ways. In 1959 Tunner was head of the Military Air Transport Service, and busy with a host of congressional hearings that would lead to the rejuvenation of military airlift in the United States. Nevertheless, he took time to write Sims's evaluation, declaring in the very first sentence Sims's "outstanding ability as an artist, designer and decorator." This officer had "accomplished all the tasks asked of him in an outstanding manner," a list that included redesigning MATS cargo aircraft "and then working with contractor to insure that weight, durability, quality and cost of materials met desired standards." He had also visited numerous bases, including the major facilities at Travis, McGuire, and Dover, and redesigned the general appearance as well as refurbishing housing and clubs. Sims stood out as "an energetic and tireless worker," someone who "cheerfully takes on any tasks assigned." Tunner concluded with the note, "This officer is eminently well qualified for promotion to colonel and I heartily recommend that he be promoted to this grade on the next list." The next year, Tunner's last in the service, he repeated that tone, starting the evaluation with "Colonel Sims has been an outstanding performer under my direct supervision in each of the major airlift exercises over the past twelve years." Tunner explained that Sims "has given the Air Force and MATS unselfishly of both his time and his exceptional talent, not only as an artist and designer, but as an expert in the area of oral and visual presentation." In the section where he had to list "Strengths," Tunner put, "His greatest strengths are imagination, his attitude of cooperation, his ingenuity, and capacity for hard work."[17]

Most important of all, Tunner did everything he could to foster and champion Sims's creative gift. Hal Sims never lost his boyhood dream, and unceasingly continued to develop his artwork and artistic talent all his life. As his family recalled, he loved painting more than anything else in the world.

Thus, whenever possible, Tunner tried to give his officer every opportunity to use that gift. Sims co-created the Berlin Airlift newspaper, the *Task Force Times,* with Ray Towne, and designed the logo. In his personal papers, he included copies of this paper with his personal comments jotted in thick marker along the sides and top. On page six of the August 3, 1949, edition, one of the last, a banner headline read, "Commanders Cite Task Force Times As Factor In Lift Success." On top of this, Hal Sims wrote, "This makes me proud to have been part of the 'TIMES,' in addition to being its founder."[18]

But Tunner did a lot more. Sims was chief navigator, so over the years of flying together, the general got a chance to witness firsthand many of the paintings Sims completed in his free time on their stops around the world. In time, the list of places they visited, and that Sims painted, included Japan, India, Egypt, Turkey, Iceland, Brazil, the Azore Islands, and Alaska. General Tunner recognized these works as a unique visual diary of the world through the eyes of a military navigator, and felt the collection told a story and should be shared with a larger audience.

Thus, because of Tunner's single-handed efforts, Hal Sims became the first living artist in American history to have a show at the Smithsonian Institution. The curators were reluctant to take this step, but they had not reckoned with William Tunner. Suzanne Baker said, "General Tunner's idea of showing Hal Sims' collection of paintings did not follow their usual routine in acquiring an artist's exhibit . . . but Tunner . . . wouldn't take no for an answer." He "kept going till it happened," till one of his men was honored in the medium he cared about most. Baker noted, in what was as obvious to the family as it was to Sims himself, that Tunner was "a great fan as far as his artwork and artistic talent."[19]

Another example of how Tunner pulled men into his orbit was the story of crew chief Earl Morrison. Morrison was a native of Long Beach, California, who settled in Oklahoma. Somehow, he came to Tunner's attention, and the senior officer must have checked him out. As Ann Tunner noted, that would have been enough; Tunner had an instinct for who would work well with him, and then acted.[20]

Morrison got the call, but at first could not figure out what was going on; Tunner explained that he wanted the tech sergeant as his crew chief and flight engineer. After some discussion, Morrison seemed to agree, but then stated one nonnegotiable qualification, that he not be forced to live in the local vicinity: "I said, 'General, if I go I don't want to move into town.'" If he had to do that, the deal was off.

That was risky business, a noncom making demands to someone with stars on his shoulders. But Tunner knew his men and would stand by them. After a prolonged conversation, Morrison finally admitted that he had just gone through a bad divorce, and if he was in town, "I'd just go crazy."

At that point Tunner asked, "Where are you living?" Morrison replied, the local barracks, and that was enough for Tunner. He picked up his new crew chief and the two went over to the billet. Tunner personally picked out the best room, had the staff sergeant who currently occupied that space moved out, and Morrison moved in.

Morrison returned that loyalty. One day during the Berlin Airlift Tunner asked Morrison, "How do you feel about going to Berlin?" This was November 30, one of the worst days, with terrible fog; only a couple of flights got in. But Tunner was bound and determined to bring tonnage in, and if he had to take it himself, so be it. He asked Morrison, "Will you go with me then?" and Morrison replied, "I sure will," adding, "He had become acquainted enough with me and how I handled those airplanes . . . he knew I'd be watching" the plane closely, that Morrison was a good man to fly with. When they finally landed, under a fog cover that was down below 200 feet, they found that when "we broke out . . . there was only three red lights left [i.e., they had only three lights left till the end of the runway]." Morrison summed up this episode by observing, "He respected me, I respected him."

That was enough to make Morrison special. On one trip to Berlin, after they landed the sergeant was putting in safety pins and pitot covers, doing his work as a flight engineer. A captain who had been on board intervened, dismissively ordering him to get Tunner's bags. Morrison just looked up and told him fine, you take care of finishing the plane then. A highly insubordinate remark delivered in a highly insubordinate tone (albeit totally accurate). Tunner just laughed his head off, so the captain knew what was what and backed off.

Tunner went even further than that; on occasion "he let me fly right-hand seat when he was flying . . . that is something else" (the copilot's seat; a real sign of trust). Even Red Foreman protested that.

But the story that best describes Tunner's special relationship with his insiders came the time his plane picked up a special passenger, William Jr., who was very young at the time. They were flying back from Berlin, and the boy started to touch things, as kids will do. Tunner blew up and started to yell at his son. Morrison was in the right-hand seat and, amazingly, he told the general, "Please don't talk to that boy like that." He explained that Tunner Jr. was "just curious," that he wanted to see what his father did. At that point, as Morrison put it, "It got so quiet I don't think the engines made any noise." After a couple of minutes Tunner left the cockpit. Morrison took the boy and put him in his lap for a while and let him touch whatever he wanted (they were on autopilot). There were not many generals who would let sergeants lecture them about how to raise their children.

Over the years at Ferrying Division and the Hump, Tunner's crew got fleshed out. Raymond Towne flew B-26 missions in Italy, but was a genius at public information and at writing up data. He became one of Tunner's closest confidants, and the general even served as best man when Towne married Dorothy Jorski. Mrs. Towne's remembrances of those years included the comment that it was "very exciting" to work for Tunner, and that "he expected personal humor in the behavior of his staff."[21]

Manuel Fernandez—known to one and all as "Pete"—went back to the early days of Ferrying Command and was Tunner's communications head, but also his chief scrounger; Morrison said that whatever one needed, "he could get it." Ann Tunner remembered Fernandez for his "wonderful sense of humor. . . . He could write so beautifully. . . . Long after the general retired and Pete Fernandez would write him letters, they were just beautiful, humorous letters. . . . He was a very, very clever man."[22]

The rest of the team included Sterling Bettinger, who served as Tunner's chief pilot during the Berlin Airlift. Ed Guilbert was director of air traffic for cargo, someone Ross Milton described as "a live wire of a ground officer," and Dee Towne believed "had a gift of organizing." When Tunner first met Orval McMahon, another regular, back in Memphis he was a staff sergeant, but by the time Berlin came up, McMahon was a lieutenant colonel. Tunner had been "impressed with his knowledge and soundness" when it came to logistics, and made him chief of supply. Ann Tunner believed the general respected McMahon "highly . . . He had a beautiful, strong character."[23]

And then there was Miss Katie. Catherine Gibson was William Tunner's secretary for most of his air force career. Back in Memphis, Tunner needed a secretary right away, so he contacted the local civil service office. It was a Friday when he got the list of candidates, and true to form, wanted to get started right away and asked applicants to be interviewed on Saturday or Sunday; that demand shortened the number of possibilities on the spot.

Gibson came out on Sunday and impressed Tunner as "proficient and intelligent, not to mention independent." Over the course of the interview, the officer sternly pointed out that "we're a few miles" out of the city, "and you will have to make arrangements to get here yourself." Calmly, sweetly, she replied, "Tell me, captain . . . just how do you think I got here this Sunday afternoon?"[24]

That was just the beginning. On the plane taking Tunner to Berlin to tackle the largest airlift in human history, "When I looked around and saw my staff of twenty handpicked officers, plus Miss Katie Gibson, I was delighted." Decades later, when the name Catherine Gibson came up, Ann Tunner just blurted out, "Oh bless her heart. . . . She went everyplace with him."[25]

T. Ross Milton came on board as Tunner's chief of staff just before the Berlin Airlift. Milton came from a military family; his father was a career officer who graduated from West Point in the same class as Douglas MacArthur. During World War II Milton headed B-17 units in the Eighth Air Force, commanding the 91st and 348th Bombardment Groups, respectively, and led the second raid on Schweinfurt, Germany.[26]

When Milton came back from the war, the air force reassigned him to ATC. The combat flyer took this decision as "a great shock" and briefly threatened to resign, but soon thought better. He realized that "it was the only thing going on. . . . I didn't like it at first," but then realized that "nobody else was doing anything." Instead, ATC was handling part of the demobilization as well as running a main transportation link to American units all over the globe. Milton realized, therefore, "we were the only ones who were busy," and as a result, "I found myself doing some fairly interesting things."[27]

Milton, by then a full colonel, wound up helping run an airlift base outside Cincinnati, as chief of staff to the brigadier general in charge. Tunner was set to take over the base, and the commanding officer was on his way out. He warned Milton about the new general's already legendary loyalty to his men, telling the aide, "you better come with me . . . because Tunner's going to bring his own men. . . . He'll fire you the day he gets here." When Tunner arrived, he called Milton and the base's deputy commander to his office, and asked each of them to state their duties. After the recitation, the new commander inquired, "Is there any reason it takes two of you to do what you're doing?" The deputy answered in the negative, Tunner told him to leave, then looked at Milton and said, "Alright [sic], you've got it. Get out and take charge."[28]

The story cited above was drawn from an interview with Milton, and it may have simplified what happened. Tunner, as noted before, made quick and insightful decisions regarding his staff, and given the amount of control he immediately gave that young officer, it is clear that he had found a bright addition to his group; as Tunner later described it, Milton "would obviously be a success in any operation he took on." Milton also agreed that Tunner had "a lot of faith in certain people."[29]

Milton stood out in the group as someone a little quieter, especially in comparison to Red Foreman. Ann Tunner remembered him as "very sophisticated . . . very smart," but also more "reserved"; while the general's son added that he was "quiet," a "good thinker," and that his father "respected" Milton.[30]

This staff provided William Tunner with many benefits, just as he did all he could to support them. First and foremost, it meant that he could respond to a crisis faster than almost anyone else, with a top-notch crew that was used to working together, ready to go. During the Korean War Tunner told a *Time* reporter, "When we start a new airlift, we start in a hell of a hurry. It is a whole lot easier to start with people you know." Ann Tunner observed that "all these men were *highly professional*" (emphasis in original) in their respective fields, and that her husband had "a loyal group that he could call on to go with him on different operations." Milton agreed, stating that Tunner's men "worked very well as a team."[31]

In addition, General Tunner drew strength from these men he cared so much about. Dorothy Towne explained that her boss was a quiet man, that "he got most of his energy by disengaging from large groups," by thinking things through and reading. "He had a few very close friends," she noted, but "not many . . . What he really loved was a quiet dinner party with very close friends."[32]

Instead, as Ann Tunner put it, "These men were his extended family. . . . He had men he knew he could trust." Members of the group and their families came by the house regularly, although generally within a sense of friendship but also formality, befitting a military relationship.[33]

Again, the best example of this came with Red Foreman. When he got married, Tunner served as best man and held the reception at his house. But shortly after that, the Berlin crisis beckoned, and they had to leave. Tunner grabbed Red, excusing himself to the newlywed wife with the line, "You'll be married a long time," but also moving her into his house, the best on the base. Betty Foreman Churchman looked back on those days and affirmed, "It was a very close-knit group . . . and stayed together for quite a long time."[34]

5 / Buildup to Destiny

William Tunner had helped make the Hump Airlift a success, setting many precedents that he would later put to use in a far more dramatic venue. First, however, after the war ended in 1945, he flirted with new career options but quickly became enmeshed in efforts to defend and then extend his vision of military airlift. At the same time, on the other side of the Atlantic, a situation developed that would challenge the Free World in a test of ingenuity and courage.

Upon his return to the United States, Tunner took over Ferrying Division once again, and eventually headed the combined Atlantic and Domestic Divisions. But he had other ideas on his mind than working for Uncle Sam, knowing that in peacetime there would be much less opportunity for promotion, that the military would be cut back.

Like many other top officers who had discovered their administrative skills, Tunner looked to the private sector. This was hardly a surprising leap, given his close contacts with men like C. R. Smith, great captains of industry. Tunner explained, "It occurred to me that a military man would work twelve hours a day, often seven days a week, to run an organization ten times as large as a comparable one in the business world," for only a fraction of the pay and benefits.[1]

The idea was to create a global carrying company called World Air Freight. Tunner and his associates made clear at the start of their proposal that "the basic operating principle of WORLD AIR FREIGHT is *large volume at minimum rates*" (emphasis in original). They planned on a fleet of fifty C-54 planes, the four-engined Douglas transports that had succeeded the C-47, which would fly a total of 12 million ton-miles a month. That was a truly remarkable figure, given that in 1945 all of the commercial airlines in the United States *combined* had managed only 24 million ton-miles, and that was their peak year of operation, ever. Furthermore, they had charged between 26 and 50 cents a ton-mile, while World Air Freight rates would start at 15 cents, and then drop to 10 cents or lower.[2]

What they were proposing, therefore, was a revolution, the first true mass air freight carrier in the country. The founders argued that the benefits of using air cargo would include not only fast shipping for seasonal goods, perishables, and new products that had to get to market fast, such as style items like fashion, but also "lower interest charges on goods in transit, reduced inventories . . . and a material reduction of warehousing costs." Decades before the term was commonplace in business circles, therefore, these entrepreneurs were advocating a practice later known as just-in-time manufacturing, and exploring how it could be accomplished.[3]

Tunner was the brains behind this plan, a man with the knowledge to put an operation of this kind together, while the rest of the key figures were financiers. He would become president at a high salary, while running an airline a fraction of the size of the divisions he commanded during the war. In addition, among the men he recommended to head the new corporation was Robert Foreman. In a letter to his backers on executive appointments, Tunner wrote of Foreman, "I consider that there is no finer pilot in the Army Air Forces. In addition, his knowledge of other pilots and of piloting is invaluable." Tunner would keep the team together, would start with his best men.[4]

Tunner eventually backed off from World Freight. In his memoirs, he gave as the reason his promotion at this time to major general, an indication that the army recognized his importance and that there would be a place for him in its future. The other reason, unspoken, was that he now had a vision, and wanted to act on it.[5]

In the postwar era, military air transport was at a crossroads, searching for an identity. No one was sure as to what role it would play in the future, if it would remain an independent branch of the service, and if so, at what scale.[6]

William Tunner had to respond to a challenge like that. In February 1947 he wrote to General Robert Webster, then head of ATC, with a coherent proposal for the organization's future. Tunner proposed that it must be set up to serve as the military's main air transport resource, capable of handling all loads, from bomber sections to cans of beans to passengers, on a 24/7 basis under all weather conditions.[7]

After considerable discussion, up to and including cabinet level, the Pentagon agreed, and the first integrated air transport unit, the Military Air Transport Service, became effective on June 1, 1948. This was basically a merging of ATC with the Naval Air Transport Service (NATS), the former clearly the senior partner. Major General Lawrence Kuter became the commanding officer, and the new force had a combined fleet of 496 planes and 27,300 personnel. In a May 17, 1948, article in *Aviation Week* titled, "World's Great Transport System," Kuter stood with his top three officers, Tunner on the far right of the photo.[8]

Throughout this period, therefore, Tunner worked as an advocate, both in the military and outside, on behalf of airlift. By then there were various components to this comprehensive vision, and he took steps on behalf of each of them.

Above all else, there was a global vision of the central role of air transport in the military, that it must replace ground and sea transportation as the fundamental delivery mechanism. He argued that "by one means we can eliminate the trains, the ports, the ships," that of "transport aircraft based at airports throughout the country, ready for instant duty." In a stirring passage from this 1946 article, the general depicted what was for many a fantasy: "These aircraft would maintain a continuous shuttle, night and day . . . never ending streams of aircraft carrying supplies and men." In fact, this was an amazingly accurate depiction of what he would operate during the Berlin Airlift, two years hence.[9]

Thus, to Tunner, this was the key to everything else, and he would dedicate his life to its realization. In a private letter written in 1946, he declared, "It is my belief—and one which I preach upon every occasion and provocation— that eventually the transportation business of our armed forces will be principally handled by air."[10]

Tunner used whatever occasion history provided to prove his point, then publicized the results. In 1946 the nation experienced a crippling railroad strike, pitting big business and the president against workers and their labor unions. To General Tunner, this was nothing more than an opportunity to show what air transport could do during a national emergency.

Thus, within twenty-four hours of the strike's commencement, what was then still ATC launched "Operation Casey Jones" to supply America by air. Five hundred military transports took to the skies, carrying stalled military car-

goes, first-class mail, and, as a last priority, some civilian passengers and shipments. Though the strike was over within a few days, there was even time for
a dramatic emergency flight, carrying a twelve-year-old child suffering from a
brain tumor from his stranded train in Arizona to a California hospital.

All of this, of course, was conveyed in a press release from the Public Relations Office of the Continental Division of ATC. This document pounded
home the critical lessons, how in this moment of danger, "with rail transportation at a standstill and commercial air carriers already overtaxed, the country
had turned to its one certain source of help—military air transport." The authors then hit on another one of Tunner's main themes, the need for a professional air transport staff in a separate command, declaring, "It was this organization: its planes, its people, its traffic and above all its 'know how' in air
transport, which made possible the swift, efficient expansion called for in the
transportation crisis."[11]

Tunner now added the next logical step, another concept that he would advocate for years; to make air transport work, the Air Force had to develop and
buy bigger, better, more efficient planes. Leaders entrusted with the nation's defense, he argued, could not accept outmoded transports any more than they
could antiquated bombers or fighters, and considerable research and allocations
had to take place if the air carrying arm was to remain capable of its strategic
mission. In a 1948 memo to the Air Force Chief of Staff, for example, Tunner
openly "requested that the Air Force undertake the necessary research and development of a modern . . . freight carrying transport airplane."[12]

Again, Tunner lost no chance to make this key point before every possible
audience. He prepared a talk on the new C-74 Globemaster, touting it as a possible answer to the transport deficiency, claiming "the huge C-74 to be the first
Air Force transport . . . capable of efficiently and adequately supplying and
supporting our Armed Forces." On May 19, 1948, he gave a speech before the
Commerce and Industry Association of New York in which he referred to airlift
as "this new factor in military power," and made clear that existing machines
were inadequate, that a new fleet of more advanced planes had to be developed
and purchased. His remarks were covered by the *New York Times,* the *New York
Herald-Tribune,* and the *New York Journal of Commerce.* On yet another occasion, when Fred Glass, president of Air Cargo, Inc., echoed this call in a well-
publicized speech, Tunner not only wrote Glass as a kindred spirit, but sent the
New York Times clipping of the speech to the Air Force deputy chief of staff, the
commander of ATC, and other officers. In one letter, he concluded, "I am con-

fident that development along the lines I have previously indicated is, without any question, the direction we must go."[13]

Similarly, when Hanson Baldwin, the prestigious military correspondent of the *New York Times,* wrote that the need for air transport was "limited," Tunner took fervent action. He wrote numerous letters to top figures throughout the Army Air Forces, including the heads of the planning departments for both the AAF and the War Department, as well as that later entity's director of research and planning. Tunner argued that Baldwin's article was inaccurate and "can do great harm unless vehemently refuted with established facts and cold logic." Above all, there was the fear that "outside limited circles, little was learned about air transport," and the clear need for vigilance on the part of air transport's guardians.[14]

By then, however, there was need for vigilance on other places as well, especially the fate of Western Europe. William Tunner was asking Ray Towne, "Are we to become the Roman Empire of the Twentieth Century? Are we Americans, together with our allies, going to be forced to man the frontiers of the free world against the Communist 'Huns and Vandals?'"[15]

In 1945, and for years to come, Berlin seemed a doomed city. On June 10, 1943, the Western Allies commenced heavy bombing raids, and continued, with the RAF at night and the U.S. Army Air Forces during the day, virtually unstopped till the end of the war. By the time Hitler lay dead in his bunker, 156 million pounds of bombs had blasted the capital alone.[16]

These powerful weapons did their job; there was not much left of the place. *Life* reported in July 1945 that over 2,700 of Berlin's 19,500 acres were completely destroyed, that the city's prewar population of 4.25 million was halved. Of those remaining, as many as 1.5 million may have been homeless, or an astounding three-quarters of the former inhabitants. Studies showed that in the center of the city, in a circle five miles across, the level of destruction was, according to the U.S. Army, "complete." In the nearby Charlottenburg district, of the 11,075 residential buildings, only 604 were left standing. Saul Kagan, who worked for the U.S. Military Government researching war crimes by German banks, remembered, "When I flew into Berlin in 1946 there was no basement I couldn't see from my plane. . . . We did a first-rate job."[17]

The infrastructure needed to keep a city alive was gutted. Water mains were in chaos, with breaks at 3,000 different places. Three out of four fire stations were destroyed. Of the 1,000 buses in the municipal fleet, only 37 were left.

When gas was available 4,000 street lights glowed, down from 125,000 at the start of the war. Before the conflict started, Berlin had benefited from the use of 600,000 private telephones. The Russians took almost all of these, so that by the time U.S. occupation forces entered, only 4,000 remained. One Russian officer observed, "If the Germans wanted telephone service, they should not have started the war."[18]

The devastation strained reporters' writing skills. The great journalist William Shirer, returning in October 1945 to the city he had covered during the rise of Nazism, declared, "Most of the little streets I knew, gone, erased off the map. The railways stations . . . gaunt shells. The Imperial palace of the Kaisers roofless, some of its wings pulverized, and here and there the outer walls battered in . . . the old spreading trees that I had known, bare stumps." Howard K. Smith noted how the roadsides were littered with "skeletons of streamlined gray Wehrmacht cars which careened to conquest over every highway in Europe. Now they lie, belly to belly, burned out and red with rust from the autumn rain. The whole desolate scene is one of crushed power." When Walter Ulbricht, later head of East Germany, came back in May 1945, days after the city fell, smoke was so dense, "we could barely find our way through the rubble." The scholar F. L. Lucas wrote, "One had heard of it, read of it, seen pictures of it; but still the reality staggered and appalled. The eye, scanning street after street of shambles. . . . Among these endless rows of gaunt, hollow-eyed facades, one felt like a mouse wandering amid the skulls of some great catacomb." That summer, the newspaper *Berliner Zeitung* predicted that it would take sixteen years to get rid of the rubble, twenty years before sufficient replacement housing was built.[19]

Life became survival. At first, Berliners got by on Allied rations, which began at 1,248 calories for the aged and unemployed, and rose to 2,485 calories for those performing difficult labor; at this time people in the Ruhr were getting 740 calories a day. Poor distribution, however, meant that, on average, only 64 percent of this got to those who needed it.[20]

Work was scarce, much of it done by *trummerfrauen,* or women of the rubble, who were paid next to nothing to help clear the streets. One woman told how she clawed through piles of debris for hours with her bare hands, earning a bowl of diluted cabbage soup.[21]

As a result, the black market flourished, and the fundamental medium of exchange became the cigarette. Under the system established by the Army Finance Department, in 1945 a mark was considered equal to ten cents in American money. Using that rate of exchange, butter cost $120 a pound, $60 bought a pound of coffee, and for $7 one could purchase stockings made out of shredded wool, impossible sums. Instead, Berlin became a city of barter, with university professors, for example, being paid three pounds of flour per lecture, on a day-to-day basis; one top nightclub comedienne charged eight ounces of bacon and a similar weight of white beans for each performance. At this time, one journalist accurately remarked, "Nobody in Berlin today can . . . buy enough food to feel really filled up."[22]

Meanwhile, another fear hung over the whole question of how and what to do with Germany, with how the reconstruction was to proceed. The West was now intensely aware of the crimes this nation had committed under Hitler, and it was not clear how much of that was regretted. As late as July 1947, a writer for the *New Yorker,* in dispatches from Berlin, observed that Germans felt no responsibility for the war, "they just say darkly, *'Fruher war es besser'* [Things were better before], meaning under Hitler," and "the bulk of Germany . . . still 'thinks brown,' meaning *Braunhaus,* or Nazi." How should the Allies treat a nation like this, deal with this situation? And what would be the relationship between the wartime Allies, a large question to be sure, but with the future of Germany a particularly delicate issue?[23]

The postwar occupation of Germany and of Berlin was created in an initial atmosphere of Allied cooperation that would not last long. The defeated aggressor was divided into four zones run by the Soviet Union, the United States, Great Britain, and France, all of whom would sit on the ruling Allied Control Council (ACC), sited in Berlin. In the U.S. zone, by 1947 one individual had assumed the key role in this setup: General Lucius Clay served simultaneously as both commanding officer of the European Command, United States Army (EUCOM); and the head of the Office of Military Government of the United States for Germany (OMGUS).

Even though Berlin was in the Soviet zone, as the former capital of Nazi Germany and home of the occupation authorities, it had a unique status. Two weeks after the ACC had its first meeting, the Allies set up a special administrative unit to run this city, the four power Allied Kommandatura, with complete authority; its first announcement began bluntly, "The Inter-Allied Kommandatura has today assumed control over the City of Berlin." By 1947 Brigadier General Frank Howley played a major role in this structure, and became the commandant of the country's U.S. garrison in Berlin.[24]

Because Berlin was occupied by all the powers, special arrangements had to be made regarding the area; among these was access to transportation routes into the city. Clay and the Western Allies took the position that there was little need for written agreements, since the very presence of a military garrison implied the need for open movement of supplies and personnel. In addition, Clay felt that by asking for an agreement on specific land routes, he would be accepting access to some, but inherently consenting to not use others. He preferred complete freedom to use all available routes.[25]

From the very first, the Soviets fought this position, and moved to severely limit land access to Berlin. Marshal Georgi Zhukov, the great World War II commander who sat on the ACC, almost immediately fought for a single highway route to the city, as well as the use of rail lines, which Clay accepted on June 29, 1945. The American general felt at the time that his broader vision of full access for the garrison would prevail in case of dispute, and there was no reason to press the Russians and precipitate a conflict this early. On September 10 the Soviets agreed to a daily quota of ten trains into the Western zones of the former capital, raised to sixteen on October 3, then later to thirty-one.[26]

On the matter of air routes, the Soviets were somewhat more forthcoming. In November 1945, despite a Western request for six passageways, they agreed to three 20-mile wide corridors into the city, originating in Frankfurt, Hamburg, and Hanover. To govern this system, the ACC promulgated a set of flight rules, published on October 22, 1946.[27]

These rules were part—but only part—of the explanation of why the Soviets treated air access with such diffidence. Air travel was a relatively new development, the high-tech innovation of its era. Flight officers feared disaster if this could not be brought under strong control, if a common system could not be agreed upon to minimize flight hazards. While politicized generals had clear ideas of what to do regarding more traditional forms of land transportation, they may have been more willing to bow to technical experts in the air realm.[28]

There was also one other reason for Soviet negligence of the air corridors, far more powerful, and that was simply that they did not care. In the winter of 1942–1943 the Soviets had engaged in a titanic battle around the city of Stalingrad. After they cut off the German Sixth Army and trapped it, Herman Goering promised that his Lutwaffe could supply the Wehrmacht with everything it needed, by airlift.

In no time at all, the minimum daily totals started getting pared down, reduced to a bare bones figure of 300 tons daily, barely enough for the army to survive. On the first day, however, the German air force delivered only 75 tons, or 25 percent of a figure already barely adequate. Over the next few days the high figure was 129 tons, the low a dismal 28 tons.

With few supplies coming in by air, the Sixth Army starved to death, and fell apart. One veteran captured the mood when he noted, "the situation had deteriorated catastrophically. We were lacking in food, weapons, rest, warmth, hope." Although some troops fought to the end, many began to discard weapons, forgo any kind of discipline, and join bands of stragglers and looters.

This struggle garnered publicity all over the world, convincing generals everywhere that airlift was a weak and ineffective tool. In America, the *New York Times* on December 22, 1942, reported, "One of the most striking phenomena of this front is the paucity of air action" by the Germans. Five days later, the paper told how, "There are other indications that the Germans are being pinched for equipment. Prisoners complained of a shortage of ammunition," with riflemen getting daily rations of only 60 bullets compared to 120 at the start of the battle, while machine gunners had only 1,000 rounds a day when previously they had received 3,500. According to the paper, "All prisoners complained about the steady deterioration of their rations," which were listed as "a small piece of meat daily, a half pound of bread and a little apple jam or hard candy in place of sugar." This was actually far more than what German troops were getting by that point.[29]

On that horrific battlefield the Russians had proved that air transport was a minor force, that it could not feed an army, let alone a city. The Soviets believed, in other words, based on ample evidence, that airlift was not a strategic factor. This view shaped their policy on Berlin, since they considered air transport meaningless, a worthless chip in their eyes, that they could easily throw at the United States as a good-will gesture of no consequence.

The situation in Berlin played itself out, in part, against a backdrop of the great events of the early cold war, as relations between the United States and the USSR reached the breaking point. While in May 1945 the two nations were wartime allies, by 1947 they had split badly, with President Harry Truman replying to Soviet-sponsored violence in Greece and Turkey with the doctrine of containment, enunciated in his famous speech of March 12, 1947.

On the crucial issue of Europe's future, and especially the fate of Germany, the superpowers had vastly different goals. Josef Stalin sought a weak continent, one ripe for discontent and Communist takeover, while the United States wanted a stable zone allied with itself.

Of all the European issues the Allies confronted, the most contentious was the fate of Germany, for emotional as well as strategic reasons. This was the nation that had launched two world wars and a holocaust, and had taken tens of millions of lives. No one in the world could take this issue lightly, least of all those who had suffered the most, and the most directly.

The Soviet Union had a clear position on Germany, and that was that it must be permanently weakened. Germany had imposed grievous losses on Russia in the struggle that commenced in 1914, and from 1941, the USSR had taken the vast bulk of the casualties in the European war and destroyed most of the powerful German armed forces.

In addition, Stalin believed firmly that, given the events of the past few decades, the next German aggression was merely a matter of time. He worried that because of its technical capabilities, the now prostrate state would recover within a few years and proceed to make war against the East, just as it had done twice before within a relatively short time, at remarkably high cost to the Russians.[30]

Simply put, the Soviet leaders had to make sure that this would never happen again and chose a dramatic course to achieve that goal. Germany's economy would be stripped, and to buy time during a future aggression, countries in a position to serve as buffers, such as Poland, had to be turned into puppet states whose primary strategic purpose was to buy time for the Soviets to mobilize.

They were not alone in some of these views, either. France, which had also felt the German heel during two occupations, sought a total breakup of the German state. In August 1945, for example, Charles DeGaulle proposed to Truman that the Rhineland be taken away from the former home of National Socialism, and that the great Ruhr industrial basin come under international control.[31]

The United States had a different view entirely. The Americans quickly came to realize that Germany held a central position in the revitalization of the European economy. If that nation languished, the rest of Europe would remain sick, while a German recovery might foster prosperity throughout the continent.

There was also another reason for putting Germany back on its feet. In the postwar era, large parts of the country—especially the big cities—literally survived on Western military rations, and the cost was substantial, with some estimates going as high as $700 million a year for the United States and Britain combined. The going rate to support the hundreds of thousands—and sometimes millions—of DPs (displaced persons) alone was sixty cents a day per person.[32]

It was not just the United States that was being effected. Britain's zone, for example, included the industrialized but now demolished Ruhr district, with little farmland; it produced only 40 percent of its food, compared to the Soviet Zone that had ample farms and coal resources as well. Taking that burden off the U.K. would help that nation with its own stalled recovery, and also ease protests at home, as citizens asked why tough rationing continued at the same time that they were paying to feed former enemies. At the same time in the United States, Congress, seeking to cut costs after a long and expensive war, continually questioned the large American outlay as well. Given that the democracy could not approve mass starvation of an occupied people, the only alternative was to work for German self-sufficiency.[33]

Thus, by the early postwar period, the United States and Great Britain sought a unified Germany in order to restart its economy. Though the justification for this was financial, the strategic ramifications were vast, and to many, frightening. The Soviets to some extent, but especially the French, had blocked this in the ACC, to such an extent that the Anglo-American forces felt they had no choice. On July 30, 1946, the United States and Britain announced that they had reached an agreement to merge their two zones, a decision immediately attacked by the other two powers as a violation of the Potsdam covenants.

Discussions of this plan continued for several years amid the increasing tensions of the cold war, till at a conference for the Western powers, held in London on March 6, 1948, France, recognizing that Soviet aggression was a more immediate danger than Germany, signed on as well.

On March 20, 1948, the Soviets took the first step in their response to this powerful development. The incident occurred during a meeting of the ACC, which had by now settled into a routine. The position of chair rotated between the great powers, and this individual not only presided, but also provided the refreshments that ended the day's events, in an attempt to preserve some sense of wartime comradeship and conviviality. At this point in time, the acting chair was Soviet marshal Vassily Sokolovsky, a somewhat pleasant host.

That afternoon of March 20 was different. Sokolovksy took the offensive, criticizing the London conference for taking place without Russian approval and demanding to know what agreements had been reached there. General Clay and the British representative, General Sir Brian Robertson, replied that they had no need to get Russian approval for their meeting; that the Russians had not been forthright on details as to what they had been doing in their own zone; and that relevant information would be available after the respective governments had signed off on the appropriate reports and documents.

Sokolovsky then rose abruptly and began reading from a text that had obviously been prepared long in advance, which did not depend on what the

Western delegates had or had not said. He claimed that the Western nations had shown contempt for the occupation mechanism and would bear the blame for its destruction. "By their actions," he professed, "these delegations once again confirm that the Control Council virtually exists no longer as the supreme authority in Germany," that they had committed "serious violations of the obligations devolving on . . . authorities in Germany by virtue of the four-power agreements," and that the conference could not "be recognized as lawful." As interpreters finished their translations, the British representative tried to reply, but Sokolovsky cut him off. The entire Soviet contingent stood in a prearranged plan, and Sokolovsky yelled, "I see no sense in continuing this meeting and declare it adjourned," and walked out with his aides. This was the first time in the history of the ACC that the chair had ever concluded a meeting without a vote of the members; and more ominously, he did not establish a date for the next meeting, which had always been standard procedure. The Allied Control Council would never meet again.[34]

The former alliance that had taken down Hitler was now split, never to be restored. Clay and Howley sensed that the Russians would now act, and the most obvious step would be some effort to force the Western allies out of Berlin. An armed attack seemed unlikely, so the alternative had to be some sort of pressure; one possibility was a blockade. Howley began to stock up on basic supplies, and set up measures by which the radio stations in West Berlin could be used for propaganda broadcasts. All at once, Berlin, which had seemed like the headquarters of a major military command just days before, began to look like an isolated island.[35]

On March 26, less than a week after the ACC meeting, the Soviet army chief of staff, Lieutenant General G. Lukyanchenko, made a public statement claiming the West was allowing and even "facilitating" the movement of criminals across their borders in Germany. In response, his army would have to protect its zone against "subversive and terrorist elements."[36]

On the day after this statement, the Soviets acted. New rules would take effect as of April 1. From that day hence, all travelers through their zone, by auto transport or rail, had to show identity papers. All freight, especially for the military, would require special permits as well. No cargo, no passenger train, could leave Berlin without the Soviet commander's permission, effectively granting him sole control of the movements of all goods and persons in and out of the city.[37]

Clay contacted Washington, explaining that he did not intend to comply with any of these new regulations. U.S. trains would try and gain free access to

Berlin, and if necessary, would fight for that right: Clay stated, "It is my intent to instruct our guards to open fire if Soviet soldiers attempt to enter our trains." Seeking permission for this powerful move, the general added, "the full consequence of this action must be understood." Officials in Washington, including the secretary of defense and the Joint Chiefs of Staff, were not ready to authorize this last step. They did, however, agree to let Clay test the new restrictions, under certain conditions: American soldiers would block any attempt by the Soviets to board the trains but could not fire unless fired upon.[38]

The test of wills began. As April Fool's Day dawned, the first train to move out was French, but it left too early; the military commander on board had not yet received orders, so permitted Soviets to search, and afterward the journey progressed as planned. After that an American train embarked, and again, the lieutenant in charge let Soviet soldiers take a look around, after which they let it proceed. *Newsweek* reported on "embarrassed superiors who spluttered darkly of court martial" for the hapless junior officer.[39]

The third trip took the charm. This train refused to pull over when so signaled and kept on going. The Soviets merely shuttled it off to a siding where it sat for several days before pulling back; Clay stated the obvious, "It was clear the Russians meant business."[40]

On April 2, Clay took one other step to deal with the crisis. He ordered Lieutenant General Curtis LeMay, commander of United States Air Forces in Europe (USAFE), to begin flying supplies to Berlin. LeMay had the Sixty-first Troop Carrier Squadron, based at Rhein-Main air base, commence flights immediately, and soon added a few other units.

There is no question that this measure was seen as a stop-gap, at best. The entire complement of the Sixty-first consisted of twenty-five C-47s, planes capable of flying only a few tons per trip, and although the aircraft was sturdy and heroic, by 1948 it was considered out of date. While the British supplied a few of their own planes, a force this size could do little more than augment current supplies just for the garrison. One commentator in the *London Times* observed, "Talk of an 'air bridge' is picturesque, but it would be foolish to suppose that, if the worst came to the worst, the Allied community and forces here could be maintained by this means alone." These words applied, of course, solely to the inability of air transport to supply the local military; no one, not Clay nor anyone else, had ever even conceived that air transport could be used to take care of a city with a population in the millions.[41]

What later became known as "the baby airlift" or "little lift" was moderately successful. During its eleven-day duration, roughly 1,300 tons of supplies in

3. C-47s line up at Tempelhof Airport. (National Archives photo, SC304538)

Berlin arrived by air, including 327 tons of food, almost all of it fresh. No one had yet thought of dehydrating food to cut down on weight in this preliminary effort. One officer at Rhein-Main, William Shimonkevitz, noted, "We carried fresh foodstuffs in—milk, eggs, cheese, meat, vegetables, et cetera—and empty milk bottles, households goods, furniture, personal belongings out."[42]

Within a few weeks, matters subsided to a level of controlled, mild hostility. Western trains began to make their way through the Soviet zones to Berlin, and Russian troops stopped trying to board them. Small acts of harassment persisted, with Eastern forces sometimes stopping a truck or slowing a train through a transfer point. Something had changed, however, something fundamental, that would not rectify itself for another half century. And it would begin in Berlin.

By 1948 the cold war was underway, but had not flared; as of March 20 the Allied Control Council had still been operating. Now, however, things were falling apart rapidly, with conflict imminent. Clay wrote his superiors on April 10, "We have lost Czechoslovakia. We have lost Finland. . . . After Berlin

4. Milk transport. (History Office, Air Mobility Command, Scott
Air Force Base)

will come western Germany. . . . If we mean to hold Europe against Communism, we must not budge" from that capital city. Nikita Khrushchev once said
that Berlin was like the West's testicles; he could squeeze it any time he wanted
to make them yelp. This was the location where the test, the split would come,
and the cold war would begin.[43]

In an April 7, 1948, dispatch from Berlin to the *New Yorker*, Bernard Taper
wrote that, "It has become obvious to everyone that the quadripartite government of Germany has failed in its purpose and just about finished. . . . the Soviets have made it clear that . . . it is now time for the Western powers to pack
their bags and leave, and that furthermore, they mean to inspect their allies'
bags when they go." To Taper, the airlift "was enthusiastically acclaimed by the
Americans as a . . . demonstration . . . of Western strength, but its practical significance is not quite clear." Berliners, he noted, "through hard experience, are

accustomed to think of air power in terms considerably more than fifty somewhat antiquated two-engine transports." Instead of relief, therefore, the mood in the city was one of impending war, with people reconstructing wartime shelters. Gallows humor among the Allied personnel included such jests as, "See you in the salt mines of Siberia," and the realization, above all, "that they were on an island, instead of at the end of a cul-de-sac."[44]

The event that precipitated crisis was implausibly enough—monetary reform. The Americans and the British had for some time openly discussed merging their two zones into one—an entity with the unlikely title of "Bizonia." It had been enough, however, to frighten the French and the Russians, both nations that had seen up close the power of a unified Germany. By April 1948, however, amid rising tensions, the French agreed to merge their area into this new entity.

The Western nations now came up with a new means of unifying Germany, not for its own sake, but to tackle the single biggest problem hindering economic expansion, the total worthlessness of German money. To battle this, they would institute a new currency good in all Western sectors, creating a single economic zone.

At the end of the war, the Allies were in charge of Germany, including its currency, the *Reichsmark*. With no assets to back it, this paper was worthless, so the victors produced their own scrip—military marks—yet in a short time this had no value, either. Some of the blame for this lay with the Russians; the U.S. mint had made up a set of plates for each of the nations that held an occupied zone, and the Russians printed up cascading amounts of paper money, partially as a cheap way of providing soldiers up to six years' worth of back pay.

The result was rampant inflation, which turned Germany into a barter economy. Instead of printed paper or even precious metal, the basic item of trade became the cigarette. Some sources claimed that one cigarette could fetch as much as twenty marks at the official rate (there were ten marks to the dollar), and that a pack of Chesterfields was sold for the equivalent of ninety dollars. Most accounts cite figures lower than that, but still indicate a skewered market. A GI could buy a carton of smokes at the PX for fifty cents, sell them at the black market price of 1,500 marks, then redeem those notes at a military exchange and send home $149.50 after deducting for his cost. Roughly $200 million got sent out of the country that way, another factor with deep impacts on the local currency. In addition, Saul Kagan claimed that the Russians were even counterfeiting Camel cigarettes from an operation run out of Leipzig, in order to profit from the exchange rate disparity.[45]

General Clay had long believed that the crucial economic reform was to create a new currency, telling Washington in May 1946 that this solution "was essential and of immediate urgency." By 1948 the Western Allies were ready to act.[46]

The step they took was far more than a fiscal fix. Instead, they decided to establish a unified West German government, bound by a common currency, the *Deutsche Mark,* that would bind the nation and invigorate the economy. The date for releasing this news was set for Friday, June 18, 1948, but the French, who had originally agreed, now balked at the thought of a strengthened and reawakened Germany. On June 17, however, they finally came on board, and the announcement went out as planned, to take effect on Sunday, June 20.[47]

The currency shift hit hard on all parties. In the Western zones, it did all that it was supposed to; as journalist Howard K. Smith put it in his memoirs, this step, "had done the trick. It poured tonic into the anemic system of Germany's economy and sopped up the inflated currency left by Hitler, gave money a value, made workers willing to work for it, and peasants and shopkeepers ready at last to sell for it." The economist Henry Wallich claimed that "Currency reform transformed the German scene from one day to the next . . . goods reappeared in the stores, money resumed its normal function, the black and grey markets reverted to a minor role, foraging trips to the country ceased, labor productivity increased, and output took off. . . . The spirit of the country took off over night."[48]

To the Soviets, it was a disaster. With no market for the old money, everyone from speculators to housewives would try and dump whatever currency they had saved or hoarded in the Eastern zone, which had of course refused any participation in this changeover, and was the only place where this money could be spent. On June 28, 1948, *Newsweek* reported, "All over Western Germany rich and poor alike spent last week trying to buy something—anything . . . they formed . . . queues at stores, theaters, railway stations." Furthermore, "Thousands tried to slip into the Soviet zone to dump their marks. One man, arrested at the . . . border, had 400,000 marks on him."[49]

This was the step the Soviets, with their own troubled economy, simply could not allow. Walter Bedell Smith, U.S. ambassador to the Soviet Union, observed that "had there been no . . . currency reform there would have been no Berlin Crisis." He pointed out that "to the Men in the Kremlin, on whose horizon

Germany had always loomed large . . . as the greatest potential threat . . . this was a direct challenge." The Soviets, in other words, felt they were witnessing their greatest fear, a revived and powerful Germany. They would precipitate the first great episode in the cold war, banking on superior strength on the ground and ignoring airlift as weak and hence irrelevant. No one at the time knew how it would turn out, except one general in Washington who had a vision few understood or would listen to.[50]

6 / Blockade

The Soviet response to currency reform was drastic, as real and severe as their fears of a new Germany. Not surprisingly, the Russians had been expecting such a move, and decided early on where to strike. As early as December 1947, the CIA had told President Truman "there was a possibility of steps being taken in Berlin by the Soviet authorities to force the other occupying powers to remove [their forces] from Berlin." On March 19, 1948, in a meeting with Walter Pieck, one of the leaders of the East German government, Josef Stalin suggested that the two nations "make a joint effort . . . perhaps we can kick them out."[1]

A rapidly escalating series of harassments began. In the first week of June several mail trains bound for Berlin were stopped at the border between Western zones and Soviet-occupied territory. On June 19, guards blocked all traffic on the autobahn and demanded that barge traffic into the former capital get special permission before proceeding. Two days later, the Russians stopped a U.S. military supply train and refused to let it proceed into Berlin; the next day they placed armed soldiers on board, hooked up a Soviet engine, and shunted it back to the West.[2]

These were just the opening rounds; the knockout blow, however, was close behind. As midnight rang in June 23, 1948, Soviet authorities, who had the master Berlin power switch in their sector, shut off all electricity flowing from Eastern generators, which provided the bulk of the city's power. After that, power would flow into the western part of Berlin only between 11:00 P.M. and 1:00 A.M. By six o'clock that morning all trains trying to get in were sent back to the West, followed by similar stoppages of motor and barge traffic. The official Soviet news release stated, "The transport division of the Soviet military administration is compelled to halt all passengers and freight traffic from Berlin . . . because of technical difficulties." An article shortly after in the *Taglische Rundschau,* a Red Army paper, followed a similar tack. "According to informed sources the technical difficulties on the . . . railroad line, which have already been announced, are much more serious than originally believed. . . . it is difficult to say at the present time when the passenger and freight service . . . can be resumed." General Clay called this "one of the most ruthless efforts in modern times to use mass starvation for political coercion." The reality was, Berlin was cut off, and it looked like no one had the power to stop the Russians.[3]

In the days prior to this ultimatum, General Clay had been warning the U.S. Army about what was coming. The morning that Berlin became isolated, a dispatch went out describing the fate of the military freight train that got stopped. On June 21 Colonel Howley began stockpiling supplies, so that by the twenty-third warehouses contained seventeen days' worth of bread and flour, thirty-two of other cereals, twenty-five of proteins such as meat and fish, and forty-two of that German staple, potatoes. Back in January, Dr. Eugene Schwartz, chief medical office in the American sector, received second-hand information about a drunk Soviet general who had snarled, "If those swine aren't out of Berlin by June, we'll close every access there is." Schwartz took the account seriously and began to stock up on medical supplies.[4]

At this point General Clay had few options open to him, and the ones he favored were badly thought out. His own personal choice was to try and ram an armored convoy through from the Western zones to Berlin. Plans were drawn up for a regimental combat team, a force of several thousand men supported by tanks and artillery. The unit would be led by Brigadier General Arthur Trudeau, to include an engineering battalion with bridging equipment to fix any thoroughfares that the Russians had "closed for repairs."[5]

Clay believed that the Russians were bluffing, and a show of force would back them down. In memoirs published only a year after the Berlin crisis ended, Clay argued, "The care with which the Russians had avoided measures which would have been resisted with force had convinced me that the Soviet Government did not want war." On the basis of this belief, he held that "the chances of . . . a convoy being met by force with subsequent . . . hostilities were small. I was convinced that it would get through to Berlin and that the . . . blockade would be ended." Nevertheless, he admitted, "No armed convoy could cross the border without the possibility of trouble," and hence, he had "made it clear" to the Joint Chiefs "that I understood fully the risk and its implications."[6]

Clay was wrong; the problem with this concept was that it failed to take into account the vast disparity between American and Soviet military strength in Europe. By February 1948 the entire U.S. military establishment, worldwide, was down to just over a million personnel, with only 552,000 in the army. This last service had ended World War II with eighty-nine divisions, but only twelve were left. Of these, most were manned by youngsters, replacing the hearty veterans who had been immediately discharged after the war. The portion of this force in Europe, the entire U.S. Army strength on the continent, was only 83,000 troops, lacking up-to-date equipment like tanks, and badly disciplined. One account referred to these forces as a "shambles," and records show that despite nonfraternization orders, venereal disease was rampant, with one remarkable unit of 1,000 men accumulating 1,200 cases within a single month. Even the vaunted First Infantry Division, the elite "Big Red One," had a combat efficiency rating of only 62, with one of its regiments down to a score of only 15.[7]

The air force was not much better. By mid-1946 United States Air Forces in Europe was down to one bomber group, two squadrons of night fighters, one reconnaissance wing, and six groups of fighters, mostly with P-47s and P-51s. Few of these were maintained, however, so by 1947 the operational strength— that is, the force capable of taking to the air—was down to three B-17 heavy bombers, two A-26 light attack bombers, and thirty-one P-47 fighters. Later, General LeMay would quip that if war had come, "we would have cleaned them up pretty well, in no time at all," but a reporter interviewing him for the *American Mercury* in 1948 expressed surprise at how weak the American air fleet seemed to be, and LeMay "agreed tacitly," blaming the problem on the overly quick and drastic demobilization. Years later, in his memoirs, Clay admitted that "USAFE would be stupid to get mixed up in anything bigger than a cat-fight at a pet show."[8]

Allied support was limited as well. In all of Germany the British could muster only 103,000 troops, the French another 75,000. Field Marshal Bernard Montgomery openly stated in his writings that the British army, part of a nation stretched thin by postwar debt, was not ready for war.[9]

The forces available to defend Berlin were even leaner. On July 9, 1948, *U.S. News and World Report* stated that the total military strength in the beleaguered city consisted of only 3,000 American, 2,000 British, and 1,500 French troops, a total of just 6,500.[10]

Facing this was a truly formidable force, especially according to the conventional wisdom of the postwar period. Though post-Soviet analysis has dramatically downgraded the size of the Soviet military after the Second World War, American commanders at the time believed they were facing a force of 175 divisions totaling 4 million personnel. Ninety-three divisions of this force, roughly 2.1 million men, were marshaled in Europe and available within several days for any confrontation with the West, along with 7,500 aircraft. The standard figure for local strength was 18,000 Russian troops in Berlin itself (a three-to-one ratio against combined Western forces) and 300,000 in East Germany, including a number of the elite Guards units, and over 2,500 combat aircraft. Frank Howley, hardly a shy flower when it came to standing up to the Russians, felt that "militarily we did not stand a chance. The Russians could have moved in and liquidated us," that "we would have got our *derrieres* shot off." Even Clay later told a biographer, "We were in no position to hold our own against the Russians in Germany."[11]

The idea of a direct confrontation was turned down by authorities at every level and in every jurisdiction. They all recognized that Clay's proposed route was 125 miles long, with an average of three bridges per mile. Secretary of State George Marshall, who led the U.S. Army in World War II, thought such a step was folly, as did the then-current army chief of staff, Omar Bradley. Bradley recognized what everyone else did, that the Russians could blow up bridges every step of the way, bog the U.S. forces down, and eliminate them in an attrition battle. Robert Lovett, undersecretary of state and the foremost advocate of air power in the Truman administration, thought the idea was "silly," that the Russians could halt the convoy and then "just sit up on the hillside and laugh." *U.S. News and World Report* cautioned that "war could easily result" over this conflict, since "Berlin is in such a tension that a shot fired by a trigger-happy soldier could start a battle. And a battle in Berlin could bring a general war." The stock market responded to the first news of the convoy idea with a sharp downturn, and even the British balked. Sir Brian Robertson, the British military governor, reminded Clay, "If you do that, it'll be war—it's as simple as that. In such an event, I'm afraid my government could offer you no support, and I'm sure [the French] will feel the same." At the same time, the Soviet General Staff, according to recently disclosed documents, had agreed to resist any efforts to break the blockade by land, and would shoot first if necessary. Clay's favorite idea, therefore, was no option at all.[12]

The Americans had another alternative regarding the use of force. Shortly after the blockade began, President Truman ordered B-29 units to fly to forward positions in Great Britain, a move attended by a great deal of publicity. To everyone in the world, this advanced craft was identified with one weapon, and that was the atomic bomb. The Americans were raising the stakes, and could possibly use this leverage to seek a settlement.

But this bluff, like a poker player betting with a pair of twos, had no basis in reality. At that time the United States had plenty of B-29s, but only thirty-two that were capable of delivering nuclear weapons. These planes were all in the 509th Bomb Group, which had never been deployed outside of the United States. It was easy to spot these weapons, furthermore, as bombers equipped to carry nuclear weapons had undercarriages painted with anti-reflective materials to help crews survive the blast, and these planes could quickly be distinguished from their conventionally armed counterparts. In addition, the total U.S. stockpile of assembled atomic bombs by July 1947 was only thirteen. It is hard to believe that the Soviets, with their advanced spy network in the United States, were not aware of all these factors. The movement of B-29s, therefore, was a good means of boosting civilian morale, but had no effect on Soviet leaders, who knew more about the reality of this step than the American people did.[13]

To put this another way, as the Berlin crisis broke out Clay was resolute, but he had few options, none of them viable. One alternative was to back down from the currency reform, but this was an agreement reached at the highest levels of different governments, and the general had no authority to negate them. The other was simply to cave in and leave Berlin, which most authorities, both military and civilian, felt was going to happen anyway. Why not do it sooner than later, with fewer casualties? The outcome, after all, in these minds, was inevitable. No one—at least no one in a position to affect the crisis at that time—had any other ideas that would actually save the city.

Many of the command generals, in fact, thought the time had come to get out of Berlin. General Albert Wedemeyer, who would be instrumental in getting Tunner to Berlin, at this early stage asked an aide to draw up "arguments in support of your initial statement, 'We do not want to go to war over Berlin.'" Among the points made to support this proposition were that the American newspaper reading public were "not going to see in the Berlin situation, the same obvious occasion for sacrifice of blood and treasure which they saw in Pearl Harbor." Furthermore, "It is certainly not realistic to discuss the matter of how many tons a month our aircraft can continue to carry . . . it is not reasonable to suppose that the Russians who have shown so much determination to evacuate us from Berlin, will continue to let us get away with this evasion which they can so easily interrupt." The conclusion was clear: "We should . . . prepare to get out of the untenable positions, be it by retreat, planning now for immediate . . . evacuation of dependants and non-combatants."[14]

Clay was moved to a response, not by insight or inspiration, but through desperation.

The original idea was British, in fact, and not American. Several days before the blockade went into effect, RAF Air Commodore Reginald N. Waite came up with the notion that an airlift might be needed again, only this time on a far larger scale. Drawing up a crude plan, he took this concept to Major General E. O. Herbert, head of Britain's Berlin garrison, who became the first—of many—to dismiss the idea as ridiculous. Waite persevered, prepared more elaborate figures, and was granted ten minutes with General Robertson. Robertson was hardly positive, but promised to show the data to Clay. The next day, Clay was no more convinced than his counterparts from across the pond.[15]

And why should he have been? The figures were astounding. The western sectors of Berlin had over two million residents. Normal incoming freight traffic on land and water routes brought in 13,500 tons of cargo each day, although quick estimates dropped this down to a survival level of 4,500 tons daily. This seemed like an insane figure, given that all of the initial fleet of planes available were C-47s, which carried 3 tons a piece, and there were only a couple of airfields in Berlin, neither of them with many runways or much in the way of unloading facilities. Yet planes would be required to fly in as much as 3 tons a day just of secondary commodities such as yeast, in order to make enough bread to feed Berliners, plus 38 tons of salt each day. Worst of all, the city needed coal, its basic source of energy, and no one had ever used planes to fly that kind of crude, bulk material. And what would happen in a couple of months, when fall and then winter set in, and planes could not fly at all? It did not look promising.[16]

Bluntly put, at that point Clay had no choice. It was not that he believed in airlift—he did not—there was just nothing else to do, or else he would have to leave Berlin altogether. He had to try something, so the general picked up his phone and sent LeMay into action.

On June 26, the day the Berlin Airlift officially started, General LeMay sent twenty-five C-47s into the besieged city carrying 80 tons of flour, milk, and medicines. The day before his chief of staff, Major General August Kissner, was preparing estimates of what USAFE could do in an all-out effort; he came up with 225 tons daily. Clay meanwhile was seeking a figure more in the range of

500 to 700 tons, possibly enough to at least supply the local military forces, but as he admitted, it would take a "very big operation" to even deliver figures like that.[17]

It was a brave beginning, but everyone—in OMGUS, in the Pentagon, in the White House, but especially in the Kremlin with their memories of the Stalingrad airlift only five years old—knew how little this was, compared to the need. Curtis LeMay later admitted, "It was a pretty modest start." Airlift was just an ingenious method to buy a little time, nothing more. It could not move mountains, work miracles, or feed a city.[18]

Clay had taken this momentous step on his own, without contacting the State Department or asking permission from anyone. It was time for the president of the United States to step in.

Harry Truman's historical image is of a leader who made tough decisions, and past scholarship portrays his reaction to the Berlin blockade as a classic example of forceful leadership. More recent investigations have called this into question.

Truman's initial reaction was at odds with Clay's determination. He preferred to remain in Berlin, but did not feel an abiding loyalty to the German people the way his military governor did, and Truman recognized the tough reality of the U.S. position.[19]

On Sunday, June 27, the day after the airlift officially began, Truman's advisors met to draw up a set of choices for the president. Kenneth Royall, secretary of the army; James Forrestal, secretary of defense; and Robert Lovett, undersecretary of state, got together in Royall's office to come up with some recommendations.

After a four-hour discussion, they arrived at a set of options that bowed to the inevitable. The United States could really only contemplate three possible actions: it could start making plans to withdraw from Berlin at a fortuitous moment; it could fight, no matter what the cost; or it could look for negotiations while trying to remain firm. General Omar Bradley later referred to this as, "get out; fight; or try to stand on quicksand, hoping for a diplomatic solution or another sudden change in Soviet policy."

The next day, Monday, June 28, the group presented their views to the president, who was firm, but less than thoughtful in his appreciation of the situation. Forrestal's diaries included the famous line that is most quoted: Truman declared that on the issue of withdrawal, "there was no discussion on that point. We are going to stay—period." But did that mean he was prepared to go to war?

Not exactly; when Royall pressed the president to mobilize the armed forces, get them ready for conflict, Truman refused, stating only that he "would have to deal with the situation as it developed." Did he support the airlift, then, as the best way to resolve this? No, the airlift could never succeed. After further questioning, Truman did little more to clarify his position. He wanted to stay in Berlin, but refused to mobilize the necessary resources to resolve the situation.

Truman had made a tough decision, but he did not lead his government. The military was especially distressed, recognizing that they would bear the brunt of any possible conflict which the president was not willing to acknowledge, and that they would be accountable for retreat as well. Bradley penned a memo, commenting, "Only future developments can determine whether we must leave in one month or in one year. Eventually, however, we will have to withdraw unless . . . Soviet policy undergoes a radical change." As Daniel Harrington, an Air Force historian, ably analyzed the situation, "On the one hand," Truman had "ruled out preparations for an evacuation of Berlin; on the other, he and the National Security Council gave military leaders insufficient guidance on which to draw up plans for war."[20]

Whatever its limits and shortcomings, a decision had been made. That night Robert Lovett sent a cable to the American ambassador in London; it read, "We stay in Berlin."[21]

At this stage, it was the virtually universal judgment of every government official, and every prominent commentator, that this was the *wrong* decision, an effort that could not end in anything but disaster. Except for Tunner, *no one* in Europe or America believed that airlift could accomplish this giant task, unprecedented in the history of the world. To put matters as bluntly as possible, at its outset, no one believed that the Berlin Airlift would be anything but a complete failure. Indeed, the chorus of voices testifying to this conclusion was both remarkable and unanimous, carrying all policy sectors.

First, it was clear that General Clay, who gave the order to begin the airlift, did not think it would work. In a Secret Priority message to Omar Bradley, army chief of staff, Clay reported that "the presently scheduled air lift will meet the food needs on a reasonable basis for the 1st 2 months" only. "However," he continued, "coal is in very short supply in Berlin and shortage of this commodity rather than food will be our most difficult problem," then added significantly, "unless surface transport reopened within next month." *Newsweek* quoted Clay in its June 21, 1948, issue to the effect that local food stocks were "very limited," and could hold for only "a number of days." The planes landing in Berlin could take care of the military force, "but could never feed the local population on a permanent basis." The day the airlift started, Clay stated flatly to Marguerite Higgins of the *New York Herald Tribune,* "It is absolutely impossible to supply the city by airpower alone." *Time* later reported a conversation between Ernst Reuter, Berlin's mayor, and one of Clay's top aides. Having just been informed of the airlift, Reuter remarked, "It's wonderful to hear Clay's determination, but I don't believe it can be done." The aide replied, "I don't believe it, either."[22]

This dismal view was shared by most top officials in the Pentagon, both civilian and military. Lovett and Forrestal believed that when the bad weather set in around October, the airlift would collapse and the administration would have to make some tough decisions. In July, Assistant Secretary of the Air Force Cornelius Whitney informed the National Security Council that "the Air Staff was firmly convinced . . . the air operation is doomed to failure." Lovett added his voice, rejecting airlift as a "temporary expedient" and "unsatisfactory." A U.S. Army General Staff study that had been prepared in January rejected emphatically the notion of airplanes supplying Berlin, and most air force generals were "flabbergasted" by the idea. One Top Secret study for Bradley claimed that despite the air force's best efforts, "all stocks of food and fuel will be exhausted by 25 October. Critical shortages of supplies other than those . . . may well have developed prior to that time." Even Curtis LeMay expressed doubts. Summing up the situation in his memoirs, he admitted, "I never dreamed how consequential this would become." Clay "kept increasing his requests, and eventually it dawned on me. . . . He was going to . . . support the city of Berlin entirely by . . . air. Not being in the airplane business, obviously Clay never realized that . . . he was talking . . . of such prodigious amounts, it was far beyond our capacity to operate."[23]

Over at the State Department, diplomats shared the warriors' pessimism. George Marshall believed that airlift was "obviously not a solution," while George Kennan, brilliant head of the State Department's policy planning staff, was even gloomier. At that time, he wrote, "No one was sure how the Russian move could be countered, or whether it could be countered at all. The situation was dark and full of danger." Walter Bedell Smith, U.S. ambassador to Moscow, had, according to one account, "little faith in the ability of the Airlift to supply Berlin," but wisely chose not to disclose his misgivings to his adversaries.[24]

America's staunchest allies, the British, shared this seemingly universal sentiment. Ross Milton, who worked closely with his counterparts in the RAF, explained that "the British were very much aware of the limitations of what we could do," while General Herbert was considerably more blunt. Prior to the airlift, he declared, "They won't do it, and even if they do, we could never hold out." By winter it would fail; the Western Allies would be out of the city by October 1.[25]

The English-speaking press took this view and broadcast it far and wide. The editors of *Time* cautioned that the air plan "could not be carried on at the summer rate when winter comes," Walter Lippmann, the most prominent journalist in the United States, felt that "to supply the Allies' sectors of Berlin by air is obviously only a spectacular and temporary solution to the . . . blockade." If continued, it could "only be carried on for a while in the summer months. But in the long run, especially in the fog and rain of a Berlin winter, the cost in lives of the pilots and crews . . . and of the money, would be exorbitant." *Business Week* counseled, "The air lift can't keep us there through the winter; we just can't step it up enough, especially when the weather gets bad."[26]

London's pundits agreed. The *New Statesman* announced, "Every expert knows that aircraft, despite their immense psychological value, cannot be relied upon to provision Berlin in the winter months." The prestigious *Times,* voice of the Establishment, went much further, arguing that, "Talk of an 'air bridge' to Berlin is picturesque, but it would be foolish to suppose that, if the worst came to the worst, the Allied community and forces here could be maintained by this means alone."[27]

One group of people who did not have to be convinced of these arguments was the Russians, the victors of Stalingrad. On June 29 Sokolovsky wrote General Robertson that the West could "provide for the continued supply of goods to the population for the next few weeks," with the clear implication that anything beyond that was doubtful. TASS reported on July 4, "Every day the food situation in the three Western Sectors of Berlin grows more and more critical," that the possibility of bringing in sufficient coal by air was "impossible." Walter Bedell Smith held that "neither Stalin nor Molotov believed that the airlift could supply Berlin. They . . . felt sure that cold and hunger, and the depressingly short, gloomy days of the Berlin winter would destroy the morale of the Berlin population and create such a completely unmanageable situation that the Western Allies would have to capitulate and evacuate the city." A British Foreign Service officer cabled that "the Russians are convinced that they hold all the cards and will be able to maneuver us into a position where . . . we have no choice but to withdraw from Berlin. Our current air effort may have disconcerted them. But I doubt whether they believe we can keep it up indefinitely and on a sufficient scale."[28]

One person defied this consensus. General William Tunner believed in airlift fervently, and he had proved what it could do back in Burma. Furthermore, he was shrewd enough to know what Europe-oriented generals on both sides of the Iron Curtain did not, that the comparison between Stalingrad and what was happening in Berlin was false. Tunner estimated, accurately, that a peacetime air operation would be entirely different from one taking place in a war zone. The air fleet would not be attrited by enemy attacks; bases could be maintained and built up, without fear that enemy forces would overrun them. Finally, while the weather in Germany was severe, and a considerable issue, it could not compare with that in Russia.

All of Tunner's confidants saw this confidence, this deep and sure belief. His son remarked, "I don't think there was any doubt in his mind" that the Berlin Airlift could work, while Ann Tunner believed, "he just knew" he could do it. Dorothy Towne reaffirmed this determination, claiming Tunner "had absolute faith" in the success of the mission. Earl Morrison added the last component, the one other reason Tunner was so sure: his beloved and proven crew would accompany him. Morrison recalled, "There was no doubt in my mind" that Tunner knew he could do this, because of "the staff he brought with him." With that team, it was clear, "He was there to do it. There was absolutely no doubt about it."[29]

Ross Milton was Tunner's chief of staff during the Berlin Airlift, the person possibly closer to this general than anyone except Red Foreman. But Milton was also a combat officer with lots of experience in conventional warfare. In a 2002 interview with the author he explained that Tunner "was probably the only person in the air force who really believed that we could do what we did in Berlin. I don't think anybody in the Air Staff believed it." Most remarkable of all, he revealed, "Most of us who worked for him didn't really think we were going to do that well." Instead of confidence, "there was a general feeling that this was the beginning of World War III and what we were doing was just stalling for time. It wasn't going to solve anything. . . . I don't think anyone really thought it could work."[30]

There was one exception to this, of course: "The guy who really thought it would work was Tunner," Milton observed. Tunner believed in the mission right from the start, "absolutely" and completely. First, however, someone would have to assign him to the job.

7 / A Cowboy Operation

The officers running the airlift had their work cut out for them in those early days; the need was enormous, and without Tunner's experienced team, they had to start from scratch.

The most comprehensive analysis of Berlin's daily food needs was a tough order to fill. Each and every day, planes would have to deliver, not just meat and potatoes and flour, but forty-three tons of milk (all dried, both skim and whole), ten tons of cheese, eleven tons of coffee, and eighty-five tons of sugar. It was a big order, and that did not include the coal.[1]

The first step was to choose a commanding officer, and on June 28 LeMay appointed Brigadier General Joseph Smith, head of the Wiesbaden Military Post. Smith would make the first steps to tackle this mission, working under LeMay's direction.[2]

Smith's initial move was to order more planes. United States Air Forces in Europe had, at that time, 102 C-47s, which carried three tons apiece, but only two of the larger C-54s, capable of hauling ten tons on each trip. Something more would be needed.[3]

On June 25, Clay contacted Brigadier General August Kissner, chief of staff at USAFE, asking him how many planes they had. According to an after-action interview, Kissner said he "told him the Air Force would do its best, that estimated tonnages would be submitted in an official message in a half hour." That follow-up promised roughly one hundred trips a day with the C-47s, and suggested that raising the 300-ton figure to 500 tons would require another thirty C-54s.[4]

5. General Joseph Smith, Tunner's predecessor as head of the Berlin Airlift. This photo was taken when he was a lieutenant general and commanding officer of MATS, 1951–1953. Smith was not a fan of Tunner. (History Office, Air Mobility Command, Scott Air Force Base, Box 7, Folder 5)

The next day, Clay's chief of staff called Kissner and told him, "Turn it on." But at the same time LeMay was contacting Lieutenant General Lauris Norstad, the deputy chief of staff for the U.S. Air Force, in Washington. LeMay asked for those thirty C-54s, with two crews apiece to keep them flying the maximum number of hours.[5]

The air force came through. On June 28 the Fifty-fourth Troop Carrier Squadron left Alaska with nine planes, while the Twentieth with its dozen C-54s took off from its home in the Panama Canal Zone; both were bound for Germany. The next day the Nineteenth Troop Carrier Squadron flew out of Hickam Field in Hawaii with eleven more, and on July 10 the Seventeenth Troop Carrier Squadron out of Great Falls, Montana, added its nine planes to the growing fleet. In total, forty-one transports joined the Berlin Airlift, enough to raise the daily figure hundreds of tons, yet nowhere near enough to feed the city once existing stocks ran out. But at least things were looking up.[6]

Another bright note in those early days was the commitment of allies. On June 25 the Royal Air Force ordered one squadron of eight C-47s to start flying supplies to Berlin, and the next day doubled that with another squadron of the same size. The first flight by a British transport took off at 6 A.M. on the twenty-eighth, and over the next twenty-four hours thirteen planes brought in forty-four tons of food.[7]

By then, it seemed like planes "were coming in so fast and furious," according to Paul Harris, who served in the Berlin Air Safety Center. In the last days of June the airlift had totaled only 1,404 tons, but the figures were climbing. On July 8 Berlin received 1,117 tons, but this dropped to 819 the next day; by July 15 it was up to 1,480 tons again. The air command began to refine operations: the original agreement with the Russians permitted three corridors. The central lane would no longer have two-way traffic and would be dedicated to outgoing flights only from Berlin, in order to increase efficiency.[8]

Coal was becoming a problem; Berlin needed a lot of it, and it was bulky and hard to manage, the antithesis of the small, high value packages most experts claimed were the only legitimate air cargo. One early experiment was to just put the coal in sacks, load these in the bomb bay of a B-29, and have the plane drop them from a low level. Fast, efficient, it did not work. Coal can not withstand that kind of impact, so all they got on that first test was a lot of coal dust. But the issue of how to transport large quantities of coal would not go away, and became one of the many crises Tunner would face when he took over.[9]

All of this was well-meaning, and effective, but nowhere near enough. The airlift needed more planes, lots of them. That kind of decision could only be made in Washington.

By mid-July it was clear that the Russians were not giving up; the United States would have to decide whether to fish or cut bait. Starting on July 19, the National Security Council held a number of meetings over what course to pursue.

At the first session, Truman remained firm and carried the tide, but many of his advisors were hesitant. Lovett argued that it was "obvious that the Soviets know that flying weather will be too bad for this operation to continue beyond October." Three days later the president convened a larger group, but also in-

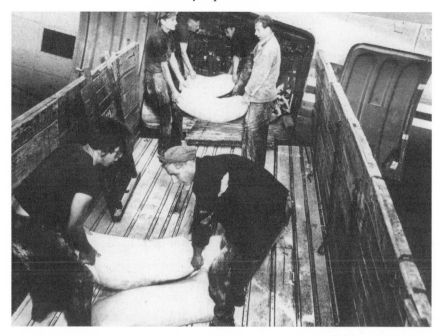

6. Loading sacks into a C-47. Note the slant to the floor. A C-54, the C-47's successor, sat on a horizontal plane, and could be loaded directly from lifts. (History Office, Air Mobility Command, Scott Air Force Base, Box 7, Folder 1)

vited General Clay, who had flown in from Germany. By that time Clay had become an airlift proselyte, and he delivered rosy scenarios of how the planes really could feed Berlin if they were just augmented by additional forces. By then the airlift was managing 1,000 tons a day by the American units alone; the commitment of another seventy-five C-54s would bring this figure up to 3,500 tons by replacing the tiny C-47s entirely, and the British (who were then managing 750 tons) could up their figure to another 1,000 tons daily. In addition, the people of Berlin were remaining firm, supportive of the American effort, and determined to make sacrifices as long as they did not starve.[10]

The major objection to this came from the air force, and for understandable reasons. In essence, Clay was arguing that the service place almost its entire strategic airlift capacity on the Berlin run. A July 18 top secret report to Omar Bradley claimed that taking on the Berlin situation would "render Military Air Transport Service practically ineffective" around the world, and thus be in no position to supply the army in case of a war. Another top secret memorandum, from the secretary of defense to the National Security Council on July 28, 1948, argued that with an all-out effort that stripped the U.S. Air Force, "minimum requirements can be met by air transport," but "for at least a considerable, though probably not an indefinite period." In other words, even by dedicating all of MATS to this, it still might not work.[11]

General Hoyt Vandenberg, air force chief of staff, pointed out that he had responsibilities that spanned the globe, not just one theater. If an emergency broke out, other crisis zones would be left shorthanded. In a worst-case scenario, if the Russians decided to fight over Berlin, a strategic asset, clustered there, might be destroyed in a hurry, leaving the United States with precious little air cargo capacity to meet any other needs of what would then be a shooting war at the international level; Vandenberg stated that his service could not conduct the airlift and a major conflict at the same time. In addition, he pointed out, such augmentation could not work without the construction of new airfields in Berlin; existing facilities could move just so many planes, and that limit was being reached quickly. This step, however, would require bringing in repair and maintenance facilities from existing locations around the world to Germany. All in all, it was, to an air force watching multiple hot spots, an incredibly risky move, placing all the eggs in one basket, and then watching to see if they got shot at. At the same time, however, the service also expressed pride, as well as the eternal call of the late-twentieth-century warrior: If the nation was to take this step, let them go all the way. Vandenberg admonished the group, "If we decide that this operation is going on for some time, the Air Force would prefer that we go in wholeheartedly. If we do, Berlin can be supplied."

The NSC took up the charge: Clay would get his planes, with more to come. They agreed to start construction on a new Berlin airfield, and "reiterated the determination to remain in Berlin in any event."

This was a drastic step. T. Ross Milton recalled, "The airlift would have failed, without any question, if we hadn't stripped the Air Force of all its transports. And there was a lot of resistance in the Pentagon to doing that. Their point was, 'Look, you're fixing things so that we can't respond to anything, anywhere else.' . . . We took every damned C-54 in the Air Force, for all practical purposes."

The July 22 NSC meeting established the fundamental commitment of the United States to the Berlin Airlift, but it did not quell doubts in many quarters, including both high levels of government and the media. The issues Vandenberg raised, and their strategic and fiscal impact, remained in play for months to come. On July 26 the Joint Chiefs of Staff issued a followup memo that reiterated most of Vandenberg's arguments. The airlift reduced MATS' ability to meet other commitments, was terribly expensive, and was using up stocks of fuel and spare parts.[12]

This refrain got taken up in *U.S. News and World Report*, which, in a series of articles over the next few months, reminded its readers of the costs and dangers of committing the American military to an airlift strategy. In an article in the August 20 issue, the magazine concluded that. "The airplane is taking on the task of supplying an entire city—a job that requires carrying bulk goods, for which an airplane is not designed." It went on to price out the cost of carrying a ton of bulk goods, then multiplying it by the figure of 4,000, to estimate how much it cost for one day's delivery, by different forms of transportation. River barge came in the cheapest, only $3 a ton for a total figure of $12,000 a day. After that came rail, at $5 a ton, or $20,000 daily. Close behind, trucks could do the job for only $6 a ton, $24,000 for a day's worth of goods. Far, far behind this was air transport, at $50 ton, $200,000 a day, or ten times the price of rail shipments.[13]

Three months later, on November 19, with winter beckoning, *U.S. News and World Report* carried an article headlined, "Real Cost of Berlin 'Air Lift.'" The opening sentence read, "'Air lift' to Berlin . . . is draining the U.S. of military air transport in other parts of the world." It pointed out that service had been reduced to Japan, Hawaii, Alaska, and the Panama Canal. The cost to the air force was up to $385,000 a day, or a yearly rate of $140,525,000, which, as the magazine pointed out, would go higher as bad weather increased wear and tear on planes and parts and men. Less than a month later, these estimates had gone up to $160 million a year, with another $200 million to pay for all the food these planes carried. Replacing worn-out machines could run another $500 million, and the total cost could go as high as one billion dollars a year, a ferocious sum in 1948.[14]

These complaints were compounded by a growing realization that the airlift, an extemporaneous solution, was less than efficient. A *Fortune* magazine writer quipped that the airlift "started in typical American style—with a hair-trigger decision based upon an underestimate of the true situation." While everyone admired the spirit of generosity and gumption that lay behind this effort, there was also a sense that steps had to be taken to provide far better organization. As one scholar explained, "The airlift was born of necessity, a product of improvisation and inspiration, eventually becoming a reality." In this initial stage, how-ever, good fellowship and rambunctiousness held sway, with no one taking the reins and turning it into a professional operation.[15]

In those early days, the airlift had all the excitement and enthusiasm of a cattle drive, but with somewhat less precision. Pilots pushed ahead in clunk-ing cargo planes, passing one another to see who would get into Berlin first or make the most trips in a day. Gail Halvorsen, who would become world fa-mous for dropping candy to Berlin's children, remembered, "It was a joke if you could take off before your buddy and get back . . . before he did. It did not mat-ter how you did it, just so you beat him." LeMay wrote in his memoirs, "No-body regarded the enterprise very soberly at first. They kidded about it, called it LeMay's Coal and Feed Company. Big joke."[16]

If these practices were "chaotic and dangerous," as one later report put it, others were terribly inefficient. An air force memo on "Difficult or Unusual Problems" with the airlift, drafted July 2, 1949, began by stating that when the operation began "there were no orders concerning duties and responsibilities," only some verbal commands. Flight operations officers, furthermore, had "no definite instructions and nothing to substantiate their responsibilities."[17]

As a result, the author continued, air traffic control was doing a poor job. Ground officials continued to demand a twenty-five-minute safety margin be-tween takeoffs, slowing things down. Radar was often "inoperative," and thus "aircraft had no positive check as to distance separation between each aircraft," so altitude became the only factor keeping planes apart. As they came in to land, there was no effort to regulate the traffic, and "controllers were attempt-ing to give all missed approaches a second attempt, resulting in congested traf-fic." Many of these craft got diverted to other bases, although some landed in terrible circumstances.[18]

One of the worst results of this situation was that there were often huge traffic tie-ups over Berlin, with planes backed up for miles and flying in ever-expanding circles over East German air space. When John Thompson, head of *Newsweek*'s Berlin office, took a trip between bases in Germany and his of-fice, he discovered that these kinds of problems plagued not just Berlin but the feeder airports as well. According to his dispatch, "At Frankfurt, Wiesbaden, and Berlin planes were stacked up at six or seven different levels; ground control occasionally directed two planes to the same level. Some pilots, too impatient to wait for 'step down' orders, slipped down to approach levels without receiv-ing authority." A reporter from *U.S. News and World Report* told how, "On one bad weather day three ships had to circle Rhein-Main for two hours, awaiting landing instructions." Only later did they discover that all three were flying at the same height of 8,000 feet in the same area, at great risk of collision. *Time* picked up this thread and reported that in one control tower a G.I. looked out at the sky full of planes and complained, "We've got to get these babies down somehow." Thompson concluded, "The airlift at that time was a magnificent, confused, slapdash performance." Dorothy Towne, remembering what this period was like and comparing it to what would come later, said simply, "There was no rhythm, no rhythm had been worked out," before the Tunner team arrived.[19]

At the same time, the planes were being worn down, as no one had made plans for replacing badly needed spare parts. Airlift planes used up six months' worth of windshield wipers in the first two weeks, and more had to be found. Engines and propellers began breaking down, and on one occasion MATS had to fly over seven power plants and eighteen tires in an emergency run from the States. A *U.S. News and World Report* correspondent told about sitting for two hours in a C-47 that never took off because it lacked a landing gear pin; without this part the wheels would not go down again, once retracted; the pilot had comforted him by noting, "You can 'belly land' a 47 and never feel the shock." Another plane had flown for ten days without a door.[20]

Things were just as bad on the ground. No procedures had been worked out to regulate deliveries, so pilots sat around endlessly on the ground after they arrived, waiting for someone to give them orders, to pick up a new load at one of the German bases, or get their craft offloaded in Berlin. Crews milled around the flight lounges and did what military men have always done in their time off: slept, ate, played cards or chess or table tennis or darts, and got thoroughly bored.

The story of the flight team of Lieutenants Robert Wilcox and Nick Nicholson highlights this lack of efficiency. On the second day after they joined the airlift, they received orders that their next flight would start out three hours after they had just returned from their first mission. Grabbing a couple of hours shuteye, they still managed to show up at 2:15 A.M. as ordered, where they were told their plane was grounded with problems, and they should come back at 12:15 P.M. They got on board that one, but shortly after takeoff the left engine went sour, so they had to return to base. After that, their next flight was at 1:15 the next morning, but around midnight, this got rescheduled to 6:15 A.M. Wilcox wrote in his diary, "It's getting so that we're living on such a confused schedule that we can barely tell what day it is."[21]

Although they uniformly tried to do a good job, many crewmen had no idea of what was going on. Major Edward Willerford, the RAF's air cargo officer, did not know at first what size load his C-47s carried. One U.S. pilot arrived in Germany with a three-day pass and asked to catch a plane into Berlin to see the sights. Told that this was against regs (all weight was reserved for flying crew and cargo), he asked, "Where can I get some information on train schedules to Berlin?" Another flight showed up with a stereotype of an American master sergeant: he stood there in the door, "carrying his spare uniform on a coathanger and holding his Alsatian dog on a lead. A bewildered Japanese woman peered from under his elbow." Looking out over the mess that was an airfield in Berlin in those frantic days, he was stunned: "God . . . Where do we live? Where do we eat? Where's town?"[22]

Sooner or later the sergeant must have found accommodations, but his troubles were only starting. With too few crews and planes for the job of feeding a major city, men reached exhaustion quickly and then flew some more. Lieutenant Robert Miller, flight surgeon for the Sixtieth Troop Carrier Squadron told how, during those early weeks, "It was a seven-day-a-week schedule, with most of the pilots lucky if they got seven hours sleep out of thirty-two." He gave examples of pilots who flew seven and a half hours, stood duty for sixteen hours, then managed only eight hours sleep before going out again. Another medical officer claimed, "Toward the close of the third week, the dangerous level had been reached." Crews came in talking about how both the pilot and copilot had fallen asleep in the cockpit, awakened by the sudden change in altitude as they lost control of the plane temporarily. The flight surgeon told how "their fatigue was shown in their irritability, and they were jagging badly on too much coffee." In addition, "the long hours, their exhaustion, and the weather was causing a lot of colds and a lot of fliers' ears. You know how painful a bad ear is in flight? Well, not a guy quit, and a lot of them were being crucified by plugged up ears."

Eventually, some of the men rebelled, but only in an informal manner; no organized solution to their woes was proposed. At the Rhein-Main field in Germany, one of the principal feeder airports, the commanding officer of the army units on the base woke his men each morning by having a cannon fired at 6:00. Requests to cease this practice, so damaging to the strained muscles and nerves of air crews on 24/7 schedules, met with no response. One night, the airmen took matters in their own hands, and using block and tackle, hoisted the offending field piece to the roof of a four-story barracks. After that the army took the hint, and the gun remained silent for the duration of the airlift.[23]

Tunner later told an interviewer, "Mechanics and flight personnel could not tell us how long they had worked, what their schedules were for the next day, or even when they were supposed to eat. They were sleeping in airplanes, in the mess hall, and anywhere else they could stretch out."[24]

Things were not so good for Berliners, either, as they struggled to survive amid the mixed results of the early airlift. The first sign of blockade was a visible one: the lights went out. With generators in the Eastern zone, power had to be cut by as much as 80 percent to both factories and homes. *Newsweek* told readers, "The lights were going out all over Berlin last week . . . and in the brief summer night the capital looked as it did during the first terrible summer after the war—an endless cavern of dark and menacing ruins."[25]

As with the lights, so went the jobs. On July 19, 1948, the *New Republic* claimed that the city already had 100,000 unemployed, and that "within a month or so, industrial production will have come almost to a halt because of lack of electricity, coal and raw materials." As many Berliners as possible, both men and women, tried to join the legions of manual laborers helping unload planes and building airports, but this was a stopgap solution at best.[26]

With the airlift still way below minimum goals, food now became a problem. One early solution was to bring in dehydrated goods only, thus saving an enormous weight in water that could be made up locally. This also meant, however, that nothing was fresh, that the only fruits and vegetables available, for example, were dehydrated.

Even with such a drastic move, the amounts were puny. One German doctor in the British zone of Berlin had a level-3 ration card, the kind handed out to white-collar workers. Contacted by Ernest Borneman, writing for *Harper's Magazine,* this medical man provided a listing of all he consumed in a *month.* During that thirty-day period he ate 26 ¼ pounds of potatoes and an equal amount of bread. He managed 2 pounds, 10 ounces of meat, or roughly 10 ounces a week, and the equivalent weight in cereals. He had only 2 pounds, 3 ounces of canned or dried vegetables that month and 1 pound, 5 ounces of sugar. He could use that in the 5 ounces of coffee he received (barely one oz. a week), and also got 11 oz of fat for cooking. Some families were down to a serving of dehydrated potatoes a day, with children having difficulty standing.[27]

Berliners legitimately blamed the Russians for their woes, but were starting to have qualms about the Western Allies as well. As rumors circulated that the Russians had moved one hundred heavy tanks and huge detachments of Mongol troops into East Berlin, there developed, as one journalist put it, "a tendency to grumble about the westerners' lack of foresight and faulty understanding both of their eastern antagonists and of the exacting requirement of a power-politics contest." Intensely aware of their pariah status, they also wondered whether or not, once push came to shove, any leader in America or Britain would, or even could, commit to a war to save Germans.[28]

Ruth Andreas-Friedrich, who had survived the war and its aftermath, kept a diary of all those years. Her entry for July 23, 1948, as the airlift ramped up, began, "No lights, no radio, no electricity to cook. . . . One eats nothing but bread with margarine and chives." She added, "One could drink water too. But since the water purification plants have stopped functioning it is advisable to drink only water that has been boiled. One can boil it at night. Between midnight and two in the morning when ration group C . . . receives its power supply for the week. Sometimes we get it as early as eleven thirty. So we sit around waiting. We grope our way around the apartment as if blind." She concluded, "It is a question of nerves."[29]

The standard term that would later be applied to the Berlin Airlift at this stage was a "cowboy operation." As one report observed, "Soon after the airlift began it became obvious that it was in trouble. . . . There weren't enough planes in Europe to carry the necessary tons of supplies Berlin would need each day. There were no standard procedures governing the flights as crews lounged in ready rooms . . . Inefficiency was rampant." The airlift was drifting, coming undone. Tunner was about to meet his destiny.[30]

After the war, William Tunner had been shuttled around to a number of posts, from Cincinnati to Memphis to Long Island to Westover, Massachusetts. In June 1948, however, General Lawrence Kuter, head of MATS, promoted Tunner to deputy commander and ordered him to headquarters in Washington, D.C. Tunner's job there was mundane, supervisor of operations and traffic, construction and communications. Some of this and that, in other words, but little in the way of direct responsibility.[31]

Even worse, the Berlin crisis was flaming white-hot. Tunner saw this immediately for what it was, the grandest opportunity to prove airlift was a force to be reckoned with. He urged Kuter, "You have just been organized as *the* air transport forces of the Department of Defense . . . it is our responsibility as the air transport experts to handle this . . . if anyone is to handle it" (emphasis in original). All the pieces were there, he argued, pieces he had been building throughout his professional life: "We have the trained people, not only the crews but the airplanes; we've got the technicians behind the crews; we've got the traffic people . . . who know how to load and unload and account for cargoes, and we have a very experienced staff who understands the business of air transportation, which is not flying bombers or fighters or something else." In one interview, he observed, "MATS had been formed with the idea in mind of taking on any airlift job that came up. We were the only organization that was qualified to run a huge airlift. To ignore us after we were formed and operating seemed kind of silly to me."[32]

Tunner gave two versions of Kuter's reply; in his memoirs he claimed the senior officer told him, "That's not the way to do it, Bill. . . . Let's just sit tight and see what happens." In an interview, the answer was, "Well, Bill, if we're going to do it, the Pentagon will tell us to do it."[33]

In either case, it was not what Tunner wanted to hear. The opportunity of a lifetime—a unique, historic opportunity for airlift—was glowing on the horizon. Tunner was in full entrepreneurial mode—passionate, dedicated, independent, and committed—and waiting for orders was not what he wanted to hear. In his memoirs Tunner claimed he dropped the matter for the moment, but in a later interview he left the impression that instead he pressed the issue: "I told Kuter that I did not think that was enough. I thought we should tell the Air Force chief that if he has gone to the trouble of forming this new command, it should be used. . . . we know the airlift business." Tunner was willing to butt heads with the Pentagon, when his superiors held him back.[34]

Tunner, angry, did not suffer rebuff easily, and his memory shifted accordingly. Later on, he told an air force interviewer that in early July Kuter took off for a tour of bases in the Pacific, just as things were heating up in Europe. But by July 2 MATS had already submitted to the NSC a plan for taking over the airlift, and on that day Kuter had alerted the various MATS commands that they might be moved to Germany with little notice. Staff worked over the Independence Day holiday drafting orders, while maintenance crews began prepping planes. So more was going on than Tunner was willing to acknowledge.[35]

But they weren't in the fight yet. Tunner was like a caged cat, pacing. As he gently put it in his memoirs, "I was beginning to get restless. With an airlift taking place in the world, I did not enjoy warming the bench. . . . I could tell, from the reports coming in, that the operation of the Airlift could stand improvement." By then Tunner was only in charge of a taskforce to round up maintenance personnel for the 200-hour checks on the C-54s. When he left for an inspection tour of bases, Tunner gave Milton strict orders to, as Milton remembered, "haunt the Pentagon and find out what was going on." Every night Tunner called in, "and he was not happy with my news, for there appeared to be no sentiment for a major effort and no mention of Tunner going over to run it."[36]

There is no clear reason as to why Tunner did not immediately receive the airlift command. One scholar speculated that Vandenberg had been a strong opponent of sending so many planes to one crisis and denuding the rest of MATS, so the last person he wanted to send was an airlift zealot who would demand even more resources.[37]

The story of how Tunner got to the Berlin Airlift does not begin with an air force leader at all, but with a United States Army general. During World War II, Albert Wedemeyer had taken over as theater commander in China toward the end of the conflict. This meant that he was almost alone, in a generation of warriors who had been bloodied in the fields and skies of Europe, in having a deep understanding of what airlift could do. As Tunner later remembered it, Wedemeyer "knew he not only lived but he fought the Japanese by virtue of the cargoes of gasoline, ammunition, bombs and people that we took over to him. It was rather amazing to him . . . as an Army officer that he could live by virtue of an airlift, but he did." Though Wedemeyer had to be aware of the air contribution to his efforts, air force records further confirm that he and Tunner met at the time and conferred on the conduct of the war. One letter from Tunner to Wedemeyer, for example, discussed the results of a conference between the two in Chungking, where Tunner, true to form, pressed "the relative efficiency of ATC transport . . . compared to those of other Army Air Force agencies."[38]

By June 1948 Wedemeyer was deputy chief of staff, U.S. Army, and director of Combat Operations and Strategy, a very powerful position. His initial reaction to Clay's armed convoy idea—an army operation—was that it was "ludicrous," because of the vast imbalance between U.S. and Soviet forces.[39]

Instead, Wedemeyer drew on his experience in the obscure CBI (China-Burma-India) Theater and suggested an airlift, and even came up with the idea that the most experienced air transport officer, William Tunner, be assigned to head it. As Wedemeyer later wrote in a private correspondence, "I had . . . as much exposure to airlifts and their potentialities as any officer in the Army, for my theater was surrounded by the enemy and my only line of communications was over the Hump. Further, in charge of that airlift . . . was one of our outstanding air officers . . . William H. Tunner." But this was a tricky business; as an army general, Wedemeyer could not command the air force to do anything and had to proceed via diplomacy.[40]

By then the airlift had begun, and at a meeting of the Joint Chiefs of Staff, Wedemeyer brought up the idea of sending Tunner over to head it. Tunner's version had it that Wedemeyer said, "You have got to have the same kind of an airlift that you had on the Hump, and you have got to have the same commander. The commander who supplied me is Bill Tunner."[41]

The response of Hoyt Vandenberg, air force chief of staff, confirmed Tunner's worst fears and violated one of his supreme commandments: air transport was the not the same as bombers or fighters, and could not be done effectively by generals with no experience; instead it must be left to the professionals. But Vandenberg had not read Tunner's playbook and his response was that "any of his officers could easily handle the matter" and that, furthermore, the man in charge was Curtis LeMay, the original can-do-it character. LeMay, a formidable force in Air Force circles and not easily budged, made clear that he supported Vandenberg's viewpoint when he told a reporter the airlift "operation can continue indefinitely as presently set up." Tunner summed up Vandenberg's state of mind as, "they were doing very well, and there was no sense in sending this hotshot Tunner over there." Tunner had ruffled feathers, and it was not helping his career, or the airlift.[42]

Wedemeyer's response was low key, but persistent. At the Joint Chiefs of Staff meeting, "I just pointed out the success that Tunner had in China but said no more." It was in after hours, however, that Wedemeyer won his case. He and Vandenberg were next-door neighbors at Fort Myer, and according to Wedemeyer, "we saw each other often, particularly at the cocktail hour when he or his wife would call and suggest the pre-dinner libation." This informal approach worked, and Vandenberg finally admitted that he had made a mistake in not initially assigning Tunner to the airlift. In all likelihood, there was also the growing realization that he needed Tunner; as Alfred Goldberg, dean of air force historians explained, Tunner was increasingly accepted as "the airlift man . . . the foremost one in the Air Force at the time."[43]

After that, Vandenberg moved with dispatch. On July 23 he ordered MATS to set up a Task Force headquarters group and move eight squadrons of C-54s to Germany, and he called in Tunner and said, "Well, Bill, it's all yours. When can you take off?" The official orders, dated July 30, began, "You are designated as Commander, Airlift task force (Provisional). The mission of the Airlift Task Force is to provide airlift to Berlin and such other places as may be directed by the Commanding General, USAFE." After that came a number of subsidiary points, but two stood out: first, the new commander "will exercise direct operational control of personnel and equipment allocated to your Task

Force," and second, he would "exercise operational control over all aircraft using the . . . Berlin air corridor and the air space allocated to your mission in any other corridor." In other words, while he was still under USAFE, he had relatively complete authority over the airlift operation, pretty much all that the independent leader, a pioneering entrepreneur-as-general could ask for.[44]

After Vandenberg gave him the good news, Tunner asked for one thing and one thing only: "Will it be alright for me to take some of my trained people along with me?" Vandenberg grumbled and asked, "How many?" still suspicious that the airlift would utilize too many resources and destroy MATS' ability to do any other job. Tunner assured him he would be reasonable, so the chief of staff went along, instructing the airlift leader to "tell Personnel the names of the people you want, and their orders will be cut right along with yours." On July 27, three days before the official orders arrived, Tunner left to set up his headquarters at Wiesbaden. The plane carried nine officers and two airmen, plus Catherine Gibson; it was piloted by Red Foreman. The next day another flight with thirteen commissioned officers, five enlisted personnel, and some civilians took off to join them; among the familiar names on the two planes were T. Ross Milton, Edward Guilbert, Hal Sims, Raymond Towne, Orval McMahon, and Pete Fernandez. Earl Morrison later remarked that this was the step that convinced him that Tunner would triumph. "There was no doubt in my mind, by the staff he brought with him," Morrison declared; "He was there to do it. There was absolutely no doubt about it." Tunner would need a lot of things to win this struggle, but the most important assets took off with him.[45]

On July 28, 1948, Tunner landed in Germany and began the work that would establish airlift as a force in military circles worldwide for ever after. Getting out of his plane—Number 5549—his men sported a sight not seen before in Germany, a white Star of India and the round sun of China, both bordered in blue, above red-and-white stripes representing the United States, the official insignia worn by veterans of the CBI theater. Brigadier General August Kissner, LeMay's chief of staff, met the party and took them to see his boss, where the reception was less than cordial. Tunner remembered that LeMay "wasn't very pleasant, he was very cold"; he simply said, "Well, you'd better get started." Tunner brusquely replied, "Tell Smith I'm here and taking over," and the two men each offered a quick, "goodbye." Tunner recalled, "And that's about all the conversation we ever had." There was a budding issue here; LeMay was in charge of USAFE, the larger command, and believed that MATS should report to him, but "Tunner felt . . . he had been ordered by higher authority to come to Germany and run the airlift," and nothing could be more important. Highlighting this conflict, one civilian employee at headquarters claimed, "Up to this point everyone had considered the operation was to be a MATS project under our own name, but after a visit to USAFE Headquarters we were quickly informed that the project was to be a USAFE operation." Later on, Tunner's relationship with superior officers at USAFE would take a turn for the worse, even beyond this rough beginning.[46]

The matter of quarters did nothing to relieve the chill. Of the eight hundred houses taken over by U.S. occupation forces, LeMay garnered the grandest, a 102-room mansion owned by the Henkell family of champagne fame, complete with fifteen servants. Tunner would not have quite the same level of accommodations, and that may have rankled.[47]

Tunner and Milton wound up in the Schwartzer Bock Hotel, which sounded good, but wasn't. All they had was a third-floor walk-up apartment that consisted of a single room, with a view of burned-out structures. Getting there was no easy matter; the elevator was out, and the entrance door opened into the bathroom. Tunner wrote that "the only way you could get into the . . . quarters of the commander of the Berlin Airlift," was to maneuver "between the tub and the commode." "It was pretty obvious," he observed, "that I was in Europe at the command of General Vandenberg, not at the request of anyone in Europe."[48]

His staff's quarters were even worse, an apartment house that "had really taken a beating. The floors were covered with debris, the walls were filthy. There were no desks, no chairs, no telephones." Located at 11 Tannus Strasse, it became known as "Tunner Strasse." In rapid order, the team set to work, pulling in some German civilians to start the cleanup, with McMahon working on getting furniture and Fernandez obtaining telephones and other communications equipment.[49]

Before them was the mission. Milton disclosed that "the sight that greeted us" at Wiesbaden "was not encouraging. It was evident that everyone—pilots, supervisors, everyone—was on the edge of exhaustion." Tunner assembled his team and told them, "We came here to work. I'm not asking you . . . to put in twenty-four hours a day, but damnit, if I can do eighteen hours a day, you can do fifteen."[50]

The first thing they did was to go out and investigate conditions. They discovered quickly how complex the job was: in India Tunner had thirteen bases with planes flying into six bases inside China, plus all the airspace in Southeast

Asia. Berlin had only two old and rapidly deteriorating airports—Tempelhof in the American zone and Gatow in the British zone—which were only four minutes' flying time apart. Instead of enjoying vast expanses of sky, he would be running the largest operation of its kind in history inside a postage stamp.[51]

Tunner hopped a plane into Berlin and found "confusion everywhere." Decades later, Milton recalled that his own first impression confirmed fears, that "when we first went over there it was an absolute shambles," with "people . . . on the brink of absolute exhaustion. . . . No attention," he explained, "had really been paid to operational procedures and basic organization. It was just a thrown-together, ad hoc organization." This was fine at first, since "its sole purpose was to hold the line while people decided what they were going to do. I don't think anyone had any idea that this little emergency airlift was going to do much more than to sustain our garrison out there while we made up our mind." But now that had changed, a decision had been made, and the airlift had to change fundamentally.[52]

The first step was to expand and restructure the staff. General Smith, Tunner's immediate predecessor, had a command staff of only three or four officers, not nearly enough to run an operation that had grown to substantial size and was about to become enormous. Tunner wanted people he not only trusted, but also that he knew were experts in their respective aspects of air transport.[53]

He was not nice about it. In the mold of a corporate executive who did not worry about firing managers when he had production goals to meet, Tunner, in the words of one airlift vet, engaged in "wholesale replacement of people in key jobs." Smith was one of those moved out, fast, and though Tunner meant nothing personal by this—it was just business—Smith took deep offense and years later would condemn Tunner as a glory hound. But in 1948 the only thing that counted for Tunner was making the airlift work, proving before the world that his vision was accurate and attainable.[54]

Tunner thought big. In early memos he laid out the fact that this was no temporary effort—he expected it would last till at least November 1—and that it would be a twenty-four-hour-a-day job. One early memo on tonnages had numbers hand-scribbled at the top: "5620 x 30 = 168,600"; he already knew what minimum monthly goals he had to meet. In addition, he began taking steps to ensure there would be no interruptions to the flow of goods, insisting "a three-day backlog of airlifted supplies" must be constantly on hand at all dispatching airports, to prevent delays and ensure sufficient time for "type-loading and arranging of the cargo," a concern of air transport experts, not bomber or fighter pilots.[55]

Even more, there was a sense of mission. On July 6 he wrote Kuter, "the lift is an opportunity for air transport to show what it can do. . . . The precedent and policy in future use of air transport is now being established." A month later, Kuter replied, reminding Tunner what the air transport man already knew so well, "Even more so than during the operation of the Hump, the eyes of the world are on you."[56]

By the third day after his arrival, the first major seismic shift rattled the airlift: crews would have to stay by their planes and could not wander off. Loading and unloading had to be done right away, so as not to waste these men's time, nor the airlift's.

Instead, they would be greeted by two vehicles. First, a jeep would appear with an operations officer and someone with weather information, providing the crew with instructions for their next trip and the conditions they would meet along the way. Alongside them was a mobile snack bar, equipped with hot coffee, doughnuts, and sandwiches. No more would airmen have the opportunity to wander around, greet friends, make a call, or catch forty winks. They ate on the tarmac and took off right away. In an effort to make this a bit more palatable, Tunner had the German Red Cross recruit the prettiest girls they could find for this job, so there was at least some solace. It was smart, but also effective; in time, turnaround would drop to less than thirty minutes per mission. Later, Tunner described the changes with the comment that, from then on, "No one leaves his airplane except to step down the ladder and get a doughnut and coffee and get back in and never go inside the Operations building. His weather will be brought out to him; his clearance will be brought out to him." Pilots sat in the cockpit the whole time, and their instructions got sent up by the jury-rigged solution of a clothespin on the end of a stick. Crews now complained that they never even got to see Berlin, that they wanted to visit the ruins: Tunner replied, "They had enough ruins in Frankfurt . . . if they wanted to see ruins."[57]

Above all, Tunner knew he needed more planes, or as he wrote General Kuter, "the key to the whole problem is big planes and lots of them." And that meant only one thing.[58]

T. Ross Milton asserted that Tunner "really waded into it when he got there. I mean he was everywhere, he was finding out . . . what we had to have, and then we began to work on the fact that we just had to get different airplanes, C-54s."[59]

7. The inside of an Airlift C-54, loaded with sacks of flour. (National Archives photo, SC304549)

The DC-4, the civilian version of the C-54 Skymaster, was an effort to expand the size and scope of the legendary plane, by making a bigger and far more capable plane, as well as increasing power from two to four engines. The army's initial reaction was that it was too much plane for too little mission; one general officer, clearly not a member of the Tunner school of airlift, brusquely asked Donald Douglas, founder of the eponymous company, "What possible use could the United States Army have for a four-engined transport?" But World War II provided the answer, and by 1943 the C-54 was rapidly becoming ATC's main long-range plane.[60]

One important reason for this change was its sheer ability to do the job. While the C-47 could only manage three tons, the C-54 could manage fourteen tons, flying at 240 mph to distances as far as 3,900 miles away on one fueling. Because the airlift asked it to do something it was never designed for—the plane was created to carry passengers long distances, not ponderous loads for short, jarring hops—loadmasters kept the weight down to ten tons of cargo per trip.[61]

The C-54 was an elegant machine, the Cadillac of its era. The wing actually had fewer parts than its counterpart in the smaller C-47, while the new cockpit, according to one flyer, "seemed . . . of conference-room size." Inside, the plane's interior could be made palatial, so that several generals, including Albert Wedemeyer, used it as a flying limousine. The White House was equally impressed, and rigged up one as FDR's private transport, the first version of what would later be labeled Air Force One.[62]

Most important of all, like its predecessor, the C-54 was a safe and reliable plane, in some ways even more so. One big change was to replace the C-47's tail dragging gear; the older plane used a low rear wheel, which made the plane sit at an angle when on the ground. The C-54 was better balanced, and had a front nose wheel that kept the plane level. This made it much easier to land, especially in severe winds, as the airlift would experience in the German winter to come, plus loading could now be done by forklifts.

The plane was a joy to fly, very maneuverable with light controls; long flights in this bird were far less fatiguing than in any other model. Ernest Gann, who went on to become a best-selling writer, was a pilot and big fan of the Skymaster. He claimed that they were "of such sturdy and reliable temperament many pilots developed a special DC-4 yawn. As an instrument aircraft they were so docile even low-time pilots could shoot a near-perfect approach."[63]

The accomplishments did not stop there. The Skymaster flew 80,000 ocean crossings during World War II, yet only three aircraft ever went down, and only one of these incidents involved fatalities. As late as 2002, C-54s were still being used to fight fires in California, what the *Los Angeles Times* called, "the final line of defense against what may be the worst onslaught of wildfires . . . in recent memory."[64]

So, not surprisingly, pilots loved the craft. Ann Tunner calmly remarked, "Douglas, I guess . . . built planes like that, they just belonged in the air." One writer said it was unlike any other plane, "in a league of its own," and a young pilot even joked to Tunner, "General, do you think the C-54 will ever replace sex?" Mercifully, the general's reply is not recorded, but it was clear that the C-54 was the plane that the Berlin Airlift would depend on for success. Tunner needed more of them.[65]

There was no question he was going to get them, either. Smith had begun this process by pushing for more planes, and Truman would help, although the air force was still hesitant and often delayed sending aircraft. Clay, above all, was now committed to the idea of airlift and clamoring for support. Tunner had a fair amount of clout, both in his new position and via Kuter. But LeMay was now under pressure, and made the first move to vastly expand the air fleet in Germany.

A couple of days after Tunner arrived, LeMay called; the new airlift commander turned to Ross Milton, his chief of staff, and told him, "Go over and see what he wants." "So," as Milton put it, "I went over to LeMay's office."[66]

LeMay had a brief but critical question for the new executive officer: "I've got to tell General Clay how many C-54s we need. And he's waiting for an answer."

This was the opportunity Tunner and Milton had been primed for; they had almost a blank check, as long as they could justify the figures. Calm heads and careful calculations must be the order of the day.

But not *that* day. Milton replied, "Yessir, I'll get right back over to the airlift headquarters and go to work on it." Milton did not get it; Clay was waiting, and LeMay was not the kind to dilly-dally. He looked at Milton, pointed to a small desk in the corner, and ordered, "Sit down here and go to work on it. What do you need?" Milton asked for a pencil and pad and a slide rule, "so he yelled out . . . to his chief of staff, told him to bring this stuff into me, and he went on entertaining foreign visitors while I scribbled away."

It wasn't quite so bad as it sounded at first telling. The Tunner team had been working on this already, and Milton knew his boss's utilization figures, how each plane was supposed to operate. With that in mind, he could start with the total daily tonnage requirements and calculate back to how many missions this would entail, how many planes per day, and then figure in things like maintenance. Milton came up with an initial estimate, a subtotal, then asked about the availability of British bases, revised his numbers and came up with a final figure.

Nice work, but it did not go as planned. Milton handed the sheet to LeMay, who picked up a phone and bellowed, "Get me General Clay." Tunner's executive officer asked, "You want me to stand by?" but LeMay answered, "Oh, I don't need ya. I can read this stuff." As Milton described it, "I went out, hung around the outside door and listened to him and he gave the wrong figure to Clay, the subtotal." Milton then went back to Tunner, told him what happened, and got the command, "Get your ass back over there right away." Back at LeMay's office, he explained the error, and the head of USAFE called Clay again and backtracked, "We've done a little recalculation here." When he hung up, he turned and said, "Thanks, Milton," a line the air officer considered "a rare encomium from that taciturn man."[67]

Milton's figure was 225 C-54s, which he said would have "stripped the Air

Force" and utilized several navy squadrons as well. By September all C-47s had been pulled from the airlift (although the British still flew them), replaced by the larger machines. Planes would continue to be assigned as late as January and even April 1949, but at its height the Berlin Airlift utilized 312 of the U.S. Air Force's 441 C-54s, or 71 percent of their total fleet, with more planes coming from the navy. Given that only 1,242 of these planes ever got built, roughly one-third or more of all the C-54s that ever existed flew to bring coal and food into a beleaguered city.[68]

On August 4, 1948, Tunner held his first press conference. Praising General Smith's work as "superb," he was aggressively upbeat about the work before him. His main point was to compare this mission to the Hump, declaring that whatever the problems, "We solved them over there. . . . We can solve them here, too." Even the factor that most concerned officials—the onset of winter and foul weather—did not seem to bother him, claiming that on "instrument days . . . we will definitely get tonnage to Berlin." Planes were landing and taking off faster than ever, and things were on the uptick.[69]

But there was still a long way to go before air transport could feed a city. It would take an unexpected crisis to kick Tunner and his team into high gear.

8 / Black Friday

William Tunner and his men thought they were prepared for the Berlin Airlift, but it took a quirky event to get them fully mobilized. It was just one of those moments, a compound of strange weather and the previous chaos.

August 13, 1948, was a Friday, although it is doubtful anyone in the airlift worried much about that. Tunner's duty that day was the kind of event commanders are often called on to attend, ceremonial and routine. Back at Wiesbaden, an old German man had approached the general: the gentleman wanted to give one of the flyers a present, a common expression of gratitude in those days. This particular gift was a bit extravagant, however, a jewel encrusted gold watch in a velvet case, handed down from his great-grandfather. The elderly fellow offered it as his thanks for what the airmen were doing, "as a little token from an old and grateful heart." Tunner accepted the gift, and promised to personally bestow it on a deserving recipient, in a proper ceremony. The pilot he picked was Lt. James Lykins, who had set a record for flying the most missions to date, forty-six round trips in forty-two days. It was to be a modestly big deal, the ceremony held at Tempelhof, with the Honor Guard of the Third Battalion of the Sixteenth Infantry there, as well as the 298th Army Band and the Berlin Military Post Fife and Drum Corps.[1]

When Tunner took off from Wiesbaden for the quick jump into Berlin that morning, the weather was fair and reasonably pleasant. His plane—5549—slipped into its assigned position in the steady flow of machines heading into the capital, with Sterling Bettinger as pilot and Red Foreman as copilot. Tunner sat in the jump seat behind them.

Germany, however, has quirky weather patterns, and things were not quite as bright over Berlin. In fact, the city was experiencing its worst storm in thirty years. Rain came down in sheets so thick that the radar was literally disabled, unable to pierce an atmospheric curtain this thick, this dense. Cloud cover was down to the floor, two hundred feet or below, a potential disaster since pilots had to fly past apartment buildings taller than that, and now they had to do it blind, both in visual and electronic terms. Sterling Bettinger later asserted that "the controllers on duty in the tower could see absolutely nothing." Even worse, the skies were becoming extremely crowded as traffic backed up; Bettinger reported, "Ahead of us, 20 C-54s stretched out like product on a conveyer belt, each one three minutes apart, holding steady at 180 mph. Behind us, plane after plane joined the convoy, reporting their positions as they entered the corridor."[2]

Over Berlin, pilots were becoming desperate to land, calling out for assistance; then things got a lot worse. Lieutenant Henry Fulton, holding for forty-five minutes over Tempelhof waiting for radar guidance, suddenly spotted a break in the clouds; on his own initiative he guided his C-54 in for a landing on visual approach. But nobody saw all that clearly in the storm, and Fulton had picked up a new runway that was still under construction, not the main airfield. He plowed into eighteen inches of gravel and rubble, badly damaging the plane and requiring emergency crews to be called on, further straining the besieged air facility.[3]

Seven minutes later disaster struck. Lieutenant Francis Adams was coming in on the airport's main runway, not a subsidiary path. He landed too fast, and only touched down on the last third of the runway. With insufficient distance to properly brake, he overshot the runway, and practically made it onto a Berlin street. His C-54 plowed into a ditch, at which point the left gas tank blew up, and the plane was an inferno. All the crew got out, but Tempelhof was a mess. And right behind Adams, another pilot—ferrying a full load of flammable coal—spotted that fire from his cockpit, braked too hard, and exploded both tires. This left a C-54 stuck in the middle of the runway and blocking everything else, with few personnel available to handle this new emergency.[4]

The controllers were now in full crisis mode and took the only step possible to them: they began to stack planes, having them fly around Berlin at every height possible within safety limits, anywhere from 3,000 to 12,000 feet, in an ever-widening circle running over into the Soviet zone. Planes bumped around in the rough weather, as "pilots filled the air with chatter, calling in constantly in near-panic to see what was going on," in Tunner's words. Even Red Foreman gasped that the planes were being stacked, "God knows how high." Tunner said what everyone must have voiced that horrible morning, "God knows why there were no collisions."[5]

But Tunner had grasped the enormity of the situation, whose consequences went far, far beyond stacked planes. As the pileup grew bigger and bigger, U.S. aircraft began to circle out past the Berlin limits—a twenty-mile radius from the Allied Control Council building—and into Soviet airspace, in total violation of the corridor accords.

This was no joke. During the airlift the Russians would inform the Americans that "all foreign aircraft appearing over the Soviet Zone of Occupation outside the limits of the air corridors and the region of Greater Berlin will . . . be forced by Soviet Air patrols to land on the nearest airfield in the Soviet Zone."[6]

Tunner's "Log of Personal Activities" in the air force files shows he was already intensely aware of this issue and of the consequences of such violations. The August 4 entry, for example, nine days before Black Friday, records, "After an incident . . . wherein a C-54 is alleged by the Russians to have been 50 miles outside the corridor, and in view of the warning that future infractions of the corridor would result in the aircraft being intercepted and forced down." As a result of that accident, air staff received new instructions. From that point on, all pilots would be "thoroughly briefed on this problem and . . . any pilot reported outside the corridor would be grounded, pending an investigation of the violation." The confirmation that the commanding officer believed fervently in these rules came in the entry for August 12, literally the day before this disaster: "General Tunner announced that he would henceforth have no sympathy for personnel . . . who exhibit 'pilot error,' poor judgment, or infractions of rules and regulations established to control operations of their aircraft." Another indication of how serious this issue was, came in a memo on August 19, that spoke of secret intelligence that "the Russians intend to interfere . . . with our operation," within days, and that one of the most likely possibilities was "the forcing down of aircraft not in the corridors." Now, in the midst of this terrible storm, Tunner saw all his rules discarded, but far more dangerous, the making of an enormous international incident that could lead to the start of hostilities and the Third World War.[7]

And that was not all. At least as important to him, Tunner was witnessing the downfall of the airlift, the project he had dreamed would prove his vision before the world. Instead, as the air force historian Daniel Harrington wrote, "The entire U.S. lift stumbled to a halt, right before Tunner's eyes."[8]

Finally, it was personal. Tunner had come to Germany as the master of efficiency, but now, as he later revealed, "it was damned embarrassing. The commander of the Berlin Airlift couldn't even get himself into Berlin." A strong man, an independent leader of powerful will and dominant ego, was being humiliated and embarrassed. This situation could not last long.[9]

Tunner said that at that point he would have "snapped my grandmother's head off." Instead, he acted.[10]

The call came through clear and sharp, electrifying ground control. "This is 5549. Tunner talking, and you listen. Send every plane in the stack back to its home base."

Shock. Silence. A request to repeat identification and the remarkable command.

Tunner's voice, determined, came on again, barking the same decree, ordering all planes returned to bases in West Germany, with immediate clearance for him to land. "Send everybody in the stack below and above me home," he stated powerfully, "Then tell me when it's okay to come down." Tunner recalled that Foreman and Bettinger "looked at me with their mouths open."[11]

It is hard to imagine the reaction of pilots, crews, controllers, ground staff at that moment. Everyone had been working flat out, albeit in a less than disciplined way, but they all believed that every flight counted. Now, in a matter of sentences, Tunner had canceled hundreds of hours of work and flight time. He also quite possibly saved the Berlin Airlift.

Another relevant question is what Tunner was actually like in those terrible moments. Clearly, he was beside himself, and with great justification. Most interviewees recalled that Tunner was not a screamer, but the master of a slow, but red-hot burn. His son remembered that the general's anger was "very controlled . . . very determined," that he "never lost control . . . He may have raised his voice, but he didn't yell." Betty Foreman Churchman, Red's widow, claimed that, "if anybody crossed him, he really showed his anger . . . You could see it boiling inside him, he would get so furious. He didn't say much, he didn't have to." Ross Milton added that it did not happen often, but "when things went really wrong"—and Black Friday was "really a dramatic day"—Tunner had "a terrific temper."[12]

This was the figure that confronted his men. After they landed Tunner turned to his crew, some of his most trusted associates, and gave them the assignments that would transform the Berlin Airlift and turn it into a success. "As for you two," he barked, "I want you to stay in Berlin until you've figured out a way to eliminate any possibility of this mess ever happening again—*ever*.

I don't care if it takes you two hours or two weeks, that's your job. I'm going to give this guy his watch and then I've got some business to attend to with those monkeys in the tower" (emphasis in original).[13]

The team was Bettinger and Foreman, Tunner's best pilots, joined by Hal Sims, navigator and artist, who would help determine flight paths, then ease the process by designing clear diagrams and useful models. No one in Berlin knew more about flying and mass air transport than these men. Bettinger said that Tunner told him, "our authority to change procedures for controlling and holding landing approaches and departures was not limited by any existing rules." Using model planes and coat hangers and string, they began work, draping the string across the room to represent flight patterns, and using small planes attached to thin hanger-wires to determine which pattern worked best. What they came up with became the basic operating structure of the Berlin Airlift.[14]

The details of this plan were important, but far more so was the philosophical underpinning of what they did. The goal was not just to make the Berlin Airlift safer and more manageable; it must, above all, be efficient. And to do that, they understood, as many procedures, as much of the flight as possible, had to be standardized. Acting like the disciples of Frederick Taylor they truly were, the Tunner team set out to eliminate as much individual initiative as possible, to get rid of cowboys and have everyone operate within an aerial assembly line.

The first thing they did was to standardize the routes, roughly the equivalent in ground terms of establishing which side of the road cars would drive in each direction. This drew on earlier decisions made by Smith, but with some refinements. From that point on, all inbound traffic came along the southern and northern routes of the three routes only, the former originated in the American zone, the latter in the British. All returning flights, going back to base after unloading in Berlin, would use the central corridor; after exiting the Soviet zone they could turn for a final brief jaunt toward their home base, well out of the way of the incoming flights. This simple step drastically cut down the chances for a midair collision.[15]

Next, all landings would be ground controlled. No more would pilots have the freedom to determine whether or not conditions were right, or what ceiling was acceptable for landing, or what approach speed was appropriate. From that point on radar would be the guiding hand, and every pilot would follow instructions from a ground controller, reading from a strict playbook.

The logic behind this was far-sighted. Visual landings by the pilots were fine in the balmy days of August, but in winter this system would fall apart and the airlift would fail its greatest test, with disastrous consequences. Under the new setup, flyers would have months to get used to GCA, ground control approach, so that when they really needed it—when it was the only way to get into Berlin—they were used to it and could depend on this method, and on themselves. The C-54, furthermore, was the perfect plane for this new procedure, since, according to John Ohlinger, who flew C-46s and C-47 in most of the theaters of World War II, the Skymaster was "remarkably stable" during instrument operations, and "precision approaches using . . . GCA . . . were no problem whatsoever. Even in severe turbulence the aircraft seemed to have an innate affinity for the straight and narrow."[16]

The logical corollary to this was a tight set of rules. There would now be specific—as in exact—speeds permitted for flying, for approach, for landing. Whether or not to land in a time of shifting cloud cover was no longer an individual choice; Tunner sent out orders that any pilot who could not bring his bird in when visibility was greater than four hundred feet would be busted down to copilot. The same fate awaited anyone who encountered visibility that was *too low,* and still tried to do a landing, despite orders from the control tower. There was now only way to do things: the Tunner way, courtesy of men like Foreman and Bettinger and Sims.[17]

Most controversial of all, pilots would have one chance and one chance only to come in. Any plane that now missed its approach would be sent back along the central corridor—fully laden—rather than be permitted to make another try.

This had a number of benefits. For one, it cut down dramatically on the stacking that had been occurring regularly. In addition, it was terribly efficient. No one spent time nursing a plane, letting it try again and again till the pilot got it right. At one time controllers spent ninety minutes to land nine planes from a standard altitude such as 9,000 feet; now they could bring down sixteen planes in the same time. Finally, it was safer, because now there was little in the way of circling or attempts to rejoin the lineup of planes aiming to land. Tunner explained, "Sometimes, on bad days, four or five airplanes would have to go back home because . . . clouds would come across the field. But there was never a day when we didn't get some tonnage into Berlin from that day on."[18]

With these steps the Berlin Airlift started down the path that would lead to its success. Bettinger referred to what they had done as the creation of a "bicycle chain" full of interchangeable, constantly rotating links, and others have used the term "conveyer belt." Whatever the descriptor, it was now becoming an industrial operation, more suited to Henry Ford's Detroit than Jesse Chisholm's trail. Over a decade after he helped design these reforms, Bettinger wrote Tunner and underlined how important this move was. "As you must remember," he began, "your directive to Red Foreman and I to 'eliminate all stacking, holding, and second passes' was the greatest single step made in permitting the volume of air traffic that was eventually realized at Berlin."[19]

Under this routine, a typical flight still started with the fellow at the controls. With the expansion of the airlift, many of these men had made rapid transitions to the C-54; Albert Lowe, for example, was a command and instructor pilot who flew 267 flights into and out of Berlin. J. B. McLaughlin had been air attaché in the U.S. embassy in Athens, when he answered the call for transport flyers; at that point he had three thousand hours in the air, mostly in fighters, with three hundred hours in the C-47. Arriving in Germany, he learned that his time in the two-engined plane qualified him as a "first pilot"; his sole training on the C-54 was a single orientation flight with someone who had flown the route already. By the time Tunner had ironed out procedures, McLaughlin, Lowe, and hundreds more would fly in twelve-hour shifts, 6 A.M. to 6 P.M., or the reverse.[20]

The plane would be waiting for these men and quickly loaded at the Rhein-Main Air Base. The cargo would be 20,000 pounds, and the trip was a short hop for a plane designed for long hauls of several thousand miles; it was only 350 miles from this airport to Tempelhof. That airport lacked refueling facilities, however, so the C-54 took off with 1,500 gallons of fuel. It would take 400 gallons for each leg of a round trip, and the extra was reserve in case of complications of any kind. The airlift also had its own unique system of assigning code numbers to planes; those flying out of Wiesbaden were "A" (as in "Able") flights, those originating from Rhein-Main were labeled "B" (as in "Baker"). A C-54 going into Berlin (that is, flying in an easterly direction) became "Easy," while a plane returning to the Western sectors got called "Willie." Thus, on any given day, the radio channels were filled with instructions for the crew of "Baker Willie" or "Able Easy."[21]

The typical plane took off and climbed to 900 feet, when it turned south and headed for the first of a series of radio beacons. These were designed to guide the pilots on a safe and true path every time. There were two of these before reaching the all-important Fulda beacon, and by that time the pilot would have the plane at the assigned altitude and speed, usually 170 mph; the C-54 could cruise at 200 mph, but with the heavy load on board, it was wiser to keep things down to a level that the plane could handle without strain. Tunner had originally set it at 180 mph, but command staff eventually settled on the 170 figure.

Fulda was the critical beacon and the best example of how a radio beacon works. Inside the plane, this signal was picked up by a radio compass, which turned in the direction of the transmitter. Thus, you could always hone in on that key point, always keep the flight going in the right direction.

But that was not all. As the plane passed directly over the beacon, the compass needle spun around 180 degrees, a remarkable moment that served several critical functions. First, if a course correction was called for (as was the case with the earlier beacons, but not at Fulda), the pilot knew that this was the exact moment when the change would be made. Second, once a plane passed the Fulda beacon, it was now in Soviet territory and no further signals would be available till it reached Berlin airspace. From here on, the pilot would have to fly by dead reckoning, by staying on a compass heading inside the twenty-mile-wide corridor. The swing in the compass needle let him know that he had reached that point in his journey. The third benefit was the most important in terms of creating efficiency and discipline in the airlift. When the plane cleared this beacon, thus beginning the main leg of the run down the Berlin corridor, the pilot had strict instructions to call out the flight number and the exact time on the radio, in the clear. By this time, planes were flying at strict three-minute intervals; now the pilots ahead and behind had a system where they could tell, based on how many minutes they were supposed to be from the broadcasting flight, if they were running fast or slow, if they needed to speed up or slow down to maintain the rigid rules of Tunner's conveyer belt.

Forty minutes later, the pilot was talking to Tempelhof air traffic control, which cleared him down to two thousand feet and 140 mph and then through a series of beacons and descents, maneuvered him to the final flight pattern and a landing. As the pilot set down, in front of him was a jeep with a neon sign on the back that glared "FOLLOW ME." Following his guide, the flyer took his plane to the assigned pad, where a sixteen-wheel cargo truck was waiting; the side door would be thrown open as soon as possible and the unloading commenced at full speed. In the meantime, the flight crew got new orders, weather conditions for the next trip, and the chance for food and coffee with the girls at the canteen truck.[22]

Ross Milton flew this mission plenty of times. He explained that after passing the Fulda signal, "you didn't talk to the GCA till you were on your base leg. You did that all by yourself." But after that, "Air traffic control would start you down. You'd make a call at a certain point coming into Berlin and air traffic control would tell you to descend to such-and-such an altitude, and then you'd turn on a beacon . . . and then the GCA would pick you up. . . . it was very orderly, very disciplined."[23]

There were still a number of factors that made this a memorable voyage. Many of these pilots had flown combat missions during World War II, and in one sense the route was familiar to them, but previously they had been in mortal danger as they flew over Germany. Now they were flying this path again, to help people they had just fought with great bitterness. Milton, for example, who led the first daylight bombing raid over Berlin, told the author, "It was a funny feeling flying over Germany at first for me. . . . It was in no sense apprehensive. It was just odd to fly over these places where I had some recent memories." In a piece for *Air Force Magazine,* he wrote how, "Even after the passage of 50 years, it is easy to remember the tension of that period. Scarcely three years had passed since we had thought of Germany as enemy territory. It still caused a flinch to lumber across, at vulnerable altitudes, those dangerous places we remembered so well."[24]

The final leg into Tempelhof was also a showstopper. Designed in an earlier era when planes were smaller and airports could be built in the middle of cities for travelers' convenience, the approach path brought planes right down a block crowded with seven-story apartment buildings. One pilot described his first flight into Berlin: "When I broke out of the clouds," he exclaimed, "I was looking into somebody's window. There were lights in there, and I could see these people sitting around a table, eating their dinner. I had heard about how narrow that corridor was, but that was my first experience. To eyeball it that close— these people eating dinner while I'm flying an airplane right by them!" Another pilot described landing as akin to "going through a door" into people's homes. One young U.S. Navy flyer—"I was just a dumb ensign flying copilot"—made several landings in the fog without realizing what was on either side of him. Finally, he came in as the fog broke, and "glanced to my side and saw people looking back at me from fifth floor apartment buildings." Adding to the excitement, "Where we stopped was only a stone's throw from more tall buildings in front of us. It was a revelation."[25]

There was also one other little wrinkle to the Berlin flights, and that was that the Russians were engaging in widespread harassment of the planes. In fact, one Soviet fighter base sat right at the entrance to the northeast corridor that went into the British zone, while American flights going into Tempelhof passed within four miles of another installation.[26]

The standard Russian procedure was to play some form of "chicken" in the sky, using Yak and MiG fighters that challenged the C-54s by flying around and toward them. One trick was to conduct air combat exercises next to the corridors, either with a tow plane pulling a banner or else targets being set up on the ground, with the armed craft shooting at them. This gave the Russian pilots—whom the Brits referred to as "Joe's Boys"—an opportunity to buzz the transports at high speed with guns blasting, an unnerving experience, at least at first. Sometimes a group of eight or ten planes did acrobatics rather close to the American and British planes, or even conducted bombing runs among them. On one occasion, a Yak broke off its straight-on run only fifty feet from the nose of a British civilian transport, which led the pilot, a man with RAF combat experience, to simply grumble that "the Russian attack approach" was "awful."[27]

There were other tricks as well. Searchlights would be put on at night, their beams going into the corridors to cause eye strain among pilots, much like headlights on the opposite side of a freeway after dark. One time the Soviets engaged in a three-hour mock battle that involved firing antiaircraft guns in the vicinity, and rockets and flares both came perilously close to the lumbering craft. In another instance the Russians dropped paratroopers not far from the planes making their way into Berlin. Overall, U.S. pilots alone reported 733 examples of harassment.[28]

Despite that last, formidable sounding statistic, there really was no threat, and pilots soon adjusted to the petty games. At no point did the Russians engage in any of the steps that could actually have shut down the airlift, such as attacking the transports en masse or blocking all radio and radar signals, which would have ended the flights immediately. Above all, they did not use their massed military power, or as *Time* put it, "The Russians threw everything they had" against the airlift, "everything except five well-equipped Red army divisions hovering under the chestnuts of Potsdam ten miles away."[29]

Tunner instructed his pilots to just fly through the games, and in time they came to ignore the nearby Ivans. A young pilot of British C-47s named Freddy Laker, who went on to found Laker and Skytrain Airlines, claimed, "The weather was more dangerous than the Russians," while Ross Milton remarked that harassment was "minimal." As far as he was concerned, "It made a good story," but nothing more.[30]

Things started to pick up. On September 30, Tunner officially eliminated all C-47s from U.S. flights, depending solely now on the C-54 to win the day (the British still flew the smaller planes). In order to clear up the chain of command and to clarify organization, on October 14 the United States and Great Britain officially signed an agreement creating the Combined Airlift Task Force (CALTF), with Tunner in charge, and RAF Air Commodore J.W.F. Merer as deputy commander. This eased procedure—the official notice stated that the "major functions of the Combined Airlift Task Force shall be . . . operational in nature rather than administrative," meaning Tunner was "given command over all U.S. units and operational control of RAF units . . . which are directly engaged in the Airlift effort." He could even "direct Wing, Base and Station Commanders, as a first priority mission, to provide . . . administrative and logistical support" for all CALTF units, including those of the USAF. Finally, he now had "the authority and responsibility to regulate all air traffic entering or leaving the air space utilized by Airlift aircraft in the delivery of supplies to Berlin." This administrative change gave Tunner enormous power and accomplished its goal of increased efficiency, but as late as July of the following year, in a review of lessons learned after the airlift ended, CALTF officers wrote that "The British believe the Task Force combined only in name."[31]

Tonnage was edging up when Tunner reached into his Burma bag of tricks to come up with another showstopper. The U.S. Air Force was the newest service, having been formed in 1947, and September 18, 1948, was now Air Force Day, its first birthday celebration. Tunner arranged with Clay to stage a virtuoso performance, and they agreed to concentrate on one cargo, coal, as a symbol of their ability to make it through the harsh months to come. For that one exhausting twenty-four-hour period, C-54s got unloaded in as little as seven and a half minutes—by hand—and the total tonnage was a remarkable 5,583 tons, with another 1,405 brought in on British planes. It was a giddy performance, but no one knew if it could last. It was time to make the airlift work, with winter just months away.[32]

9 / Solving Problems

Now it had sunk in; the sea of problems before Tunner was enormous. Berlin was not Burma; the need was far greater, and there was no time to gradually build up a successful operation. Everything had to be working, immediately, since canceled flights just meant hunger for millions of civilians.

Raymond Towne recounted a story a colonel had told him, that if Tunner was running the Barnum and Bailey circus, the lion would put his head in the general's mouth. Thus, if he was to run this show the way he wanted it, the first thing the commanding officer had to do was work harder than anyone else, be in charge of every detail of the operation. British squadron leader J. C. Douglas believed Tunner worked twenty-three out of every twenty-four hours, and was thus informed on every aspect of the airlift. Earl Morrison, his crew chief, remarked, "I couldn't believe how that man worked"; while Gail Halvorsen, who would become famous as the Candy Bomber, said that Tunner "came across as a man with a mission."[1]

Tunner used this energy to lead his men, or to use the air force historian Daniel Harrington's phrase, it was "management by walking around." Morrison claimed, "He would show up unannounced wearing that old flight jacket," so that often you did not even know who he was, but Richard Bodycombe, another airlift vet, noted that while he definitely recalled seeing Tunner check things out, the general remained both recognizable and "an imposing figure." Tunner himself wrote that he would make himself "available to the pilots and crew members, seeking them out and listening to their complaints." Some of this was done at night, and even if the only exchange was a quick greeting, or a few minutes standing next to a flight controller, the effect was still powerful: the general was omniscient and omnipotent, always on top of things.[2]

In all fairness, this meant he drove his men hard, had little patience for less than perfection. Edwin Glazener, flight surgeon at Wiesbaden, remembered how Tunner dressed him down in front of his staff, a terrible breach of military protocol. Even decades later, Glazener told an interviewer, "I could not abide the man, and I really mean it."[3]

The log of Tunner's daily activities provides ample evidence of the level of work he took on to get the airlift running at full steam. On July 30, for example, the results of a staff meeting list twelve different new initiatives, ranging from checking on the assignment of C-54s at Rhein-Main to working on "possible improvements to Tempelhof airport," to looking into a cargo backlog, to figuring out what statistics the operation would need. The August 2 report started with a list of nine key decisions made, and moved on from there to eleven other items.[4]

There are also hints of the approach Tunner would take to making the airlift work. On August 28 the staff began a time study of unloading procedures which would speed up this process and provide more flying hours for each plane. On August 31 Tunner directed that from that point on, each craft would have an operational record detailing hours flown, time spent in maintenance, and how many minutes and hours were dedicated to loading, unloading, and servicing. As the log noted, "It is the history of the plane during each 24-hour period." With this data, Tunner and his staff could now get a clear picture of how their fleet was being used, and where they could gain greater efficiency. Tunner dreamed of a goal of one plane landing in Berlin for each of the 1,440 minutes in a day, but eventually had to settle for one every three minutes.[5]

Before this could become a reality, however, he had to use that prodigious energy to solve a myriad of problems. First on the list was improvements in Berlin's airports, and if possible, construction of new facilities.

The need was fundamental, but the problems were immense. Local airports, like everything else in this recently destroyed city, were in poor shape, way beyond what would seem adequate for an air mission of this magnitude, and their shortcomings extended to matters both large and small.

Firefighting apparatus, for example, remained grossly inadequate throughout the airlift, as detailed in a May 1949 report on Rhein-Main. The authors claimed that "proper fire fighting equipment was difficult of procurement, causing extensive maintenance thereby adding to the overloaded Motor Pool and Shops." They found that "only 10% of the 2.5 and 1.5 inch hoses . . . were serviceable," that "the balance failed on pressure tests no doubt due to improper storage and handling." As a result, "The Base is still shy roughly 5000 feet of hose of all sizes," a safety factor exacerbated by "a serious shortage of extinguishers of all types."[6]

The only way to tackle problems like this was on a case-by-case basis, starting with the existing facility in the American sector, Tempelhof. The airport had started as a military parade ground, and in 1909 hosted the first German air flight; by 1929 twenty-nine different airlines used it. Its architecture also spoke of different eras, both civilian and military, starting with the broad arching half-moon sweep of the main building, a graceful semicircle without columns that extended for 4,000 feet, or more than a kilometer long; the hangers were 682 feet long with sliding doors; the award-winning architect Sir Norman Foster has described Tempelhof as "the mother of all airports." Earlier guide books in the twenties had recommended to tourists that they visit the airdrome at night to see how the neon lights illuminated the flight paths of ascending and descending planes, and suggested the *Flughafen* Restaurant as being of particular interest for its panorama of air traffic. Tempelhof, in other words, was created at a time when airports were radical pieces of architecture, instead of utilitarian structures to handle increased loads of traffic.[7]

The problem was, for all its beauty, it was an inadequate place to land large numbers of planes. Runways, designed to handle modest German transports, were made of sod; would buckle under a C-47, let alone a C-54; and were only long enough for small aircraft and fighters. Tunner commented that while Tempelhof had "been designed by architects who were the greatest, the field itself had been designed by engineers who were the worst," and Milton described it as "a wicked little airport."[8]

Magnifying the problem, by 1945 it was in disrepair. Its main landing strip had taken punishment in the bombing raids and was no longer being used.

Thus, when the Americans took over this sector they set up a utility structure, a base of rubber and rubble surmounted by pierced steel planking, creating one runway 4,978 feet long by 120 feet wide, along with aprons and taxiways. Adequate for the occasional flight of dignitaries, this could not last long once the airlift started, and fifteen days after the first flight, General Smith learned that his main runway had a life expectancy of only sixty days more. The first solution was to simply place 225 civilian workers on the edges of the strip; after each plane landed they would rush in with steel sheets and wheelbarrows filled with rubble, and try to repair what they could before the next plane zoomed in. This was, to put it mildly, a temporary solution, so on July 9 Smith requested the authority to begin construction on a new runway. He got it, and construction proceeded, to be directed later by Tunner's new team. The Americans used 13,000 cubic yards of rubble to lay the foundation for this second road, and opened it on August 28. By November CALTF was working on a third strip as well, this one with an asphalt surface.[9]

Even with this effort, something more was needed, a new airport altogether. Planners quickly located a large rolling field 8,000 feet long and 4,000 feet wide in the French sector, near Tegel Lake, which had been used to train Luftwaffe anti-aircraft units. Unlike Tempelhof, which sat in the city center, this was in the suburbs, and there were no tall buildings around. The French quickly agreed to let the Americans use this land, in return getting rights to operate the airfield after the emergency ended and thus gaining the first such facility in the Gallic sector. The runways would be 5,500 feet by 1,500 feet, topped with asphalt.[10]

Tunner took a personal interest in what would become Tegel Airport. Ross Milton told how his commanding officer intervened, in a manner that demonstrated the senior officer's intense dedication to detail, always aimed at the same incorruptible goal of increased production.[11]

As Milton told it, "Tunner sent me up there with our engineer. . . . And the engineer and I agreed on the orientation of the runway." That seemed to be that, but they hadn't reckoned with the mind of someone who saw every action as an opportunity to boost airlift. When Milton told Tunner about his analysis, "he damn near took my head off: 'Goddamnit,' he said, 'That isn't the way to do it. The runways should all be in the same orientation. Gatow, Tegel, Tempelhof. Can't you see that?'"

This was Tunner's genius: he wanted every runway in Berlin—both on present and proposed airports—to be parallel, so that there would be no crossed flight paths, and the number of flights would not only be smooth and relatively risk free, but could also be maintained at the maximum level. Milton explained that Tunner "treated all three of them [i.e., Tempelhof, Gatow, and Tegel] as one airport, you see. Even though they were seperated." In other words, in Tunner's far-reaching mind, they were all just part of one air system.

Milton continued, "So we laid out the Tegel airport exactly parallel to Gatow and to Tempelhof. And then air traffic control had no concerns about intersecting flight paths." Pilots now flew always on the same heading whenever they came into Berlin, and ground control could always keep them on a straight line coming in. In other words, Tunner figured every possible way "to make sure the Airlift operated as efficiently as possible."

Construction began on August 5, and every aspect of the work was unusual. The scale was large; in addition to the runway, engineers planned for 6,020 feet of taxiway, 4,400 feet of access roads, and over a million square feet of apron, plus support buildings ranging from a control tower to a fire station. This meant a lot of building materials—the foundation of the runway was to be two feet thick, although in some places it reached five feet to compensate for the roll of the terrain—and again, it came from the ruins of the city. Berlin agreed to take down any structure deemed 60 percent destroyed and have its bricks ground into rubble for ballast on the runway.[12]

Almost all of this work was done by hand, and many of those appendages had once been delicate in nature. To accomplish this task, the Americans recruited seventeen thousand civilian laborers, 40 percent of them women, who worked around the clock in eight-hour shifts. Wages were 1.2 Deutsche marks per hour (officially rated as the equivalent of 36 cents), and a free hot meal each shift, which made these jobs particularly attractive; one U.S. officer remarked, "These people would work for one ladle of potato soup and a big chunk of black bread. And they moved the earth by hand." The work force varied from peasants in wooden shoes to ladies in elegant attire, although in the hot summer months many individuals of both sexes showed up in bathing suits to perform hard manual labor. Milton narrated how, "When we built Tegel, that was the damndest sight I ever saw. . . . There were people obviously unsuited for manual labor out there pushing wheel barrows, women in dresses and old guys who were probably doctors or lawyers . . . thousands of them."[13]

But there was some work that even dedicated manual workers could not do, and heavy equipment was required. After scouring the city, however, American engineers found there was almost nothing of this sort left in Berlin.

This began one of the quirkiest episodes in the entire airlift. H. P. Lacomb was one of those characters who would have been written up in *Reader's Digest*'s "Most Interesting Personalities" feature, but is now lost to history. Lacomb was a welder, but so much more, a veritable maestro with a blowtorch. Years prior, he had been working on the construction of a Brazilian airfield, when the project faced the dilemma of how to get large earthmoving vehicles into the jungle. Lacomb looked over the big machines and proceeded to chop them into pieces, his own personal, oversized jigsaw puzzle. These more manageable sections were marked, flown to the site along with their creator, who promptly welded them back together again. Someone in the airlift remembered this feat, and word went out that his services were needed again. Not exactly an internationally renowned figure, Lacomb was nowhere to be found. The air force asked agents of the Federal Bureau of Investigation to take on the task, and in quick order G-Men found the weld master working at a small midwestern airport.[14]

The airlift was now a national priority, so there was no problem getting Lacomb to Germany in a hurry. He took one look around and dove in, doing what he did best. Circling earthmovers like a painter surveys a model, he began furiously marking with chalk, then whipped out his equivalent of a sculptors chisel, the oxy-acetylene torch, all in front of a curious crowd; one journalist described the scene: "For reasons that only Lacomb knew, it was important where the cuts were made. Then he donned his face-protecting mask, lit the blue flame of his torch, and applied it to the end of a chalk line." The air force flew the segments into Tempelhof, where Lacomb began putting the pieces back together. In time he had a whole team of welders under his supervision, a crew that managed to get eighty-one different pieces of mighty equipment into the trapped city. They began to tackle bigger and bigger projects, eventually figuring out how to break up and then reassemble a gigantic electrical generator, which became the largest unit of its kind in West Berlin once they got it together again.

With this new help, airport construction flew at an accelerated pace. Work began on August 5, to be completed by January 1. Instead, on October 29 officials showed up for dedication ceremonies, and the first plane landed on November 5. Tunner was on board, along with a cargo of ten tons of cheese, and Clay came to meet him. He landed on the longest runway in Europe, 5,500 feet in length. By March of the next year, they began work on a major expansion that would include a second runway.[15]

There was still one big problem. The two transmitting towers of the Communist Berlin Radio were in the French sector, their offices were in the British area, but everything was run by Russians and their German allies. And those tall, lean towers—240 and 360 feet high, respectively—were 1,500 feet just off the main runway's center line. General Jean Ganeval, commandant of the French sector, a tough fellow who had survived the Buchenwald concentration camp, told the head of the radio station that the masts would have to be taken down and reassembled elsewhere. Not once, but three times. Nothing was done.[16]

In a formal letter, Ganeval politely informed the Russians that the towers "would no longer be available after 15 December." Promptly at 9:00 A.M.

on December 16, French military police surrounded Tegel Airport and shut it down. Taking over the control tower, they told the American personnel there to evacuate the area, and to instruct the crews at Tempelhof and Gatow that henceforth all planes would be diverted to their fields. Next to the towers was a small shack used by Russian personnel, and as they frantically tried to call for help, it became apparent that all the phone lines to their building had been cut. They were escorted to safety, as French engineers began their work.

Ganeval, meanwhile, invited roughly twenty American officers to his quarters, where he had laid out an elegant buffet of champagne and food. They also noted that he had locked the door.

At 10:45 A.M. he asked them to look out the window, and gave the signal. A massive explosion blasted against the windows; the room literally shook. One witness to the event observed that it was "a very neat bit of demolition. The tower rose about fifty feet in the air, then laid over and broke in two on landing." The general turned and modestly told his audience, "You will have no more trouble with the tower."

The Russians were beside themselves. Colonel Sergei Tulpanov was in charge of the local detachment of the Soviet Information Bureau and an official of the NKVD. Upon hearing the news, he suffered a gallstone attack so severe that doctors had to administer morphine. General Alexander Kotikov, commandant of the Soviet sector of Berlin, meanwhile, was in bed, suffering from heart problems. Tulpanov had enough clout to order the general off his sickbed to present a personal protest to Ganeval. The French officer's reply is possibly apocryphal, but so delicious it deserves to be quoted anyway. When a sputtering Kotikov yelled, "How could you do such a thing?" Ganeval calmly responded, "With dynamite." But they also agreed to give the Russians a small section of land in their sector that had previously been set aside for an airport, an issue that Tegel had made irrelevant and thus was an easy chip to give away.

Tegel now had the longest runway of any of the three West Berlin airports and became a major factor in the success of the airlift; Milton observed that it was the best of the three airports, because it had "good approaches and a nice long runway." More than half a century later, it reigns as Berlin's senior air facility. But for Tunner, more problems with airports lay ahead.[17]

Early on, he recognized one of the incongruities of the airlift. The Americans were flying the bulk of the missions, yet the route from the British zone to Berlin was substantially shorter than the route from the American zone. Distance equaled time, and time was everything. A shorter route meant more flights, and meant that the shorter path would be used by the larger C-54s, instead of the C-47s the British still had in service. Put another way, a base in the British zone meant that American planes launched from there would only have a one-hour trip, instead of a one-and-a-half-hour journey from bases like Rhein-Main and Wiesbaden; they could make five trips a day, compared to three and a half from the American bases. Figures like that were too important to ignore.[18]

Tunner chose the British facility at Fassberg for an American takeover. One of the Luftwaffe's largest facilities, it would have room for the sixty-five C-54s the general planned to base there, and the British had built it up by laying 3.6 million square feet of concrete in seven days. They were even able to deal with one particular flight problem—flocks of sparrows that slammed into windshields and got churned by propellers—in a distinctly English way. One non-commissioned officer was a falconer back in Blighty, and he asked his mates back home to ship him some hunting fowls. The sparrows did not last long.[19]

Neither did the British. On August 22, 1948, the first American C-54s began to land.

At first this appeared to the Americans as a plush assignment. Fassberg had been one of the most elegant Luftwaffe bases, and servicemen could stare at the magnificent porcelain vomit bowl attached to the wall in the dayroom, not to mention the massive armchair rumored to have been reserved for use by Herman Goering himself. In addition there was that best friend of military personnel, a well-stocked gym with an indoor pool.[20]

This euphoria did not last long. While the needs of those planning to hurl their food seemed well taken care of, nothing else was. Living quarters consisted of tiny rooms with double-decker beds, cubicles so small that wardrobes, chairs, or tables could not fit inside the space; one medical officer reported that the rooms were "similar to those found in concentration camps." Clothes hung from overhead beams, and letter writing, an essential to morale, became an impossible feat.[21]

That was just the start of the problems. The British, it seemed, did not believe in hot water, so there was precious little available for showers or shaving; even the water was bad, unchlorinated, which seemed backward and dangerous to the Americans. On top of all this, medical facilities were nonexistent; 3,000 troops located 100 miles from any major medical facility had only a 35-bed dispensary, and anything major had to be handled by air evacuation. Between March 1 and September 29, 1949, alone, the U.S. Air Force would have to fly 616 patients out for a total of almost 162,000 miles. In addition, that distance also highlighted one of the other shortcomings of Fassberg; it was isolated and far from both dependents and any zone of recreation.

All of this was exacerbated by a divided command structure. Fassberg had become an American base, but the British were still in charge administratively. Group captain Wally Bigger ran the place, but was equal in rank to the USAF colonel who headed the unit there; and in a short time, three different American commanding officers would cycle through this tough assignment.[22]

Despite this precarious situation, it was clear that the hosts expected the Yanks to adapt to their ways. The movie theater, for example, used a class system to assign seating, which rankled the democracy-raised Americans. One of the worst offenses came on the first morning of the American occupation; striding into the mess hall to throw down a strong platter of ham and eggs, they were served kippered herring, which emanated a fishy odor so pervasive it reached outside the building and snared passersby. Brussels sprouts, a standard item on the dinner menu, also did not resonate well with many American palates.[23]

It got bad, really bad. Milton eventually had to stand up at a staff meeting and give a direct order: every officer would henceforth have to report, each and every day, what he had done to improve conditions at Fassberg within the previous twenty-four-hour period. One British airman, a devout chap, followed this up by sincerely inquiring, "Do we remember Fassberg in our prayers?" breaking up the meeting into roars of laughter.[24]

Headstrong, Tunner now made a lousy situation much worse. His model always was derived as much from private business as it was from the military, and he decided to adopt a business approach at Fassberg, or as Milton described it, "Tunner tried to run Fassberg as though it was United Airlines." This meant abolishing the core units, the squadrons, and the military structure; instead, men were to work on whatever needed to be done, regardless of who was flying in and out. Unit pride was gone. Hours also became longer and longer, which Tunner justified as the kind of work that employees in the private sector also performed sometimes, during rush periods. Except no one was getting any overtime pay in the military.

As one air force historical monograph on the airlift concluded, "The experiment failed miserably." Milton told how, "Morale was very low and finally . . . we, meaning several of us . . . went to work on him and said, 'Look, this isn't United Airlines, this is the Air Force. These guys have to have some identity. There's no overtime or the things airlines pay.'" Tunner, however, was lost in the entrepreneurial model and obsessed with making airlift work on the largest scale possible; Milton reported, "It was very hard to sell it to him," but eventually their arguments, backed by the weight of evidence, prevailed.[25]

Fassberg was never an ideal spot to spend the airlift, but it soon became a great deal better. Tunner reestablished the squadrons, providing something for the men to rally around, and he began organizing liberty runs to Hamburg and Copenhagen.[26]

Next to restoring unit identity, the best thing Tunner did to fix the problems at Fassberg was to finally hit on the perfect commanding officer. Colonel J. Theron Coulter was commander of the Sixtieth Troop Carrier Squadron and a resident of Beverly Hills. It was there that he met his wife, who proved invaluable in helping to make the base livable.[27]

Coulter was a pleasant man, a good diplomat, and an effective organizer, someone dedicated to fixing the situation. Even more impressive, however, was his spouse, the film actress Constance Bennett. Glamorous, a star in her own right, Bennett proved herself the antithesis of a Hollywood bimbo, and became the steadiest player of them all. She had followed her husband to Germany when the airlift started, and now took up residence with him at his new post.

As the wife of the American commanding officer, Bennett took it upon herself to make the new garrison work. Ross Milton noted how, "Connie, to everyone's surprise, trotted right along with" Coulter, and immediately proved that she was "basically pretty damn tough. . . . She really organized things up there." She had no qualms about the most mundane tasks, such as handing out doughnuts to flyers; Ann Tunner called her "a great trouper. She used to go out and work on the flight line with the Red Cross girls . . . a great sport." Far more important, one of her specialties became getting resources no one else could attain; Milton explained that "she went over everybody's head to get what she needed," and described her as "one of the most formidable scroungers in any service." In time, furniture and other amenities appeared, and life at Fassberg began to become tolerable.[28]

Supplies filtered into Berlin, but each commodity brought with it unique problems. Food, for example, the most essential cargo, was taking up too much room, so they decided to bring in flour rather than bread, and to dehydrate potatoes, a staple of the German diet. This became so much a part of the Berlin scene that one local cartoon showed a stork flying over the city with the traditional bundle in its beak, labeled, "Powdered Baby."[29]

Coal actually made up more weight in airlift cargoes than food and became a concern that was never fully conquered. The first method of transporting the stuff was in G.I. duffle bags. These were big and handy—there were several million left over from the war—and just the right size for packing a dense commodity without getting so heavy they could not be loaded and unloaded easily. Unfortunately, the thick canvas used in these sacks was extremely porous, so dust crept through at an awesome rate. Planes became clogged with coal dust and had to undergo cleanings more often and of a more rigorous nature. One pilot explained how, "After each day's coal-laden flight, I headed for the shower. The coal dust choked my hair and ran down my body. I had to get it washed out."[30]

Nothing seemed to end the wave of coal dust. First, the logistics crew began to wet down the satchels, but the amount of water required for a ten-ton cargo added significantly to the plane's weight, and the idea was rejected. They tried bags made out of hemp, and eventually settled on five-ply paper bags, that were only good for a few trips. These were made in Germany (ironically, in a plant in the Frankfurt suburb of Sachsenhausen), at such a low price that the cost of coal satchels dropped from $250,000 to $12,000 a month. Even these, however, turned out to be too porous, and the final accommodation was to lay a tarpaulin on the floor of each plane hauling coal, and then shake it out afterward. This had both up and down sides; for one, it meant that the canvas sheets would retain literally tons of coal that could be put to use. On the other hand, this meant accepting the fact that there really was no solution, that no bag could ever keep coal dust from taking over a plane. One Navy R5D (their version of the C-54), returning to the states for its one-thousand-mile servicing, turned out to be half a ton overweight from coal dust that had seeped into every crevice in the craft. As late as the 1960s, mechanics servicing planes that had been in the Berlin Airlift still found holdings of coal dust in out-of-the-way places.[31]

Another related commodity was what the air force called POL—Petroleum, Oil, Lubricants. One problem was the increased use of aviation gas by the airlift as a whole; prior to this operation USAFE used about 30,000 gallons a month, but by July 1949 this had increased almost ten-fold, to 291,000 gallons, and overall, the lift consumed over 100 million gallons of this high-test product. Navy tankers brought the fuel to Bremerhaven, from whence it traveled by rail and pipeline to the USAFE bases. At the height of operations the navy was bringing over 12 million gallons a month.[32]

There was still the problem of getting fuel into Berlin; though the local airports did not service the C-54s, gas and oil were required for all the vehicles in the city, both military and civilian. At first this arrived in the old-fashioned 55-gallon drums, but right away this was seen as inefficient. For one thing, the drums weighed 365 pounds when full, and were difficult to manhandle. Even empty, they represented unnecessary weight on both the inbound and outbound flight that was paid for in fuel bills and cargo not carried. Drums also had to be steam cleaned after each delivery, further slowing down what Tunner perceived as a fast moving and inexorable process.[33]

The British—but not the RAF—came up with the solution to this one. The UK had a fleet of forty-two air tankers of all sorts in the hands of various civilian companies; the airlift simply contracted with them to handle all fuel deliveries into the city. These planes could collectively handle 550 tons of liquid each day, enough to keep the city going. Gatow, the British airfield, originally could handle only two tankers at a time, but by March 1949 the RAF had sufficiently expanded their facilities that they could defuel fourteen planes simultaneously. The liquid ran through pipes into huge storage tanks with 108,000-gallon capacity, from whence it was drained into tank trucks and distributed throughout the city.

Besides these basics, Tunner's men had to provide for a plethora of different goods, some of them cantankerous. Salt, for example, is one of life's basics, but is also corrosive. British flying boats had been designed to handle this, with high overhead cables that had been treated to resist damage from salt water, and hulls that were electroplated to protect them. These ships flew onto Lake Havel as long as the weather was good, and then after that a Halifax bomber equipped with a pannier in the bomb bay took over the task.[34]

After that the list of necessities grew long. Berliners needed clothing, so between August 16 and December 16 the lift flew in 803 women's dresses, 500 children's dresses, 348 pairs of boys' underwear, 48 sets of boys' trousers, and even 70 towels; there were also 82,644 pairs of shoes for all genders and ages, but pilfering by the unloading crew resulted in these being shipped in mass bundles of right- and left-only footwear. Planes carried two thousand hot-water bottles, a load of ten tons of fresh herring (which melted and became part of the plane's interior decoration; the pilot remarked, "I was very happy when it became time for my aircraft to be returned to the U.S. for major inspection"), and even kosher meat for the small remaining Jewish population; for Passover 1949 they would bring in ten tons of matzo, four tons of matzo meal, and three thousand bottles of Kosher Passover wine. The only time the lift turned down a request was when the National Institute of Diaper Services of America offered to provide twelve thousand diapers a week for the mothers of Berlin, as long

8. The Berlin Airlift provided everything the city needed, even supplies for Passover 1949 for the city's small remaining Jewish population. (National Archives photo, SC320133)

as CALTF agreed to not only fly in the clean ones but carry out this gigantic load of soiled laundry. The all-male leadership turned this down quite easily, but they did agree to make space for newsprint to keep a free press going in the blockaded city.[35]

That newsprint also created jobs, another issue Tunner had to keep his eyes on. If he did not fly in raw materials factories would close and mass unemployment, already a problem, would skyrocket. And if he did not fly out manufactured goods, thus slowing down turnaround time in Berlin so these goods could be loaded, there would be no profit and no companies in business for very long.

Just prior to the blockade, Berlin's industries had been enjoying a modest revival. In April 1948, for example, German technicians had come up with a way to make high-strength rayon from beech-wood pulp, a product so strong it could successfully be used in the manufacture of auto tires. Between April 1 and mid-July, factories in the city applied for permits asking permission to ship

12 million marks worth of exports; the Siemens electrical parts factory alone made 672 requests.[36]

Now, however, disaster beckoned. A *Life* story that extolled the growth in Siemens and other factories also asked questions in tense tones. "How tightly must Berlin be choked," they queried, "before factories start closing, unemployed men start rioting and Communist 'action committees' go to work?" In the first seventy-five days of the blockade, thirty-five hundred firms shut down, mostly for lack of electrical power to keep them going, and others operated for only four hours a day. What was once a twenty-four-hour city ground to a halt as all public transportation shut down by 6 P.M. Exacerbating matters still further, much of Berlin's manufactured goods had been sold in the Soviet Zone, and while some traffic still continued, most of this was blocked. Unemployment soared, as the number of workers without jobs went from 30,000 at the start of troubles to 150,000 in May 1949, with another 100,000 doing part-time work only. With a working-age population of 800,000 this meant that the number of families with inadequate income was as high as 31 percent. In its October 21, 1949, edition, several months after the airlift concluded, *U.S. News and World Report* headlined an article, "Hungry Berliners Turn From U.S.," and reported, "Every third person in the combined . . . sectors of Berlin at present is living on relief. Every fifth worker is unemployed."[37]

Berlin had certain advantages in this struggle, such as the fact that it maintained many small handwork shops that did not require bulk shipments, and had an electrical industry that produced small, high-value goods. But, the variety of enterprises also meant that the different kinds of raw materials would be vast, and that many of the components would be of odd shape, weight, and density, hard to pack or stack.[38]

Tunner never fully recognized the importance of this issue, and instead concentrated on large bulk loads that could be handled in assembly-line fashion. A program to bring in 102 tons a day of raw materials starting in October 1948 failed to meet its quotas—one of the few in the history of the airlift—and the average for the lift overall was seventy tons daily. By spring 1949, however, these numbers did start to pick up, and in April the lift was bringing in 100 tons a day for Berlin industry.[39]

The other problem was getting exports out to their markets, and again Tunner balked, grand vision getting in the way of other concerns. His mission was not just to feed a city, but to above all prove mass airlift worked; that meant getting immense supplies of goods in, and not stopping to take them out. The British fought this, and resented the American position; one insightful RAF officer said the resistance came from the fact that the Yanks did not want to do anything to disrupt their turn-around times—which were "very good indeed" and because they "hate to spoil their performance."[40]

Tunner hated this concern about bringing goods *out* of Berlin. As early as August 1948 he complained to Clay about requests to fly out household goods, which would cause disruption to his schedule, how, "to ensure maximum utilization of aircraft . . . ground times must be kept to a minimum." In another memo, he pointed out that "a careful study has been made of the effect which bringing cargo out of Berlin will have on the tonnage which can be brought into Berlin." Trying to remain patient, he explained, "We are trying to maintain split-minute timing on loading, unloading, servicing, and clearing of aircraft. Any new factor which is injected into the overall problem has a definite cost which adversely affects the total number of trips into Berlin and, consequently, the total tonnage."[41]

The British took up this slack as best they could with their limited resources, and Tunner always allowed some goods to be loaded into his departing planes. Manufactured goods frequently had a bear—the city's ancient symbol—stamped on them, with the slogan, "Made in Blockaded Berlin." The first British flight took off on August 5, 1948, and soon almost nineteen tons a day were outbound. In January 1.5 million lightbulbs made that journey, and Tunner could even write in his memoirs about goods ranging from loudspeakers to small locomotives that his planes carried back to West Germany. The Office of Military Government in the Berlin sector reported, in fact, that in December 1948, a peak month, 13 million marks worth of goods were exported from the British sector, while another 7 million marks worth of product had left from the U.S. area.[42]

Thus, life in the blockaded city became a complex tale. According to a May 1949 census, the western sectors of Berlin had a population of 2,056,000; that meant a lot of flights were needed. But Berliners were starting to believe the airlift could save them: polls done by the military's Opinion Surveys Branch showed that in July only 45 percent of Berliners thought the planes would bring in enough supplies to make it through the winter, but by September this figure was up to 77 percent. Residents in the besieged city began to get used to the omnipresent sound, although visitors or newcomers took a while to adjust and at first did not sleep at night. Locals, however, not only slept, but also became attuned to the rhythm of planes coming and going overhead. Some claimed that if anything stalled the flow, that change in sound would jolt them out of a deep sleep, because intuitively, they knew that something had happened to endanger them. Karin Hueckstaedt recalled that she "felt secure. As long as we heard those planes flying, we felt like everything was all right. But I remember waking up sometimes and thinking something was wrong. There was no plane."[43]

Something was changing in attitudes as well. Berliners responded, not only to the reality of beating the blockade, but also to a major shift in world outlook. Just a few years previous, they had been pariahs, survivors of one of the vilest regimes in history. Paul Fussell, a great literary critic and historian, said, "It is not easy to recall that when the war ended, the Germans, large and small, civilian and military, were despised as loathsome sadists who by their behavior, their laws, and their extermination camps, had earned widespread contempt and deserved serious punishment." Now, instead, some of the conquering nations were going to incredible lengths to save them. Ross Milton, who had been wounded by shrapnel from a 20mm exploding round and had no reason to appreciate Teutons, remembered, "I developed quite an admiration for the people in Berlin during that airlift. They struck me as being much like the people in London had been during the air attacks," quite an accolade. Berliners, in turn, would do almost anything to show their gratitude, not just for the goods being brought in, but for being restored to the status of human beings. They would show up at the airport with beloved trinkets, a final, incredibly emotional symbol of a previous, comfortable existence, and beg to be able to give it to one of the pilots as a token of gratitude. When planes crashed and Allied lives were lost, Berliners cried and somehow found endless amounts of fresh flowers to place at memorial plaques.[44]

Not that it was easy; to paraphrase Karin Hueckstaedt, Tunner had to make sure that Berliners did not have to experience "no plane." But even so, there would be shortages. Every food was rationed, from the small pieces of meat (all deboned in West Germany to save weight) to the generic product called "nourishing material," which probably was, but would never be consumed by anyone not trapped and hungry. Condiments and seasonings were nonexistent, so food was bland; as an American academic wrote, in the homes of German women, "The lowly onion is a luxury!" One man who labored at Tempelhof had to make do for breakfast with a piece of bread smeared with fat.[45]

Power was also an issue, for heat and light. Coal was severely rationed, so families bundled up in whatever they owned. Housewives continued to wash clothes in cold water, just as they had during the worst of the war years. Bakers had to produce a predetermined amount of bread for each one hundred pounds of coal they received, or else were cut off completely from supplies of both flour and fuel.[46]

Electricity came in blocks of just a few hours, but at all times of the day or night. Citizens of Berlin would get up at odd hours to cook or just to read, the rest of the time sitting in the dark once the sun set. One dentist had a bicycle contraption that his wife peddled to provide power for the drill, and a hair-dresser made appointments at midnight so he could see the hair he was about to cut. Generators came in to help keep the hospitals open, but nightlife ended; friends were told to drop by at strange times, whenever the lights might be on, and share some tea, the only opportunity when acquaintances could look at one another.[47]

Housewives had a devil of a time. Some families ate whenever the lights came up and let their bodies adjust; in other cases the head of household pre-pared the food at these strange interludes, then wrapped the dishes in what-ever insulation they could manage—feathers, cotton bunting, blankets—so that returning workers could enjoy a hot meal, even if they fed themselves in the dark. Washing up had to be done with cold water, and soap was available in only the smallest of quantities. One female American writer, surveying the "Women of Berlin," observed that after a few months in Germany, when she spent a night in a small American hotel, "The soap in my room was a month's ration in Berlin, and the towels were beyond what even the VIP guesthouses run by our Military Government, can offer." She added that in Berlin, "A cake of good soap is one of the most acceptable gifts one can make."[48]

There was also harassment by the Russians. Commandant Frank Howley received telephoned threats, or there would be the implied danger of a phone ringing but no one on the other end, a doorbell clanging but nobody on the threshold. Most of this behavior was directed at Berliners who worked with the Westerners; Hans Hoehm, a clerk in the office of the U.S. Military Govern-ment got a call one night. A voice on the other end intoned, "You are a traitor because you work for the Americans. All traitors will be shot when the Ameri-cans leave Berlin." Hanging up the phone fast, he was too frightened to tell his wife about the call.[49]

Even worse, Russian troops and agents would sometimes abduct Berliners, a task made easier by the fact that the city was blacked out, without power to keep the streetlights lit. One time Saul Kagan, a top official in the U.S. Mili-tary Government dealing with banking, had to meet with the man who would later become a leader in the Finance Ministry of what became West Germany, a Dr. Haas. Kagan journeyed to Haas's home for an appointment, traveling in an official U.S. military vehicle with a driver.[50]

Some time after they arrived, as Kagan and Haas were working, Kagan's driver stuck his head in to alert them to the fact that a Russian military vehicle filled with soldiers had circled the block three times. Haas's face lost all color instantly; decades later, when the author asked what the German looked like at that moment, Kagan pointed to a ream of crisp white typing paper.

Kagan responded authoritatively, immediately placing a call to the U.S. military authorities, requesting assistance. Fifteen minutes of "terrible tension" passed before a group of American MPs showed up to protect them. It turned out that the Russians were nothing more than a group of drunken soldiers. With all the lights out during the blockade, they had gotten lost and were just driving in circles in the dark as they tried to figure out what to do.

General William Tunner could not solve all of these problems; there was nothing he could do about Russian harassment of Berlin's residents, for example. But he had to solve some of these, to make the process so efficient it could even beat nature, in the form of the cold winter approaching fast. The airlift needed more solutions to the ever-expanding list of obstacles and problems.

10 / Finding Solutions

Tunner saw immediately, knew on an intuitive level, that in order to make the Berlin Airlift work—to make *airlift* work—he could not just improve the system. Instead, he had to totally remake military air transportation, make it different from what anyone else had ever conceived, along lines he had pioneered on the Hump. In Berlin, Tunner was not just trying to feed a city; he was attempting to prove a holy grail existed, that airlift was a strategic necessity in the modern era.

The key to his approach, as Ross Milton put it, "was basically discipline." This started at the top; Tunner himself, in the words of Dorothy Towne, had "great personal discipline" and "was always well groomed. . . . I imagine when he lived in a tent in Burma he was very well groomed."[1]

Tunner saw the airlift as a business operation, and his whole approach was to impose the most methodical corporate procedures he could adapt to the situation. Daniel Harrington, an air force historian, insightfully wrote, "The airlift's goals were humanitarian, but Tunner's methods were—because they had to be—ruthlessly mechanical." Towne observed that Tunner "was thinking in terms of running a factory, like a production line," and airlift vet Charles Ernst recalled that his boss "wouldn't tolerate anything but perfection."[2]

Like all great corporate innovators, his great ally was data. Time-motion engineers checked and calculated every aspect of the airlift; Red Foreman's widow explained that her husband used to go out with a stopwatch to make sure that planes were taking off and landing when they should, down to the minute.[3]

Ground zero for all data was the charts room. Tunner set aside one space just for all his charts—more than fifty—providing every kind of data possible, from missions flown to unloading times at every airport to maintenance breakdowns. These tables did not sit in fancy binders waiting for inspection, either; they were tacked to the wall so that Tunner could walk around and analyze everything, grasp everything within the time it took him to cover that one room. These were not only maintained on a 24/7 basis, they were updated every hour; one account by a reporter noted how he walked in at 3:40 one afternoon, and the latest information had just been posted at 3:30 sharp. Milton remarked, "We had all these charts around the room . . . and he knew what each of one of them meant. He used to come in and study these stat charts every day." If any number was dropped or seemed off, Tunner brought it up with staff. That image of a leader very much in charge of the operation was typical at that time in, say, the automobile industry, but this became the first example of its kind in the history of military air transport. Milton added that Tunner had incorporated into his thinking a lot of knowledge from commercial airlines, all kinds of procedures and concepts that were "something new because none of us had ever heard of aircraft utilization and commercial charges." Tunner, he concluded, was "very modern . . . quite ahead of his time."[4]

Everything came under scrutiny. Before, two planes could fly vastly different distances carrying the same tank of gas. Now, calculations took into account speed, load, altitude, wind, outside temperature, and as a result officers could figure out practically to the mile how far a plane could go with a specific load under a given set of conditions. Refueling time was also cut, from thirty-three minutes to only eight. Planes that missed their scheduled departure— one account claimed this was regulated to the second—moved back in line and waited for holes deliberately inserted into the traffic flow to accommodate such screwups and to keep load rates as high as possible. As early as October 1948, a few months after Tunner took over, *Newsweek* reported that the airlift "is Big Business, organized and operated with typical American commercial efficiency." Gatow, in the British sector, became the busiest airport in the world, handling *three times* the planes and cargo of the next biggest, LaGuardia in New York City.[5]

Red tape became the enemy of efficiency, so military procedures got streamlined. This may have ruffled feathers among the higher-ups, may have gotten Tunner into trouble with superiors, but in Germany, those issues did not matter.

Instead, the Encyclopedia Britannica's online edition now cites the airlift as the first example of e-commerce, how Tunner's man Ed Guilbert got rid of the multiple—if not endless—requisition forms, and began to order directly by phone, telex, and teletype. When Captain Carl Virgin, a traffic control officer, arrived at Tempelhof from his previous duty assignment at Wright and Patterson fields in Ohio, he was "amazed" at how much nonsense had been eliminated from his job. "I just can't believe my eyes," he exclaimed, "an operation as great as the airlift going on with so little paper work."[6]

Tunner did not mind spending money as long as his unit costs went down. A report covering the month of April 1949 showed that the cost of the operation went up over $2 million, but that the task force had flown 9 million more ton miles than the previous month. Between January and June of that year, flying costs per ton dropped from $38.61 to $34.68, or 9 percent.[7]

Tunner loved those numbers, explaining in his memoirs that he sought "precise rhythmical cadence . . . This steady rhythm, constant . . . became the trade-mark of the Berlin Airlift." Dorothy Towne added that to Tunner that sound, the steady drone of planes in lockstep, "was just like a piece of music" to his ears.[8]

Pilots now had to toe the line; no cowboys, no mavericks allowed. Tunner's wife, Ann, in a recent interview, told how he would "cruise the line . . . He would see what was going on." By then, he had gained the nickname "Willie the Whip," but it did not faze him; years later, Ann Tunner explained that when it came to discipline, his attitude was, "He's not running for election. This wasn't a . . . popularity move."[9]

By spring of 1949 the Tunner team had created and distributed a "Manual of Aircrew Ground and Flight Procedures for Airlift Aircraft," a good indication of how thorough their command of the airlift had become. The guidebook covered every detail, from the initial section on how to "Report to Operations" to chapters on "Engine Run-Up," "Cruise," and "Securing Aircraft," to make sure all of these procedures were done according to form. The manual had twenty-two major sections, twenty-three subheadings, and another twenty-three sub-subheads.[10]

But this manual also exposed one of Tunner's most deeply held concerns, safety. "Emergency Procedures" was the last of the twenty-two sections but also the biggest, covering more than a quarter of the entire volume. The endless regimentation meant that pilots now *had* to do the right thing, that personal error would be minimized, and that the safest and best procedures would be discovered and implemented. The airlift, for example, maintained emergency corridors, so that troubled craft could be directed to these safe zones where they would receive maximum priority without endangering anyone else. Overall, between June 1948 and May 1949 eighty-five individuals died during the Berlin Airlift in either air or ground accidents, including thirty-two Americans, thirty-nine British, and fourteen Germans. While each of these lives lost is tragic, in all fairness the accident rate remained remarkably low, especially given the twenty-four-hour nature of the lift, and the tough winter weather that had to be challenged over and over again. Compared with U.S. Air Force operations worldwide for the same period, airlift pilots maintained a rate for all serious accidents—not just fatal ones—of 2 percent, compared with 5 percent for the service as a whole.[11] Tunner's procedures, in other words, meant that there were less than half as many incidents under his command as was typical for the U.S. Air Force at the same time, leading Dorothy Towne to observe that the general "was a perfectionist when it came to safety." Gail Halvorsen also remarked, "I credit him with saving my life through the procedures he set up."[12]

Halvorsen's story is relevant in another way. Not only is he the most famous airlift veteran by far, much more so than General Tunner or even Lucius Clay, his story reveals a lot about Tunner's ceaseless quest for efficiency. As the airlift heated up, Tunner became so focused on his mission—of saving both a city and the concept of airlift—that he lost sight of the sheer humanity of what he was accomplishing.

Gail Halvorsen is the closest the Berlin Airlift ever came to creating a living legend. In 1948 he was serving at Brookley Air Force Base in Mobile, Alabama; on June 10, Halvorsen agreed to go to Germany to help with the lift. Fighting a bad cold, he stuffed his duffle bag with handkerchiefs.[13]

Once he hit Berlin, Halvorsen did what every other serviceman did, became a tourist, complete with camera, setting off to see the ruins and whatever else he could take in. He did not get far.

Just outside Tempelhof, the flyer came across a group of children, about thirty in all, who, like all children everywhere in the world, were fascinated by planes and airports. This naturally gentle man stopped and talked, answering the barrage of questions that followed: How much food did each plane hold? How fast did they go? What was the cargo capacity? Was it really true that they flew in real milk for babies?

Then it happened. Halvorsen made an observation that has been picked up and made part of the American legend. And while these stories are real and true, they are also too sweet and simple and leave out the rest of the story, the part that shows just how complex a man Gail Halvorsen really was.

The tale goes like this. Halvorsen was turning away to go about his business, when he realized that these kids were different. He thought about this, trying to put his finger on something, when it hit him: they did not beg. As he described this revelation, "In South America, Africa, and other countries, an American in uniform was fair game for kids with a sweet tooth. Thousands of American G.I.s filled the special craving of countless little ones. . . . It became a conditioned response: a group of kids, their immediate, strong request, hand in the pocket for pre-placed goodies for such an encounter. . . . Here there had been no request."

Halvorsen's description reads like a postwar comic involving Italian orphans; it smacks of naiveté and innocence, but also almost a condescending attitude. It is the story repeated in all accounts; it is accurate. But it is also only part of what happened, and it does not do him justice.

That afternoon, Halvorsen noted the failure to beg, but he also saw much more. His first conclusion was to recognize the incredible maturity of these children. When they asked questions, they had more than childhood fascination in mind; they wanted to know if the airlift would work. This was particularly brought out by one tiny girl of roughly twelve years of age, who wound up lecturing Halvorsen, a World War II vet. She pointed out that American bombers had destroyed most of her city, and that many of the children had had loved ones killed in the air raids. But after that they experienced the communist system close up, and made choices. "We don't need lectures on freedom," she insisted. "We can walk on both sides of the border. What you see speaks more strongly than words you hear or read." Halvorsen understood immediately: "It was freedom, not flour, that they were concerned with that warm July afternoon in 1948." This in turn shaped his response to the begging, in ways overlooked in the Norman Rockwell images of a carefree American flyer helping some kids. Halvorsen grasped that there was something more to their behavior, that the real reason they did not beg was because "they were so grateful for freedom and our desire to help them with these meager food supplies that they refused to tarnish their feelings of gratitude for something so nonessential."

Still, he wanted to do something. But his pocket contained nothing of value to a child, except two lonely sticks of Wrigley's Doublemint gum. Even after he split each of them in half, there was still not much for thirty kids. He reached out his hand, and stood there transfixed as they grabbed for the treasures, even taking the tin foil wrappers and tearing them into strips so that even more could get some taste or smell, some hint of the riches.

And then genius struck. Impulsive, glorious, sweet-natured genius. Gail Halvorsen found himself telling the throng that the next time he flew over he would drop them some more candy in parachutes from his plane. Always the fair father figure, he added that this would only happen if they all took a solemn pledge that no matter who caught a packet, it would all be shared equally among the group. In shouted cries of "Jawohl, jawohl," everyone agreed—of course.

The small girl had become their spokesperson now, due to her good English skills and better common sense, and voiced the fears that every child there carried that moment. "They want to know what aircraft you will be flying," she explained. "Such a small package would be too easily lost, especially if you come late and we have tired by watching all day in vain." How could they recognize his plane among the hundreds in the sky? Who could argue with such hardcore logic?

Halvorsen had no idea of which plane he would be in, so could not give out identifying numbers. Instead, he enjoyed a second flash of inspiration, and decided he would simply signal them by wiggling his wings, just like he did as a rookie flyer back in his hometown of Garland, Utah.

That was more easily thought than translated. No words could close the gap surrounding "wiggle," so Halvorsen finally wound up extending his arms and giving "a demonstration that could have won an Oscar," and definitely earned laughs.

It was not hard to prepare. Take some of those handkerchiefs he had in abundance, collect some extra chocolate and candy bars and gum from the guys, and make up a few parachutes and parcels. On his next flight, coming in at about 1,500 feet and closing fast, he saw the same group. Halvorsen noted that the crowd was still about thirty, that the kids had not let anyone else in on the secret; these were nobody's fools. All he had to do was open the door to a small chute in the cockpit's side wall, put there for firing distress flares, and out went the bundles. That was all there was to it. He would do it a couple of times more, and this gentle man's gesture would be done.

Hardly. One version has it that what brought this to the public's attention was the sacks of mail that started arriving from Berlin's children addressed to "Uncle Wiggly Wings" or the "Schokoladen Flieger" ("chocolate flyer"). Another has it that one of the parcels almost clobbered a reporter from a German paper, who wrote up the story.

Whichever was true, Halvorsen's gesture had caught the public's eye. In an age of fear, what he did was simple and generous and good, and always would be. In a new century that is smarter and more cynical than ever, Gail Halvorsen is still loved in Berlin, and for good reason. Neither the memories of Lucius Clay nor William Tunner can make that claim.

The pace quickened. Everyone wanted to get in on this wonderful act, so by now, whenever Halvorsen returned from a flight, the space around his bunk would be crowded with cases, cartons, boxes of every kind of confection the PX could spare. The hankies went fast; Halvorsen and his mates resorted to stripping off the sleeves of old uniforms, till a supply sergeant delivered three parachutes which were promptly cut up into smaller versions good for dropping candy.

By now Halvorsen had become famous, both in Berlin and in America. Children wrote asking that Uncle Wiggly Wings remember them in his flights, and many of the letters opened up doors for friendships that Halvorsen cherished long after the youngster had become an adult, although not all of them. One of his favorite stories involved a young, serious Berliner named Peter Zimmerman, who wrote an excruciatingly detailed letter that included not only a map, but precise directions as to where to go and when to drop his bundle: "After take-off fly along the big canal to the second highway bridge, turn right one block. I live in the bombed-out house on the corner. I'll be in the back yard every day at 2 PM. Drop it there."

No one, especially a good-natured fellow like Halvorsen, could resist such a command, so the next flight went according to plan. A follow-up letter, however, explained that Peter "didn't get any gum or candy, a bigger kid beat me to it." More flights, more lack of success. Peter became desperate; he would always include drawings, child's drawings of animals or planes, and on one, across the tail fin of a crude C-54, he penciled, "No chocolate yet." Finally, beyond consolation, he burst: "You are a Pilot? I gave you a map. How did you guys win the war anyway?" Halvorsen put together a healthy package, and quietly mailed it to Peter the next time he hit Berlin.

Back in the states, Halvorsen had become a celebrity. The folks of Chicopee, Massachusetts, took over a recently retired fire station and turned it into a central depot for receiving donations from around the country, including the twenty-two schools that signed up to offer whatever support their kids, parents, and teachers could muster. By January 1949 they were shipping eight hundred pounds of candy and parachutes *every two days* to Halvorsen and all the other flyers who were by now participating as well.

Halvorsen had done something special by any account, and Tunner's response to this event reveals a lot about his remarkable dedication to efficiency. Most accounts seem positive: Ann Tunner referred to Halvorsen as "a dear, dear person," quite a true statement; Earl Morrison recalled hearing Tunner say to the flyer, "I want to thank you for what you started here." Halvorsen himself remembered Tunner calling him in several times to offer praise. In addition,

Milton pointed out how important this all was to a man who missed no opportunity to bring attention to his mission; as he aptly put it, Uncle Wiggly Wings
"was an astonishing public relations gambit thought up by some amateurs."[14]

There is some other evidence, however, that indicates that Tunner was not
so glowing in his assessment of Halvorsen's contribution to the lift. While he
speaks highly of the flyer in his memoirs, published fifteen years later, the official history of the airlift put out as a publicity document in 1949 and monitored closely by Tunner told a different tale. Out of endless pages on maintenance, logistics, and the wonders of ground control approach, Halvorsen
received a total of one paragraph only seven lines long.[15]

There are other, more powerful indications that Tunner's reaction was mixed,
that he questioned whether or not this was a useful contribution to the airlift,
and worried whether it would impact the tonnage figures negatively. Dorothy
Towne remembered that "at first Tunner didn't feel at home" with what Halvorsen was doing. "We had to concentrate on safety and efficiency and that
didn't fit in the program. . . . At first it was seen as a diversion," although the
general did eventually warm to the idea. Sterling Bettinger claimed that when
Halvorsen appeared before Tunner, "the commander first expressed his extreme
displeasure with the candy drops . . . then told Halvorsen it was a good thing"
and "said he should continue." Ross Milton, however, went much further, stating that Halvorsen "used to drive Tunner nuts. . . . He really wanted no part of
this. As far as he was concerned it was a distraction" from the relentless drive for
productivity and efficiency.[16]

The best indication of how Tunner must have felt, however, can be deduced
from a story told in Halvorsen's memoirs. By that point the chocolate flyer was
a celebrity, and had gone back to the United States on a publicity tour, winding up on the interview circuit in New York City. One afternoon he showed up
for a midday meal at the Manhattan Hotel (where the place setting had "four
forks! I'd never been to a four-fork lunch"), with John Swersey of the American
Confectioners Association. Swersey pulled no punches. "I represent the confectioners of the United States and you have already received quite a few supplies. We are really excited about what is going on over there and want to do
more. What can we do?" That sounded an awful lot like a blank check, and
Swersey confirmed it by asking bluntly, "How much of this stuff can you use,
Lieutenant?"[17]

Talk about a kid—or at least a very, very nice man—in a candy store. Halvorsen made some rough guesses, then threw out a figure "I thought would give
him indigestion. . . . It must have been ridiculous. He didn't bat an eye."

Soon after, Halvorsen was on his way back to Germany. He reported to Tunner, then went back to being an airlift pilot, hauling coal and flour and mail, occasionally dropping something through the flare chute to kids waiting below.

A month later, he had landed at Rhein-Main after a Berlin flight, when an officer drove up in a jeep and demanded that Halvorsen join him. A quick drive took them to the railroad yard, and a freight car guarded by several armed members of the U.S. military. Halvorsen thought it was a VIP and blurted, "Who have you got in the box car?" "It isn't who," he was told, "it is what." Or more specifically, 3,500 pounds of candy bars and gum—close to two tons' worth—from "some guy in New York named Swersey." The next week Halvorsen received a shipment of 3,000 pounds more.

That was an awful lot of sticks of gum, enough to create a dilemma. No matter how diligent they were, no matter how many partners in crime they enjoyed, they could never drop that much candy. But by now it was December, and the answer became obvious, that they should throw the biggest Christmas party imaginable for the children of Berlin.

And so it was. Just to set the scene, this was not only a terrific thing to do; it was a public relations gift from heaven, highlighting not only U.S. good will, but also the epitome of airlift, the force that could deliver everything, even Christmas. But it also meant that the men of the Combined Airlift Task Force were doing something other than hauling goods during a terrible, crucial winter month.

The parties—they were held all over the city, there was so much candy—went just as planned. Due to the time of year and the lack of electricity, all events took place during the afternoon of Christmas Eve, and Berlin had a far more magical Christmas than anyone had ever guessed was possible.

What was Halvorsen, the creator of this publicity bonanza, doing that glorious afternoon? In his memoirs, he mentioned that "unfortunately I was not able to attend any of those parties. But the fireworks were very much in evidence, late on Christmas Eve, as we flew . . . on our way to Berlin with a load of dried potatoes." For Tunner, no matter how noble the cause, nothing could be allowed to break the endless rhythm of the Berlin Airlift. He was so committed, nothing—not even the nicest guy and the biggest publicity coup of the airlift—could be allowed to drop the tonnage figures by even one planeload's worth.

Instead, rules of efficiency had to be applied to every aspect of the operation. Ground logistics procedures became the subject of scrutiny, to wring out precious minutes and enhanced systems for the handling of cargo. The leaders of Fassberg, for example, realized early on that there was no warehouse for their supplies and spare parts, just an open hangar. Without security, and with material just piled willy-nilly, taking an inventory was impossible. One report on the problems there noted that "thousands of items were received without paper work." Tunner's men divided the hangar into bays, moved all items till they were in their proper categories, and gained accounting control over shipments, while placing guards to cut down on pilferage.[18]

But that was just a start. Every aspect of the handling of goods had to be regulated. Tunner traveled to the freight yards where soldiers loaded the coal into sacks, and "found that there was great carelessness on the part of the Army . . . that some bags which were supposed to weigh 100 pounds would be 120 or 80." That would not do; it meant that loads could not be planned, that planes flew over- or underloaded, each of which caused different kinds of problems. In no time at all, in Tunner's words, "we got uniformity in that." But he also added a line that pounded home his main theme. The reason why this had happened was because the service had failed to use its professionals. Even in something like coal loading, it took expertise, not amateurs; "things like that," Tunner noted, "are what a transport man knows."[19]

The restructuring of logistics began with the plane itself. Careful study produced a diagram showing the load-bearing capacity of each section of a C-54's or C-47's cargo space. Copies of this were placed in each plane so that crews could get just the right items in the right places to create a full and balanced load.[20]

On the runways and arrival areas, similarly, nothing was left to chance. Every base had a production control officer who stayed in constant touch, not only with the local commander, but also with Air Traffic Control and the Chief of Operations at CALTF. This meant he had a lot of strings to pull if things got rough, a necessity, given that his duty was to "expedite all activities pertaining to aircraft turnaround." Below this were the ramp officers, who, according to a memo from Tunner's Director of Traffic, "patrolled" their zones "constantly" to make sure no glitches occurred, and to solve them when they did as quickly as possible.[21]

The planes were positioned according to plan, so that as many as ten to twenty craft would be lined up, not coincidentally, "like the production line in some aircraft assembly line"; industrial analogies were always apt in describing a Tunner operation. As soon as the plane touched down and the switches were thrown, the flight engineer threw open the cargo doors, as fuel trucks pulled up to begin refueling. Another ground vehicle carried the loading supervisor

9. Troops supervise local workers loading and unloading planes. (National Archives photo, SC305829)

and his crew, who usually were hired local workers of various nationalities. The very first group put to work, for example, was made up of Lithuanian refugees, followed by a contingent of Poles.[22]

Loading time varied depending on what was put on board or taken off. One-item shipments such as coal were easy, compared to manifests that ranged from food to small- and odd-sized manufactured goods, or pierced steel planking. But it was always fast, a striking fact given that almost all the work was done by hand; the air force historian Roger G. Miller accurately noted that "most of the . . . cargo delivered to Berlin was carried at least part of the way on someone's back." Filling up a C-54 generally took from fifteen to thirty minutes, and at the height of the lift, a team of twelve laborers could take ten tons of coal off that same plane in under ten minutes, or less than a minute for each ton. In one test, conducted on a randomly selected team at Fassberg, the loaders packed a C-54 with ten tons of coal, tied down the cargo, and closed the plane's doors, all in less than six minutes, a remarkable figure of close to two tons per minute. Tunner even used his old methods of pitting one group against another in contests—not the last time he would try this on the lift—offering prizes to crews that could load the fastest. In his memoirs, he claimed that one winning team managed their ten-ton burden in five minutes and forty-five seconds, and gained a full pack of cigarettes for each man on the crew.[23]

Experts monitored every aspect of this, and instituted better procedures. Time-motion study personnel with stopwatches stood out on the runways to analyze the loading process down to the second. To make sure that everyone understood the larger plan of things, their part in it, and how it fit with everything else, each base had a model of the complete airlift including flight paths and radio and radar stations, in the Operations and Briefing rooms.[24]

The best indication of the depth to which Tunner's men took this attention to detail is the discussion of "Cargo Tie Down" in CALTF's final publicity report. Not exactly the kind of topic that produces best-selling novels, it was something that only airlift men could take that seriously. Several pages described the different kinds of strappings and locks used and their relative merits. At several points, the authors noted that although "continuous research was carried on to determine the most efficient tie-down procedure . . . this is a problem on which much additional research is needed."[25]

The nerd-like quality of these lines testifies to the single-minded focus of the airlift officers and their total professionalism, but it also underlies the importance of the issue. Most of the traditional tie-down materials, such as plain rope, faltered under the constant wear and tear they were now subjected to, with a spike in replacement costs, and cargoes damaged because they shifted when the straps could not stand the strain and broke. This was serious business, but no one had ever considered it before. Airlift experts had to find solutions.[26]

Tunner was in charge of all this. Milton told how his boss "considered any minutes spent on the ground . . . that was tons that weren't getting delivered. So we used to have to keep track, every day, of how long it took to turn an airplane around." If, for some reason, the numbers climbed instead of dropped "somebody had to go up there and find out what had gone wrong." To Tunner's industrial way of thinking, "you multiply one minute by twenty-four hours, that's a lot of minutes and how many tons does that cost you?"[27]

At the same time, he never lost sight of the fact that men had to do all this work. Tunner may have worked the dickens out of them, but morale was always a significant issue for him.

This would be a tough battle. With the onset of the blockade, followed by the rapid expansion of what became CALTF, many officers and airmen had

10. Workers load a C-54. Note how level the fuselage is, facilitating quick handling of cargo, unlike the C-47, which used a low-mounted tail wheel. (National Archives photo, SC304539)

been sent to Germany with little or no notice. Some of these came from bases with a tropical climate, so the transition to colder, damper Germany would be hard. Making matters even worse, the Air Force set a limit of either forty-five or sixty-five pounds of luggage, and any professional devices got included in that total. Mechanics, for example, carried their own tool boxes, and had little of the weight allowance left for clothing. Although the local bases provided winter garments, any personal items, including the little things that helped one adjust to foreign places, got sent as "unaccompanied baggage," which took from three to six months to arrive.[28]

Even worse, most of these men had been assigned to temporary duty, and they took the adjective seriously. They logically assumed that "temporary" meant "for a limited time only," but instead their tours got extended over and over again, with no end in sight; one December 1948 Pentagon briefing on air-lift personnel matters stated that "we have extended periods of temporary duty to 180 days." After that, the air force simply posted them to the area as permanent troops, usually without allowing anyone to go home to settle affairs. Tunner told how he "woke up one morning and someone said, 'I read your name in the paper this morning.' I said, 'Well, what did it say?' 'It said you were assigned here on permanent duty.' And that was the first I knew about it."[29]

This wreaked havoc on marriages. Captain Ken Herman told an interviewer, decades later, "There were a lot of divorces being threatened as a result of pilots being ordered over there, and some of those marriages collapsed under the pressures caused by the airlift." The dependents had a good point, too: "Many wives felt they had sacrificed enough during World War II, and that they shouldn't have to go through this only three years later."[30]

There were all kinds of problems involved with maintaining relationships. Mail shipments into Berlin went from 83,000 pounds in August 1948 to 92,000 by October, only to plummet to 53,000 in the harsh winter of January 1949, and as late as March was still only 80,000 pounds. Personal contact could be even harder; Tech Sergeant Sebastian Raffa of the Thirty-ninth Troop Carrier Squadron had become engaged to Lorraine Coy back in June 1947, but he was assigned to Tokyo before they could get hitched. When his unit got the call to join the airlift, he wired her to meet him at a California base they would be stopping at, cabling, "Will be there a few days, and we can get married." But the minute he landed, orders came to push ahead to San Antonio, Texas—before Lorraine Coy could get to the West Coast, of course. She bought a new train ticket for her person and her trousseau, but then got a wire that he was moving on to Germany immediately. Late in the airlift he was scheduled for rotation, but had still not seen his bride-to-be, and cracked that, "With my kind of luck, I'll get back to the States just in time to learn my girl is on her way to Europe to visit me."[31]

Even when dependents connected, there were all kinds of matters that had to be resolved. Housing was always short; even through to the end of the operation, an official history of billeting reported, "our biggest problem still remains that of housing the large number of dependents awaiting quarters." Perishable food, even milk for babies was in short supply, and cooking was a chore under the strained circumstances. In one case the electricity cutoffs in Berlin forced one ingenious American housewife, an OMGUS dependent, to come up with a novel solution to make a roast; she would shuttle the meat from one oven to another all over the city as power flicked off and then on somewhere else. A lamb entrée set the record, with a total of twenty-two hours between traveling and cooking before it was done.[32]

All this took its toll on the airmen. The Red Cross director at Fassberg told an interviewer he had "never seen so much anxiety" as he did there, particularly among the men with families left behind. Despite a non-fraternization policy, rates of venereal disease soared; the leading medical study on the operation declared, "The incidence of venereal disease among Airlift personnel was excessive," and bluntly stated, "The chief cause for this . . . was the fact that persons suddenly removed from their established homes and placed in a new environment made hasty heterosexual adjustments." In the worst cases some men tried to cut down on the number of missions they flew, or even refused to take off, and were sent home immediately, although with no other disciplinary action taken.[33]

Tunner took every step he could to turn this situation around, starting with the basics. He began a rotation policy so that troops would feel there was an end in sight, and he created a Dependent Housing Office. With many of the bases in isolated areas, he pushed to improve facilities on base, to reverse what the medical report called, "the fact that acceptable recreational outlets were . . . overcrowded" and too few in number. At Rhein-Main, for example, the movie theater was completely redecorated from a shabby, flimsy structure to a modern emporium with red leather seats. He saw to it that the library got new books and new chairs, then expanded the photo lab and gave all personnel access to it, instead of just the officers. On every base, clubs with pretty hostesses opened for the men, and ham radio facilities became available so that there was contact with the outside world. Basketball and baseball teams sprouted, and boxing matches became a common occurrence. At Fassberg, always a tough base to spend time in, a little matter like scheduling movies three times a week made a big difference.[34]

Tunner also sought as many chances as he could conjure up to display the good side of the airlift. Notices would appear about how an air force father and son had been reunited in Germany, to offset all the stories about family separation. Articles on the success of Anglo-American cooperation at various bases appeared, to calm the grumbling about bad food and cold water. A front-page headline, complete with several pictures, brought the message, "First Groups to Leave Wiesbaden, Fassberg On Rotation Policy."[35]

Above all, Tunner sought to praise his men in public and to distribute that information as widely as possible. As early as September 1948, with a long way to go, he had a letter printed in the most important CALTF medium, the *Task Force Times*, with the strongest words possible from a man with Tunner's beliefs. "You, the men who are making the airlift possible," he wrote, "have shown the world the undreamed-of potentialities of air freight transportation. You have proved conclusively that the Air Force can carry anything, anywhere, at any time."[36]

That meant an awful lot to William Tunner, but it is doubtful that it rang so true with an ordinary grunt who did not philosophize about the future of airlift. Tunner had to make them care, make them believe his vision.

He started by simply highlighting men who had set records. Anyone who did something special, something better than anyone else in the same job, became a big shot, got some publicity and some badly needed attention. As early as August 1948, *Stars and Stripes* had a front-page story on the top airlift flyer, the Texan who had made forty-six round-trip journeys in forty-two days and got the gold watch from Tunner on Black Friday. In January, with bad weather all over, *Task Force Times* praised plane No. 407, and Captain H. A. Reynolds, who made the Wiesbaden-Tempelhof run in a record four hours, compared to an average of four and a half hours. Even the loading crews got attention, as the time a sixteen-man cadre "made Vittles history" (Operation Vittles was the official name of the airlift) when they managed to hurl nineteen tons of coal into two C-54s in seven minutes. For all of these men, the Berlin Airlift had become a source of pride and not anxiety, something they could throw out their chest and brag about, rather than a source of gripes.[37]

From that came the next logical step; Tunner borrowed a gambit from his experience on the Hump, and began to encourage his men to compete with one another. As early as August 23, the *Task Force Times* noted that CALTF had set a new record, but this was light stuff compared to what was to come.[38]

The idea was to pit one squadron, one team, one wing against another to see who could be the best at making Tunner's dream work. One article reported that a landing crew at Tempelhof had unloaded and turned around a C-54 in eighteen minutes; that meant that the plane had landed, disgorged ten tons of cargo into waiting trucks, received flight plans and weather information, and was off the ground again in little more than one quarter of an hour. Truly this was an amazing feat, worthy of notice. But just behind the headline, in the second paragraph, came the ominous words, "This bettered a turn-around time of 19 minutes established at Fassberg recently." Somebody had been shown up, and now they would have to work harder to regain the title. At the end of March 1949, there was even a call to the entire operation, a bright announcement that the "Lift Sets Weekly Mark, Threatens Monthly Figure." Inside, readers of the *Task Force Times* learned that, with just a few days left in the month, previous weekly records were a bad memory, the daily record could be

11. C-54s lining up for takeoff. (History Office, Air Mobility Command, Scott Air Force Base, Box 7, Folder 1)

beat in the next period of good weather, and the old monthly record was surely a loser. It was clear that anyone who did not share this excitement, this commitment, was the worst kind of slacker.[39]

The men bought it, big time. Every first-person account of the airlift included stories of the competition, which many claimed made the World Series seem like a poetry contest. One reporter walked into an operations room to hear an officer yell into the phone, "Your tonnage figures are goddamn cockeyed. The 317th topped you; we can prove it." After that the phone slammed down on the receiver, as the competitor glared at everyone around him and barked, "Who the hell did they think they're kidding?"[40]

While that may have been a rhetorical question, the reporter asked a noncommissioned officer what was going on. The sergeant replied, "Figures. . . . Everybody's tonnage-whacky. He's claiming the tonnage high for the day. Somebody in Wiesbaden gave it to the 313th or some other Group. You'd think this was the Kentucky Derby."

Soon, every unit was vying to be the best, in Tom Sawyerish fashion. Different bases, different units, even the reputation of the air force versus the navy was at stake. When an airlift article in *Newsweek* praised one particular unit, an Alaska-based naval squadron, the periodical received a letter written at two A.M. in an engineering office in Germany. Sergeant W. V. Ratagick of the Twentieth Troop Carrier Squadron generously began that while "the Alaska Squadron, no doubt is good, I will place the record of our outfit against that of any outfit on the field and if we don't top them all, in airplanes in commission, trips flown, and tonnage hauled, I will eat my hat." After that the niceties were over, as Sergeant Ratagick added, "We don't doubt that the snowball boys do a good and tough job up there in the Aleutians, but over here they are in the big league and are going to have to hump to keep up." Finally, Tunner's men had pride, and would bust guts to make the lift work.[41]

There was one other ingredient in the formula, the oldest of all, and that was humor. Tunner eased up on a lot of regulations; he would treat his men like adults and make them work hard but overlook a pinup where it should not be. One of his best decisions involved on-air conversations; technically it was illegal to make a joke in a radio transmission, with stiff fines. Those rules did not apply to the Berlin Airlift, by order of the commanding officer. After that, Texans played the mouth organ into their mikes, while pilots referred to MiGs in disparaging terms. Even the reserved Brits got in on the act, in one case a pilot describing his cargo dryly but irreverently as "a mixed load of coal, flour, dried fruit and two Brigadiers."[42]

Tunner even relaxed the rules about his own public image. When it came to real issues, to making the airlift work, he was a powerful presence, but on smaller matters he would brook little indiscretions. There were countless stories of an officer in a rumpled leather flight jacket coming on a pilot at night or in a hurry, getting rough treatment and backing off. In one case he approached a flyer engrossed in prepping his plane for the next trip out. Tunner, whose outfit that day did not include stars, determined after a couple of questions that this was the young man's first mission, then asked if he would mind if the senior man took over. The hot shot replied, "You're darned right I would mind, I want to fly it myself," and Tunner just smiled and walked off.[43]

That story appeared on the front page of the CALTF's newspaper, in the upper left-hand corner. Tunner, in fact, had a remarkable sense of humor, as long as one of two conditions was met: it was for the good of his men, and/or it was from someone he trusted.

The vehicle for all this was the *Task Force Times,* founded by Hal Sims and Ray Towne. This was Tunner's prime means for getting his message out, to boost morale and publicize the airlift.

Above all, it was designed to create competition. Every issue included a

"Howgozit Board," a feature listing different units and the tons carried, number of trips made, and aircraft utilization rates. These categories remained consistent, and the column appeared from the start to the end of the operation. It was the men's personal version of the baseball standings, except that they were the players. Every week, in other words, Tunner had a way to stoke the desire to exceed limits.

Tunner also used the paper to boost morale. The headline of the October 29, 1948, issue bore the momentous headline, "HORRAY! A'LIFT ROTATION ON WAY!!!," announcing that some men would begin heading back to the states. To impress on the men that what they were doing really mattered, the October 1 paper carried a story, "Airlift Seen as Key to World Peace." By the fall, most editions also carried a regular feature, "Fassberg Jottings," giving attention to that beleaguered outpost. There were also plenty of photos, mostly of visiting dignitaries or airmen who gave something special to the lift. One image was missing however; in the entire run of the *Times,* few if any pictures of Tunner ever appeared. This was for the men.[44]

There was one other thing that made *Task Force Times* special, or rather, one other person. From the start there had been space for a cartoon, but quickly this became the personal domain of Jake Schuffert. Growing up in the coal-mining regions of Pennsylvania, Schuffert found school boring ("I was in my 12th year of ducking truant officers, harassing teachers, and drawing cartoons of everyone connected with the education racket. . . ."); and farm work down in Florida earned meager pay, so he joined the Army Air Forces eleven days before Pearl Harbor. Although trained in radio, he held a number of jobs during and after the war (Schuffert drew nose art for the 464th Bomb Group until "the crews learned every plane I painted was lost in action"). He eventually became Tunner's radio operator, where higher-ups discovered his talent. As Milton explained, Schuffert drew pictures "to amuse himself"; one time, on a long flight, for example, Milton went to lie down, and his radioman did a cartoon of the senior officer getting up and wondering where they were.[45]

In the pages of *Task Force Times,* however, Schuffert came into his own. His cartoons were witty and clear, but above all irreverent. Often dripping with sarcasm, they would poke fun at the leadership of the airlift and all of their machinations, with no sacred cows. Efficiency experts were ridiculed in an image of Russian spies who declare, "This airlift job will be simple, all we have to do is steal their slide rules." One picture showed an airman tied to the blades of a helicopter, while a shark-toothed officer is getting behind the controls as he gloats, "So you want to be rotated, eh??"

12. (Sergeant Schuffert, *Task Force Times*, November 1948)

13. (Sergeant Schuffert, *Task Force Times*, March 25, 1949)

14. (Sergeant Schuffert, *Task Force Times,* May 18, 1949)

Raymond Towne pointed out the importance of this work, that because they were in the airlift's official paper put out by headquarters, "every coal heaver, net twister, and airman knew that his problems were known to the Old Man, even if he couldn't do anything about them immediately." Tunner, instead, supported the cartoons, never censoring a single one unless it was for what Towne referred to as "latrine humor." The general even wrote a foreword to a compilation of these works, telling how "Schuffert's cartoons were good for at least one laugh each day to the thousands of men who were struggling with dirty planes and difficult and crowded living conditions while keeping the airlift running," and noted, "Task Force men clipped them from the *Times* to grace their desks, office walls, and living quarters."[46]

But the masterpiece was not a Schuffert effort at all, but an extended story written by a public information officer entitled, "Fassberg Diary." It opens as a weary traveler first encounters the airlift base, when from a distance, he hears a "weird unearthly sound"; it is singing, but "whether the choir was of celestial origin or straight from the depths of Hell I was unable to say." Soon, the words become clear:

Holding back on defecation
Leads the way to constipation
All of which bears no relation
To the feeding of a nation:
Our moral indignation
Stems from simple consternation:
Commendation, approbation
Are a crock of affectation—
You may have your admiration
And your little tin citation.
Flights of fancy, inspiration
Take us back to our home station
All we want is just
ROTATION.

The traveler soon discovers the Airwick Task Force (so named because it smells so bad). The crew of this operation report, "We are all much happier today," despite the fact "our composite morale is hovering in the vicinity of Kelvin Zero." Nevertheless, they have read that "Uncle Tumbler says our morale is very high. We did not know this before, now that we know it we feel much better." On another occasion, in the mess hall, they thank a local waitress, who instead of being beautiful is "bovine." In reply to their kind words, she says "Bitte" (or "thanks" in German). The men yell back, "Bitte? Of course we're bitte! You'd be pretty god-damn bitte yourself, Sis, if they snatched you over here on twenty-two seconds notice and left you here for the rest of what might have been your life!" The dartboard on the wall is described by one senior officer as hanging between "the VD chart and the picture of me getting my fifth Spittles Citation from General Tumbler." At the mention of this godlike figure's name, "all bowed their heads," as would occur whenever Tumbler is mentioned.

This remarkable work expressed the fears, anger, frustrations of the individuals making airlift work. The real General Tumbler loved it, and kept a copy in his personal files.[47]

The biggest solution to the problems of airlift, however, was a dream, albeit a grand one. Tunner quickly realized that his vision of the future depended on machines as well as men, and the current versions were frankly inadequate.

15. (Sergeant Schuffert, *Task Force Times,* February 25, 1949)

16. (Sergeant Schuffert, *Task Force Times,* December 28, 1948)

17. (Sergeant Schuffert, *Task Force Times,* December 11, 1948)

They had been designed by men bound by earthly concepts, rather than a higher sense of what this medium could accomplish. He would need better planes, bigger transport planes than anybody had built yet or were even on the drawing boards. To accomplish this, General William Tunner became a virtually ceaseless advocate of larger cargo aircraft for the military, a cause he would pursue for the rest of his life.

This was no easy task, and never would be. By the time Tunner became converted to this cause, World War II was in full bloom and cargo planes stood far behind bombers and fighters when it came to prioritization. Douglas began work on the massive C-74 in 1942, but in 1944 the air force investigated the company over charges it was favoring production of this plane (with postwar commercial possibilities) instead of building A-26 attack craft. As a result, instead of building three a month, Douglas only managed to finish one before the war ended, and thirteen overall, of which twelve remained in existence by 1948. In the case of the C-97, a cargo version of the B-29 bomber, the government gave it only a 2-C priority rating and Boeing found it was hard to find enough workers to build it; in 1945 only two had been accepted by the Army Air Forces.[48]

By then Tunner was a visionary, a change agent in society, and such parochial attitudes would not deter him. He was particularly enamored of the C-74 Globemaster, which had a cabin 75 feet long and could haul 25 tons for 2,100 miles. As early as July 10, 1948, there was discussion in the Pentagon of sending these planes to the airlift, but planners decided to allocate only one such plane to the new mission, keeping the rest on traditional routes in the Caribbean.[49]

Instead, Tunner gobbled up all of these planes, and made the most out of them. From the start, the fleet got placed under the aegis of the Atlantic Division of MATS, which meant Tunner had a lot of leeway here, so he assigned them to hauling C-54 engines from the States to Germany.

The one C-74 he could bring to Berlin became a combination showpiece and demonstrator of what could really be done if air transport only had the right planes. On August 17, this giant plane landed at Gatow with twenty tons of flour, and then proceeded to prove what a remarkable craft it was by backing it into its parking space. Over the next six weeks, the craft flew twenty-four more missions, bringing in almost one and a quarter million tons of supplies, and on Air Force Day in September made six round trips and brought in a quarter million tons of coal.[50]

After that, it started bringing in heavy construction equipment, including graders and bulldozers. Tunner wrote Donald Douglas how this was "equipment which would be impossible to move in any other Air Force aircraft."

After that, the C-74 left the lift, in large part because its bulk tore up the runways. In the short time he had it, however, Tunner did everything he could to publicize what the plane could do, holding briefings as often as possible that highlighted just how much the airlift could accomplish if it used these planes instead of the standard C-54s. The *Task Force Times* carried articles whenever the Globemaster flew, pointing out the capabilities of the large aircraft. Photos appeared in the local press of dignitaries, dwarfed by the plane, and stories began to run in the American press. A piece in the *Washington Daily News*, for example, bore the provocative headline, "70 Globemasters Could Feed Berlin—If We Had Them," and opened with the sentence, "The C-74 Globemaster now doing a brief tour of duty on the Berlin Airlift . . . offers an example of what might have been."[51]

This was not the only plane he experimented with. The C-82 was the first of the cargo planes with back-loading clamshell doors and a high ceiling, so that despite its limited capacity of roughly five tons, it was ideal for mobile loads that could be driven aboard, such as jeeps or light earthmoving equipment. By September Tunner had five of these planes working the airlift, even though some of the flights were tricky. Richard Bodycombe, later a major general, piloted one load so big that it required mechanics to remove the tail doors, at which point Bodycombe discovered that the plane in that condition "wasn't aerodynamically perfect. It was like a backwards plate flying through the air." But he managed to complete the trip successfully, and *Time* mentioned the big craft in its articles.[52]

That was what Tunner really sought, a means to put pressure on the military leadership in every way possible, from traditional channels to any other medium he could think of, which may have been outside the normal chain of command, but had the potential to be far more effective. Again, its effect on his career was not a consideration.

Thus, when the *New York Herald-Tribune* carried a story in its "Air World" column that began, "Never again will there be a time when a major air-lift project somewhere is not requisite to the maintenance of human society," Tunner had it reprinted in full in the *Task Force Times. Aviation Week* did an article, "More Lessons From the Airlift—An Analysis," which included a note that "large, long-range transports . . . have proved themselves in the air support operations," and did a full page on an exhibition in the Pentagon that compared load-carrying abilities of various four-engined transports. Tunner even persuaded Ernst Bevin, Britain's foreign minister, to take a tour of the C-97 during that official's visit to Berlin, to the deep consternation of aides who feared the worst as the overweight Bevin—who had just recuperated from a heart attack—huffed and puffed as he climbed aboard. Above all, by the end of the airlift Tunner's staff had whipped up a chart that was a model of persuasion, using straightforward bar graphs to compare the C-47, the C-54, and Tunner's plane of the future, the C-74, posting how many trips, how much flying time, how many crews, aircraft, maintenance men, and how much gasoline each model would have required to conduct the airlift all by itself. The results were clear, simple, and irrefutable. In an interview with the *Bee-Hive,* house organ of the United Aircraft Corporation, Tunner uttered the words of a prophet that "the airlift stands out in aviation like the first page in a wholly new chapter of history." He yanked out the faithful chart and started reeling off numbers, how the C-74 could fly a fraction of the trips the others made, at a greatly reduced cost.[53]

By then Tunner had gone even further. Experience merged with ideals, and he began designing the ideal transport plane for a subsequent era, fleshing it out to the point of a detailed model. That was not enough, however, so he began to publicize this whenever he could, in every available forum. A piece in *Aviation*

Week headlined, "Tunner Outlines 'Ideal' Cargo Plane," and then provided a list of his specifications. By April 1949, with the airlift under control, Tunner took the time to write a memo to General Muir Fairchild, Vice Chief of Staff of the U.S. Air Force, on "strategic, heavy duty transport aircraft" that stretched through four single-spaced pages with an equal size appendix that listed two pages of "Built-In Maintenance Items Desired" and another two on "Communications Requirements."[54]

Some members of the air force hierarchy listened and understood, but not all. Hoyt Vandenberg, for example, the man who had initially refused to send Tunner to Berlin, wrote that Tunner "has convinced us . . . that we can fly anything, anywhere, anytime," then added "that the future of military air transport is in big aircraft." Not all of these leaders were quite so enamored of Tunner and his passions, however, which would have important repercussions for both the airlift and for Tunner's career.[55]

11 / Rebellion

Maintenance seems prosaic; everyone changes the oil in their car. But it is also a necessity, since without it, machines stop running. Because of its critical role in keeping the airlift efficient, it caused Tunner to take dramatic steps, sparking a rebellion that revealed just how single-minded a leader he really was, regardless of the rules surrounding the uniform he wore. It also led to his most epic struggle with authority, a prolonged battle with serious consequences for him.

Maintenance, back in the days of the cowboy operation, was at times an improvised affair. On some occasions, to service the nose gear, personnel would move as many locals as they could to the rear of a C-54 till the plane tipped back onto its tail and permitted easy access to the front wheels.[1]

Tunner would have none of this. His first directive on this subject was the most important: maintenance schedules, the checks done every fifty, two hundred, one thousand hours of flight time, would now be followed scrupulously, no matter how many planes it took out of the air. Without this system, he understood, in time there would be no planes flying at all. One study showed that "the 'aircraft in commission' . . . figure has even more effect on tonnage into Berlin than the weather." At the height of the airlift, with 354 planes assigned to it, only 128 were actually flying at any time.[2]

Part of the problem was the airlift's enormous appetite for spare parts, as C-54s flew more in a month than they would in a year of normal service. A stock of windshield wipers expected to last six months evaporated in two weeks. Tires became a scarce commodity as did brakes and spark plugs. Other items became almost impossible to repair: high-tech radios, for example, clogged with coal dust and flour.[3]

Tunner's team used their usual methods, instituting a new form which kept a detailed history of every plane, and publicizing ideas for improved procedures that again covered every detail from air compressors to auxiliary generators.[4]

Above all, he instituted the same assembly-line maintenance procedures he had pioneered during the Hump. Once again, there were no crew chiefs, but a series of stands where mechanics performed the same operations over and over again. The C-54s arriving for the 200-hour checkup came in covered with oil and grease, with black coal dust fused into the wood flooring. The first stage, therefore, was to wash down the plane with a chemical solution under fifty pounds of pressure, followed by a water rinse that came out of the hose twice as hard. Some parts of the interior were still hand brushed when all else failed to remove the grit, and as much as fifty pounds of sugar, macaroni, coal dust, and flour could be removed from under the cargo floor. Even worse was the grime collected on the top of the plane, which resembled lamp black and could not be washed off. To remove this powerful residue, engineers took a thirty-six-foot-long de-icing cloth and rigged up a machine to run it across the upper part of the fuselage like a giant shoe-shine rag. Overall, getting the plane as clean as possible became a six-hour operation involving sixteen men.[5]

This was only the first stage. After that the craft moved to platforms where mechanics ran up the engine and performed diagnostic tests, basically writing the game plan for the rest of the inspection. From there the C-54 went through stages where experts repaired different systems, such as electronics or hydraulics, and then on to the sixth form where everything was checked to make sure that the work had been done satisfactorily.

But Tunner had hit a problem, in that there were not enough trained personnel to do the job. His staff had determined that to keep things going around the clock, they had to relentlessly maintain a crew of fifteen mechanics on every plane being overhauled, but as late as February 1949 only seven were assigned to the job.[6]

To make up the difference, he resorted to a strategy he had created back in Burma, to use locals to fill positions for the air force. As had happened in Asia, there were quite a few difficulties with this approach.

The initial hurdle was a stiff one. Though Tunner overcame it with stealth and tact, it revealed the cause of future problems. This crucial difficulty was the need to get approval for many of his ideas from higher authority.

Despite his all-powerful position running CALTF, Tunner was still in an or-

18. Mechanics at the Rhein-Main Air Base near Frankfurt work on a C-54 motor. Maintenance was a constant problem for Tunner and sparked his most dramatic challenge to authority during the Berlin Airlift. (National Archives photo, SC304550)

ganizational bind when it came to dealing with higher-ups, individuals whose approval he needed for many of his schemes. As one example, he had no authority to speak directly to Lucius Clay, head of the U.S. Military Government in Germany; all such requests, especially for parts and tools, had to go through the head of USAFE, at that point Curtis LeMay, who could alternatively be helpful or grumpy. If the latter, Tunner would effectively be hamstrung, not a position this activist entrepreneur enjoyed or took lightly.[7]

The fact was, Tunner had a serious organizational problem. Even though he was the commanding officer, Combined Airlift Task Force, this was still a part of USAFE, and he depended on them for all support functions, such as providing equipment and spare parts. This had the potential for turning into a monumental problem: not only could this administrative arrangement become a serious bottleneck, it was stealing credit from MATS, as Tunner was trying to establish this branch as the master of airlift. In a memo to Kuter on July 6, Tunner pointed out how this was the big moment for the United States to show what air transport could really do, and, "The unit *organized* specifically for heavy, sustained airlift is MATS" (emphasis in original). A month later he would write his boss, "The organization is not what you wanted, nor what I would have preferred, but higher authority determined it should be under USAFE."[8]

Mitigating this was the fact that LeMay used a light touch, giving Tunner a lot of leeway to run his own show. In August the CALTF commander wrote Kuter, "We have received magnificent cooperation in every respect. This job is the hottest thing . . . and they have given us top priority in everything." In his reply, Kuter remarked favorably on the "type of cooperation [we are] getting from Clay, LeMay & Co. in Germany."[9]

Sometimes, however, it was rough going. As Tunner gently put it in his memoirs, his Hump ideas "were not always understood" in LeMay's office, and by inference, the idea of using civilian German mechanics was one of those notions that did not get sent up to Clay.

Instead, chance intervened when, according to Tunner, he happened to be making a routine inspection at Tempelhof just as Clay was boarding a plane there, and the two exchanged greetings. The odds that this really was an accident, that the savvy Tunner did not plan to be there, seem as likely as the possibility that Tunner would become an advocate of rail service.

According to his account, Tunner claimed that at one stage in the cordialities, Clay asked him if he had any problems. In what must have been the most casual tone of voice, the airlift general replied that he did have a lack of maintenance men, "But I think I can whip it . . . if you will allow me to hire some skilled German mechanics." Clay replied quickly and easily, "Go ahead and do it. . . . Tell Curt I said it's O.K." That was that.

It was not so easy, by far; besides having bypassed chain of command and possibly irking USAFE staff, Tunner had actually taken a most controversial step. On the emotional level, there was the question of employing Luftwaffe veterans; it was one thing to hire women and children, or even men, to do manual labor; now the airlift was rewarding skilled personnel who had serviced the Nazi's air force.

There were also very serious security issues. All Germans hired by the U.S. military had to be screened to "prevent employment of undesirable individuals," especially war criminals. According to a report on Intelligence during the airlift, security officials had to create files for more than 5,000 individuals hired during the blockade. One occupation forces memo, for example, that was stored in a folder labeled "Suspicious Jokers," discussed the applications for work by four Berlin residents, who had files in the "NSDAP records at the

Berlin Documents Center." These searches, furthermore, would be conducted by a Counter-Intelligence Section that was overworked and never augmented, despite the radical increase in their workload. Even the Air Police Squadron at Rhein-Main received more resources than that, growing from 70 to 185 enlisted men to handle the expanded security needs of the airlift's key facility. As a result, many key steps, such as fingerprinting and issuing security badges, were handled in a haphazard manner. This would also be the first time in occupation history that German civilians would be allowed to do this level of work on air force planes, and as one precaution "no one individual would be given knowledge of the full operation of the airlift." CALTF received warnings that Germans would commit sabotage, ranging from bombs in the coal to tools in the machinery.[10]

Tunner ignored all these admonitions. According to his logic, "When a man has got a wife and children, and he is living in your community, he is depending on the pay you give, and his wife and children are depending on the pay he gets, do you think he is going to sabotage your planes?" Experience proved the accuracy of this judgment; there were no such incidents involving the use of German mechanics on the airlift.[11]

One of the first people he hired was the former Luftwaffe major general Hans Detlev Von Rohden, an air transport officer who had served at Stalingrad and who had authority among veterans; his former rank was as high as the one Tunner held while running the airlift. Von Rohden immediately took on several crucial tasks, such as recruiting workers and seeing that translators started working on the C-54 repair manuals. In addition, Tunner simply assigned him the job of personally vouching for anyone hired; years later, when asked if he had "any way of screening these mechanics," Tunner replied, "No. We had to rely on this German general."[12]

Most sources follow Tunner's manuscript in claiming that skilled workers flocked to the job after that, but military records show that it was a lot tougher. The CALTF took out ads in the Frankfurt papers and local radio stations (Rhein-Main is located just outside that city), as well as posting notices at the labor office, all with minimal results. Subsequent discussions revealed that while there were enough mechanics in the larger area, few of these men lived in Frankfurt, which had not had any aircraft industry facilities before the war. In addition, getting to and from Rhein-Main was difficult; seven miles from downtown was a long walk, one way.

Again, they found solutions. At a time when only half the roster of mechanics required had been signed up, CALTF agreed to find housing for the

German civilians on base, thus eliminating most of the problems. Improved local transportation cleared up much of the rest, and the employment quota was met. By the end of the airlift, there were German supervisors and technical translators working alongside these mechanics, workers whom the head of maintenance at one base claimed were "good—better than the G.I. with a sheet-metal M.O.S." (Military Occupational Specialty). Tunner wrote that by the end of his mission, there were actually more German mechanics than American working on airlift planes.[13]

These were all crucial issues to Tunner; he understood completely that no operation could continue for long if the planes were not kept up in a regular and professional manner. Dorothy Towne stated that Tunner was "a perfectionist when it came to maintenance of aircraft" and that he expected the same from every one of his mechanics: in his workshops there was "no dust on the floor." Ann Tunner also pointed out that her husband was "very, very strict" on this issue, how, "it wasn't just getting that tire fixed; that tire had to be mounted just right." This was an issue about which he showed no tolerance, and she added that "he wasn't very patient about mistakes on the ground. They were too costly once the mistake was put in the air."[14]

Thus, if there was one problem, one obstacle, that would set off a headstrong, entrepreneurial general who was conducting a holy crusade, it was this one. Maintenance would lead to his greatest rebellion against the lack of innovation that could sometimes overtake a hierarchical organization, and though he would win the battle, he would also acquire a reputation as a troublemaker in some powerful districts of the Pentagon, to the detriment of his career.

To put this in perspective, as the Berlin Airlift geared up, General William Tunner was at the height of his powers, locked into a crusade that he had come to believe in with the passion of a prophet. In his memoirs he declared that, "If the Berlin Airlift was to be successful—and I never had any doubts but that it would be—then it would be more than just an airlift." He had become a captain of industry, a Donald Douglas forcing innovations that would change the world for the better, someone who had a vision and the drive to see it through to reality. But his dream meant he was trying to transform a branch of the armed services, an institution with extreme structure and rules; as Red Foreman's widow put it, "He didn't strike me as being as military as some of the other men."[15]

Tunner's nemesis arrived that fall. In late September the Pentagon ordered Curtis LeMay to Omaha to take over the Strategic Air Command. His replacement was a lieutenant general named John Cannon, and nothing would be the same on the airlift after Cannon arrived.[16]

Unlike Tunner, Cannon was not a West Pointer; instead he graduated from Utah Agricultural College and entered the army in 1917 as a second lieutenant. By 1942 he was leading fighter and bomber units in the North African campaign and by December 1943 had become commanding general of both the Twelfth Air Force and the Mediterranean Allied Tactical Air Force, which ran all fighter units during the battles in Sicily and Italy. Even more important for Tunner, from August 1945 to March 1946 Cannon had headed USAFE, the post he was now returning to. This was a figure who was used to command, to running his own show, an air force model of a fighting general with lots of ties to the honchos running the service.[17]

There were plenty of reasons for him to clash with Tunner, too many. Part of it was the difference in age and careers; Cannon was a traditionalist, who worked his way up the ranks in standard fashion. Tunner, on the other hand, was what a later generation would call a "whiz kid." West Point at sixteen, with a fast career trajectory, so that he was always younger than the other men holding positions at his level, often by many years. His wife made the comment that "General Tunner was always young," and added judiciously about his opponents, "These were very educated and powerful generals, leaders in their own right . . . and looking back I can see it was probably a thorn for them to have this younger man come in and take over."[18]

But there was a far bigger gap in their experiences than just age. Cannon was a combat commander, not a transportation man, a difference that would cause outrage in both of them. One historian perceptively wrote that "Cannon, like . . . other combat fliers seemed . . . to look on the operation as a perhaps rather demanding but not essentially remarkable parcel-post service—just put the packages on those planes and get them off again. The proper business of a military pilot was to destroy the enemy, not deliver groceries." That flew in the face of everything Tunner believed with his heart and soul, everything he stood for and had staked his career on.[19]

Adding to this were problematic elements of Cannon's administrative style; the new head of USAFE was an extremely hands-on manager. In printed works Milton described Cannon as having a "love of detail, even trivia, and a desire to know everything that was going on," but in an interview with the author he was blunter, branding Cannon as "a nit picker kind of guy." This was the last thing Tunner could tolerate in the midst of the airlift.[20]

At the most basic level, there was a fundamental clash over who was in charge. Back when he had run USAFE the first time, Cannon had received a letter from Hap Arnold that "as top Air Advisor in Europe, you would have the facilities for coordinated action on all important air problems in Europe." Cannon's reply is significant; he wrote back that he was "in complete agreement with your thought for the establishment of a 'senior Army Air Force representative in Europe.' It is fundamental." He then went on to discuss some problem areas, even at that early stage: "An official communication from your Headquarters to *Air Transport Command,* the Group Control Councils and the AACS . . . would undoubtedly clarify the situation for all concerned" (emphasis added). Cannon, therefore, had already tangled with Tunner's outfit over issues of hierarchy and control. As Ann Tunner diplomatically remarked, always keeping the mission in mind, "I think it was . . . in all consideration, very hard for Joe Cannon—who was not a transportation person—to have someone at this particular time . . . come in and be telling everyone what to do." Her husband was less cordial, bluntly telling an interviewer, "General Cannon came over, apparently, with the idea that he was going to run the Berlin Airlift and I was determined he wasn't."[21]

More than at any other point in Tunner's career, this would be the prime example of how the air transport leader's entrepreneurial personality clashed with the hierarchical structure of the military. On the one hand, Tunner clearly had the expertise to run the show, and he was right on how to go about it. But in the air force, on the other hand, just like in any other service, rank commands. Cannon was the boss, and Tunner had an obligation to get along with him. There would be precious little evidence that Tunner did much to accomplish that goal, resenting any kind of direct supervision of the type that Cannon was far too willing to apply. There was no effort from him to smooth things over, to work within the structure and get what he needed that way. As the air force historian Daniel Harrington noted, "Reform and innovation don't occur in the abstract; they occur in institutions, and being right is just the start of the process."[22]

The two men clashed from the very start. Just days before Cannon's arrival, after long negotiations, the United States had signed an agreement with the British creating CALTF, with Tunner as commander, and a British officer as deputy commander. The purpose was obvious, to set up a unified command structure to run the airlift, eliminating friction and inefficiency. LeMay signed an agreement that joined the two nations' work "in order that the resources of each participating service may be utilized in the most advantageous manner," with a simple, straightforward goal that must have warmed Tunner's insides, to deliver to Berlin "the maximum tonnage possible."[23]

Then General Cannon arrived, thinking the situation was going to be just like it was when he ran USAFE back in 1945, when Hap Arnold had made him a most supreme of commanders. And even Tunner admitted that at that moment he was "forty-two, cocky and confident in my knowledge of air transport and the ability of my staff to carry out its duties, and I did not feel that I needed any advice from an aging combat man of fifty-six years."[24]

Cannon took one look at the new agreement and exploded, yelling, "What the hell is this? . . . What are you trying to do to me?" While the source is Tunner's writings, it rings true, the kind of thing a powerful officer would bark at a cheeky subordinate. It was also foolish policy, given the necessity for the kind of command structure Tunner then enjoyed. Tunner smoothed over things for the moment, telling the head of USAFE that this had been worked on for some time, and that they had, in fact, sought to complete the matter before Cannon arrived, so that he did not have to waste time getting brought up to date on a complicated and delicate matter.

If that pacified Cannon, it was only a brief respite. Soon after came the written orders that would be the bane of Tunner's airlift existence. From that point forward, Cannon informed him, he could have no contact with any higher-up in any part of the service. This was not only final, but comprehensive; Tunner could not even contact his own outfit, MATS headquarters in Washington, to ask for help or supplies. That last point was a real sore spot, and it meant immense trouble for the airlift. Up till then, when Tunner was running short of anything—parts, people, or planes—he contacted Kuter, who, not surprisingly, given their relationship and shared belief in air transport, came through for Tunner. He claimed that up till this time, "General Kuter turned out to be 'true blue' . . . and when I needed something, he would provide it." Now instead, Tunner had specific written orders, reinforced verbally in a session that can only be imagined, that he was not, under any circumstances whatsoever, to contact MATS in any way, shape, or form. Instead, all requests would be handled through the offices of USAFE. This was a direct order, presented in both typed and oral form.[25]

The worst part was not Cannon's constant interference from that point on, although that was tough enough. Tunner wanted to be left alone to carry on his mission, the individual entrepreneur breaking down barriers, while Cannon, whom he referred to as his "American master," was constantly demanding explanations and data, asking, "Why did I do this, why did I not do this?" That kind of intervention—common in the military—must have gotten under Tunner's skin something awful, but it was not a threat to the operation and was not what led him to fight back.[26]

The real issue was a slow down in operations and materials, keys to good maintenance and a constant supply of planes. As the airlift grew, as the mission got more complex, obstacles cropped up, except that now Tunner had no authority to kick butt and make things happen if the problem was not under his direct command. The 1,000-hour inspections, a major overhaul, had to be done back in the States, but something had gone afoul with that pipeline. In November he reported to Cannon that a job that should have taken twenty-two days per plane had instead ranged from forty-four to eighty-eight days, with an average of fifty-seven. By then sixty-seven C-54s had been sent back home, but only eighteen had come back.[27]

Even the European situation was worsening when it came to maintenance. The most important stage of the schedule was the 200-hour check, originally done at a USAFE base in the German town of Oberpfaffenhofen, which Americans never learned how to pronounce. Tunner assigned Major Jules Prevost, who had been a maintenance executive at Pan American Airlines before the war, to institute the assembly-line system, but this facility was small and with limited space, much of it outdoors. Tunner had to find something better.[28]

The answer was the base at Burtonwood in England, which had been used during the Second World War as a major Eighth Air Force repair depot. Clearly it was large enough to take over full responsibility for 200-hour checks for what was becoming one of the world's great air fleets; the perimeter alone was over seventy miles long.[29]

That was the good news; there was plenty of bad as well. Burtonwood was just outside Liverpool, and had been run down—Tunner described it as "dingy, dirty, and depressing looking. Living quarters . . . were cold and dank. The chow was greasy and tasteless." One of the G.I.s in the first detachment to check out the new base reported, "We climbed off a TWA Constellation and into mud." Lumber was nonexistent locally, so crews at Oberpfaffenhofen actually had to build work stands then have them flown back to England and reconstructed at the new facility. Housing was a huge problem, as England was still in the midst of severe shortages and little could be spared by way of construction materials, and it was even a big deal to get U.S. personnel assigned there. The cold war became the first time in seven centuries that foreign military forces were established in Great Britain during a time of peace, and special arrangements of all sorts had to be made.[30]

Within no time, Burtonwood was falling behind. In November, when the transfer took place, Oberpfaffenhofen, which was being phased out, still managed to complete 45 inspections, compared to only 18 at Burtonwood. But there were lots more planes in the lift by then, so as a result of Burtonwoods' failure, 102 others had to receive their 200-hour care at all the other bases on an ad hoc basis, 24 at Rhein-Main and 9 at Fassberg, for example, sites that had their hands full with daily maintenance and just making sure planes got off the ground fully loaded. In addition, they had had mechanics stripped from their workforce and reassigned to Burtonwood, in order to centralize this function, making this an even more severe burden. By December, Burtonwood was up to 49 inspections, but this was still far below expectations, only a quarter of what Tunner had expected they could handle by then. That was actually fewer than 2 planes a day, at a time when Tunner had expected 7 C-54s to be processed in that same twenty-four-hour span. He was now facing a shortfall of 35 planes a week, and again, the local bases had to take up the slack.[31]

In the face of this dramatic shortfall, Tunner was helpless. While Oberpfaffenhofen had been a CALTF facility, Burtonwood was strictly USAFE. Tunner flew over, his experts flew over, recommendations were put in writing, and everything got blocked by air materiel officers at USAFE. At the same time, he was restricted by direct order from contacting anyone in Washington for help, and could not even ask for assistance from maintenance specialists in the Pentagon. One sympathetic historian wrote that Tunner was "reduced to listening to excuses and empty promises."[32]

As deadly serious as this was, it was still not Tunner's foremost vexation. Dorothy Towne commented that "General Tunner knew it could work if we had what we needed." This was a general who believed that his men should be worked hard, but also backed by every resource the service had. Now the pipeline had clogged; whereas before Tunner—and the airlift—could often get what they needed within four days, it took that long for a requisition just to make it through the USAFE labyrinth.[33]

For the first time, Tunner's men did not have supplies and tools, down to basics like wrenches and screwdrivers. It was one thing to face the weather, to make men work in cold conditions for long hours; to begrudge them the very instruments and parts they needed to do their jobs was intolerable. A seventy-two-hour supply of all critical materials was downgraded to less than twenty-four hours' worth, a dangerous situation; at one point a plane sat on the ground for five days without parts, till the necessary components arrived. Ann Tunner told how her husband's "big worry always was equipment for his crew chiefs. . . . He used to beg for screwdrivers and pliers."[34]

In reports covering October through December, Tunner tried to bring attention to his shortfalls. These documents described a situation where service personnel at the Rhein-Main Air Base had "no overcoats, winter underwear and winter socks." It was becoming apparent that "the real threat to successful operation of the airlift was not weather but unavailability of parts." During October, for example, more planes were grounded at the end of the month than at the beginning, because "the increase in the assigned fleet had not been met by a proportionate increase in availability of parts."[35]

Making this even worse, Tunner was convinced that everything he needed was available locally. He could not get his hands on any of it, however, not just because of USAFE's poor attitude, but due to what he felt was sheer incompetence and bureaucratic butt covering. According to his memoirs, just outside of Munich, in a town called Erding, was a depot that had been used as a dumping ground by the U.S. military after the war for surplus items. Everything and anything had wound up there, tons and tons of supplies of every kind, including tools and airplane parts. No one, however, had kept any record. But the goods were there.[36]

As a result of this unusual situation, USAFE became hesitant to either inventory Erding, or to request additional supplies from stateside. If they had done the former, the information would have been used as an excuse to cut back the current flow of supplies, and if they went too far in following the later course, they risked being told that the request was excessive, in light of what might be found near Munich.

This contradictory state of affairs incensed Tunner. He wrote that pettiness of that sort "was no concern of mine. I needed those replacement parts and tools right then and there. I didn't care where they came from." Through the rage came the mission, and also the greatest fear. "I had a daily tonnage to meet," he admonished. "If I was short one day, I would have little opportunity, particularly with the weather . . . to make it up. On November 30, for example, one of those pea-soup fogs began to close in on Berlin. You couldn't drive a car in the city that day, much less land a plane. Of forty-two planes that took off for the city, one landed." There was only one answer: "To make it up, I needed the full support and cooperation of the headquarters directed to furnish that support."

Tunner never forgot this affront—not only to him but to his mission and his men—and never forgave. In a post-airlift CALTF report on training and operations, for example, the message got rammed home as often as possible. One section began by pointing out that "The accomplishment of the Communications section was hampered by the existence of a dual command which caused many delays, conflicting orders, and retarded efficiency." A project to increase the Rhein-Main telephone exchange by two hundred lines had been "delayed by the difficulty experienced in obtaining the equipment which was available in the zone," and work that should have taken fifteen days to accomplish required six months, "due to the existing supply set-up." In addition, the failure of USAFE to provide procedures for the use of air-ground radio "caused much confusion and was responsible for the illegal use of this facility by many organizations. . . . The Communications Officer took this matter up with headquarters, USAFE but no tangible action was ever taken to eliminate the problem." In a 1961 interview, Tunner declared, "I could not get parts, engines, and supplies directly. I had to go through someone else to get them. That took time, and it was aggravating. Time was crucial."[37]

Things came to a boil at Christmas, and the catalyst was, of all people, Bob Hope. The great entertainer had scheduled a holiday show for the men of the airlift, and Washington turned it into a legitimate extravaganza of support for the troops. Besides entertainers like Hope, Irving Berlin, and Jinx Falkenberg, the roster would include Vice President Alben Barkley, Secretary of the Army Kenneth Royall, and most intriguing of all, Secretary of the Air Force Stuart Symington. Everyone from Tunner to the lowliest private was inundated with advance publicity on every media from *Stars and Stripes* to Armed Forces Radio, and as the big date wound near, they were primed for a good time.[38]

On December 23, at the very last minute, Tunner got the schedule. There would be two shows, the first on Christmas Eve at USAFE headquarters in downtown Wiesbaden, another on Christmas Day in a similar central location in Berlin. Both spots were far, far away from any CALTF air base, and it was unlikely that many of his men would ever be able to make the show.

Tunner was livid over this slight to the men he believed in so dearly; "It was my Airlift boys, working their butts off around the clock, who deserved that Hope show." The official record of the staff conference that afternoon stated, "General Tunner expressed his extreme displeasure over the Bob Hope show which had been billed as a show for the Airlift," but he candidly corrected this later with the line, "Extreme displeasure indeed! I was mad clear through."

Even that barely cuts the surface of the anger he must have felt—and would display to his superiors.

Tunner "knew full well that events of this magnitude . . . had certainly been approved by General Cannon, but that didn't stop me." He immediately blasted off a memo to USAFE that either Hope appeared at CALTF bases, or he would insist that all mention of the airlift—the fundamental reason Hope had chosen to visit at this time—would be removed from advance notices and publicity of all and any kinds. That was a powerful threat and an effective one. USAFE ruled that CALTF personnel had priority at both the Wiesbaden and Berlin events, and got Hope to schedule three more performances at the airlift bases themselves, including one at beleaguered Fassberg. Hope, with no idea of the behind-the-scenes drama, graciously and easily agreed to the extra performances. As a result, a great many airmen who would otherwise have been frozen out at a lonely time in a cold place, got to see something special.

But Tunner's rebellion did not stop there. On Christmas Day, Secretary Symington, the official most concerned with how the airlift was going, asked for and received a thorough tour of Rhein-Main Air Base. Tunner served as guide, although naturally and legitimately, Cannon tagged along; no commanding officer ever would, or should let a dignitary of that rank go unattended.

According to Tunner, Symington was the epitome of the concerned professional, asking about every iota of how things were running, including speaking to the men, asking them "intelligent and pertinent questions."

The story Tunner told about his big breakthrough went like this: Symington stopped in front of a mechanic; suddenly confronted by a lieutenant general, a major general, and a civilian who looked mighty important, he wisely moved to put down his tools and salute. The secretary of the air force told him, "Relax," introduced himself, and added, "Just wanted to see how you're getting along with that engine." The mechanic replied, "Oh, I'm going to get it fixed all right, sir . . . but I could do it better if I had better tools."

That fat was in the fire now. Symington pressed, "What's the matter with your tools?" At the point the serviceman picked up a screwdriver, wrench, and pliers. "See these?" he barked, "Well I bought 'em myself here in Germany and they're all I got, and I can't get any more, and they ain't worth a good goddamn."

Silence. Tunner quietly beaming, Cannon quietly seething. Then it was all out in the open, as Symington turned to the head of CALTF and grumbled, "This is what you've been telling me all along." Tunner knew he had won the battle to get what his men needed, and wisely kept his mouth shut, as Cannon turned the shade of a cooked lobster.

Afterward, Symington wanted to know everything, in black and white, and roughly yesterday. Tunner and all his team spent Christmas Day and the day after working without stop to prepare the monumental report, "Supply and Maintenance Problems—First Airlift Task Force." Everything from poor tools to worse facilities was documented, with recommendations for improvement in every category. USAFE received a carbon copy.

All this has gone down in history in Tunner's words; there is little in the way of a corroborating account. Evidence in the files of Air Mobility Command (MATS' successor), however, shows that there was more to the story than Tunner described. First, the general and Symington were old acquaintances. In August, for example, the secretary, along with air force Chief of Staff Hoyt Vandenberg, traveled to Germany, according to Tunner, "for the express purpose of looking over this operation." The CALTF commander had "several informal conferences with both of them," and the visitors even "showed considerable interest in the maintenance setup."[39]

Thus, it is likely that the story was embellished, that Tunner had much easier access to Symington than his account indicates. Nevertheless, the CALTF commander had his staff draft a powerful memo. Back in October, Tunner had sent Symington a list of what was required to make the airlift work. Now, reviewing what had been accomplished and what had failed, the memo noted that the earlier piece had called for "an adequate stock and flow of supplies and equipment including C-54 spare parts, engines, tires, communications equipment, etc. in order that the Airlift Task Force will not be grounded by shortages or deficiencies." Instead, the new memo argued, "Stock and flow of supplies and equipment have not been adequate." This document was dated December 23, just around the time of the incident Tunner talked about in his memoirs, and after that supplies began to flow again. The fact was, whatever the background story, Tunner had gone directly to senior authority, over the head of Cannon.[40]

Tunner had been right in everything he asked for, but it was a pyrrhic victory. Raymond Towne wrote humorously, "Let us draw the curtain of charity over the choleric effect this had on the theater commander," but Milton was much more blunt. Tunner, he explained, "thought nothing at all of bypassing military chains of command to get what he wanted, so he went straight to the Secretary or anybody he thought could help. The airlift as far as he was concerned was the most important thing." But this came at high cost, "He didn't

care the least whose feet he stepped on to get what he needed. You make enemies when you behave that way, but he didn't care, it didn't bother him." Tunner would not submit to military hierarchy—would not give a hoot about it if
it threatened the mission.[41]

The conflict did not end there, in a welter of different, little ways. One
memo late in the airlift on "Air Installation Difficulties" stressed that of all the
problems they faced, dual command was "the worst headache . . . a situation
with which it was most difficult to cope." Cannon, on the other hand, retali-
ated whenever and wherever he could. One of Tunner's pet projects was a final
report on the airlift, a work that could be used to show just what airlift could
accomplish. By the time it was due to appear in late 1949 Tunner had already
been reassigned, and Cannon did everything in his power to block publication,
and even attempted to impound the copies in a move that was possibly against
air force regulations.[42]

Throughout these disagreements, Tunner remained true to his nature. He
was the innovator, and this was the crucial moment that would make or break
his dream of military airlift. But that drive, that vision, that entrepreneurial
personality also made him single-minded and even thoughtless, and did not
win him any friends in the highly structured air force. Milton remembered that
Tunner "wouldn't make any effort" to calm the waters with higher-ups in his
passion to make the airlift work, that "he didn't seem to care about how he got
along with his contemporaries. He didn't seem to care." No one—in business
or the military—can afford that kind of attitude. Tunner was blind to anything
but his cause.[43]

In the long run, Tunner's intransigence hurt him more than the airlift. The
planes flew, and the city was saved. But his career was not.

William Tunner paid a price for his dreams and his drive, his unwillingness
to let anyone get in the way of his vision or hurt his men. Some of the leaders
in the Pentagon recognized what he had done for the air force; others resented
his overt rebellion against superior officers and took umbrage at it, regardless of his accomplishments; in some circles, Tunner was a troublemaker. On
April 8, 1949, for example, as the airlift peaked, General Muir Fairchild, vice
chief of staff of the air force, wrote Tunner about some recent correspondence
he had gotten from the airlift leader. Tunner had stressed the need for "strategic, heavy-duty transport aircraft," in all likelihood not the first memo he had
sent on this subject. Fairchild bluntly replied, "You know the present picture
on" these types of planes, "and consequently . . . you realize that it will be a long

time before any . . . of your suggestions would materialize." The senior officer concluded, "We are proud of the job you and your people are doing on the Airlift." There was a compliment in this reply, but also a reprimand.[44]

This was not an isolated case. In December 1948, at the height of the airlift with transport showing what it could do on a global scale, the air force held a series of analytical discussions at Maxwell Air Force Base. These were attended by top staff, including General Hoyt Vandenberg, air force chief of staff, its highest officer.

It did not go well for air transport, despite what they were doing across the Atlantic. Kuter, who was present, felt that "the period for commentary and questions, after the MATS presentation, opened in a tone that was neither absolutely objective nor noticeably sympathetic." It was so bad, he felt compelled to write Vandenberg to complain and set the record straight.[45]

More drastic steps would follow in the years to come. In 1950 Tunner got passed over for the job of commanding MATS, an unbelievable slight given that at that point he was the foremost authority on military transport in the world. Instead, the position went to Joseph Smith, the hard-working, more senior but establishment officer who had preceded Tunner in getting the airlift started, back in the days of the "cowboy operation." But Smith was also a confirmed Tunner opponent, who felt the airlift commander was a glory hound. In a later interview, Smith said of Tunner and CALTF, "He didn't create this MATS command for anybody but himself, for his own glorification."[46]

That same year, the air force appointed General Nathan Twining as deputy chief of staff for personnel, later raised him to vice chief of staff, and then in 1953, to chief of staff for the United States Air Force. During the Second World War, he had headed the Fifteenth Air Force in Italy and the Mediterranean Allied Strategic Air Forces, the bomber equivalent of the tactical command Cannon held. It is inconceivable that the men were in anything but close contact. In his new executive capacity, Twining would write in Tunner's efficiency report that the younger man had, according to one account, an "irascible personality," which had a "detrimental effect . . . on his leadership ability." Tunner's methods and personality were not always appreciated in the air force, and this affected his career in substantial ways.[47]

12 / The Test

Now, however, as the weather darkened, any difficulties with Cannon, any concern for career, were overshadowed by the supreme test. Germany in the winter becomes a nightmare; it lies on roughly the same latitude as Labrador, but serves as the meeting ground for cold North Sea gusts blowing south, which confront the warm air of the Gulf Stream. The result is moisture and blinding fogs, and above all, some of the most unpredictable weather patterns in the world, the last thing that Tunner, with his drive to regulate and industrialize airlift, could have wanted. One French diplomat exclaimed, "It is customary in Berlin to mention the weather only when it is a clear day." In order to highlight the difficulties, one air force historian pointed out that in ranking the weather at American airports, Pittsburgh would come in near the bottom. If it was set against German cities, however, it would jump right to the top; Daniel Harrington explained, "In other words, the worst American weather was better than the best German weather—and Berlin had the worst flying weather in all of Germany."[1]

Everyone knew this was coming; in July *U.S. News and World Report* had declared, "The United States can fly in food, but it cannot fly in enough coal for the Germans. That is when the real crisis may come." Now that crisis had arrived. A writer in the *New Republic* reported, "Nights are growing chilly, and every Berliner knows that when the hard winter comes he will be at best cold and hungry," amid "fears that he will have no coal and less food than during any previous winter since the end of the war—there are rumors that there will be no space heating, that is, no heating of places where ordinary people live." He remarked on the sense of dread, how the threat of cold and suffering "breaks down the defiant, desperate hope that Americans *will* stay, that the airlift *will* continue through the winter and that things will *not* be as bad as they might be" (emphasis in original). *Collier's* claimed that Berlin's "pace slowed ominously until, suddenly, nearly everyone was cold and afraid." One lady told their reporter that "you can always tell what kind of winter it will be in Berlin by the number of people who kill themselves in November," amid widespread rumors that suicides had hit an all-time high. Ruth Andreas-Friedrich wrote in her diary, "The nights are getting longer, the days are getting cooler. Whenever one runs into an acquaintance on the street, he asks, 'Do you have coal? Do you know where there is any coal?'" During a giant rally near the Brandenburg Gate, demonstrators clashed with Russian soldiers who fired on some of the protesters and wounded them; nevertheless, the civilians managed to pull down the flag the Soviets had set atop the monument, and a small boy ran off with the splintered pole. When quizzed by a reporter from the *Christian Century* as to why he had done such a courageous thing, the child replied, "The winter is coming. We need firewood."[2]

The Russians just laughed. They had seen what had happened when one tried airlifts in the winter, and Stalingrad put paid to that. A cartoon in an East Berlin paper mocked everything the West was attempting: under the caption, "Winter in Berlin," a pilot was seen dropping a single lump of coal attached to a small parachute. The message was clear; the airlift would fail in a few months, and the Western Allies would starve or leave.[3]

Pressure built on Tunner from all sides. Twenty years later, knowing what had happened, he still described the impending climate change as "a North German winter with little daylight and with rain and fog and snow which seemed to hang on day after day through this mean season." Even worse, despite the weather, the pace of shipments now had to *increase* in order to bring in the extra amount of coal needed to heat homes as the temperatures dropped. Burtonwood was still only performing a fraction of the maintenance checks it would have to complete to keep his planes in the air, and would not meet the quota till March, after the crisis had passed. The Russians then added to his misery by clamping down on the West-East Berlin gateways; before they had been lenient, and Westerners could augment rations by trading with the Communists. In October, even this was no longer possible as guards shut down all pathways. Everything they needed to make it till the spring had to be brought in by Tunner's planes.[4]

But the stakes had now become much higher than even the lives of two million Berliners. *Newsweek* wrote, "The dispute over Berlin has gone far beyond a wrangle over currency, beyond retaliation for the establishment of a Western German State, beyond Soviet determination simply to make Berlin untenable for Western powers." Instead, "it has now become a vast test of strength and prestige in which the West so far has defeated the Russians at their own game by means of the airlift—the airlift that has inspired even Berliners to turn on the Soviets with a sort of rabbit-bites-dog courage." Berlin, in other words, had become the first true and great East-West confrontation of the cold war, the first epic battle between the United States and the Soviet Union, and victory could only be achieved by Tunner's airlift, a mission that at one time only he thought possible.[5]

As October merged into the cold month when Americans celebrated Thanksgiving, the forecast was troubling. On November 13 one of the all-time great fogs in European history settled on Berlin, a blanket one thousand feet thick that his weather forecasters told Tunner might last for weeks; on November 18 only twenty-five planes took off from the big U.S. base at Rhein-Main. Over the next month, Fassberg had to reduce its flights by 23 percent—almost one-quarter—and Gatow was down 18 percent. British Sunderland flying boats could no longer land, so these missions had to be scrubbed, and on some days in December, only ten planes made it to Berlin.[6]

The numbers began to drop. In September CALTF had managed 19,766 flights, but in October this dipped slightly, down to 18,235. November, however, was a potential disaster, with half the month covered in that thick fog; flights plummeted to a figure of 13,574, a 31 percent downturn from September. During October, the airlift had managed to still average 4,761 tons a day, just over the 4,500 ton minimum, but during the first week of November all they could do was 2,700 tons a day. On November 3, pilots managed to bring in only 2,000 tons, the worst they had managed since Black Friday back in August. The eleventh month had 720 hours, and during 210 of these—a full 30 percent—the weather numbers were below even minimum flying conditions, 444 had conditions so bad that even instrument landings were precluded, and a scant 63 hours in the month had skies clear enough to allow visual flight rules to take effect. When the weather finally broke one day, Tunner pushed everyone to deliver maximum loads, writing the air force assistant vice chief of staff, "everyone stays on his toes awaiting the weather breaks," then "we use every hour that is available for flying." Nevertheless, as one air force historian lamented, "One clear day simply added to the frustration of many bad ones." December was a little better, but still low, with 16,405 flights. British pilot

Howard Myers described what it was like those days, flying on a "miserable, cold, snowy night." Ice plated his wings and became lodged in his carburetors. He had to feather one engine in his C-47, but even that was not enough as he lost speed and altitude. The only solution left was to jettison cargo, and years later he still wondered "what people on the ground over Soviet-controlled East Germany must have thought as over 4,000 pounds of macaroni came raining out of the sky on that cold winter night."[7]

Back-stocked supplies in Berlin began to reach dangerously low levels. By January, there was only a thirty-one-day supply of food left, just a month, and even less coal: nineteen days, or less than three weeks, before the city went dark and froze. Fog returned in February, and the Berlin airfields had to shut down for 122 hours, a 40 percent increase from the average of 87 hours. The RAF began flying out children, more than fifteen thousand of them. On November 22, Ruth Andreas-Friedrich confided to her diary, "Our reserves are depleted. When we go to bed we dress as if heading for an expedition to Greenland."[8]

Tunner took emergency steps. Whenever the weather cleared, they would fly their hearts out, fill the skies with planes; on December 11, at Gatow, CALTF planes made 278 landings in two hours. In addition, he pulled the last of the C-47s from the American routes; to maximize tonnage, the only plane in use would be the larger C-54. It was not enough, however, and new ways had to be found to beat winter, one of humankind's oldest and most-enduring enemies.[9]

The first answer was science, providing eyes that could see through storm clouds. General Smith had taken a small step in that direction, asking the armed forces radio to stay on the air all night, providing an electronic fix for pilots flying in.[10]

Tunner went much further. To give some idea of what it meant to rely on electronic aids, in 1948 radar was less than fifteen years old, and thus a younger technology than the personal computer at the time this book was written. The experts in Berlin had wanted a huge AN/CPN-18 system, but it was too big to fit in any plane that was flying into that city. Instead, by November, crews were starting to install a large CPS-5 radar at Tempelhof, with completion on December 27, a slightly delayed but extremely welcome Christmas gift. This new system could pick up planes eighty-five miles out, well back in the corridors; by the time the planes were fifty miles away, controllers were doing precision spacing adjustments. By early spring, this system was controlling traffic at all three airports, overseeing that common incoming path that Tunner had pioneered during the construction of the Tegel Airfield. Inside the radar facility were six 12-inch screens, assigned in pairs to each of Berlin's three airports. The first controller tracked each plane from the farthest point then handed the craft over to his twin, hunched over what became known as a "feeder scope," who then vectored them from the main route into the local system, to each individual airport's GCA (Ground Control Approach) controller. This meant that the main control for all landing fields was centered in one room, and that landing officers could see and understand what was going on in the skies all around the city. If there were difficulties at one field, for example, that knowledge was known instantaneously by everyone, and adjustments could be made immediately. After the CPS-5 got working, there was never again a midair collision on the Berlin Airlift.[11]

For the final approach, Tunner arranged for smaller ground control radars to be installed at each airport. These were not as up-to-date as the CPS-5; the systems were MPN-1s, the oldest GCA units in use among American forces. They had come out of the factory in 1943 and 1944, and each had several thousand hours of use already behind them. By modern standards, these were beyond primitive, using 700 vacuum tubes. At each airport, a trailer big enough for the machine plus four operators housed this equipment, tracking the pilots and bringing them in at night, in fog, in snow, and in rain. They used a system designed by the American physicist Luis Alvarez, that employed two radio beams, one laying out an ideal flight path, the other tracking an incoming plane, and then comparing the two. As the landing proceeded, the controller would constantly refer back and forth, talking the pilot down to a safe landing.[12]

One of the reporters covering the airlift wrote, "The pilot must have complete faith in the GCA man's ability to keep him from flying into the ground." Finding men who could do this job was no easy task, as most of the air force's controllers had left the service after World War II. After Black Friday, this had come up in the comprehensive review of procedures Tunner had ordered, and he was well aware of the shortcomings of the system he inherited, and what that meant for the upcoming winter campaign. As early as August 21, 1948, he informed his boss at MATS, General Kuter, that "one fact that [has been] brought out very forcibly is that there appear to be no traffic controllers in the Air Force . . . they are traffic followers rather than controllers." This was acceptable during the summer, but as things got cold, "the magnitude of this operation and the tight schedules which we must maintain with split-minute timing have showed how critical this lack is. . . . I foresee great difficulty if we are not furnished with some competent traffic controllers soon," and requested twenty-eight experienced personnel be transferred to him at once.[13]

Kuter came through. By September 2 he could write Tunner that twenty new men were coming over, many of them called back from civilian work with the Civil Aviation Authority on a Priority One basis; one fellow got word on Saturday that he was back in uniform, and by Friday was bringing in planes over Tempelhof. The unit in charge of this, known as AACS (Airways and Air Communication Services), eventually had 408 men working the airlift from all the bases, with 129 of them stationed in Berlin. One of these men told how "they came at us in blocks of 18 planes. There were usually three aircraft on final approach, and that took a lot of concentration."[14]

This system, in the infancy of an electronics revolution, may have been pioneering, but like all first efforts, was extremely limited. Unlike today's ever-constant Doppler radar, the antenna in those days turned only five times a minute, a sweep every twelve seconds; one controller, looking back, exclaimed, "Thank God, planes flew slow in those days." A pilot flying this route claimed that GCA "brought us all the way in until we either broke out or ran out of guts"; his personal minimum was a scant one hundred feet or one-quarter mile of visibility, although this went out the window once Tunner's rules went into effect. Some pilots wound up earning a nickname as a "senior smogger and fogger," someone who landed in any kind of weather.[15]

Despite this, the new electronic age worked, and did a lot to beat the weather and save the airlift. In a speech delivered in January, General Kuter claimed that GCA was working "five times as fast as it has ever done before," landing a plane at one of the Berlin airports every fifty seconds around the clock (the real figure was more like one every three minutes). He also quoted the Civil Aeronautics Board's air safety inspector to the effect that what Tunner was doing "has advanced the art of traffic control ten years." As early as October, before the big new radar arrived, but after Black Friday and the GCA rule, AACS controllers somewhere in the operation had radio contact with an airlift plane on the average of four a minute; Tempelhof alone was contacting one plane for each minute of the day. By the end of the crisis, that one airport was making more GCA approaches than occurred at all the airports in the United States combined, only 2 percent of which resulted in a missed opportunity and a return to Germany, despite weather. One experienced airman explained, "When we came in and set up the task force, I would have sworn . . . that you could not make GCA landings at intervals better than twenty minutes apart," and marveled at the three-minute precision that soon became common.[16]

Pilots spoke of miracles; a typical flyer, Jack Bennett, told how "the radar coverage from the ground was incredibly accurate. If our plane crept or fell back, even a few feet . . . radar would warn us to adjust our airspeed. . . . We couldn't believe it was possible to fly this accurately." In addition, the controllers learned to be the human voice, the sound that brought peace to a scared pilot. Gail Halvorsen said, "With radar the fellow could pick you up about half-way to Berlin and say, 'I've got you on radar,' and his voice is calm no matter what the weather." Ross Milton always remembered his favorite controller, a Sergeant McNulty, who went beyond the formalized traffic commands and added little touches like, "Ahh, that's nice. You're perfect. You're right in." Milton remarked, "He amused us because he was very good at his job and seemed to take a lot of pleasure in it."[17]

In time, pilots would land planes in fog that became so thick that once on the ground they could not find their unloading stands, and had to follow the rear lights of a jeep to get into position. Roger G. Miller, an air force historian and author of a book on the lift, stated, "The extensive use of GCA . . . aided by the close relationship between the controllers and the aircrews, was probably the most important single technical factor in the success of the Berlin Airlift."[18]

It was not, however, the only technical aid Tunner brought out to try and make the airlift work during those cold months. He also had installed new and powerful sodium approach lights, a project fraught with difficulties. It turned out that the best place for the lights was along an approach path that came down over a cemetery. Installing lights meant moving graves, which Berlin officials readily agreed to, but it provided the Communists with images of Americans committing sacrileges against the dead. After that came the problem of what to put the lights on top of; with building materials in short supply, the lights would sit at ground level at the end of the runway, but rise in height to 75 feet as they extended along the flight path. Airport workers noticed the one supply that came in regularly, the pierced steel planking used to maintain runways, and began welding them together to create makeshift towers. The lights that topped these installations were the best of their kind in the world, and Gatow got theirs before the main airport in London, Heathrow.[19]

The pilots and controllers may have been able to see better, but bad weather could still force planes to stay on the ground. Ice was a major worry, able to clog control surfaces and add so much weight to a plane that it became unmanageable. There was not much Tunner could do for planes that began icing up in the air, beyond making sure the standard systems were up to par, but he could definitely improve conditions prior to takeoff. The first idea was to sluice down iced-up planes with a mixture of kerosene and alcohol, but eventually a strange hi-tech solution came into place. Maintenance workers mounted a fully functioning jet engine on a truck bed, and then brought over planes—carefully, and at the proper distance—to get a defrost in the quickest manner imaginable.[20]

The general also had to know as much about atmospheric changes as possible; if intelligence wins battles, the airman's version is often weather forecasting. The difference of a quarter mile in ceiling height, for example, often decided whether a flight could make it in or had to be turned back.

Men had to know what the weather was like if the airlift was to succeed. At one point every seventh C-54 had an order that the radio operator must call in conditions at four points along the line, so that headquarters got an accurate reading of changing atmospheric patterns. At a time when the entire U.S. Air Force had only ten B-17s specially equipped for gathering weather data, Tunner managed to get several of them assigned to his command, and one of these rode shotgun, above the corridors of C-54s, as often as was necessary to give flight officers the information they needed. Tunner got more and more weather squadrons assigned to CALTF, till, in typical business fashion, he centralized authority of local operations by creating a Master Control Weather Station to coordinate all information. Finally, he insisted that all this effort had to produce results that could keep planes in the air; before Black Friday weather reports got issued every six hours, but after that the general made clear that hourly updates would be new standard operating procedure.[21]

The goal, of course, was to keep every possible plane in the air at all times. Tunner now commanded a fleet that included most of the United States military's air transport, but he also needed enough pilots to keep these planes in the air. This was no easy task, as new airmen assigned to the lift had a difficult time adjusting to the difficult circumstances there; many had never even flown the C-54 before. Tunner knew that during winter everything had to go up as soon as the weather cleared; he had no minutes left over for a pilot learning how to land at Tempelhof and missing his approach.

The ever-reliable Kuter established a unique training base for Tunner's pilots. It turned out that the weather in Montana was similar to that in Germany, and MATS turned the Great Falls Air Force Base into as close a recreation of Tempelhof, Wiesbaden, and the other lift bases as they could manage. Everything was done to duplicate conditions overseas, as pilots flew C-54s laden with ten tons of sandbags on the same magnetic headings as were used in Germany, and landed on a shortened runway to get a feel for what it was like to come into Tempelhof; local conditions provided constant fog and heavy icing. During a three-week course, students ranging from pilots to flight crews received 133 hours of training, and participated in three landings. Once things got going, twenty-nine full crews graduated each week. Great Falls gave Tunner the pilots he needed, but it also provided something beyond value for many of the men stuck in Germany on short notice. The new flow of officers and airmen now made possible a rotation policy so that some lift veterans could finally go home.[22]

No one ever thought it was possible, but General William Tunner, his handpicked team of experts, and the men of CALTF beat winter and made airlift an established part of military operations. Part of this was sheer luck; Berlin enjoyed one of the mildest winters in history, although parts of it were still horrendous. A lot of it, however, was the ingenuity and persistence of Tunner and his command, to feed Berlin no matter what, to prove that air transportation could be a force *majeure.*

It was the tale of the tape that counted. The magic number was 4,500 tons a day for survival, or 135,000 tons over a thirty-day month. By October CALTF had managed to bring in 147,581 tons on 18,235 flights, beating the minimum. November hit hard; the CPS-5 radar was not up yet, and it had the worst spell of fog that season. Productivity dropped to 113,588 tons on only 13,352 flights, an average of only 3,664 tons a day.[23]

After that nadir, however, things started to pick up. In December the airmen brought their total back up to 141,438 tons on 16,492 trips; this figure stands out, since the days between December 6 and 9 would be the second lowest in the history of the airlift, with numbers plummeting on the eighth down to near bottom. For the monthly figures to rise that high, it become clear that Tunner engaged in an almost desperate struggle, using his controllers to schedule every possible flight, the crews in the air and on the ground working at a frenzied pace when the skies cleared. This was no short burst, either; in January the numbers rose again, despite the fact that January 24–27 became the single worst patch in the entire airlift, with the fewest tons and number of flights on those days since the early period when a few C-47s flew the routes into Berlin.

By March the sun was shining. Burtonwood was operating as planned, with planes getting checked and repaired in record numbers. Replacement pilots flew from Montana to Berlin, well trained and ready to fly. Morale climbed as facilities like Fassberg steadily boasted better housing and food and recreation. It was time to soar.

That month seemed glorious. Tonnage skyrocketed to 196,161 tons on 22,163 flights, for a daily average of 6,328 tons, enough to pull Berlin off the hardest of the rationing. On March 31 Winston Churchill saluted the airlift in a speech in Boston, where he told the audience that across the Atlantic, "time, though dearly bought," had "been gained for peace." The airlift had, in fact, been shaping the postwar world, as "the spectacle of the British and Americans trying to feed the 2,000,000 Germans in Berlin, while the Soviet Government was trying to starve them, has been an object lesson to the German people far beyond anything that words could convey." As Tunner predicted, the airlift had become of the highest strategic importance.[24]

Tunner had by then shifted strategy, coming up with a new plan that only a visionary could have conceived. Instead of meeting a daily quota, the airlift now would have no fixed ceiling. Each day CALTF would try and bring the largest tonnage possible into the besieged city, and the only figures they had to beat were yesterday's records.

Milestones got passed like markers on an autobahn. Back in February the airlift decided to celebrate Washington's Birthday by bringing in 7,513 tons; learning that the day after would be Red Army Day, the crews decided to let the Soviet military know what they thought of the blockade, and flew in 7,897 tons. On March 14 a new weekly record of 45,684 tons lasted only fourteen days, broken on the twenty-eighth by a figure of 51,049 tons. West Berliners now had a daily ration of 2,000 calories, 270 more than when they had received supplies overland before the blockade started. To celebrate the spring, airlift planes flew in 2 million pine seedlings to repopulate the local woods.[25]

The airlift had succeeded, but the strain on the man had been unbearable. William Tunner had committed himself, not only to feed two million people, but to make airlift a reality, and some time during the winter, he broke.

It was not that Tunner was some kind of lightweight. He slept only four to six hours a night, and as Earl Morrison noted, he could deal with just about anything, "normally he took these situations in hand." But there was no question as to what kind of pressure he was under, and what it was doing to him. Sonia Tamara, in an article for the *New York Herald-Tribune* entitled, "Air Lift at Grips With Winter," stated what everyone knew, "No better commander than General Tunner could have been chosen." Just him, no one else; Milton claimed that Tunner "pretty much kept his hand on everything" and did not always delegate much authority, often pushing subordinates "to carry out what he wanted to do." Add to that the stress of having a boss he could barely tolerate, the fact that he was a chain smoker, and the reality that, despite his robust constitution, as Dorothy Towne, explained, "they had very little sleep over there."[26]

As true as all these factors were, it was above all the reality of what he was trying to accomplish that most weighed on him. Ann Tunner observed that "responsibility is a great adrenaline and he felt his responsibility heavily," and Milton agreed that his boss was "so focused on trying to make it work." Winter was a desperate time, with the whole affair a close-run thing. Milton remembered how Tunner became "like a man possessed," driving everyone, creating an "oppressive atmosphere."[27]

Something had to give, and the first sign was physical breakdown. As the worst moments passed and he let down his guard, Tunner became ill, though still driving himself and the rest of his crews at a ferocious pace. On March 4, according to his personal log, he "went to the hospital with a very bad cold"; but subsequent entries indicate that Tunner maintained a full load, giving orders covering every aspect of the airlift, even supervising minute details. As a result, he was out again only three days later, and on March 14 he was "temporarily suspended from flying . . . because of his recent illness."[28]

It was Milton who forced a showdown over the obsessive drive for results: "One day it just got more than I could take and I went into his office. He had a captain who always sat in his office and acted as kind of an amanuensis and I walked in and told the captain, 'Get out.'" After that the airlift's chief of staff turned to his boss: "And then I said to Tunner, I said, 'Sir, I don't think I can do this pretty good anymore'"; Milton wanted to be clear as sunlight, so added, "Just so you don't understand, I'm not trying to go home. I'll stay over here as long as there's an airlift going on. I'll fly an airplane, send me to Berlin, do anything you want. I just can't do this anymore.'" Tunner turned pale. "He was really very steamed up about the fact that the airlift might fail. He got up, put on his hat and just stormed out of his office." Roughly an hour later, Milton got the summons; Tunner's secretary informed him "the General wants to see you in his quarters." Milton knew what this meant, what happened to disrespectful subordinates in any military organization, and figured, "Oh well, this is the end of my military career." But instead Tunner just ignored the outburst, and when Milton appeared, the general merely asked his advice on some travel plans for a few days of badly needed vacation. When Milton asked how they should proceed in his absence, Tunner looked up at him, and in sheer frustration barked, "You run the damn thing."[29]

Milton solemnly believed that the point of this story was that it showed how big a man Tunner really was, big enough to recognize when he was wrong, and to act on that admission. That undoubtedly is true, and it also demonstrates his loyalty to staff, but historically there was a larger significance. The incident showed just how heavy the burden of the airlift had become, how much the founder of airlift had been affected by the strain of doing the impossible. Tunner had finally snapped.

It would not last long. On March 24 he left for a ten-day trip to Spain, where he soaked up sunshine and recuperated quickly. Milton agreed that his boss "did get better after" his rest, and that the atmosphere at CALTF was very solid.[30]

Tunner had returned, and with the warm weather, the airlift was running like he had always imagined it, as an industrial factory in the sky. He had proven his revolutionary notion, that air transportation could do even better than ground traffic, at a lot faster pace. Now it was time for a masterstroke, a spectacle so grand the whole world would pay attention.

It was a typical Tunner stunt. By late March things had become too stable, so the general decided to come up with something to bust his people out of complacency, and achieve new goals.

Tunner came up with a dream and a method. The vision was based on one essential fact: there were 1,440 minutes in a day. If a ten-ton load landed in Berlin for every one of these minutes, they could deliver 14,400 tons in one 24-hour period, roughly double the 7,000 plus figures that had become standard by then, or triple the earlier minimum of 4,500 tons. The method was competition. Just as he had done back on the Hump, Tunner would schedule an all-out day, and get each squadron to joust with the others to prove who was best. Now all he needed was a date, and Easter Sunday beckoned; as Tunner described it in his memoir, they would "have an Easter Parade of airplanes, an Easter Sunday present for the people of Berlin."[31]

The operation began to take shape. To increase efficiency, only one cargo would go out that day, so that procedures could be standardized and improved by repetition; Berlin would receive a lot of coal that Sunday. Planners arranged flights and determined quotas for each base. In addition, General Cannon was away, so there would be no interference from higher-ups, no questioning of why or how this mission had been attempted till it was all over.[32]

The airmen were not stupid, and everyone knew something was up. When the sergeants posted the quotas for that day, however, everyone howled. Then they pitched in to prove they could do it.

Tunner did not sleep for the entire twenty-four-hour period, and made three flights in and out of Berlin during this time. In some places he had to urge men on, in others he gave them a hearty "well done." At Fassberg, Constance Ben-

19. At the finale of the Easter Parade, April 15–16, 1949, airmen paint
the triumphant numbers on the nose of a plane. (National Archives photo,
SC320227)

nett was on the flight line with other wives dishing out the coffee and doughnuts; her husband, base commander Jack Coulter, told Tunner exuberantly that
his men were running ten percent *over* quota. Unfazed, the general replied that
that was wonderful, "but of course it's not up to what they were doing at Celle
[another base]. They're really on the ball over there." Coulter ran off to spur his
men on. Tunner never said so, but it would not have been surprising if he had
then gone to Celle, to tell them just how great a job those guys were doing over
at Fassberg.[33]

It worked magnificently. On one of his flights that day, Tunner was accom-
panied by Milton and Earl Morrison, his crew chief. Morrison was taking a nap
in the back when Milton came in and woke him, saying, "You have to see this!"
The entire corridor was literally filled with planes at perfectly spaced intervals.

Morrison remembered how he thought, "It was beautiful . . . I said, 'General, you're making history,'" and Tunner laughed.[34]

Tunner did not quite achieve the 14,400-ton mark, but came astoundingly close. When the last plane flew in, an anonymous crewman ran up with a bucket of red paint and a paintbrush, and dabbed on the results for all to see: 1,383 flights carrying 12,849 tons; later analysis would raise these figures, to 1,398 and 12,941, respectively. Overall, airlift pilots flew 78,954,500 miles during the Easter Parade, and a plane landed in Berlin every sixty-three seconds. All of this was done, furthermore, without a single accident; Tunner refused to relax any safety requirement for the big push. Colonel William Bunker, an army transportation officer, told them they hauled as much coal that day as six hundred railroad cars. "Have you ever seen a fifty-car coal train?" he asked. "Well you've just equaled twelve of them."[35]

This was no idle feat. Conventional wisdom was that the show might have been grand, but it was a one-shot affair, and could not be kept up. Milton believed this, and it was the key argument Tunner confronted when he had to report to Major General Robert Douglass Jr., Cannon's deputy commander. Douglass argued that after the all-out effort of Easter Sunday, "your tonnage is going to go way down; your people are going to be worn out; and for the next week you will have very low tonnage, and you will have defeated everything you are trying to do, which is to get more tonnage into Berlin."[36]

Cannon's headquarters was clearly not the Tunner cheering section, but the head of CALTF had answers. He responded that the parade had invigorated his troops, and that furthermore, "my people are going to find shortcuts which they haven't tried before to accomplish this mission."

The numbers showed that Tunner was right. Prior to Easter Sunday, the airlift had broken the 7,000-ton barrier only three times; during the week prior the average had been 6,729 tons daily. From the day after the parade to the end of the airlift, however, CALTF crews delivered an average of 8,893 tons a day.[37]

William Tunner had always argued that airlift meant power, and May 1949 proved the accuracy of his vision. On the fourth of the month, the great powers reached agreement that the blockade would be lifted on May 12. The night before that happened, as dusk fell on the eleventh, the Soviets flicked a switch and let electricity flow once more to West Berlin. For the first time in almost a year, the lights came on—all of them. At a few minutes past midnight, a jeep with two U.S. soldiers left Berlin and traveled west, while a train left Germany

20. Americans celebrate the end of the airlift. (History Office, Air
Mobility Command, Scott Air Force Base, Box 7, Folder 1)

for the British zone at 1:23 A.M. Several hours later, at 5:05, the first American
rail transport began its journey from Helmstadt, with a cargo of milk, escorted
by eight soldiers and with five civilian passengers.[38]

Still the planes flew. Before this sudden end, Tunner had been making plans
to carry on the airlift for years to come. General Clay also requested that a
stockpile be created in case the Soviets decided to reimpose restrictions, a reserve of 1.1 million tons. For the next twenty-nine days after May 12 the airlift averaged 7,371 tons a day.[39]

A week before the last flight a British C-47 took off from Lubeck with a note
stenciled on its nose that this was the last mission from that base, along with
the inscription, "Psalm 21, Verse 11." That part of the Bible reads, "For they
intended evil against thee; they imagined a mischievous device, which they are
not able to perform." On September 30, 1949, a C-54 loaded, not coinciden-

tally, with coal, the cargo that made up the bulk of airlift shipments, took off from Rhein-Main, headed for Berlin with Captain Harry Immel, one of the lift's earliest flyers, at the controls. General William Tunner was in his office at Wiesbaden, working alone.[40]

There were many reasons the Soviets backed down; negotiations at the highest level of diplomacy had preceded the events of May. Yet, at the same time, it was clear that Stalin had realized that the blockade had failed, and that his country looked like a thug in the world's eyes, rather than the defender of freedom against a rising German state.

Credit for this goes to Tunner's planes, which could feed the city for eternity, it seemed. In April, one Russian officer assigned to monitor Western air traffic angrily complained that there were so many flights, "I can't keep my records straight." Tunner always felt that the Easter Parade broke the back of any Soviet resistance, and just before the end declared, "We can keep pouring it in for twenty years if we have to."[41]

Others recognized the contribution. On May 11, Secretary of State Dean Acheson stated, "We are where we are in regard to the lifting of the Blockade because of the superb performance of the pilots and the supporting crews." General Tunner received his third Distinguished Service Medal, a decision made by General Hoyt Vandenberg, who called the airlift, "the Air Force's Number One Achievement." Later Tunner was given a rare private audience with Their Majesties, King George VI and Queen Elizabeth of Great Britain, in recognition of his service on the world stage.[42]

What had Tunner, his close staff, and the men of CALTF accomplished? Flying prop-engined planes, they delivered 2,325,937 tons, making this the largest airlift in the history of the human race, as of the time this book was published. In the peak month of May 1949, planes delivered 250,819 tons of supplies, an average of 8,091 tons a day. By way of perspective, between July 1992 and January 1996, a period of three and one-half years, an international coalition flew 177,067 tons of relief supplies into Sarajevo; this was less than Tunner's men did just in March 1949, and every month thereafter till the airlift ended. Of the grand total, the United States handled 77 percent of the load, or 189,963 flights, while the British and civilian contractors made up the rest of the total of 277,569 missions. On the basis of weight, more flights carried coal than anything else, even food, 68 percent for the dusty fuel compared to 23 percent for comestibles. One other indication of the magnitude of all this is that during the initial seven months of the airlift, U.S. planes alone flew over

145 million ton-miles. During that same period, the combined total of all domestic carriers operating at home was only 136 million ton-miles. At this time Gatow replaced LaGuardia Airport in New York as the busiest airfield in the world, and by a titanic margin; during the airlift it handled three times as much traffic.[43]

All of this was done with an accident rate 50 percent below the service average in all theaters. During these ten months, Tunner's crews flew 5 percent of all of the U.S. Air Force's flying hours, but suffered only 2 percent of the major accidents.[44]

Numbers, however, tell only part of the story. Berlin really was the rubicon of the cold war; before the blockade, many considered the Soviets an ally from the last war, and Germany as the defeated enemy. Now these roles changed, and public sentiment and policy both would move to oppose the Iron Curtain and rebuild the nation that had birthed Nazism. These lines would stay in place till 1989, when Berlin once more took center stage as the Wall fell.

It was also a formidable way to start a cold war; the authors of one book on the airlift stated bluntly, "The Berlin Airlift was the first Cold War victory." The Berlin crisis caught the Soviets acting like a hideous blackmailer, while the Western Allies stood up for freedom. Along with the Marshall Plan, the airlift placed the United States' generosity on display, and highlighted their technical might as well. As the author Andrei Cherny put it, "all around the world the Berlin Airlift had become a symbol of an America that was not only strong but good."[45]

There were other impacts as well. On a small scale, many of the procedures commercial airlift had used since its infancy were improved. Packaging was redesigned for ease of handling, and pallets became more common. Air traffic control, whether for passenger, cargo, or military uses, began to adopt the methods pioneered by Tunner's team in Berlin. One writer for *Fortune* told his readers, "It is no exaggeration to say that the lift in four months has taught Americans more about the possibilities of mass movement of goods by air than they would have learned in a decade of normal development."[46]

Tunner would also begin the struggle for bigger and faster planes, the kinds of vessels that could handle his vision of airlift. This was a fight he would pursue till the end of his military career, but as early as February 1949 he was making powerful nonmilitary friends who would make a big difference within a few years. That year Congress debated a bill that would have authorized the government to develop new and larger transports, then pay for the construction of a fleet that would be leased to the airlines. The sponsor of this bill in the House, a man who clearly saw this as the future of America, was a young congressman named John Kennedy.[47]

Tunner's vision of a place at the table for military air transport got increasingly accepted, till it became standard procedure. By the summer of 1949 the U.S. Marine Corps was using planes to move 12,700 of its Reserve troops for that season's exercises. Sixteen years later, the corps would begin the start of the American buildup in Vietnam, and while some of the first troops traveled by sea, all of the rest, plus the bulk of the immense American presence there, got carried by air. This was Tunner's triumph; whereas during World War II soldiers traveled in troop ships, now they were flown to the combat theater in large aircraft. Much of this change, of course, was due to improved technology, but it was Tunner who got the armed services to embrace the new machines and newer concepts.[48]

During the airlift, Tunner told the press, "We look upon the airlift not as an end in itself. It is an exercise in the technique of using big airplanes in a manner hitherto unknown," and later remarked, "We are close to something new and revolutionary and universally important." One journalist, who had encountered Tunner several times before, remarked that "it wasn't until now that the completeness of his air freight thinking broke upon me. I've met air freight boosters before, but not one will go as far as Tunner."[49]

T. Ross Milton observed of the Berlin Airlift, "I don't think anybody really thought it would work, except Tunner. I mean anybody in the whole military structure. He was kind of the lone prophet. He deserves that credit." Beyond that event, Tunner "really knew what he was doing. . . . He was a zealot about air transport. He wasn't really interested in anything else in the Air Force. . . . He had a lot of ideas . . . and his ideas proved pretty much to be right." Dorothy Towne believed that airlift was "the sort of things he dreamed about," that "Nobody had thought in the way that General Tunner had thought about logistics." Ann Tunner, a pilot in her own right who understood her husband's dreams, called him "a visionary. He believed in air transport and knew that people would soon be depending on it. And he just knew this. He believed it deeply."[50]

While others—from President Truman to General Clay to Berlin's politicians—made a host of critical decisions, it is fair to say that William Tunner is the one who actually got the Berlin Airlift to work and is most responsible for its success. By so doing, he not only fed millions, but also helped win the cold war. Above all, he changed the structure of the world's military forces forever.

13 / Korea

After the Berlin Airlift, Tunner returned to his post as deputy commander of operations at MATS, with authority over all air transport divisions. He and his boss, General Laurence Kuter, made up, according to one account, a "good cop, bad cop" team, with Kuter playing the softer role. One writer said he "ran the new command, refined its doctrines and voiced its goals with deft diplomacy." Tunner, meanwhile, "was perfectly happy to thunder around as the airlift operational leader, hawk big aircraft to anyone who would listen, and surge through his circling critics like a lion in a room full of terriers. . . . He was hardly the one to stay away from confrontation." Kuter would "check his enthusiasm . . . until the time was right to turn him loose."[1]

Tunner still found plenty of moments to show off his new doctrines. In April and May 1950 the army and the air force joined together for Operation Swarmer, to see if U.S. forces could deploy an entire infantry division by air, then keep it supplied in the same manner. This exercise was somewhat different for Tunner, in that most of the action would involve troop carrier planes launching paratroopers, not air transports landing the men directly onto the ground. Tunner had not usually been involved in this aspect of air operations,[2] but Lieutenant General Lauris Norstad, deputy chief of staff for the air force and air commander for Swarmer, recognized Tunner's expertise and picked him to command all airlift operations. This gave him control of a unified command, and his units dropped four 1,700-man regimental combat teams and air landed a fifth. Overall, his planes got 14,000 troops and 2,900 tons of equipment into the airhead established in the North Carolina woods for this exercise.

Tunner saw Swarmer as another way to prove that airlift could get the job done, and nothing was more important than that goal. Milton recalled that Tunner and the army officers differed as to what the top priority of MATS should be during the exercise; the army wanted specific items, while Tunner sought to maximize tonnage, always trying to prove what air transport could do. Tunner turned to Milton, "And he said to me, 'What do you think?' and I said, 'Well I agree with the Army.'" And I've never seen him so mad in my life. When we left the meeting, he had a riding crop, I forget why, and he started hammering it on an automobile, and luckily not me." Tunner yelled at Milton, "You just screwed up the whole damn maneuver." But "that blew over and everything was fine" pretty quickly.[3]

What did not change were Tunner's chief concerns. Looking at the lessons from Swarmer, Tunner stayed, as he always would, straight on focus. He advocated a unified transport command, which in this case meant moving troop carrier units from tactical air (where they were subordinate to the ground commanders they served), over to MATS (where they would be run by airlift professionals). Subsequent events would confirm this approach in Tunner's mind, but would also lead to considerable conflict with foes from his past as well as those to be made anew. Ground generals could never understand why they, the men facing the enemy directly, should not dictate airlift priorities, and would often challenge Tunner for control of the cargo planes.

In addition, he would use this episode to advocate big airplanes, a step he took on all possible occasions. Never stepping off message one jot, Tunner told the Commerce and Industry Association of New York that while air transport in the United States benefited from solid organization and a glut of experienced personnel, what they really lacked were "a great pool of large transports."[4]

Tunner did not have much time to pursue the matter. On June 25, 1950, North Korean troops, equipped with T-34/85 tanks, surged over the 38th parallel and invaded the South. Two days later, the United Nations Security Council called on member nations to assist South Korea, and President Truman committed U.S. forces to this conflict. The Korean War had begun.

Airlift did not do too well at first. Its resources were diminished; less than a year after the Berlin crisis, MATS would have fewer than three hundred aircraft, a postwar low. That figure was going down fast; the very first U.S. plane lost in Korea was one of their C-54s, destroyed at Kimpo Airfield on the opening day of hostilities. Four more became casualties by June 30, so that MATS had the dubious distinction of suffering as many aircraft casualties as the fighters and bombers during this initial phase of the war. Conditions on the ground were dismal; the remaining airfields were so small that C-54s could not land, and C-47s, with only a fraction of their cargo capacity, became the plane of choice. There was little in the way of electronic navigational aids, no radar or even radio beams for the pilots to home in on, so dead reckoning became a second-rate substitute. Weather forecasts did not exist. Scheduling was as chaotic as it had been during the early days in Berlin, and all flights ended at sundown, as none of the airfields in the U.S. sector of Korea at that time had landing lights. Years later, when an interviewer asked Tunner, "How unprepared for the Korean War was MATS?" he succinctly replied, "Very unprepared."[5]

Tunner was on an inspection trip in Alaska when the war broke out. He had along several of his stalwarts, veterans of the Berlin command staff like Pete Fernandez and Orval McMahon, but they were relatively isolated at some of the outposts. Finally General Nathan Twining, at that point commander of U.S. Forces in Alaska, appeared and asked, "Don't you fellows ever read a newspaper?" Tunner replied that there was no such luxury up at the top of the world, and Twining informed them the country was at war: "Didn't you know that Mr. Truman has practically declared war on North Korea, and here we are practically fighting them?" In fact, they did not know, and hurried back to Washington.[6]

Kuter had been organizing resources, setting up a Pacific Airlift using planes from MATS, the United Nations, and commercial airlines. Tunner offered to survey the routes and operations, to help get this setup established, and in Japan reported to Lieutenant General George Stratemeyer, head of the Far East Air Forces (FEAF).[7]

There was serendipity here. Stratemeyer had just requested an expert to take over airlift operations in the theater, and the Pentagon assigned Tunner. The airlift leader was ahead of his orders by now, so first learned of his transfer when he hit Tokyo. Stratemeyer complimented him on showing up so quickly, and Tunner was nonplussed, figuring he was still running late because of the side trip to Alaska. It took only minutes to straighten things out, and Tunner asked only that he be allowed a week or two to get back and straighten out his personal affairs; by then he was a widower, and he needed to make arrangements for his two young sons. Stratemeyer granted this request, and in due course, Tunner had finished his business and was heading back to Asia to take on another air transport challenge. With him on that plane were Red Foreman, Pete Fernandez, and Hal Sims; whenever possible, the general would always make use of his experienced group of stalwarts.[8]

Tunner's job was to impose order and discipline. The first thing he did was to create Combat Cargo Command (CCC), which brought under its wing all the air transport assets in the theater. This was no mean feat; traditionally troop carrier units had been separate from the outfits that hauled boxes, because commanders in the field wanted to have the availability of a paratroop drop at all times. Tunner pointed out that while they were waiting for such an opportunity, all those planes were sitting on the ground, their capacity for assisting other situations wasted. There was also the issue of separate services; Marine support units fought for independence, instead of being subordinate to an air force commander. There is no detailed record of what this fight was like, but Tunner admitted that there were "protestations" and that "Prying these aircraft loose from the organizations to which they were already assigned was not accomplished over night, but I was persistent." In the end, however, "I had the planes—all of them." Again, Tunner won his fight, but made enemies.[9]

In the quest for efficiency, Tunner created a unified airlift organization; he did not seek total power, however. FEAF established the Far East Command Air Priority Board, based in Tokyo, which made day-to-day decisions on how these planes would be utilized; these were the life-and-death choices, figuring out what embattled units in the field would receive and in what order. Tunner stated that "CCC's responsibility was not to allocate, but to deliver tonnage." Nevertheless, this was the first true air transport command in a combat zone in history, reporting directly to the chief air officer, and on a par with the tactical fighters and strategic bombers. One student of airlift called it the only "complete consolidation of Air Force theater airlift . . . "; its command structure was "self-contained, preventing other units from diverting transport aircraft, and was flexible enough to allow . . . diversions to support emergency requirements." In personal terms, it reinforced Tunner's view of how the air force should organize airlift in the future and gave him a taste of how potent his vision truly was.[10]

Tunner employed his successful Berlin model. Korea now had a Transportation Movement Control (TMC), which scheduled flights, established radio channels to give directions and instructions, and created a record of all departures and arrivals, a basic step that had not been taken previously. Specific air routes became standard, as did the altitudes pilots were allowed to use. Tonnage figures climbed.[11]

Tunner established one system he had not needed before in any of his experiences, and that was a medical evacuation unit. When the war started, most casualties traveled by bus and train to Pusan, and then took a ship to Japan if they needed further treatment. The head of airlift asked the obvious question that no one had posed before: as he flew more and more supplies into Korea, there was plenty of space on the return flight; why not use this to get wounded soldiers to Japan's hospitals as quickly as possible? The logic of this query, along with Tunner's determination in the face of obstacles both practical and political, made the change possible. Whenever possible, cargo planes got refitted so that they could handle patients, and doctors and nurses began to fly on the return trips. In the month and a half from mid-September to the end of October 1950—one of the worst periods of fighting of the entire war—CCC planes flew out 25,000 injured soldiers, and by the end of the conflict that number had climbed to 314,000. This made it the largest medical use of aircraft in history up till that time, far beyond the numbers in World War II. As one air force document put it, "Air evacuation of wounded came of age during the Korean War."[12]

This accomplishment, however, underlined one very vital difference between Berlin and Korea; the latter involved a shooting war with its unpredictable nature, while the former had taken place during what was virtually peacetime. The notion of a totally regimented system would not work now, as warfare created new demands. This was the great concern of the ground commanders, but Tunner showed that he could respond to a crisis or an operation when the call went out.

A good example of what Tunner and the CCC were capable of came in October 1950, when MacArthur planned to drop the 187th Regimental Combat Team in the area around Sunchon-Sukchon, behind enemy lines; the idea was to hold crucial transportation junctions and block retreating enemy forces. The operation required the use of forty C-47s and seventy-six C-119s, the big new transport known as the "flying boxcar." Although this plane had only two engines instead of the C-54's four and lacked capacity for extended range, it incorporated for the first time a huge clamshell rear door that could be used to launch paratroopers and bundles at an unprecedented speed. To put what was known as Operation Chromite into effect, all these planes had to be pulled off their usual schedules, moved to new bases, and the crews reoriented to serve combat commanders, rather than the regular flow of cargo.[13]

Tunner supervised the entire operation. On October 20, the launch date, rain and severe overcast seemed to preclude operations, and Stratemeyer urged delay. Tunner had become used to depending on forecasters, however, and his men counseled fairer skies later on in the day. To prove his point, the general took off in his own C-54 before any other plane, and found that the weather over the drop zone was, in fact, favorable. By a little past two in the afternoon, the big planes were in the skies; of seventy-six boxcars, seventy-four made it to the designated area, and seventy-one dropped their loads, an unprecedented rate. Overall, 2,860 armed troopers landed, backed by 301 tons of supplies, including heavy equipment such as jeeps and trucks, plus 105mm howitzers and their ammunition. Korean War historian Clay Blair declared, "Compared with most World War II operations, the jump was outstanding—indisputably the best combat jump the Army had ever staged." In recognition of this achievement, MacArthur awarded Tunner the Distinguished Flying Cross. From the standpoint of effective air organization, however, the other great accomplishment was that this entire fleet would again be turned within a matter of days and returned to regular duties. Tunner had demonstrated that airlift could be flexible as well as systematic.

Shortly after Tunner set up the CCC, Douglas MacArthur launched the invasion of Inchon, an end run on the enemy forces in which he staged an amphibious assault halfway up the western coast of South Korea. This was depicted—both at the time and historically—as a masterstroke that changed the war, and in many ways it was; nothing succeeds like victory, and North Korean troops fell back all the way to the Chinese border. This should not, however, disguise the fact this was also a tough gamble, one that airlift helped make a success. Inchon lies at the end of a narrow channel, easily mined; the loss of a single ship could have blocked the entire invasion. Once ships got through, furthermore, they faced some of the most extreme tides in Asia; deep draft vessels could use the harbor only twice a day for only hours at a time, while for the rest of the time there were only mud flats for 6,000 yards out, as the water level dropped 33 feet. Thus, if the landing forces got into trouble they could not be supplied for as much as twelve hours. Landing, too, was a problem, as troops would have to deal with concrete sea walls twelve to fourteen feet high.

American planners and fighting troops defeated all of these obstacles. On September 15, minesweepers cleared the channel, and during high tide landing craft loaded with Marines rammed themselves into the sea wall by gunning motors. Ladders went up, troops scaled the wall, took the harbor, and MacArthur had accomplished one of the great flanking maneuvers of all time.

He could not keep these forces supplied, however. As noted, cargo could only come ashore for six hours out of any given twenty-four-hour period, and the limit seemed to be 6,000 tons a day, far below what was needed to maintain the tempo of combat operations; at one point thirty-two ships sat offshore waiting to unload their cargoes. Ground commanders clamored for more support from every source possible, including the CCC.

On September 18, military units reclaimed Kimpo Airfield outside Seoul. The main runway was 6,200 feet long and 150 feet wide, with 750,000 square feet of parking area, three times as much as the next largest facility in Korea. The next day, at 10:55 A.M. Tunner ordered that flights could land at Kimpo, and the first plane came in at 2:46 P.M. that day. By September 24, the CCC had brought in 1,445 tons of supplies, mostly fuel and ammunition for the First Marine Air Wing that was giving so much support to the ground forces, with more arriving daily.[14]

Tunner's most momentous achievement in Korea, and one of the highlight's of his career, came at a relative low point of American fortunes in the war. While most of MacArthur's forces fought up the western coast of the peninsula, on the eastern shore, the X Corps consisting of the First Marine Division with army units in support, was conducting a campaign in the area of the Chosin Reservoir. In late November, a Chinese Communist army of ten divisions, with over 100,000 men, attacked in force. The Marines now had only two choices: to either surrender, or conduct a fighting withdrawal back to the coast and the port of Hungnam. The first option was unthinkable, and the second seemed impossible. These were Marines, however, and their commanding officer, Major General Oliver Smith, captured their spirit with one of those immortal lines that it seems the corps comes up with more than anyone else. When reporters suggested that the division was heading back where they came from, were in retreat, Smith replied in immortal language, "Retreat hell. We're just attacking in a different direction." The Marines would make it to the sea in orderly fashion, taking all their tanks and trucks, all their equipment, and above all, every last one of their dead and wounded with them. This was no rout; it was Marines fighting and moving in battle order.[15]

Towns along the way became way stops to refit and rearm, places that are now in Marine Corps history books, like Hagaru-ri and Koto-ri. By then the temperatures had turned bitter cold, well below zero, with a fierce wind. Tunner put Red Foreman in charge, and soon CCC's planes began a massive campaign of airdrops. The C-119 Boxcars began flying in on a level flight path to maximize the drop's precision into small one-hundred-yard drop zones; this system also provided the best target possible to enemy gunners. Early drops included a sixteen-ton prepackaged kit of the basics—replacement weapons, ammo, food, water, medical supplies—called "Baldwins," but after that anything and everything that could be hooked to a parachute was flown to the embattled gyrenes. By December 1, all C-119s, with their big back doors and rollers on the floor to ease out heavy loads, were assigned to this mission. Over the course of one crucial six-day period, from December 1 to 6, the C-119s got 971 tons to the Marines, 298 of them just on December 5 alone.

It was not enough to get supplies in, however; the wounded also had to be evacuated. The main Marine base by now was at Hagaru-ri; the airstrip there was only 2,500 feet long and 50 feet wide, with a water-filled dike at one end and a hill at the other. It was also only 40 percent completed.

Only one plane could manage conditions like that, the old C-47 workhorse. At 2:30 P.M. on November 30, the first one landed at the Marine base, and shortly after, it took off with 24 wounded American servicemen. Instead of a usual load of 12 to 18 passengers, one flight loaded up with 42 casualties, plus extra crew, a pilot, and a copilot, for a total weight of 46 humans plus assorted medical apparatus; somehow it managed to wobble into the air and get those men out of there. Other flights kept a promise Marine general Smith had made, that no one would be left behind, and brought dead bodies back to a place where they could receive an honorable burial. Tunner flew in on one of the early flights to organize things and get everything running in as systematic a fashion as was possible under the circumstances. In that early, desperate period, his planes had evacuated 4,312 wounded and frostbitten men, as well as 137 corpses.

This work, as important as it was, did not get the biggest headlines for airlift. Tunner had always said that he could get anything, anywhere, and the Chosin campaign provided the supreme test for that claim.

As the Marines fought their way back to the sea along the Main Supply Route, they made it from Hagaru-ri to the next main base camp at Koto-ri, eleven miles down the line, in the face of heavy Chinese resistance. Three and one-half miles south of there, however, the force faced what seemed like an unbeatable obstacle. At the sixteen-foot-wide Funchilin Pass the Chinese had blown up the only available bridge, and there was no way to build a bypass road. A narrow footpath would allow infantry and the wounded to get out, but as one historian of the campaign put it, "more than twelve hundred tanks and other vehicles would have to be shoved over the side. The Marines hadn't come this far, through so much blood, so much shot and shell, to build the world's largest junkpile." General Smith stated, "The enemy could not have picked a better spot to give us trouble."[16]

Lieutenant Colonel John Partridge, commanding officer of the First Engineer Battalion, came up with the idea of parachuting sections of a treadway bridge to the Marines. There was only one problem: no one had ever done anything like this before. Smith asked Partridge, "To your knowledge, have bridge sections ever been dropped by parachute?" The engineer replied, "Never heard of it, general."[17]

There was good reason for skepticism. Each section was sixteen feet in length and weighed 2,900 pounds. The bridge used four sections, and as backup they wanted a second structure to ensure that traffic made it over, meaning eight sections would have to be flown in.

A preliminary test back at Kimpo did not go well. Two large 24-foot parachutes billowed out, but they were not enough. The span picked up speed, and crashed into the ground, destroying itself. Tunner now obtained gigantic 48-foot parachutes, along with a crew of army rigging specialists.

On December 7, the C-119s flew into position, initially at 800 feet, but soon this went up to 1,000 feet to give the chutes time to grab more air and slow things down. Along with padding and parts, each section now weighed two tons. One of the big chutes anchored each end, and husky airmen pushed the loads along the rollers on the floor of the cargo bay and out the rear door. A small chute popped first, to catch the wind and yank out the big boys, and soon the bridge section drifted safely down to earth. Six of the pieces made it, one was damaged, and one landed behind the Chinese lines. Two days later, at roughly 3:30 P.M., the bridges were in position, and American units began to make it across the pass.

As Partridge had remarked, no one had ever done this before. It was the kind of spectacular stunt the press loved, and they paid homage to the master of airlift, giving Tunner the greatest publicity bonanza of his career. For its December 18, 1950, issue *Time* chose for its cover a portrait of the general, while just above his head flew, not just a section but an entire suspension bridge (hardly what had been dropped), propelled by giant wings. The caption read, "GENERAL WILLIAM TUNNER, AIRLIFTER. In the midst of the enemy, a bridge from the sky."[18]

Cargo Command continued to operate for a couple of months. By the time it stood down in early 1951, Tunner's pilots and crews had brought in 130,170 tons of supplies and evacuated 72,960 casualties, all with only one fatality en route.

Tunner now turned to reorganizing airlift in Korea. CCC was a temporary command, and back in October, when the war was going well for the United States Tunner had recommended that a permanent command be established to take over these duties for the duration of the war. Stratemeyer had agreed with this idea in theory, but the Chinese intervention brought more pressing matters to the fore. By early 1951 the worst had passed, and the head of FEAF implemented Tunner's proposal, on January 25, 1951, disbanding Combat Cargo Command, and creating the 315th Air Division (Combat Cargo), a regular unit within the air force. Tunner oversaw the transition, and then left to return to the states on February 8. At that point in history, there had been four great airlifts: Stalingrad, the Hump, Berlin, and Korea, and William Tunner had been in charge of the three that succeeded.[19]

This record did not keep him out of trouble, and in fact may have exacerbated problems, as he now had every right to feel his judgments on airlift were sound, and should be followed without much debate. Tunner was still the business executive, the person who had founded not just an organization but an industry, except that he wore the uniform of a firm steeped in rank and hierarchy.

Tunner got into a bind, for example, because of restrictions on his planes imposed in Tokyo; as noted, a command board set priorities, not the CCC. What bothered Tunner was not the choices they made, but the fact that they restricted his flight hours; he later claimed that he could fly planes only three hours a day, when they should have been in the air for twelve out of every twenty-four hours.

To a man who believed in production that did not sit well. In harsh terms, he described these limits as being "rather stupid . . . because anything can happen in a war . . . You've got to be ready for emergencies." At the same time, every ground commander clamored for more supplies, so Tunner let the cat out of the bag. To one high-ranking officer who complained that his men needed ammo while planes sat on the ground, Tunner—in his own words—"stuck my neck out and told him the truth." A cable went forthwith to the air force chief of staff, General Hoyt Vandenberg. According to Tunner, "Vandenberg got mad at 'Stratty,' and 'Stratty' got mad at me for telling him this." Nevertheless, orders changed, more planes flew, and supplies got to the men.[20]

Another incident also stemmed from Tunner pushing his ideas on airlift. In November 1950 he wrote that the C-119, which loomed to become the standard medium transport, should be reconfigured by stripping all equipment for troops or specialized cargo needs, thus adding two tons to its lifting capacity. The logic was classic Tunner: What could be more important than bringing in the maximum weight of badly needed goods? Any other demands could be dismissed; as he wrote the Pentagon, the current state of affairs "simply means that . . . tons of vitally needed cargo is still in Japan, which might have been in Korea."[21]

That was not all. A month later, in December 1950, he returned to another of his core beliefs. His experience in Korea had confirmed the notion that all military transport should be centralized under one command and that only people experienced in this field should be in charge. The previous arrangement had been that troop-carrying planes—such as those used to fly paratroopers—came under Tactical Air Command; during the exigencies of those first rough months in Korea, all units had reported to Tunner, and he was now urging this be adopted by the air force, as a model of efficiency.

Both these arguments, no matter how valid, stepped on the toes of TAC; Tunner was suggesting that their planes be altered, and that part of their mission be shifted to MATS. That political factor did not prevent Tunner from fighting for what he thought was right, nor did the fact that TAC was commanded at that time by Lieutenant General John Cannon.

There was no love lost between these two. Cannon wrote back that the real weight savings would be only 350 pounds and that was not worth stripping planes of their ability to fly paratroopers. Above all, he argued that flying troops was a tactical mission and not a cargo one.

This argument was not a high point of theoretical discussion in the air force. One student of the dispute wrote that when it came to how much tonnage saving was really involved, "it is difficult to determine which apples and oranges the generals were comparing." Many of Cannon's arguments were weak; he stressed that combat missions were complex and required close coordination and the use of forward air strips, for example, something that TAC was used to doing in its close air support missions for the army. Tunner, however, had proved in Burma and Berlin that conventional airlift could handle the most extraordinary tasks, and Korea had been proof that cargo planes could use the roughest of runways when it came to helping ground troops. At the same time, Tunner's high tonnage for its own sake engendered the belief that he would downgrade tactical missions and give them short shrift. In the short run, Cannon won, and the planes stayed with TAC in their original configuration.

The tussle with Cannon, like the one with Stratemeyer, had a common denominator. Tunner was a visionary who understood military airlift far better than anyone else in the world; in many ways he truly saw the future, and hence was compelled to fight for it. The air force would not always listen, but that did not stop him from speaking whenever he could, as forcibly as he could.

At one point during the Korean hostilities, with "war now raging," William Tunner gave a talk on "Global Air Transportation" before the Air Command and Staff School. In front of this powerful and prestigious audience he presented a tour de force of all his biggest ideas.[22]

He did not beat around the bush; by the sixth paragraph he was telling officers that "the military air transport service is one of the least spectacular but most convincing lessons to come out of World War II: air power is not expressed by bomber and airlift alone, but by the total air effort of a nation." This includes "transport, and other manufacturing and support functions along with the striking force."

From this understanding flowed all the subsidiary arguments. While "all military campaigns will have a definite and vastly increasing requirement for transportation," the old ground systems of rail and truck could not deliver the cargo in anywhere near the timely manner and tonnage that airlift could. In Korea, "much of the engineers' effort which went into building railroads and maintaining bridges and docks," should have gone "into airdrome construction instead." Tunner went so far as to argue that "airlift would even exceed the dependability of surface transportation in Korea, where I know of cases where trains and trucks and vessels failed to arrive at all or were days or even months late."

Changes would have to be made. Airlift must be put on a permanent basis, and no longer "considered an emergency force, a fire engine racing in at the last minute to save an unforeseen situation." In addition, air transport was "scattered throughout many commands as well as services," a major impediment to its ability to carry out missions with utmost efficiency. Only centralization into a significant command at the same level as SAC and TAC could redress both of these problems. That command, furthermore, had to be firmly in the hands of airlift professionals; to assign commanders whose expertise lay elsewhere would be ridiculous. Tunner dismissed the idea by quipping, "We might just as well place bombers and fighters in a troop carrier or air transport unit."

It was a mighty agenda. William Tunner had less than ten years left in his military career to fight for these ideas.

14 / Final Battles

After Korea, the logical next step for General Tunner should have been back to MATS, in a position to head the organization as soon as Laurence Kuter stepped down. It was not to be.

Tunner came back from Korea and was at MATS only briefly when Chief of Staff Hoyt Vandenberg called him in. In spite of all he had done with airlift, Tunner would be assigned as deputy commander of Air Materiel Command (AMC), which handled supplies and inventories, and helped develop new products for the air force. Vandenberg told his subordinate he needed the training at different jobs, to learn about other aspects of the air service as preparation for bigger things to come.

It was not a felicitous assignment, and there is reason to be suspicious as to its intent. The obvious question was why he did not go to MATS as commanding officer; instead, in 1951 the U.S. Air Force appointed Lieutenant General Joseph Smith, Tunner's predecessor in Berlin, to this post. One source claims that while Smith got the job because he was "an excellent officer, and it was his turn to command," other factors also played a role besides seniority. At that time the service was stressing the importance of nuclear-armed bombers, and the last thing they wanted was a powerful voice calling for more airlift. Kuter felt strongly that he too would be pushed out because of his advocacy, and his next assignment, as deputy chief of staff for personnel, does not indicate that he was held in high regard. Smith, however, firmly believed in the bomber mission and a diminished role for MATS, not to mention the fact that he was more gentlemanly and less pushy than the visionaries; he referred to Kuter's idea of a larger airlift command as "empire building." He would remain in charge of military airlift until 1958—an extraordinary long time to hold one post—during the period when bombers were the supreme instrument in the U.S. military and received the most prestige and the greatest funding. As one student of this era wrote, "he was a respected shepherd, who simultaneously quieted the troublesome, out-of-step 'bleatings' of Kuter and Tunner, and guided MATS into obedient and productive compliance with Air Force strategic priorities."[1]

Tunner clearly did not like going to AMC; he told interviewers in 1976 the move was something "I didn't look forward to with any pleasure." Part of the problem was the atmosphere; the operation was run by business school grads, bean counters. Tunner had no such educational background, and while he subscribed to many of their methods, he remained an independent, an entrepreneur, rather than having a middle-level mindset. Even worse, the move defied one of his basic principles, to remain a professional in one area and fight for that bailiwick. Tunner did not seek to be chief of staff, did not need to learn about every aspect of a far-flung service. His view, instead, was that "you've got to have specialists in the Air Force. A man who is a general doesn't have to be a jack of all trades just because he is a general." Tunner knew who he was and what he wanted: "I did know the air transport business . . . better than anyone in it, and I wanted to stay with it."[2]

All in all, it was a curious appointment, for the obvious reasons. In addition, as Raymond Towne pointed out, if Tunner was slated for leadership roles, why had he been kept at the two-star level, while many of his contemporaries with fewer victories had gone on to an additional star or two? Tunner's past decisions were haunting his career advancement.[3]

Stationed at Wright-Patterson Air Force Base, Tunner did his work, but took every opportunity to follow airlift and insert himself into the public discussion of military strategies and needs. When the U.S. Air Force introduced the C-124 cargo plane and the *Washington Daily News* did a story on it, they interviewed an officer referred to in the article as "the top Air Force expert on mass transport," who explained that with planes of this size, the United States could run both the Berlin and Korean airlifts simultaneously. Tunner also published an article, "Technology or Manpower," in *Air University Quarterly Review*, which recapitulated the familiar arguments on the larger role air transportation must play. One of these was a claim that the D-Day operation would have been better served if post-invasion logistics had been done by air instead of by sea, with the Allies building rudimentary airstrips instead of wasting so much time building harbors.[4]

By then Tunner was frustrated. He began the piece with a quote from Tennyson's "Locksley Hall," in which the narrator strives to see forthcoming events. After these immortal lines, Tunner added, "Tennyson, peering into the future, was attempting to see the great forests—the big picture—without singling out individual trees. He had more luck than most of us today, who seem to find the individual trees obscuring our vision."[5]

Regarding the post at AMC, Tunner claimed that he "tolerated it long enough to get out of it." One of the chips he called in came up during a conversation with Lauris Norstad, then head of USAFE; Tunner asked him if there was any assignment open in Europe. Norstad had a better idea, and in 1953, after two years at AMC, Tunner became commander of USAFE, gaining an extra star in the process, so that he was finally a lieutenant general. Tunner liked this position, and stayed there for four years. In 1957 his next assignment was back in Washington, as deputy air force chief of staff for operations, a position so close to MATS and yet so distant it became one of the worst periods of his professional life; he referred to this period as "a frustrating year . . . in the Pentagon."[6]

William Tunner wrote in his memoirs, "Of all the jobs in the Air Force, the one I wanted most was the command of the Military Air Transport Service." In 1958 he got that appointment, and on July 1 began work at his dream job, the one that he seemed destined to hold.[7]

It was not a good time to take on this role, or in fact, to even be in the U.S. military—unless you were a bomber leader. Throughout the 1950s Congress and the administration cut back drastically on military spending. Instead of a diverse force, the supreme emphasis was on the delivery of nuclear weapons by manned aircraft, so this became the heyday of SAC, with its magnificent B-47 and B-52 bombers, the most advanced aircraft on the planet. All other parts of the military—not just outfits like MATS, but the U.S. Army, Navy, and Marine Corps, had to fight to be recognized and get even slivers of the reduced budgetary pie. Brigadier General Robin Olds commented that in those days, "SAC was the be-all, know-all, have-all."[8]

In some ways it was worse in the air force, however. The newly minted service was attempting to establish an independent identity, which the uniqueness of nuclear war readily bestowed upon it. Any claim by MATS that its mission was important, too, undercut the single-minded emphasis, by pointing out that there could still be a need for supply during and after a nuclear exchange, or even worse, that there was still the possibility of a conventional war. In addition, their effort to support the army dimmed the image of a separate, independent service that stood above all others, and again pointed to other means of conducting war. During one congressional hearing on what to do about air transport, the vice chief of staff and former head of SAC Curtis LeMay told representatives that any money they gave him for planes would be spent on bombers, not on MATS. There were no other voices to challenge LeMay's either; when Congress asked the air force to send their senior commanders for hearings, only the heads of SAC, TAC, and the Air Defense Command appeared.

With this diminished vision of MATS' role in the U.S. warfighting structure, another threat appeared from the civilian sector. In 1955 a committee headed by Herbert Hoover recommended that MATS divest itself of most of its airlift capacity, and that instead it be given a fund to purchase the services it needed from commercial airlines. This resulted in a flurry of lobbying on Capitol Hill from those interests which stood to secure enormous profits from such a move.

One positive move for MATS during this period came in 1956, under what was known as the "single manager" program in the Department of Defense. Under this concept, different parts of the services would acquire full responsibility for certain missions, with units shifted across service boundaries to ensure a unified command. The air force became manager of all airlift operations, to be housed under MATS. In practical terms, the organization acquired a number of troop carrier squadrons that had been shifted to TAC and full responsibility for ferrying infantry to combat zones. This took effect a year later, and soon after Tunner would use it to demonstrate on a large scale how important airlift was and how far it had fallen behind in its capabilities.[9]

In 1958 Joseph Smith retired from the air force, opening up the position of commander of MATS, and Tunner became his replacement. His recent stint in the Pentagon did not hurt, as he may have caught the eye of the new secretary of the air force, James Douglas, who had ideas on where the service should be headed, that were far more expansive than to just support SAC. The ceremony marking the change in command was strained and formal; Smith would be presented the Distinguished Service Medal, the U.S. Air Force's highest noncombat decoration, by the chief of staff, General Thomas White. Tunner would look on, but he cannot have endorsed the award; he and Smith had become enemies since the days of Berlin, and their differing views on the role of military airlift in the 1950s put them at loggerheads. Rumors circulated that the two had nothing to do with each other, and that Smith exited through one gate as Tunner came in another.[10]

None of that slowed the new commanding officer down; he had waited too long for this, and the situation had deteriorated too far. Tunner, in words taken from a particularly insightful doctoral dissertation, "blew into MATS like a bobcat in a hen house: all motion and meanness." One of the first things he did was get rid of some of Smith's commanders and bring in his own people. Raymond Towne took over as public affairs chief, and Red Foreman, by then a brigadier general, was running one of the subordinate commands in New Jersey, not far from MATS' home in Washington, D.C.[11]

Tunner felt his back was against the wall by that point, with nothing to lose. He later compared himself and the organization he loved to "the Marines at Hagaru-ri—surrounded." This was a delicate situation; he knew that fighting back meant going public, that "there was a danger that the impending controversy might be bad for the Air Force, bad for the airlines." But to a visionary like Tunner, there was no choice, "If I had failed to fight, our strategic airlift would . . . be in pitiful shape."[12]

Despite this rhetoric, the tides of political fortune had already changed, and with Tunner's strong and well-developed concepts, he became the right man at the right time. Led by defense intellectuals, by the late 1950s Washington was seriously considering the new concept of flexible response, the idea that wars could be fought at a level below an all-out strategic nuclear exchange. Maxwell Taylor, who during World War II had led the 101st Airborne Division, the Screaming Eagles, stepped down as army chief of staff in protest over the single-minded emphasis on big bombers, and wrote that the United States had to "provide for mobile, ready forces prepared for rapid movement to areas of strategic importance overseas." Lieutenant General James Gavin, former commander of the Eighty-second Airborne Division and another advanced military thinker, called for limited nuclear war involving ground troops. Studies began to come out about the use of tactical nuclear weapons, and even the possibility of using conventional forces exclusively in a future combat situation. All of these scenarios required a strategic airlift force dedicated to military needs, capable of getting troops and advanced equipment anywhere in the globe on a moment's notice.[13]

This also meant that for the first time, MATS had an incredibly powerful ally. Tired of being considered the old-fashioned alternative, the U.S. Army took up the idea of flexible response as a critical lever to get back to the forefront of national defense. To do this, however, they not only had to develop units that could move quickly, they also needed a branch of the military that would get their men and material to hot spots in a hurry. For much of the decade, short distance transport had been in the hands of the Tactical Air Command, which also ran the fighter squadrons. Its generals, who had come up from the ranks of units that flew fast and glamorous planes like the P-51, P-47, and P-38 in World War II, were not inclined to grant high priority to ferrying the army. Their version of the flexible response doctrine would be to use fighters equipped with tactical warheads, not assisting in a ground war. The only place the army had to turn if it was going to get back in the game was MATS.

Tunner pulled out everything from the bag of tricks he had been developing since his days back in Ferrying Command. He argued that even SAC would need planes to carry its big bombs and that a fleet of bigger and better transports could even haul the new ICBMs, faster and safer than rail could. In a nuclear crisis, furthermore, the ability to get these missiles from industrial or military depots into position in the quickest time imaginable might mean the difference between defeat and national survival. MATS planes were also needed to deliver supplies—from nukes to parts to fuel—to the forward bases SAC had set up for its bombers around the world. By March 1959 Tunner was in contact with Major General John Mills, air force deputy chief of staff for development, over the "need for an instantaneous reaction transportation capability direct from factory to the using organization," in which "flexibility was mandatory."[14]

Tunner also had no qualms about using publicity to get attention, to build pressure on Congress. Articles appeared in military trade papers on how MATS was "battling for its life." The author of a piece in *Air Force and Space Digest* with the ominous title, "The Gap In Our Military Air Transport," told his influential audience that, despite the fact that the service "moves almost all of its personnel by air," its transports were all still in the World War II prop era, at a time when everything else in the air force was jet powered and capable of speeds in the range of Mach 1. As a result, he concluded, "modernization of MATS is now crucial."[15]

Even the popular press got involved. The *Saturday Evening Post* ran an article pathetically titled, "Uncle Sam's Orphan Airline," which rebutted both the argument that civilian airlines could do MATS' job, and that SAC did not need any transport backup; "as SAC increased in size and readiness, it called upon MATS to help lift not only bombs but also advance-base people and materiel," the *Post* reported. Their writer stressed the need for a new generation of

larger and jet powered transports, and discussed the problem of "sagging morale" in this neglected branch of the military. One of the officers he spoke to,
who went on record, was by coincidence the commander of the MATS facility
at McGuire Air Force Base, a one-star by the name of Red Foreman. *Business
Week* ran a story entitled, "MATS' Wings Still Clipped," that explained how
"many U.S. military strategists believe that . . . nuclear war is unlikely ever to
be fought. . . . They are convinced that the threat of local limited wars . . . is . . .
much more serious," and that the air force had to be prepared to get troops to
this new kind of war. Dorothy Towne said Tunner was behind all these stories,
that he would lobby editors, and because of both his knowledge and sincerity,
he would get them so excited and enthused about the idea they that would authorize a piece on MATS.[16]

Tunner's most elaborate effort to publicize the need for airlift and reinforce
crucial alliances was a multi-service exercise. By the late fifties the army had
given up the idea of rapidly shifting large forces to a combat zone, but Tunner
came up with a major operation to prove that such efforts could succeed.

The idea was to airlift a significant army unit into a hot zone. Ground force
commanders saw this as a limited operation, and recommended using about
6,000 troops backed up by 6,000 tons of equipment. That was not at all what
Tunner had in mind; he was looking for a showcase for what MATS could—
and could not—do, so he pushed for 20,000 troops and 10,000 tons of equipment, figures that flabbergasted the army. The head of airlift was playing hard-
ball now, however, with his back to the wall, so he began pushing the suggestion
that MATS might work with the Marine Corps instead, something the army
"did not view with favor," according to the official report, but which forced
them to move in Tunner's direction. In the end, the final figure would come out
far closer to Tunner's than what the army had originally envisioned.[17]

Planning proceeded accordingly, and after much deliberation, the final site
became Puerto Rico. The exercise now carried the code name Big Slam/Puerto
Pine, the first half referring to the MATS operation, the second to the movement of troops from the continental United States to this Caribbean island,
and then back home again, as there was no spot available for large-scale maneuvers. Fourteen air bases in the United States alone would be required to handle
all the traffic, and the operation would take fifteen days to complete.

Big Slam/Puerto Pine commenced early in the morning of March 14, 1960;
a few days earlier Tunner told a congressional committee that it would be "the
first real maneuver of this magnitude between MATS and the Army . . . since
the war," how it was "the largest peacetime airlift exercise ever conducted." De-

spite stormy weather along the route—some of it, according to the air force, "more severe than ever before recorded"—the planes got through, with 93 percent of all trips arriving on time. MATS used a large portion of its entire fleet to do the job, 222 out of a total of 447 planes, but the operation went off, in typical Tunner style, with an almost perfect safety record. At any given moment, one hundred planes were in the air, and one of these craft arrived at either of the two Puerto Rican airfields every 7.5 minutes. By the time it was over, MATS had flown a force of 21,092 troops and MATS personnel on a round trip—in other words 42,184 passenger trips—plus 10,935 tons of cargo. All of this, while still maintaining its regular service for SAC, TAC, and the rest of the military all around the world.[18]

Big Slam/Puerto Pine garnered extensive coverage; Tunner had invited aboard every relevant member of Congress imaginable, as well as 352 reporters and editors. Raymond Towne estimated that in total the country's papers devoted 33,000 column lines to the exercise. In the midst of the operation, the *New York Times* referred to it as "valuable training, the first of its exact kind. It is a public relations tour de force directed toward Congress. . . . It is also a field laboratory that may produce . . . answers to some of the major difficulties . . . that have complicated the issue of military air transportation." The *Air Force Times* quoted a final report that put paid to the idea that civilian carriers could do the job of MATS, stating that they did a fine job on normal routes, but were "not practical" for trips into combat zones. One editor who hitched a ride on a Big Slam plane headlined the story, "You Can't Run A Cold War With Businessmen Pilots," and began his article with the line, "I saw first hand the might of the U.S.A. unleashed here today as the Army and the Air Force teamed up in the largest military airlift exercise ever conducted in peacetime." He concluded, "As far as this observer is concerned, MATS proved its case. Commercial air carriers do a marvelous job of flying people from one place to another. But when strict military discipline is necessary and orders must be swiftly given and instantly carried out to the letter, it is a job for men in uniform, not civilians."[19]

After that it was a matter of sorting out the appropriate lessons. During the fifteen days of Big Slam, MATS personnel toiled an average of twelve hours a day, or eighty-four hours a week. While Tunner praised his men for working so hard, he also pointed out the severe shortcomings of their equipment: planes that were so antiquated by that era that they could not bring in any heavy equipment, such as modern tanks for the army; and how a limited operation of this sort required such an extreme commitment of existing resources. The leading U.S. military transport at that time was the prop-engined C-124, which could not fly very fast in a jet age, and also carried the burdens, as the final report on Big Slam noted, of "excessive maintenance . . . out-of-date communications and electronics equipment, and steep loading ramps." The transports in MATS' fleet were too few, too small, too slow; as a result, Tunner remarked, "it took so many airplanes and so much effort to do such a small job."[20]

Other conclusions put an end to some arguments, and reinforced new friendships. Commercial carriers, it now became clear, could not do MATS' job. The exercise had come off as well as it did, furthermore, because of the close cooperation between air transport and the army, which should be continued well into the future by means of regularly scheduled operations of this nature.

Congress got the point. By then there was a vocal opposition, men who were up-and-coming or already established leaders like John Kennedy and Lyndon Johnson. The biggest supporter of airlift, however, was a devout southerner, Congressman Mendel Rivers from South Carolina, who sat on the Armed Services Committee. Rivers's overall record is mixed, to be polite; he was an arch segregationist and racist, someone constantly fighting, not just the civil rights movement, but the 1861–1865 conflict itself.

As with his sentiments on race in American society, when it came to military airlift, similarly, Mendel Rivers made clear which side of the issue he clearly sat on, except that here was a stalwart of progress. In 1958 Rivers conducted hearings in which the subcommittee found itself "astonished and deeply concerned at how people with responsible areas are unaware of the clear and extensive military need for MATS." Two years later, he got authorization to convene an even more thorough investigation as the head of a Special Subcommittee on National Military Airlift, with hearings conducted from March 8 to April 22, 1960. It was in the midst of these critical sessions that Tunner had deliberately scheduled Big Slam/Puerto Pine.[21]

Rivers scheduled sixty witnesses, but he planned to rely most of all on Tunner and the MATS staff. As Ann Tunner pointed out, this made sense: "Transportation was General Tunner's profession. He practically started it, so he knew every nuance of transportation and continued to perfect it and fight for . . . its recognition." That had been true for some time, however; the difference in this case was that someone in authority recognized the importance of both the individual and his chosen field.[22]

Tunner knew an opportunity when it came running at him, and he held nothing back. He pointed out that MATS was still flying C-54s and labeled the fleet as being 90 percent obsolete. "The present force," he made clear, "cannot meet the time limitations established for the airlift of army forces," a claim supported by one of the other men who took the stand, General Bruce Clarke, head of the U.S. Army's Continental Command. In a prescient nod to the great crisis that loomed over the horizon, Rivers even asked Tunner if he had the capability of flying sizable ground forces to Southeast Asia. Tunner had to reply, "No sir, not within a reasonable time limit, or the time limit desired by the Chief of Staff of the Army." Rivers was not through, however, pressing the point home by asking, "And the reason . . . is because of the obsolescence of your present inventory?" Tunner now agreed, arguing that "quantitatively we probably have enough, but qualitatively—that is, with the speed and capacity we don't have enough." By the end of the hearings Tunner was laying out the precise details of a replacement fleet of large turbojet transports.[23]

The Final Report of the Rivers Subcommittee was testimony to all that Tunner had worked for since the 1930s. Its "Summary of . . . Recommendations" began with the warning that the group had concluded "that within the first 20 days of either general war, without warning, or limited war under any current . . . planning purposes, that strategic airlift capabilities are seriously inadequate." In order to rectify this condition, Congress and the military should fund development and purchase of a large turbine jet-powered transport, in significant numbers. MATS should be modernized, and the Civil Reserve Air Fleet—the civilian carriers who could be called upon in an emergency—should be viewed as an adjunct to, rather than a replacement for MATS. Finally, in a last recommendation that encapsulated all that Tunner believed, the Subcommittee intoned, "The Military Air Transport System is a weapons system . . . required in the performance of military missions." As such, it "should have a designation which is more consistent with its mission. Accordingly, the subcommittee recommends that the Military Air Transport Service be designated the 'Military Airlift Command' (MAC)," on a par with organizations such as the Strategic Air Command (bombers) and Tactical Air Command (fighters).[24]

This was Tunner's moment, and at last he had allies. Rivers told the *Christian Science Monitor* how "everyone has been going hog-wild on push-button warfare and forgetting what the Army has been saying. . . . Everybody has overlooked the possibility of a limited war." Part of the answer had to be placing MATS "on equal priority with the other services," recognizing its importance. At the same time, C. R. Smith, president of American Airlines and Tunner's old acquaintance from Ferrying Command, gave a speech before the Aviation Writers Association in which he called for the development of a supersonic transport, with the U.S. military taking the lead.[25]

Congress listened. In May 1960 the House voted a record appropriation for

MATS of $370 million, of which $250 million should go toward obtaining a jet transport fleet.[26]

Tunner was within a month of retirement, but he had won his war. Airlift was now accepted as an important part of the U.S. military. The new president, John F. Kennedy, had been an ally for some time, but even more important, came into office with a vastly revised view of what the military was and how it should operate. He and his team were critics of the all-nuclear strategy and began to build up conventional and even nonconventional forces, such as the Green Berets. All of these would need cargo planes to get them to their destination, and in his first State of the Union address, Kennedy announced "prompt action to increase our airlift capacity. Obtaining additional airlift mobility— and obtaining it now—will better assure the ability of our conventional forces to respond, with discrimination and speed, to any problem on the globe at any moment's notice."[27]

The ultimate artifact of this change was the C-141, the first jet-powered long-range transport in history, known as the Starlifter. Kennedy personally made the announcement in March 1961 that Lockheed had won the contract for the new plane in order to highlight its importance, and the first test flight took place on December 17, 1963. Leo Sullivan, chief engineering test pilot for the company, laconically explained, "we just rolled down the runway until there was nothing left to do but fly. So we flew." It was a picture-perfect episode, and the cherry on top was when someone noticed the date: this was the sixtieth anniversary of the Wright Brothers' flight at Kitty Hawk. The first Starlifter came to MATS on April 23, 1965.[28]

The plane was a gem. It could fly 25 tons for 4,600 miles, or 10 tons between California and Japan (6,325 miles), thus eliminating the need for refueling bases in the Pacific. When it came to passengers, this big bird could handle 154 combat soldiers or 123 paratroopers, and became the first jet these elite forces ever jumped out of, courtesy of an internal cargo box with dimensions of 70 feet by 10 feet by 9 feet, later extended to 93 feet and a clamshell rear door. All of this, and a top speed of over 500 mph. In addition, it became the first cargo plane to have a computer installed as part of its basic equipment.[29]

The C-141 revolutionized military airlift. On short hauls it could carry 35 tons, so it could have handled the Berlin Airlift with only one-quarter the number of flights, and done it a lot quicker given that the Starlifter flew two and one-half times faster than the C-54, and was far easier to load and unload because of its straight-through design. In 1981 it carried almost 34 tons of cargo from New Jersey to Saudi Arabia nonstop, refueling in flight three times.

It maintained one tradition of MATS' earlier craft, however, and that was reliability; one historian noted that "it was not the biggest airplane ever built, nor was it the fastest, and it could not carry the heaviest loads. But it could carry larger and heavier loads faster and further than any other plane then flying, and it could do this day after day, mile after mile, with a minimum of down-time for service and repairs." One pilot simply called it "the most forgiving airplane I ever flew," making it a legitimate descendant of the legendary C-47.[30]

Tunner was out of the air force by the time the Starlifter first flew, but there was no way he could let an occasion like this go by without comment. Always the visionary, he looked beyond steel and wires and claimed that "this plane is more than an aircraft. . . . It is a symbol of a basic change in our national attitudes toward survival." General Howell Estes, who in 1964 took over as head of MATS, claimed that the C-141 should not be viewed as the conclusion of an effort, but as merely the start of an entirely new era in airlift. If his voice was different, the words sounded familiar, as Tunner had created the modern arguments for military air transportation, and everyone else was, in essence, his follower.[31]

Tunner and Estes were right; it was only the start. In 1966, MATS became MAC, or Military Airlift Command, and received equal status with SAC and TAC in the air force hierarchy. By then the United States was building up a large force in Vietnam, and for the first time, the bulk of the troops did not travel by ship but by plane. The entire culture of war had changed; images of World War II travel consisted almost exclusively of crowded ships scurrying to avoid U-boats, whereas everyone who served in, or even watched the Vietnam War, saw planes landing in Saigon disgorging what would eventually be a major U.S. ground force.[32]

This trend has never reversed itself, and instead is now standard practice worldwide, for whoever can afford it. During the Falklands War, the British dispatched their forces by sea, but as soon as victory was complete, established air bases at Port Stanley so they could move troops in and out as fast as possible. By the time of the second Gulf War, the United States could mobilize not only MAC, but a powerful civilian adjunct as well. During the period of the formal conflict in 2002 alone, these carriers moved 500,000 troops in and out of theater, and brought in 160,000 tons of equipment, almost the weight of four *Iowa*-class battleships at standard loading. On April 8, 2003, a 60-ton M1A1 Abrams tank drove off the back of a C-17 onto Bashur Airfield, the first time that a tank had been air landed directly into combat, a feat that previously only the British had tried using gliders and light tanks in World War II.[33]

Decades after he fought to prove that airlift had an important role in the military structure, Tunner's ideas had become part of the conventional war fighting mechanism. The military history writer James Dunnigan stated, "Gone are the days when a president would order the troops to some distant nation and everyone would wait for weeks while the troops got on ships and slowly steamed off to war. We expect instant response, and that means flying the troops in." If Dunnigan had added, "with all their equipment and supplies," the man who started it all could not have said it better.[34]

Epilogue: Starlifter

In 1958 William Tunner suffered a heart attack. By then he was thick in battle to save MATS, and later wrote an acquaintance, "to be perfectly frank, it has been a very tough year for me." Tunner wanted to retire as soon as possible for health reasons, but MATS was moving from Andrews Air Force Base outside Washington to Scott Air Force Base in Illinois, and the Pentagon asked him to oversee the transition. By the end of the Rivers hearings a date had been set for him to step down, and the congressman paid Tunner homage by publicly asking the general's pardon as he got "just a little bit nostalgic." Mendel Rivers acknowledged that "it hasn't been easy in recent years to carry the banner of MATS," but Tunner had done the same fine job he had for years. Looking back over the Hump operations, Berlin, and Korea, Rivers acknowledged, "We owe a great deal of the success to your leadership, and your everlasting and untiring endeavors." In the end, he summed up the obvious, "If anybody in America today has justly earned the title of 'Mr. Airlift,' that would be you."[1]

William Tunner retired from the United States Air Force, the service that he had dedicated his life to, but which had also resisted his visionary ways and entrepreneurial personality, on May 31, 1960. He had served as head of MATS, the post so rightfully his, for less than two years, although his impact was, of course, infinitely greater. At the ceremony celebrating his departure, Chief of Staff General Thomas White awarded Tunner the Distinguished Service Medal, the service's highest peacetime honor; the citation read, "by his skillful and forceful leadership and exceptional ability," Tunner had been "eminently successful in welding the various services of the Military Air Transport Service into a cohesive and outstandingly effective organization." During the subsequent parade, among the dignitaries who were permitted to join the official party in the reviewing stand was Congressman Mendel Rivers of South Carolina. West Germany later made Tunner a Knight Commander of the Order of Merit, and named a street after him in the city he had saved—Berlin—to honor his name and memory.[2]

In some ways it was fortuitous timing. With a new administration, a new attitude toward airlift, and money flowing, the time for bureaucratic infighting was over; MATS needed a soothing administrator, not a devoted advocate. There was still built-up resentment in the air force against someone who had, in pursuit of ideals, sided with Congress and the army against their own ranks. As one scholar put it, "What MATS needed was a commander with a good understanding of airlift, wide respect and trust within the Air Force community, and the ability to maintain the progressive alliance." In the end, Tunner's ideas would triumph, but the military had had a hard time with someone who acted more like the creator of giant industrial complexes than an anonymous square in an organizational flow chart.[3]

The likelihood that Tunner would remain idle was nil. When a new Berlin crisis broke out in 1961, the world wondered if the city could once again be saved if blockade reappeared. *Life* naturally interviewed the man they referred to as "the world's most successful operator of airlifts," who told them that of course the United States could duplicate the effort, but it would work even better now, because larger planes were available, then offered details of how many planes, flights, and airports would be needed this time around.[4]

The grand themes of his life continued to dominate, and Tunner now had more time to write about them. In "Strategic Airlift," an article that came out in early 1961, he pushed for supersonic transports and a larger role for MATS. Four years later, in "Do We Want a Supersonic Transport Or an $89 Trip to Europe?" he argued against a Mach 3 transport in favor of a jumbo jet that could haul vast quantities of passengers or cargo for both the civilian airlines and the military. In familiar language, he observed that a plane like that could start "a revolution."[5]

His biggest literary project, however, was an autobiography. This was a frustrating project; Tunner had to work with a ghost writer, and the first wordsmith to take on that task turned in a glib, facetious chapter and had to be dropped. Although a second choice turned out to be better, Tunner always refused to let history be glamorized and popularized instead of sticking to facts he considered dramatic enough, and hence suffered repeated rejections from publishers. On one occasion, his amanuensis discussed possible magazine ad-aptations, but gave a clear picture of how Tunner failed to understand the business side of publishing: "The *Post, Look* and *Life* are fighting a bitter circulation battle; they want exciting and provoking stories. You've got to come out swinging and you did not choose to do so," writer Booton Herndon observed, then added, "This is by no means a criticism. Your book will be a constructive contribution to history and I am proud and satisfied with my part in it. But I don't see it on the cover of the *Post*." Most galling of all, this implied that the public was losing interest in the great events that Tunner had been a part of, a shift underlined when a German publisher turned down the rights on the grounds that "more than 15 years will have elapsed since the event of the Berlin Luft-brucke [Airlift]," and that furthermore, since then, many books have come out on the subject, "written in a journalistic manner with a corresponding appeal to the general public." Tunner could only write Herndon, "I think I have . . . a good story, still untold. . . . I don't understand the rejections at this time with airlift taking such a large part of our tax monies and being declared so vital to military readiness under the new concepts."[6]

Over the Hump was published by Duell, Sloan & Pearce in 1964, and the process was not all misery. Not only did Tunner have a public record of a proud career—Lucius Clay said publicly that everyone in the U.S. military should read the book—there had been a reopening of memory. The most poignant artifact in his research notes, for example, is a chart labeled, "Characters who were on my staff at various times," a typed list of names and their relations to Tunner during various assignments from Memphis in 1940 to commander of MATS. Once again, the roll call of Tunner's men and women appeared, each with their own record of success noted as well. Raymond Towne had started out with Tunner as a first lieutenant, but by the early 1960s was a colonel in charge of public relations at MATS. Harold Sims had gone from second lieutenant to lieutenant colonel, and Ross Milton had advanced from a colonel to a two-star general running the USAF in Asia. Robert Foreman ("Red" was in parentheses next to his formal name) now commanded MATS operations in Europe, and "Miss Catherine Gibson" was still there, referred to as "My good secretary at various times."[7]

Not surprisingly, many of these individuals kept in touch with their old boss. Months after Tunner had stepped down from the air force, Colonel Sterling Bettinger wrote to let him know "how happy and excited everyone in MATS is—now looking forward to the introduction of modern equipment. . . . The new and promising era for MATS has begun." Ross Milton penned a note asking how the retirement was going, and Charles Murphy, who had done a glowing piece on the airlift for *Fortune* back in 1948 and still remembered the extraordinary men who had led that effort, grumbled, "It is hard for me to understand how the Air Force can get along without your unique talents and imagination."[8]

Tunner was hardly idle after leaving the service. In 1958 he and his wife, Ann, bought a farm in Ware Neck, Virginia, but had not been able to move in till after his retirement, and now worked at running the place. He was on the board of directors of Seaborn & Western Airline, a leading cargo carrier across the Atlantic, and consulted with Douglas Aircraft, flying out to Santa Monica once a month. In 1968 UNICEF sent him to Biafra to report on the humanitarian airlift there. On the local scene, Tunner got involved in a host of civic causes, from the library to a day school. On April 6, 1983, he passed away, although Ann Tunner reported that "he was still writing letters to the Pentagon about airlift right up to before his death."[9]

Of all the components of the air service, transportation was the last to gain legitimacy. Fighters garnered national attention as early as the headlines for World War I aces, and by the Second World War bomber generals were coming into their own, to dominate the scene in the postwar era. Airlift barely existed before that second global conflict, and, even after the Berlin episode showed what could be done, was not accepted into the halls of power within the Pentagon.

That has all changed—airlift is now equivalent to strategic and tactical air— and it is largely because of one man. William Tunner was what is now referred to as "a transformation agent," someone who causes change to occur by means of ideas and force of personality; it was not a coincidence that he carried the nickname, "Willie the Whip."

Early on, Tunner developed a single-minded vision and entrepreneurial personality that would force the military to recognize the importance of airlift, but also get him in trouble with leadership. In essence, his career asked the question, how far can and should the military—the most regimented institution in our society—go in permitting innovators to challenge established procedures?[10]

Looking back, it is easy to see which mavericks should have been listened to, but in their own era the story was generally far less sanguine. They fought lonely battles, and frequently found their careers lagging behind those of more conventional peers. If they lacked respect, furthermore, we should recognize that sometimes this was because their ideas were too unconventional to be accepted, sometimes their ideas were really off base and should have been rejected, and sometimes, in their pursuit of a vision, they lacked any kind of advocacy skills; diplomacy helps genius. The key, for the military, is to determine which is which, hardly an easy assignment, and one in which ego and tradition should be balanced by insight and judgment.

Thus, Tunner serves as a model of a controversial, recurring issue within the armed services, how to handle innovators. This has been true for a long time.

Sometimes the story turns out poorly. Isaac Lewis invented one of the first practical light machine guns just before the First World War, but this officer was also, as one historian put it, "no respecter of person, rank or position in life," and became known as the "stormy petrel" of the army. He immediately came into conflict with the vain, arrogant head of the Ordnance Department, General William Crozier, who rejected Lewis's effort out of hand. Flemish and British companies, instead, spotted the gun for what it was, a pioneering piece of work, and began production. Shortly after, war in the trenches proved what a fine weapon this really was, and the British would eventually have 30,000 Lewis guns at work, firing 15 million rounds a day with superb reliability.[11]

In other cases, the story had a more positive ending. By the late 1960s, the U.S. Air Force was experiencing severe difficulties in how its planes and pilots fought the air war over Vietnam. A cadre of officers offered innovative ideas, and despite some resistance, turned things around so that by the 1970s America had again achieved world-class skill in fighter tactics. Officers like Larry Keith, who took over the Fighter Weapons School at Nellis Air Force Base, managed to introduce innovative ideas to great effect.[12]

Tunner's rebellion, however, was far greater than either of these examples, in which agents of change sought to either introduce new weapons or modify the use of existing ones. The founder of airlift, on the other hand, was after something more vast, a shift in the most fundamental doctrine of the air force, a reinterpretation of what the basic components of the air arm would be. He was asking the military, in other words, to rethink their basic assumptions of mission, and to assess what units would be required to carry this out. Adding to this challenge, he would also take on the culture of the service, introducing new personnel—such as women and locals—that overturned the status quo and could cause extreme discomfort. One of the things that makes a rebel a rebel is a willingness to go beyond accepted norms—persistence was everything, even at the cost of personal advancement.

William Tunner forced the U.S. Air Force to listen to his ideas, no easy task, and one not for weaklings or those who worried about their self-image. He would get the job done—*no matter what it took*—and if toes got stepped on, that was the very least of his worries. His approach highlights the choice of many of these change agents—whether to stick within the system or suffer personal derision in pursuit of a goal. Years after, when we can see what they have wrought, we praise whistle blowers and creative spirits, but forget that many of them do not return to jobs at the same level they had before they fought for changes. There is still a stigma to those who break with conventional wisdom, especially in such a tradition-bound institution as the military.

As a result, the armed services are always forced to deal with innovators, always torn between blocking change and leaping on its bandwagon, with risks in either choice. William Tunner's struggles do not stand in isolation, but are symbolic of an ongoing quandary that the Pentagon and its counterparts around the world perpetually grapples with. Tunner's oversized agenda highlights one of the most basic issues surrounding the military and transformation—namely that this institution must always be in a state of tension. On the one hand, the need for discipline inculcates conservative thinking and a resistance to change. At the same time, the pressure of life-and-death decisions compels innovation, often at a frantic pace. Their success in managing this paradox often determines the outcomes of wars, and hence of nations themselves.

From the time he found his life's calling, William Tunner became a man on fire. In describing her husband's life, Ann Tunner said, "He was adamant that anything the United States would move, he would move it, no matter what plane he had." That idealism, that persistence, changed the nature of warfare; the fact that the U.S. Air Force can carry just about anything, anywhere, anytime is testimony to the ideals and personality of airlift's founder. Later, in October 1989 William Tunner was posthumously inducted into the Airlift/Tanker Hall of Fame. The citation read: "His vision of the role airlift plays in our national defense capability is as valid now as it was in China or Berlin," then summed up his work: "Lt. Gen. Tunner's outstanding contributions to our airlift heritage warrant his recognition as 'Father of the Military Airlift Command.'"[13]

Notes

Chapter 1

1. *Time,* December 18, 1950; Flint DuPre, *U.S. Air Force Biographical Dictionary* (New York: Franklin Watts, 1965), 239.

2. William Tunner, *Over the Hump* (1964; repr., Washington, D.C.: Office of Air Force History, United States Air Force, 1985), 5.

3. U.S. Air Force Oral History Interview with Lt. Gen. William H. Tunner, October 5–6, 1976, K239.0512-911, Air Force Historical Research Agency, Maxwell AFB, Montgomery, Ala. (hereinafter referred to as AFHRA), 1.

4. *Time,* December 18, 1950; Tunner, *Over the Hump,* 6.

5. *Time,* December 18, 1950; W. Tunner interview, AFHRA, 2.

6. *Time,* December 18, 1950; The Howitzer Board, *The Howitzer* (Rochester: Du Bois Press, 1928), 319.

7. Tunner, *Over the Hump,* 6.

8. Ibid., 6; W. Tunner interview, AFHRA, 4; William McKinney, "Lieutenant General William H. Tunner, Father of the Military Airlift Command," Report Number 87-1700, Air Command and Staff College, Air University, Maxwell AFB, Montgomery, Ala., 3.

9. Tunner, *Over the Hump,* 6; W. Tunner interview, AFHRA, 6–7; DuPre, *U.S. Air Force Biographical Dictionary,* 239; letter from Curtis LeMay to William Tunner, June 1, 1959, Roll 34909, AFHRA.

10. W. Tunner interview, AFHRA, 7–14; DuPre, *U.S. Air Force Biographical Dictionary,* 239.

11. W. Tunner interview, AFHRA, 15–16.

12. Tunner, *Over the Hump,* 17.

13. Lieutenant General Harold George, "History of the Air Transport Command,"

American Airlines, n.d., in the Personal Estate of Harold Sims, 2; Carl Christie with Fred Hatch, *Ocean Bridge: The History of RAF Ferry Command* (Toronto: University of Toronto Press, 1995).

14. Christie with Hatch, *Ocean Bridge,* 3.

15. Tunner, *Over the Hump,* 16.

16. The full text of the letter appears in Tunner, *Over the Hump,* 18–19.

17. George, "History of the Air Transport Command," 3; Oliver LaFarge, *The Eagle in the Egg: The Story of the Coming of Age of Military Air Transport (Boston*: Houghton Mifflin, 1949), 11.

18. Robin Olds, http://www.af.mil/news/airman/1296/olds.htm, August 31, 2004; Tunner, *Over the Hump,* 19; W. Tunner interview, AFHRA, 17; telephone interview with Robin Olds, September 1, 2004.

19. Wesley Craven and James Cate, *The Army Air Forces in World War II, Vol. Seven: Services Around the World* (Chicago: University of Chicago Press, 1958), 9.

20. LaFarge, *Eagle in the Egg,* 13; Tunner, *Over the Hump,* 19.

21. Tunner, *Over the Hump,* 20; Christie with Hatch, *Ocean Bridge,* 126.

22. W. Tunner interview, AFHRA, 17, 19; telephone interview with Robin Olds, September 1, 2004.

23. Tunner, *Over the Hump,* 20–21; W. Tunner interview, AFHRA, 19.

24. McKinney, "Lieutenant General William H. Tunner," 7–8; Craven and Cate, *Army Air Forces in World War II: Services,* 7–8; George, "History of the Air Transport Command," 4; Tunner, *Over the Hump,* 22.

25. Tunner, *Over the Hump,* 22.

26. The Army Air Corps became the Army Air Forces on June 20, 1941.

27. McKinney, "Lieutenant General William H. Tunner," 8–9; "Routes of the Air Transport Command." Roll 34920, AFHRA; LaFarge, *Eagle in the Egg,* 60–61; Craven and Cate, *Army Air Forces in World War II: Services,* 14.

28. "Airlift/Tanker Association Hall or Fame: Lt. Gen. Harold L. George," http://www.atalink.org/hallfame/george.html, September 1, 2004; "Lieutenant General Harold L. George," http//www.af.mil/bios/bio.asp?bioID=5516, September 1, 2004; Craven and Cate, *Army Air Forces in World War II: Services,* 12.

29. The account of George's appointment comes from George, "History of the Air Transport Command," 6–7.

30. LaFarge, *Eagle in the Egg,* 51; W. Tunner interview, AFHRA, 23; Tunner, *Over the Hump,* 28; Memo from J. M. Harper to All Officers Concerned in the Preparation of Messages, July 27, 1942, Roll 34916, AFHRA.

31. Craven and Cate, *Army Air Forces in World War II: Services,* 19; LaFarge, *Eagle in the Egg,* 4, 264; Stanley Ulanoff, *MATS: The Story of the Military Air Transport Service* (New York: Franklin Watts, 1964), 17.

32. Memo from General H. L. George to Commanding Officer, Ferrying Division, February 9, 1943, Roll 34916, AFHRA; unattributed, undated article, "Over Unmarked Jungle and Glacier They Take Planes to Battle Lines," Roll 34916, AFHRA.

33. Memo on Factories Served by the Ferrying Groups, Roll 34916, AFHRA.

34. Tunner, *Over the Hump,* 28–29; Robert Sterling, *When the Airlines Went to War* (New York: Kensington Books, 1997), 80.

35. Gene Autry, *Back in the Saddle Again* (Garden City, N.Y.: Doubleday, 1978), 85–86.

36. Sterling, *When the Airlines Went to War,* 80.

37. Tunner, *Over the Hump,* 41–42.

38. W. Tunner interview, AFHRA, 28; Sterling, *When the Airlines Went to War,* 68.

39. LaFarge, *Eagle in the Egg,* 52–53; Craven and Cate, *Army Air Forces in World War II: Services,* 19; Tunner, *Over the Hump,* 11–12.

40. Memo from William Tunner to Bob Nowland, November 9, 1945, Roll 34916, AFHRA.

41. My sincere thanks to Roger Miller for this insight.

42. Tunner, *Over the Hump,* 24, 41.

43. LaFarge, *Eagle in the Egg,* 15.

44. The story of George and Smith is drawn primarily from George, "History of the Air Transport Command," 8–10. See also "A Brief History of American Airlines," March 1976, 2, provided by the National Air and Space Museum Library and Archives, Washington, D.C.

45. Material on Smith from Sterling, *When the Airlines Went to War,* 172–174.

46. Tunner, *Over the Hump,* 23; Sterling, *When the Airlines Went to War,* 171, 205–207; Robert Owen, "Creating Global Airlift in the United States Air Force, 1945–1977" (Ph.D. diss., Duke University, 1992), 23.

47. Discussion on Donald Douglas comes from Henry Holden, *The Legacy of the DC-3* (Brawley, Calif.: Wind Canyon Books, 2002), 11, 17.

48. *Time,* December 18, 1950.

49. LaFarge, *Eagle in the Egg,* 61.

50. See William O'Neill, "Transformation," *Proceedings of the U.S. Naval Institute,* March 2002, 100–104; Roger G. Miller, *Billy Mitchell: Stormy Petrel of the Air* (Washington, D.C.: Office of Air Force History, 2004), 22.

Chapter 2

1. Williamson Murray and Allan Millett, *A War to Be Won: Fighting the Second World War* (Cambridge, Mass.: Harvard University Press, 2000), 303.

2. Pete Daniel, "Going Among Strangers," *Journal of American History* 77 (December 1990): 907–908; Richard Lingeman, *Don't You Know There's a War On?: The American Home Front, 1941–1945* (New York: G. P. Putnam's Sons, 1970), 323.

3. Material on anti-Semitism in the military comes from Joseph Bendersky, *The "Jewish Threat": Anti-Semitic Politics of the U.S. Army* (New York: Basic Books, 2000). See esp. 240–41, 252, 259–63, 290–307.

4. Jeanne Holm, *Women in the Military: An Unfinished Revolution* (New York: Ballantine Books, 1992), 24, 26, 37; Leisa Meyer, *Creating GI Jane* (New York: Columbia University Press, 1996), 77.

5. Holm, *Women in the Military,* 50, 53; Jeanne Holm and Judith Bellafaire, eds., *In Defense of a Nation: Servicewomen in World War II* (Washington, D.C.: Military Women's Press, 1998), 82; Susan Godson, *Serving Proudly: A History of Women in the U.S. Navy* (Annapolis: Naval Institute Press, 2001), 115; Emily Yellin, *Our Mothers' War: American Women at Home and at the Front in World War II* (New York: Free Press, 2004), 130.

6. Meyer, *Creating GI Jane,* 25, 41.

7. Ibid., 77, 81; Yellin, *Our Mothers' War,* 132.

8. U.S. Air Force Oral History Interview with Lt. Gen. William H. Tunner, October 5–6, 1976, K239.0512-911, Air Force Historical Research Agency, Maxwell AFB, Montgomery, Ala. (hereinafter referred to as AFHRA), 29; interview with Ann Tunner, October 15, 2000.

9. This biography of Nancy Love is drawn primarily from "Nancy Harkness Love," http://www.pbs.org/wgbh/amex/flygirls/peopleevents/pandeAMEX03.html.

10. Adele Scharr, *Sisters in the Sky: Volume I—The WAFS* (St. Louis, Mo.: Patrice Press, 1986), 3.

11. The story of Fay Gillis comes from her obituaries in the *New York Times,* December 9, 2003, and the *Los Angeles Times,* December 12, 2003. The letter from Love is in "History of the Air Transport Command: Women Pilots in the Air Transport Command," 3. This appears in two places in AFHRA: at call number 300.0721-1 and on microfilm reel 34418. Page numbers, unless mentioned otherwise, are from the former document.

12. William Tunner, *Over the Hump* (1964; repr., Washington, D.C.: Office of Air Force History, United States Air Force, 1985), 34–35.

13. Ibid., 35. There is absolutely no record of anything other than a professional relationship between Tunner and Love.

14. Ibid., 36; "Women Pilots," 22.

15. Scharr, *Sisters in the Sky,* 14; "Women Pilots," 14–15; Wesley Craven and James Cate, *The Army Air Forces in World War II, Vol. Seven: Services Around the World* (Chicago: University of Chicago Press, 1958), 528.

16. "Women Pilots," 15–17.

17. Ibid., 18.

18. W. Tunner interview, AFHRA, 30–31; "Women Pilots," 22.

19. "Women Pilots," 24, 30.

20. Material on the first cadre of women pilots in WAFS is found in ibid., 30–35.

21. Jacqueline Cochran biographical material comes from Dean Jaros, *Heroes without Legacy: American Airwomen, 1912–1944* (Niwot: University Press of Colorado, 1993), 49–51; Jacqueline Cochran and Maryann Bucknum Brinley, *Jackie Cochran: An Autobiography* (New York: Bantam, 1987), 7–49; Col. Flint DuPre, *U.S. Air Force Biographical Dictionary* (New York: Franklin Watts, 1965), 42–43; "Jacqueline Cochran— (Biographical)," 220.0721-12, AFHRA.

22. DuPre, *U.S. Air Force Biographical Dictionary,* 43; "Cochran," AFHRA; Cochran and Brinley, *Jackie Cochran,* 5–6, 352–354; http://www.centennialofflight.gov/

essay/Explorers_Record_Setters_and_Daredevils/cochran/EX25.htm, September 15, 2004.

23. Craven and Cate, *Army Air Forces in World War II: Services,* 528; Scharr, *Sisters in the Sky,* 6.

24. Jaros, *Heroes without Legacy,* 56–58; Cochran and Brinley, *Jackie Cochran,* 167–68, 173.

25. "Women Pilots," 6.

26. Ibid., 6; Scharr, *Sisters in the Sky,* 8.

27. Scharr, *Sisters in the Sky,* 8.

28. Cochran and Brinley, *Jackie Cochran,* 187, 197; Jaros, *Heroes without Legacy,* 59–60; "Women Pilots," 55.

29. U.S. Air Force Oral History Interview with Ann Tunner, October 6, 1976, K239.0512-912, AFHRA, 6; Jaros, *Heroes without Legacy,* 59; Craven and Cate, *Army Air Forces in World War II: Services,* 530–31.

30. Website "Nancy Harkness Love"; W. Tunner interview, AFHRA, 34; Oliver LaFarge, *The Eagle in the Egg: The Story of the Coming of Age of Military Air Transport* (*Boston*: Houghton Mifflin, 1949), 132.

31. "Women Pilots," 77; LaFarge, *Eagle in the Egg,* 132.

32. Jaros, *Heroes without Legacy,* 60–61; website "Nancy Harkness Love"; Weatherford, *American Women,* 43–44.

33. "Women Pilots," 42, 51–52.

34. LaFarge, *Eagle in the Egg,* 133; "Women Pilots," 52, 92.

35. "Group Manual," Reel 34916, AFHRA; "Women Pilots," 87–88.

36. Jaros, *Heroes without Legacy,* 63.

37. LaFarge, *Eagle in the Egg,* 135–36.

38. Ibid., 135–37; website "Nancy Harkness Love"; W. Tunner interview, AFHRA, 33.

39. Tunner, *Over the Hump,* 37–38.

40. The account of this incident, unless cited otherwise, comes from "Women Pilots," 83–86.

41. W. Tunner interview, AFHRA, 36–37.

42. Ann Tunner interview with the author, October 15, 2002.

43. "Women Pilots," microfilm version, 129; W. Tunner interview, AFHRA, 30.

44. Ann Tunner interview with the author, October 15, 2002.

45. W. Tunner interview, AFHRA, 31–32, 35.

Chapter 3

1. Philip Jowett, *The Japanese Army, 1931–1945 (1)* (London: Osprey, 2002), 14.

2. Quoted in Maj. William McKinney, "Lieutenant General William H. Tunner, Father of the Military Airlift Command," Report Number 87-1700, Air Command and Staff College, Air University, Maxwell AFB, Montgomery, Ala., 11.

3. William Koenig, *Over the Hump: Airlift to China* (New York: Ballantine Books,

1972), 22; John Garraty, *The New Commonwealth, 1877–1890* (New York: Harper & Row, 1968), 80.

4. Otha Spencer, *Flying the Hump: Memories of an Air War* (College Station: Texas A&M University Press, 1992), 20–21; Jowett, *Japanese Army,* 17.

5. McKinney, "Lieutenant General William H. Tunner," 11; Koenig, *Over the Hump,* 24; Charles Miller, *Airlift Doctrine* (Montgomery, Ala.: Air University Press, 1988), 49; Roger Launius, "The Hump Airlift Operation of World War II," *Airlift* (Fall 1985): 9; Nicholas Williams, *Aircraft of the United States' Military Air Transport Service, 1948 to 1966* (Leicester: Midland Publishing, 1999), 12–13.

6. Launius, "The Hump Airlift Operation," 9; Williams, *Aircraft,* 13; Spencer, *Flying the Hump,* 12.

7. Roger Launius, "The Hump Airlift and Flight Safety," *Flying Safety* (November 1991): 25–26; Stanley Ulanoff, *MATS: The Story Of the Military Air Transport Service* (New York: Franklin Watts, 1964), 18; McKinney, "Lieutenant General William H. Tunner," 11; Koenig, *Over the Hump,* 51; Jon Sutherland and Dianne Canwell, *The Berlin Airlift: The Salvation of a City* (Gretna, La.: Pelican Publishing, 2008), 174.

8. Quoted in C. V. Glines, "Flying the Hump," *Air Force Magazine,* March 1991, 103; McKinney, "Lieutenant General William H. Tunner," 3; Edwin White, *Ten Thousand Tons by Christmas: A Comprehensive Story of Flying the Hump in W. W. II by an Officer Who Was There* (St. Petersburg, Fla.: Valkyrie Press, 1975), 97.

9. Spencer, *Flying the Hump,* 54–55, 117; White, *Ten Thousand Tons by Christmas,* 67, 77–78, 196; William Tunner, *Over the Hump* (1964; repr., Washington, D.C.: Office of Air Force History, United States Air Force, 1985), 55.

10. Henry Holden, *The Legacy of the DC-3* (Brawley, Calif.: Wind Canyon Books, 2002), 161; Launius, "Flight Safety," 26; Gene Autry, *Back in the Saddle Again* (Garden City: Doubleday, 1978), 86.

11. Launius, "The Hump Airlift Operation," 9–10.

12. Oliver LaFarge, *The Eagle in the Egg: The Story of the Coming of Age of Military Air Transport* (Boston: Houghton Mifflin, 1949), 109; Spencer, *Flying the Hump,* 52–53.

13. LaFarge, *Eagle in the Egg,* 118–99.

14. Glines, "Flying the Hump," 104.

15. Spencer, *Flying the Hump,* 91; LaFarge, *Eagle in the Egg,* 126.

16. Koenig, *Over the Hump,* 115–17; White, *Ten Thousand Tons by Christmas,* 242–43; LaFarge, *Eagle in the Egg,* 125.

17. Interview with Ann Tunner, October 15, 2002.

18. Ibid.; J. B. McLaughlin, "Berlin Airlift," *IFR,* June 1998, 6–7.

19. Robert Sterling, *When the Airlines Went to War* (New York: Kensington Books, 1997), 57, 59; Carroll Glines and Wendell Moseley, *The Legendary DC-3* (New York: Bantam Books, 1979), 92–93.

20. Glines and Moseley, *DC-3,* 113–14; C. M. Daniels, "The Douglas DC Legend," *Airpower 3* (July 1973): 16.

21. Dan Downie, "The First Real Airlift," *Air Progress* 23 (November 1968): 18; White, *Ten Thousand Tons by Christmas,* 191, 197.

22. Wesley Craven and James Cate, *The Army Air Forces in World War II, Vol. Seven: Services Around the World* (Chicago: University of Chicago Press, 1958), 137–38.

23. U.S. Air Force Oral History Interview with Lt. Gen. William H. Tunner, October 5–6, 1976, K239.0512-911, Air Force Historical Research Agency, Maxwell AFB, Montgomery, Ala. (hereinafter referred to as AFHRA), 38; Tunner, *Over the Hump,* 51; Letter from William Tunner to Boo, June 25, 1962, Roll 34938, AFHRA, 1.

24. W. Tunner interview, AFHRA, 38.

25. Tunner to Boo, AFHRA, 2.

26. Tunner, *Over the Hump,* 57.

27. Ibid., 87, 113.

28. Material on Tunner's rotation policy comes from ibid., 88–90.

29. Tunner to Boo, AFHRA, 5–6; Launius, "The Hump Airlift and Flight Safety," 27; Tunner, *Over the Hump,* 104.

30. Tunner to Boo, AFHRA, 5–6.

31. Tunner, *Over the Hump,* 102–104, 106; Spencer, *Flying the Hump,* 142–43.

32. Tunner, *Over the Hump,* 107. A nice introduction to Andrew Carnegie's obsession with data and efficiency can be found in David Brody, *Steelworkers in America: The Nonunion Era* (New York: Harper & Row, 1960).

33. Tunner, *Over the Hump,* 81–82.

34. Ibid., 98; Glines, "Flying the Hump," 105.

35. Tunner, *Over the Hump,* 100.

36. "Accident Rate By Station" in unnamed document, Roll 34918, AFHRA; McKinney, "Lieutenant General William H. Tunner," 13.

37. Tunner to Boo, AFHRA, 7.

38. Spencer, *Flying the Hump,* 141; Tunner, *Over the Hump,* 91; W. Tunner interview, AFHRA, 39–40.

39. Tunner, *Over the Hump,* 90–91.

40. Interview with Ann Tunner, October 15, 2002; W. Tunner interview, AFHRA, 39.

41. W. Tunner interview, AFHRA, 40–41.

42. Spencer, *Flying the Hump,* 141.

43. *Hump Express,* January 18, 1945, Roll 34919, AFHRA.

44. "Skootering," Roll 34919, AFHRA.

45. Interview with Ann Tunner, October 15, 2002.

46. Tunner to Boo, AFHRA, 2.

47. Koenig, *Hump,* 143; Craven and Cate, *Army Air Forces in World War II: Services,* 138.

48. Tunner, *Over the Hump,* 65, 94.

49. Miller, *Airlift Doctrine,* 55.

50. W. Tunner interview, AFHRA, 48; Craven and Cate, *Army Air Forces in World War II: Services,* 140–41.

51. Tunner, *Over the Hump,* 95.

52. Spencer, *Flying the Hump,* 144.

53. Craven and Cate, *Army Air Forces in World War II: Services,* 138; document titled, "U.S. Army, India China Division, Air Transport Command," Roll 34919, AFHRA; Spencer, *Flying the Hump,* 144–45.

54. Quoted in McKinney, "Lieutenant General William H. Tunner," 14.

55. Every account of this day draws on Tunner, *Over the Hump,* 132–34.

56. Craven and Cate, *Army Air Forces in World War II: Services,* 146, 150–51; Glines, "Flying the Hump," 105; Spencer, *Flying the Hump,* 8–9.

57. LaFarge, *Eagle in the Egg,* 114.

58. Craven and Cate, *Army Air Forces in World War II: Services,* 150–51; Launius, "The Hump Airlift Operation," 15; Roger Launius, "The Berlin Airlift," *Airlift* (Summer 1988): 10.

59. W. Tunner interview, AFHRA, 61.

60. *Time,* December 18, 1950, 28; Tunner, *Over the Hump,* 59; interview with Ann Tunner, October 15, 2002.

61. W. Tunner interview, AFHRA, 59.

62. Spencer, *Flying the Hump,* 22.

63. The term "age of big business" in reference to Tunner's arrival is used in Craven and Cate, *Army Air Forces in World War II: Services,* 139; Keonig, *Hump,* 143, 153; and Spencer, *Flying the Hump,* 137. See also "U.S. Army, India China Division, Air Transport Command," Roll 34919, AFHRA, 1.

64. Letter from Catherine Gibson to William Tunner, November 4, 1960, Roll 34938, AFHRA.

65. Interview with Ann Tunner, October 15, 2002; interview with Dr. William Tunner, February 3, 2003; Tunner, *Over the Hump,* 135.

Chapter 4

1. Interview with T. Ross Milton, September 14, 2002; interview with Sybil Sims and Suzanne Baker Sims, both on January 18, 2003; telephone interview with James Breedlove, April 13, 2003; telephone interview with Dr. William Tunner, February 3, 2003. See also Raymond Towne, "Tunner and the Saga of Airlift," *Air University Review* 16 (November–December 1964): 96.

2. Telephone interview with Dr. William Tunner, February 3, 2003; and telephone interview with Dorothy Towne, March 31, 2003.

3. William Tunner, *Over the Hump* (1964; repr., Washington, D.C.: Office of Air Force History, United States Air Force, 1985), 104–105; memo from William Tunner to Major Tilley, October 22, 1948, Roll 34928, Air Force Historical Research Agency, Maxwell AFB, Montgomery, Ala. (hereinafter referred to as AFHRA).

4. Major Edward Wittel, "Interview: Mr. Airlift, Lieutenant General William H. Tunner," *Airlift Operations Review* 3 (April–June 1981): 3; interview with Ann Tunner, October 15, 2002; telephone interview with Dr. William Tunner, February 3, 2003.

5. William Tunner to C.L.R. Barrett, September 13, 1944, Roll 34909, AFHRA.

6. Interview with Major General Russell L. Waldron, February 6, 1987, AFHRA, 10.

7. Oliver LaFarge, *The Eagle in the Egg: The Story of the Coming of Age of Military*

Air Transport (Boston: Houghton Mifflin, 1949), 47; *Time,* December 18, 1950, 28; interview with T. Ross Milton, September 14, 2002.

8. Telephone interview with Betty Foreman Churchman, May 20, 2003.

9. Interview with T. Ross Milton, September 14, 2002; telephone interview with Betty Foreman Churchman, May 20, 2003; Tunner, *Over the Hump,* 14, 66–67, 163; telephone interview with Dorothy Towne, March 31, 2003.

10. Interview with T. Ross Milton, September 14, 2002; Tunner, *Over the Hump,* 66–67.

11. Telephone interview with Dr. William Tunner, February 3, 2003; interview with Ann Tunner, October 15, 2002; Tunner, *Over the Hump,* 66–67.

12. Interview with Ann Tunner, October 15, 2002

13. Interview with T. Ross Milton, September 14, 2002.

14. T. Ross Milton, September 14, 2002; interviews with Sybil Sims and Suzanne Sims Baker, January 18, 2003.

15. Tunner, *Over the Hump,* 165; interview with Suzanne Sims Baker, January 20, 2003; e-mail from Suzanne Sims Baker, October 9, 2004.

16. Documents in the Personal Estate of Harold Sims.

17. Ibid.

18. Ibid.; interview with Suzanne Sims Baker, January 20, 2003.

19. Interview with Suzanne Sims Baker, January 20, 2003; e-mail from Suzanne Sims Baker, October 9, 2004.

20. The discussion of Earl Morrison is based on a telephone interview with him on March 12, 2003.

21. Tunner, *Over the Hump,* 164; telephone interview with Dorothy Towne, March 31, 2003.

22. Tunner, *Over the Hump,* 163–64, 176; telephone interview with Earl Morrison, March 12, 2003; interview with T. Ross Milton, September 14, 2002; interview with Ann Tunner, October 15, 2002.

23. Interview with T. Ross Milton, September 14, 2002; telephone interview with Dorothy Towne, March 31, 2003; Tunner, *Over the Hump,* 163; interview with Ann Tunner, October 15, 2002.

24. Tunner, *Over the Hump,* 13.

25. Ibid., 165; interview with Ann Tunner, October 15, 2002.

26. Interview with T. Ross Milton, September 14, 2002; U.S. Air Force Oral History Interview with Gen. Theodore R. Milton, April 9, 1976, K239.0512-1466, AFHRA, 1; "Biography, United States Air Force: Milton, Theodore R., General," attached to U.S. Air Force Oral History Interview with Gen. Theodore R. Milton, July 9, 1982, K239.0512-1339, AFHRA; U.S. Air Force Oral History Interview with Gen. Theodore R. Milton, K239.0512-917, n.d., AFHRA, 17–18.

27. Air Force interview with Milton, July 9, 1982, 28, 39–40; interview with T. Ross Milton, September 14, 2002.

28. Interview with T. Ross Milton, September 14, 2002.

29. Tunner, *Over the Hump,* 164; interview with T. Ross Milton, September 14, 2002.

30. Interviews with Ann Tunner, October 15, 2002, and Dr. William Tunner, October 15, 2002.

31. *Time,* December 18, 1950, 28; interview with Ann Tunner, October 15, 2002; interview with T. Ross Milton, September 14, 2002.

32. Telephone interview with Dorothy Towne, March 31, 2003.

33. Interview with Ann Tunner, October 15, 2002; interview with Dr. William Tunner, October 15, 2002.

34. Interview with Ann Tunner, October 15, 2002; telephone interview with Betty Foreman Churchman, May 20, 2003.

Chapter 5

1. William Tunner, *Over the Hump* (1964; repr., Washington, D.C.: Office of Air Force History, United States Air Force, 1985), 155.

2. "World Air Freight, Inc.," 1, Roll 34920, Air Force Historical Research Agency, Maxwell AFB, Montgomery, Ala. (hereinafter referred to as AFHRA).

3. Ibid., 7.

4. Letter from William Tunner to William Loucks, March 31, 1946, Roll 34920, AFHRA, 2.

5. Tunner, *Over the Hump,* 155.

6. Charles Miller, *Airlift Doctrine* (Montgomery, Ala.: Air University Press, 1988), 165–68.

7. Ibid., 169.

8. Ibid., 174; "NATS and ATC are Merged Into Single Military Transport Service," *Aviation Week,* February 9, 1948, 10; "World's Great Transport System," *Aviation Week,* May 17, 1948, 11.

9. "Army Transport of the Future," Roll 34920, AFHRA, 1.

10. Letter for William Tunner to Luke Finlay, July 29, 1947, Roll 34920, AFHRA.

11. "Operation: 'Casey Jones'," Roll 34920, AFHRA.

12. Memo from William Tunner to Chief of Staff, United States Air Force, May 4, 1948, Roll 34919, AFHRA.

13. Tunner's talk, "Douglas C-74 Globemaster Story," and material on his speech before the Commerce and Industry Association are in Roll 34920, AFHRA; the clipping on Glass's speech and Tunner's follow-up letters are in Roll 34919, AFHRA.

14. Material on Tunner's response to the Baldwin article is in Roll 34919, AFHRA. The quotes are from Tunner to General August Kissner, May 2, 1947.

15. Colonel Raymond Towne, "Tunner and the Saga of Airlift," *Air University Review* 16 (November–December 1964): 98.

16. Michael Haydock, *City under Siege: The Berlin Blockade and Airlift* (Washington, D.C.: Brassey's, 1999), 2; Joel Sayre, "Letter From Berlin," *New Yorker,* July 28, 1945, 52.

17. Haydock, *City under Siege,* 2; "Berlin," *Life,* July 28, 1945, 19; "Out of Death, Life," *Time,* July 30, 1945, 40; interview with Saul Kagan, October 16, 2002.

18. Robert Jackson, *The Berlin Airlift* (Wellborough, Northamptonshire: Patrick Stephens, 1988), 20–21; D. M. Giangreco and Robert Griffin, *Airbridge to Berlin: The Berlin Crisis of 1948, Its Origins and Aftermath* (Novato, Calif.: Presidio Press, 1988), 59; Haydock, *City under Siege,* 6, 22.

19. William Shirer, "End of a Berlin Diary," *Atlantic Monthly,* May 1947, 108; Howard K. Smith quoted in his obituary in the *New York Times,* February 19, 2002; Walter Ulbricht quoted in Alexandria Richie, *Faust's Metropolis: A History of Berlin* (New York: Carroll & Graf, 1998), 608; F. L. Lucas, *The Greatest Problem and Other Essays* (New York: Macmillan, 1961), 38.

20. Haydock, *City under Siege,* 14; Jackson, *Berlin Airlift,* 21; Howard K. Smith, *The State of Europe* (New York: Alfred A. Knopf), 1949), 115.

21. Jackson, *Berlin Airlift,* 13; Richie, *Faust's Metropolis,* 609.

22. Joel Sayre, "Letter From Berlin," *New Yorker,* August 4, 1945, 49, 50; Haydock, *City under Siege,* 39.

23. Genet, "Letter From Berlin," *New Yorker,* August 2 1947, 42.

24. Office of Military Government, U.S. Sector, Berlin, *A Four Year Report* (Berlin: Office of Military Government, Berlin Sector, 1949), 25.

25. Roger G. Miller, *To Save a City: The Berlin Airlift, 1948–1949* (College Station: Texas A&M University Press, 2000), 6; Mark Magnan, "The Berlin Blockade" (M.A. thesis, George Washington University, 1956), 10–12.

26. Magnan, "The Berlin Blockade," 10; Haydock, *City under Siege,* 41; Max Charles, *Berlin Blockade* (London: Allan Wingate, 1959), 15.

27. Giangreco and Griffin, *Airbridge to Berlin,* 98; my thanks to Roger G. Miller for bringing the original Western request to my attention.

28. Magnan, "The Berlin Blockade," 12.

29. *New York Times,* December 22 and 27, 1942.

30. Hannes Adomeit, *Soviet Risk-Taking and Crisis Behavior: A Theoretical and Empirical Analysis* (London: George Allen & Unwin, 1982), 125–26.

31. Giangreco and Griffin, *Airbridge to Berlin,* 51.

32. Haydock, *City under Siege,* 76; Yehuda Bauer, *Out of the Ashes: The Impact of American Jews on Post-Holocaust European Jewry* (Oxford: Pergamon Press, 1989), 207.

33. Avi Shlaim, *The United States and the Berlin Blockade, 1948–1949* (Berkeley and Los Angeles: University of California Press, 1983), 19.

34. Ibid., 113–15; Richie, *Faust's Metropolis,* 659; Jackson, *Berlin Airlift,* 34–35; Ann and John Tusa, *The Berlin Airlift* (New York: Atheneum, 1988), 102–103.

35. Shlaim, *The United States and the Berlin Blockade,* 118–19.

36. Charles, *Berlin Blockade,* 27.

37. Ibid., 27–28; Miller, *To Save a City,* 20.

38. Thomas Parrish, *Berlin in the Balance, 1945–1949: The Blockade, the Airlift, the First Major Battle of the Cold War* (Reading, Mass.: Perseus Books, 1998), 133–34; Miller, *To Save a City,* 20; Giangreco and Griffin, *Airbridge to Berlin,* 78.

39. *Newsweek,* April 12, 1948, 32; Haydock, *City under Siege,* 126–28.

40. Parrish, *Berlin in the Balance,* 136; Miller, *To Save a City,* 20.

41. The *Times* is quoted in Charles, *Berlin Blockade,* 34.

42. Miller, *To Save a City,* 21; "A Report on the Airlift," 165.7158-293, AFHRA; Stewart Powell, "Berlin Airlift," *Air Force Magazine,* June 1998, 52.

43. Richie, *Faust's Metropolis,* 662; Haycock, *City,* xiii.

44. Bernard Taper, "Letter From Berlin," *New Yorker,* April 17, 1948, 92, 94–95; Richie, *Faust's Metropolis,* 661–62.

45. Parrish, *Berlin in the Balance,* 35, 156; Haydock, *City under Siege,* 39; interview with Saul Kagan, October 16, 2002.

46. Adomeit, *Soviet Risk-Taking,* 90.

47. Giangreco and Griffin, *Airbridge to Berlin,* 82–84.

48. Howard K. Smith, *The State of Europe* (New York: Alfred A. Knopf, 1949), 123; Daniel Harrington, "The Berlin Blockade Revisited," *International History Review* 6 (February 1984): 96; Richie, *Faust's Metropolis,* 660.

49. *Newsweek,* June 28, 1948, 33.

50. Smith is quoted in Magnan, "Blockade," 32. See also Walter Smith, *My Three Years in Moscow* (Philadelphia: J. B. Lippincott, 1950), 231.

Chapter 6

1. The CIA quote is in Alexandria Richie, *Faust's Metropolis: A History of Berlin* (New York: Carroll & Graf, 1998), 1059n176; Roger G. Miller, *To Save a City: The Berlin Airlift, 1948–1949* (College Station: Texas A&M University Press, 2000), 3.

2. Arthur Pearcy, *Berlin Airlift* (Shrewsbury: Airlife, 1977), no pagination; Miller, *To Save a City,* 31.

3. Max Charles, *Berlin Blockade* (London: Allen and Unwin, 1959), 46; Mark Magnan, "The Berlin Blockade" (M.A. thesis, George Washington University, 1956), 37; John Man, *Berlin Blockade* (New York: Ballantine Books,1973), 43.

4. Michael Haydock, *City under Siege: The Berlin Blockade and Airlift* (Washington, D.C.: Brassey's, 1999), 134.

5. Miller, *To Save a City,* 43.

6. Lucius Clay, *Decision in Germany* (Garden City, N.Y.: Doubleday, 1950), 374.

7. *Time,* June 23, 1947, 21; Hannes Adomeit, *Soviet Risk-Taking and Crisis Behavior: A Theoretical and Empirical Analysis (London*: George Allen & Unwin, 1982), 139; Michael Haydock, *City under Siege,* 104; Brian Libby, "Policing Germany" (Ph.D. diss., Purdue University, 1977), 7; Miller, *To Save a City,* 28–29; *Army Times,* August 6, 2007, 16.

8. Haydock, *City under Siege,* 105, 141; Eduard Mark, *Defending the West: The United States Air Force and European Security, 1946–1998* (Washington, D.C.: Air Force History and Museums Program, 1999), 31; Frank Kluckhohn, "Behind the Scenes in Berlin," *The American Mercury,* November 1948, 522–23; Curtis LeMay with MacKinlay Kantor, *Mission With LeMay: My Story* (Garden City, N.Y.: Doubleday, 1965), 411.

9. Miller, *To Save a City,* 29; Magnan, "Berlin Blockade," 76.

10. *U.S. News and World Report,* July 9, 1948, 12.

11. *Time,* June 23, 1947, 20; *U.S. News and World Report,* July 9, 1948, 11; Adomeit, *Soviet Risk-Taking,* 140; Robert Jackson, *The Berlin Airlift* (Wellborough, Northamptonshire: Patrick Stephens, 1988), 39; Henrik Bering, *Outpost Berlin: The History of the American Military Forces in Berlin, 1945–1994* (Chicago: Edition Q, 1995), 86; Frank Howley, *Berlin Command* (New York: G. P. Putnam's Sons, 1950), 235–36; Jean Smith, *Lucius D. Clay: An American Life* (New York: Henry Holt, 1990), 498. An important assessment of Soviet troop strength in this era can be found in Matthew Evangelista, "Stalin's Post-War Army Reappraised," *International Security* 7 (1982–1983): 110–38.

12. Miller, *To Save a City,* 43, 48–49; Adomeit, *Soviet Risk-Taking,* 141; Avi Shlaim, *The United States and the Berlin Blockade, 1948–1949* (Berkeley and Los Angeles: University of California Press, 1983), 131; Haydock, *City under Siege,* 143, 145, 151; Walter Isaacson and Evan Thomas, *The Wise Men: Six Friends and the World They Made* (New York: Simon and Schuster, 1986), 456; *U.S. News and World Report,* April 9, 1948, 30; *Nation,* July 31, 1948, 116; Thomas Parrish, *Berlin in the Balance, 1945–1949: The Blockade, the Airlift, the First Major Battle of the Cold War* (Reading, Mass.: Perseus Books, 1998), 176.

13. Shlaim, *The United States and the Berlin Blockade,* 237–38; Russell Buhite and William Hamel, "War For Peace," *Diplomatic History* 14 (1990): 383; Adomeit, *Soviet Risk-Taking,* 141–42; Daniel Harrington, "The Berlin Blockade Revisited," *International History Review* 6 (February 1984): 103; Miller, *To Save a City,* 46–48.

14. Memorandum for General Wedermeyer, July 21, 1948, Record Group 319, Series P & O 092 (Section ix-c), National Archives, College Park, Md.

15. Pearcy, *Airlift;* Haydock, *City under Siege,* 143; Shlaim, *The United States and the Berlin Blockade,* 202.

16. Charles, *Berlin Blockade,* 59; Haydock, *City under Siege,* 148.

17. Parrish, *Berlin in the Balance,* 198; Miller, *To Save a City,* 44; Charles Murphy, "Berlin Airlift," *Fortune,* November 1948, 90.

18. LeMay and Kantor, *Mission with LeMay,* 415; Parrish, *Berlin in the Balance,* 194.

19. The account of Truman's decision is drawn from the following sources: Walter Millis, ed., *The Forrestal Diaries* (New York: Viking Press, 1951), 452–54; Haydock, *City under Siege,* 152; D. M. Giangreco and Robert Griffin, *Airbridge to Berlin: The Berlin Crisis of 1948, Its Origins and Aftermath* (Novato, Calif.: Presidio Press, 1988), 96; Parrish, *Berlin in the Balance,* 181; Harrington, "Revisited," 98–102.

20. Parrish, *Berlin in the Balance,* 183; Harrington "Revisited," 102–103.

21. David McCullough, *Truman* (New York: Simon & Schuster, 1992), 630.

22. Record Group 260, Entry 20, Box 5, Airlift Correspondence Folder, National Archives, College Park, Md.; *Newsweek,* June 21, 1948, 31; Marguerite Higgins, "Obituary of a Government," in Arthur Settel, ed., *This Is Germany* (New York: William Sloane Associates, 1950), 322; *Time,* July 4, 1949, 18.

23. Roger Launius, "The Berlin Airlift," *Airlift* (Summer 1988): 12; Harrington, "Revisited," 99; Ann and John Tusa, *The Berlin Airlift* (New York: Atheneum, 1988), 104–105; Adomeit, *Soviet Risk-Taking,* 164–65; Shlaim, *The United States and the Berlin Blockade,* 204; Memorandum for the Chief of Staff, U.S. Army, July 18, 1948,

Records Group 341, Entry 335, Box 807, Folder Berlin, June 15, 1948, National Archives, College Park, Md.; LeMay and Kantor, *Mission with LeMay,* 415.

24. Mark Arnold-Foster, *The Siege of Berlin* (London: Collins, 1979), 49; David Clay Large, *Berlin* (New York: Basic Books, 2000), 403; William Tunner, *Over the Hump* (1964; repr., Washington, D.C.: Office of Air Force History, United States Air Force, 1985), 216.

25. Interview with T. Ross Milton, September 14, 2002; Haydock, *City under Siege,* 125.

26. *Time* and Walter Lippmann quoted in Giangreco and Griffin, *Airbridge to Berlin,* 107; *Business Week,* July 24, 1948, 15.

27. Frank Donovan, *Bridge in the Sky* (New York: David McKay, 1968), 69; Charles, *Berlin Blockade,* 34.

28. Walter Smith, *My Three Years in Moscow* (Philadelphia: J. B. Lippincott, 1950), 231; Adomeit, *Soviet Risk-Taking,* 165; Shlaim, *The United States and the Berlin Blockade,* 211, n. 38.

29. Telephone interview with Dr. William Tunner, February 3, 2003; interview with Ann Tunner, October 15, 2002; telephone interview with Dorothy Towne, March 31, 2003; telephone interview with Earl Morrison, March 12, 2003.

30. Interview with T. Ross Milton, September 14, 2002.

Chapter 7

1. "A Special Study of Operation 'Vittles,'" *Aviation Operations* 11 (April 1949): 16.

2. Roger Launius and Coy Cross, II, *MAC and the Legacy of the Berlin Airlift,* K300.04-61, Air Force Historical Research Agency, Maxwell AFB, Montgomery, Ala. (hereinafter referred to as AFHRA), 10; Roger Launius, "Berlin Airlift," *Air Power History* 36 (Spring 1989): 10; "Interview of Brigadier General A. W. Kissner, USAF, Chief of Staff, USAFE," 2.5234-1, AFHRA, 1.

3. Launius and Coy, *MAC,* 11; Launius, "Berlin Airlift," 10.

4. "Kissner," 1.

5. Ibid., 1; Launius, "Berlin Airlift," 10.

6. "Vittles," 8–9.

7. Arthur Pearcy, *Berlin Airlift* (Shrewsbury: Airlife, 1997), no pagination.

8. Ann and John Tusa, *The Berlin Airlift* (New York: Atheneum, 1948), 168; Stewart Powell, "Berlin Airlift," *Air Force Magazine,* June 1998, 53.

9. David Tragg, *Airlift* (Novato, Calif.: Presidio Press, 1886), 78.

10. The account of the NSC meetings is drawn from Roger G. Miller, *To Save a City: The Berlin Airlift, 1948–1949* (College Station: Texas A&M University Press, 2000), 81–83; Launius and Cross, *MAC,* 16–17; Haydock, *City under Siege: The Berline Blockade and Airlift* (Washington, D.C.: Brassey's, 1999), 178; interview with T. Ross Milton, September 14, 2002.

11. Memorandum for Chief of Staff, U.S. Army, July 18, 1948, and "A Report to the National Security Council by the Secretary of Defense," July 28, 1948, both in

Records Group 341, Entry 335, Box 807, Folder Berlin (June 15, 1948), National Archives, College Park, Md.

12. Miller, *To Save a City,* 83.

13. *U.S. News and World Report,* August 20, 1948, 16.

14. Ibid., November 19, 1948, 25, and December 17, 1948, 22.

15. Charles Murphy, "Berlin Airlift," *Fortune,* November 1948, 90; Mark Magnan, "The Berlin Blockade" (M.A. thesis, George Washington University, 1956), 84–85.

16. Dave Bettinger with Brigadier General Sterling Bettinger, "Year 2000 Emergency Management: A Parallel to the Berlin Airlift," http://www.year2000.com/archive/bettinger.html, October 7, 2002; Henrik Bering, *Outpost Berlin: The History of the American Military Forces in Berlin, 1945–1994* (Chicago: Edition Q, 1995), 90; Tusa and Tusa, *Berlin,* 180–81; Curtis LeMay with Mackinlay Kantor, *Mission With LeMay: My Story* (Garden City: Doubleday, 1965), 416.

17. Bettinger, "2000," 4; E. H. Kirkland to Commanding General, 1st Airlift Task Force, July 2, 1949, Roll 34926, AFHRA, 1.

18. Kirkland, 5–6; Michael Haydock, *City under Siege,* 164.

19. *Newsweek,* October 18, 1948, 50; *U.S. News and World Report,* August 6, 1948, 61; *Time,* July 19, 1948, 28; telephone interview with Dorothy Towne, March 31, 2003.

20. Thomas Parrish, *Berlin in the Balance, 1945–1949: The Blockade, the Airlift, the First Major Battle of the Cold War* (Reading, Mass.: Perseus Books, 1998), 220; *U.S. News and World Report,* August 6, 1948, 61.

21. Haydock, *City under Siege,* 155–56.

22. Daniel Harrington, "Against All Odds," *American History Illustrated,* February, 1982, 14; Richard Malkin, *Boxcars in the Sky: The Thrilling Story of Flying Cargo* (New York: Import, 1951), 270; Robert Rodrigo, *Berlin Airlift* (London: Cassell, 1960), 70.

23. Frank Donovan, *Bridge in the Sky* (New York: David McKay, 1968), 47–48; Paul Fisher, "The Berlin Airlift," *The Bee-Hive* 23 (Fall 1948): 8; D. M. Giangreco and Robert Griffin, *Airbridge to Berlin: The Berlin Crisis of 1948, Its Origins and Aftermath* (Novato, Calif.: Presidio Press, 1988), 101.

24. C. V. Glines, "Berlin Airlift Commander," *American Heritage* 20 (October 1969): 45.

25. Tusa and Tusa, *Berlin,* 165; *Newsweek,* July 19, 1948, 22.

26. Frederick Ford, "New Marks, Old Mistakes in Berlin," *New Republic,* July 19, 1948, 12.

27. Ernest Borneman, *Harper's Magazine,* August, 1948, 64; Anthony Atwood, "Operation Vittles," *Naval Aviation News* (May–June 1998): 37.

28. Ford, "Marks," 12; *Newsweek,* April 26, 1948, 32.

29. Ruth Andreas-Friedrich, *Battleground Berlin: Diaries 1945–1948* (New York: Paragon House, 1990), 234–35.

30. Bettinger, "2000," 2.

31. U.S. Air Force Oral History Interview with Lt. Gen. William H. Tunner, October 5–6, 1976, K239.0512-911, AFHRA, 77–81.

32. W. Tunner interview, AFHRA, 81–82; Major Edward Wittel, "Interview: Mr. Airlift, Lieutenant General William H. Tunner," *Airlift Operations Review* 3 (April–June 1981): 4–5.

33. William Tunner, *Over the Hump* (1964; repr., Washington, D.C.: Office of Air Force History, United States Air Force, 1985), 159–60; Wittel, "Interview," 5.

34. Tunner, *Over the Hump,* 160; Wittel, "Interview," 5.

35. W. Tunner interview, AFHRA, 82; Launius and Cross, *MAC,* 21–22.

36. Tunner, *Over the Hump,* 159–60; Charles Miller, *Airlift Doctrine* (Montgomery, Ala.: Air University Press, 1988), 177; T. Ross Milton, "Inside the Berlin Airlift," *Air Force Magazine,* October 1998, 49.

37. Parrish, *Berlin in the Balance,* 217.

38. W. Tunner interview, AFHRA, 83–84; William Tunner to Albert Wedemeyer, August 22, 1945, Roll 34927, AFHRA.

39. A. C. Wedemeyer to William Tunner, November 23, 1960, Roll 34938, AFHRA; A. C. Wedemeyer to Nicholas Pasti, January 21, 1974, K168.16-17, AFHRA.

40. Wedemeyer to Pasti, AFHRA.

41. W. Tunner interview, AFHRA, 85.

42. Wedemeyer to Tunner, AFHRA; Wedemeyer to Pasti, AFHRA; Tunner interview, AFHRA, 85; M. H. Froelich, "Air Lift Breaks the Berlin Blockade," *Flying* (October 1948): 76.

43. Wedemeyer to Pasti, AFHRA; Wedemeyer to Tunner, AFHRA; telephone interview with Alfred Goldberg, November 26, 2002.

44. W. Tunner interview, AFHRA, 86; Memo, "Instructions to Commander, Airlift Task Force (Provisional), Brigadier General August Kissner to Major General William H. Tunner," July 30, 1948, Roll 34922, AFHRA.

45. Tunner, *Over the Hump,* 162–63; W. Tunner interview, AFHRA, 86; Launius and Cross, *MAC,* 29; Milton, "Inside," 49; telephone interview with Earl Morrison, March 12, 2003.

46. Haydock, *City under Siege,* 181–82; W. Tunner interview, AFHRA, 86; Parrish, *Berlin in the Balance,* 219; Launius and Cross, *MAC,* 31.

47. Haydock, *City under Siege,* 182, 219.

48. Tunner, *Over the Hump,* 166.

49. Ibid., 166–67; Berlin Airlift Files, Box 1, Folder 1, History Office, Air Mobility Command, Scott AFB, Ill.

50. Milton, "Inside," 49; Tunner, *Over the Hump,* 167.

51. Tunner, *Over the Hump,* 168.

52. Ibid., 167; interview with T. Ross Milton, September 14, 2002.

53. W. Tunner interview, AFHRA, 96–97.

54. Telephone interview with Howard Fish, April 13, 2003; U.S. Air Force Oral History Interview with Lt. Gen. Joseph Smith, July 22–23 and November 16, 1976, K239.0512-906, AFHRA, 234–35.

55. "Plan for Task Force Vittles"; "Operation 'Manna'"; and Memorandum to Gen-

eral Cannon, October 20, 1948. All in Box I, Folders 1 and 4, Berlin Airlift Files, History Office, Air Mobility Command, Scott AFB, Ill.

56. Memo from William Tunner to Laurence Kuter, July 6, 1948, Box 1, Folder 1; memo from Kuter to Tunner, August 13, 1948, Box IV, Folder 31. Both in Berlin Airlift Files, History Office, Air Mobility Command, Scott AFB, Ill.

57. D. M. Giangreco and Robert Griffin, *Airbridge to Berlin: The Berlin Crisis of 1948, Its Origins and Aftermath* (Novato, Calif.: Presidio Press, 1988), 121; Parrish, *Berlin in the Balance*, 224; W. Tunner interview, AFHRA, 99–100.

58. Miller, *To Save a City,* 159.

59. Interview with Milton.

60. Tunner, *Over the Hump,* 71.

61. Miller, *To Save a City,* 151; Bill Gunston, *American Warplanes* (New York: Crown Publishers, 1986), 78; Tunner, *Over the Hump,* 181.

62. E. E. Burton and Charles Wood, "Design of the DC-4," *Canadian Aviation,* November 1944, 113; Otha Spencer, *Flying the Hump: Memories of an Air War* (College Station: Texas A&M University Press, 1992), 177; John Ohlinger, "C-54 Skymaster," in Robin Higham, *Flying American Combat Aircraft of World War II: 1939–45* (Mechanicsburg, Pa.: Stackpole Books, 2004), 125.

63. Ohlinger, "C-54," 127–28; Gann material comes from Ernest K. Gann, *Ernest K. Gann's Flying Circus* (New York: Macmillan, 1974), 152–53.

64. Nicholas Williams, *Aircraft of the United States' Military Air Transport Service, 1948 to 1966* (Leicester: Midland Publishing, 1999), 27; *Los Angeles Times,* July 20, 2002.

65. Interview with Ann Tunner, October 15, 2002; Robert Sterling, *When the Airlines Went to War* (New York: Kensington Books, 1997), 52; Tusa and Tusa, *Berlin,* 266.

66. The account of Milton's calculations is drawn from my interview with Milton. On LeMay's personality, see Donald Miller, *Masters of the Air: America's Bomber Boys Who Fought the Air War Against Nazi Germany* (New York: Simon & Schuster, 2006), 104.

67. LeMay's compliment is in Milton, "Inside," 49.

68. Interview with Milton; Miller, *To Save a City,* 163; Gunston, *Warplanes,* 78.

69. Clippings on the press conference are I Roll 34928, AFHRA.

Chapter 8

1. Michael Haydock, *City under Siege: The Berlin Blockade and Airlift* (Washington, D.C.: Brassey's, 1999), 189; Frank Donovan, *Bridge in the Sky* (New York: David McKay, 1968), 105.

2. Dave Bettinger with Brigadier General Sterling Bettinger, "Year 2000 Emergency Management: A Parallel to the Berlin Airlift," http://www.year2000.com/archive/bettinger.html, 6.

3. Haydock, *City under Siege,* 189; Bettinger, "Report," 6.

4. Arthur Pearcy, *Berlin Airlift* (Shrewsbury: Airlife, 1997), no pagination.

5. William Tunner, *Over the Hump* (1964; repr., Washington, D.C.: Office of Air Force History, United States Air Force, 1985), 153; Robert Rodrigo, *Berlin Airlift* (London: Cassell, 1960), 59.

6. C. K. Gailey to General Luyanchenko, November 10, 1948, Record Group 260, Entry 20 (A1), Airlift Correspondence Folder, National Archives, College Park, Md.

7. "Log of Tunner's Daily Activities," August 19, 1948, Roll 34920, Air Force Historical Research Agency, Maxwell AFB, Montgomery, Ala. (hereinafter referred to as AFHRA); Robert Jackson, *The Berlin Airlift* (Wellingborough: Patrick Stephens, 1988), 32.

8. Daniel Harrington, *The Air Force Can Deliver Anything! A History of the Berlin Airlift* (Ramstein Air Base, Germany: USAFE Office of History, 1998), 47.

9. Tunner, *Over the Hump,* 154.

10. Ibid., 153.

11. Ibid., 154.

12. Telephone interview with Dr. William Tunner, February 3, 2003; telephone interview with Betty Foreman Churchman, May 20, 2003; interview with T. Ross Milton, September 14, 2002.

13. Tunner, *Over the Hump,* 154–55.

14. Bettinger, "Report," 7; Rodrigo, *Berlin Airlift,* 60.

15. Bettinger, "Report," 7; Lt. Col. Billy Hoppe, "Lieutenant General William H. Tunner in the China-Burma-India 'Hump' and Berlin Airlifts," Air War College, Air War University, Maxwell Air Force Base, Montgomery, Ala., 1995, 17–18.

16. John Ohlinger, "C-54 Skymatser," in Robin Higham, *Flying American Combat Aircraft of World War II: 1939–45 (Mechanicsburg,* Pa.: Stackpole Books, 2004), 128.

17. Frank Donovan, *Bridge in the Sky* (New York: David McKay, 1968), 119; U.S. Air Force Oral History Interview with Lt. Gen. William H. Tunner, October 5–6, 1976, K239.0512-911, AFHRA, 97–98; Tunner, *Over the Hump,* 173–74.

18. Clayton Knight, *Lifeline in the Sky: The Story of the US Military Air Transport Service* (New York: William Morrow, 1957), 62–63; W. Tunner interview, AFHRA, 98.

19. Bettinger, "Report," 7; Sterling Bettinger to William Tunner, October 10, 1960, Roll 34938, AFHRA.

20. Albert Lowe, "The Smell of C-54 Engines, Rain and Snow," http://www .konnections.com/airlift/lowe.htm, August 16, 2004; J. B. McLaughlin, "Berlin Airlift," *IFR,* June 1998, 6.

21. Michael Froelich, "Air Lift Breaks the Berlin Blockade," *Flying,* October 1948, 23; Robert Sterling, *When the Airlines Went to War* (New York: Kensington Books, 1997), 268; "A Special Study of Operation 'Vittles,'" *Aviation Operations* 11 (April 1949): 38–39.

22. The best descriptions of a typical flight are in Roger G. Miller, *To Save a City: The Berlin Airlift, 1948–1949* (College Station: Texas A&M University Press, 2000), 128–29, and "Vittles," 21–22. There is a very clear map of these flight paths in Clayton Knight, *Lifeline in the Sky: The Story of the US Military Air Transport Service* (New York:

William Morrow, 1957), 59. Haydock, *City under Siege,* 239–40, gives a good description of how the Fulda Beacon worked. See also Tunner, *Over the Hump,* 173.

23. Interview with T. Ross Milton, September 14, 2002.

24. Ibid.; T. Ross Milton, "Inside the Berlin Airlift," *Air Force Magazine,* October 1998, 49.

25. Thomas Parrish, *Berlin in the Balance, 1945–1949: The Blockade, the Airlift, the First Major Battle of the Cold War* (Reading, Mass.: Perseus Books, 1998), 274, 290; Miller, *To Save a City,* 167.

26. Tunner, *Over the Hump,* 168.

27. Robert Rodrigo, *Berlin Airlift* (London: Cassell, 1960), 182; Ann Tusa and John Tusa, *The Berlin Airlift* (New York: Atheneum, 1988), 180; Tunner, *Over the Hump,* 185; Robert Jackson, *The Berlin Airlift* (Wellingborough: Patrick Stephens, 1988), 125, 129–30.

28. Jackson, *Berlin,* 130; Tusa and Tusa, *Airlift,* 249; David Tragg, *Airlift* (Novato, Calif.: Presidio Press, 1986), 81; "A Personal Account By: Col. Charles S. Allen," http://www.konnections.com/airlift/callen.htm, August 16, 2004; Frank Donovan, *Bridge in the Sky* (New York: David McKay, 1968), 128; Major Edward Wittel, "Interview: Mr. Airlift, Lieutenant General William H. Tunner," *Airlift Operations Review* 3 (April–June 1981): 6; Richard Collier, *Bridge Across the Sky: The Berlin Blockade and Airlift* (New York: McGraw-Hill, 1978), 164.

29. *Time,* July 5, 1948, 22.

30. Henry Holden, *The Legacy of the DC-3* (Brawley, Calif.: Wind Canyon Books, 2002), 181; interview with T. Ross Milton, September 14, 2002.

31. Miller, *To Save a City,* 96; Combined Airlift Task Force, "A Report on the Airlift, Berlin Mission," 168.7158-293, AFHRA, 18–19; "Points of Disagreement on Preliminary Analysis of Lessons Learned," Roll 34921, AFHRA.

32. Miller, *To Save a City,* 162–63.

Chapter 9

1. Raymond Towne, "Tunner and the Saga of Airlift," *Air University Review* 16 (November–December 1964): 95; Robert Rodrigo, *Berlin Airlift* (London: Cassell, 1960), 67; telephone interview with Earl Morrison, March 12, 2003; Gail Halvorsen, *The Berlin Candy Bomber* (Bountiful, Utah: Horizon, 1997), 64.

2. Daniel Harrington, *The Air Force Can Deliver Anything! A History of the Berlin Airlift* (Ramstein Air Base, Germany: USAFE Office of History, 1998), 105; telephone interview with Earl Morrison, March 12, 2003; U.S. Air Force Oral History Interview with Maj. Gen. Richard Bodycombe, May 28–29 and September 25, 1985, K239.0512-1691, Air Force Historical Research Agency, Maxwell AFB, Montgomery, Ala. (hereinafter referred to as AFHRA), 11; William Tunner, *Over the Hump* (1964; repr., Washington, D.C.: Office of Air Force History, United States Air Force, 1985), 177.

3. Edwin Gere, *The Unheralded: Men and Women of the Berlin Blockade and Airlift* (Victoria, B.C.: Trafford Publishing, 2003), 119.

4. "Log of Tunner's Daily Activities," Roll 34920, AFHRA.

5. Roger G. Miller, *To Save a City: The Berlin Airlift, 1948–1949* (College Station: Texas A&M University Press, 2000), 91.

6. Memo, "Narrative of Air Installation Difficulties During Period of 26 June 1948 to Date," May 21, 1949, Roll 34926, AFHRA.

7. "Closing of Berlin Airport Turns a Page of History," *International Herald Tribune,* July 20, 2004; "A Special Study of Operation 'Vittles,'" *Aviation Operations* 11 (April 1949) 58; *Grieben's Guide Books: Berlin, Potsdam and Environs* (Berlin: Albert Goldschmidt, 1929), 21, 36; *New York Times,* May 20, 2008.

8. Tunner, *Over the Hump,* 169–70; interview with T. Ross Milton, September 14, 2002.

9. Arthur Pearcy, *Berlin Airlift* (Shrewsbury: Airlife, 1997), no pagination; Charles Murphy, "Berlin Airlift," *Fortune,* November 1948, 91; Michael Haydock, *City under Siege: The Berlin Blockade and Airlift* (Washington, D.C.: Brassey's, 1999), 32; Miller, *To Save a City,* 61; "Vittles," 58.

10. Thomas Parrish, *Berlin in the Balance, 1945–1949: The Blockade, the Airlift, the First Major Battle of the Cold War* (Reading, Mass.: Perseus Books, 1998), 274.

11. Interview with T. Ross Milton, September 14, 2002. Milton's story is confirmed in a reference in the February 3, 1949, entry in "Log of Tunner's Daily Activities," Roll 34920, AFHRA.

12. Miller, *To Save a City,* 110; "Vittles," 60–62.

13. Robert Jackson, *The Berlin Airlift* (Wellingborough: Patrick Stephens, 1988), 61; Parrish, *Berlin in the Balance,* 275; interview with T. Ross Milton, September 14, 2002.

14. As noted, H. P. Lacomb was impossible to find. His story is drawn from John Man, *Berlin Blockade* (New York: Ballantine Books, 1973), 90–91; Frank Donovan, *Bridge in the Sky* (New York: David McKay, 1968), 133, 135.

15. Miller, *To Save a City,* 108–10; Max Charles, *Berlin Blockade* (London: Allen and Unwin, 1959), 113.

16. The story of taking down the Tegel towers comes from Mark Arnold-Foster, *The Siege of Berlin* (London: Collins, 1979), 65; Ann and John Tusa, *The Berlin Airlift* (New York: Atheneum, 1984), 305; Haydock, *City under Siege,* 248; Donovan, *Bridge in the Sky,* 138; Parrish, *Berlin in the Balance,* 277; Tunner, *Over the Hump,* 213; Miller, *To Save a City,* 113–14; Jackson, *Berlin,* 64. See also Memo, C. D. Sullivan to Commanding General, USAFE, October 28, 1948, in Berlin Airlift Files, Box II, Folder 9, History Office, Air Mobility Command, Scott AFB, Ill.

17. Daniel Harrington, "Against All Odds," *American History Illustrated* (February 1982): 35; interview with T. Ross Milton, September 14, 2002.

18. Tunner, *Over the Hump,* 170; Parrish, *Berlin in the Balance,* 288.

19. Miller, *To Save a City,* 50; Haydock, *City under Siege,* 195; Donovan, *Bridge in the Sky,* 68.

20. Tunner, *Over the Hump,* 209; T. Ross Milton, "Inside the Berlin Airlift," *Air Force Magazine,* October 1998, 50.

21. Material on Fassberg's shortcomings comes from Parrish, *Berlin in the Balance,* 302 and Harry Moseley, "Medical History of the Berlin Airlift," *United States Armed Forces Medical Journal* 1 (November 1950): 1252–58.

22. Haydock, *City under Siege,* 195; Jackson, *Berlin,* 73.

23. William Tunner, "A Case of Identity," *Aerospace Historian* 16 (Summer 1969): 32; Parrish, *Berlin in the Balance,* 302; letter from Catherine Gibson to William Tunner, November 4, 1960, Roll 34938, AFHRA.

24. Letter from Catherine Gibson to William Tunner, November 4, 1960, Roll 34938, AFHRA.

25. Roger Launius and Coy Cross, II, *MAC and the Legacy of the Berlin Airlift,* K300.04-61, AFHRA, 42–43; interview with T. Ross Milton, September 14, 2002.

26. Milton, "Inside," 61.

27. Richard Malkin, *Boxcars in the Sky: The Thrilling Story of Flying Cargo* (New York: Import Publications, 1951), 271.

28. Milton, "Inside," 61; interview with T. Ross Milton, September 14, 2002; interview with Ann Tunner, October 15, 2002.

29. David Clay Large, *Berlin* (New York: Basic, 2000), 406.

30. The discussion of coal and the airlift comes from Donovan, *Bridge in the Sky,* 67; Harrington, "Against," 14; D. M. Giangreco and Robert Griffin, *Airbridge to Berlin: The Berlin Crisis of 1948, Its Origins and Aftermath* (Novato, Calif.: Presidio Press, 1988), 171. See also Gere, *Unheralded.* P. 120.

31. Franklin Davis Jr., *Come as a Conquerer: The United States Army's Occupation of Germany, 1945–1949* (New York: Macmillan, 1967), 215; Miller, *To Save a City,* 155.

32. Giangreco and Griffen, *Airbridge to Berlin,* 130; "Airlift to Berlin," *National Geographic Magazine,* May 1949, 531.

33. Information on Berlin's POL comes from Combined Airlift Task Force, "A Report on the Airlift, Berlin Mission," 168.7158-293, AFHRA, 51; Arthur Pearcy, *Berlin Airlift* (Shrewsbury: Airlife, 1997), 80.

34. "Report on Airlift," 51; Miller, *Save,* 155–56.

35. Rodrigo, *Berlin Airlift,* 230–31; Eric Morris, *Blockade: Berlin and the Cold War* (New York: Stein and Day, 1973), 116; Henrik Bering, *Outpost Berlin: The History of the American Military Forces in Berlin, 1945–1994* (Chicago: Edition Q, 1995), 110; Tusa and Tusa, *Airlift,* 258; Donovan, *Bridge in the Sky,* 153; Arnold-Foster, *Siege,* 80; Memo to Economics Branch, OMG, March 10, 1949, Records Group 260, Entry 1259 (A1), Box 492, Folder Miscellaneous—Airlift In, National Archives, College Park, Md.

36. *Business Week,* April 10, 1948, 116; *Life,* July 19, 1948, 75.

37. *Life,* July 19, 1948, 75; Deane and David Heller, *The Berlin Crisis: Prelude to World War III?* (Derby, Conn.: Monarch Books, 1961), 96; *Newsweek,* May 9, 1949, 32; Joseph Loeb, "Opportunity in Berlin," *New Republic,* November 7, 1949, 14; Office of Military Government, U.S. Sector, Berlin, *A Four Year Report,* 1949, 42, 119; *U.S. News and World Report,* October 21, 1949, 28.

38. "Report on Airlift," 52.

39. William Stivers, "The Incomplete Blockade," *Diplomatic History* 21 (Fall 1997): 584; *Task Force Times,* April 1, 1949.

40. Tusa and Tusa, *Berlin,* 262.

41. Memo from HQ AIRLIFT TASK FORCE PROV SGD TUNNER to CIN-CEUR, August 8, 1948; memo from William Tunner to Commander in Chief, European Command, Berlin, August 7, 1948. Both in Records Group 260, Entry 20 (A1), Box 5, Airlift Correspondence Folder, National Archives, College Park, Md.

42. Bering, *Outpost,* 112; David Wragg, *Airlift* (Novato, Calif.: Presidio Press, 1986), 79; Tusa and Tusa, *Berlin,* 263; Donovan, *Bridge in the Sky,* 189; Tunner, *Over the Hump,* 206; *Four Year Report,* 40.

43. *Four Year Report,* 62; "Berlin Attitudes On The Air Lift—Future Trends," Report No. 141, Opinion Surveys Branch, Information Services Division, Records Group 260, Entry 118 (A1), Box 457, Folder 141, National Archives, College Park, Md.; Howard Siepen, "Berliners Dauntless," *Christian Science Monitor,* November 13, 1948, 5; Parrish, *Berlin in the Balance,* 224–25.

44. Paul Fussell, *The Boys' Crusade: The American Infantry in Northwestern Europe, 1944–1945* (New York: The Modern Library, 2003), 161; interview with T. Ross Milton, September 14, 2002; Alexandria Richie, *Faust's Metropolis: A History of Berlin* (New York: Carroll & Graf, 1998), 668; Tunner, *Over the Hump,* 217.

45. Arnold-Foster, *Siege,* 82; Haydock, *City under Siege,* 263; Chase Woodhouse, "Women of Berlin," *Survey Graphic,* December 1949, 6.

46. "Special Study," 14; Woodhouse, "Women," 496.

47. *Four Year Report,* 61; Miller, *To Save a City,* 171; Ruth Andreas-Friedrich, *Battleground Berlin: Diaries 1945–1948* (New York: Paragon House, 1990), 246.

48. Woodhouse, "Women," 496; Tusa and Tusa, *Airlift,* 271; Frank Howley, *Berlin Command* (New York: G. P. Putnam's Sons, 1950), 231.

49. Jackson, *Berlin Airlift,* 88; Richard Collier, *Bridge across the Sky: The Berlin Blockade and Airlift* (New York: McGraw-Hill, 1978), 56.

50. Interview with Saul Kagan, October 16, 2002.

Chapter 10

1. Interview with T. Ross Milton, September 14, 2002; telephone interview with Dorothy Towne, March 31, 2003.

2. Daniel Harrington, *The Air Force Can Deliver Anything! A History of the Berlin Airlift* (Ramstein Air Base, Germany: USAFE Office of History, 1998), 44; telephone interview with Dorothy Towne, March 31, 2003; telephone interview with Charles Ernst, April 14, 2003.

3. Harrington, *Deliver Anything,* 44; telephone interview with Betty Foreman Churchman, May 20, 2003.

4. Roger Launius, "Berlin Airlift," *Air Power History* 36 (Spring 1989): 13; Thomas Parrish, *Berlin in the Balance, 1945–1949: The Blockade, the Airlift, the First*

Major Battle of the Cold War (Reading, Mass.: Perseus Books, 1998), 302; interview with T. Ross Milton, September 14, 2002.

5. Launius, "Berlin Airlift," 15; Robert Owen, "Creating Global Airlift in the United States Air Force, 1945–1977" (Ph.D. diss., Duke University, 1992), 70; *Newsweek,* October 18, 1948, 50; Ann and John Tusa, *The Berlin Airlift* (New York: Atheneum, 1984), 256.

6. Vladimir Zwass, "E-Commerce," *Encyclopedia Britannica Online,* April 2, 2003; *Task Force Times,* April 14, 1949. In the 1960s, while working for DuPont, Guilbert devised a standard form for electronic messages used for tracking shipping cargoes.

7. Memo to General Tunner, May 30, 1949, Roll 34921, Air Force Historical Research Agency, Maxwell AFB, Montgomery, Ala. (hereinafter referred to as AFHRA); Combined Airlift Task Force, "A Report on the Airlift, Berlin Mission," 168.7158-293, AFHRA, 51.

8. William Tunner, *Over the Hump* (1964; repr., Washington, D.C.: Office of Air Force History, United States Air Force, 1985), 174; telephone interview with Dorothy Towne, March 31, 2003.

9. Interview with Ann Tunner, October 15, 2002.

10. "A Manual of Aircrew Ground and Flight Procedures for Airlift Aircraft," April 15, 1949, Roll 34927, AFHRA.

11. In all fairness, the service was training beginners, flying combat aircraft, and transitioning to jets. My thanks to Roger G. Miller for putting this into context.

12. "Report on the Airlift," 41–45; Press Release, May 13, 1949, "Summary of the Berlin Airlift," Roll 34921, AFHRA; telephone interview with Dorothy Towne, March 31, 2003; telephone interview with Gail Halvorsen, April 21, 2003. The best source on fatalities is the comprehensive record in Roger G. Miller, *To Save a City: The Berlin Airlift, 1948–1949* (College Station: Texas A&M University Press, 2000), 204–209.

13. Halvorsen's story comes from Gail Halvorsen, *The Berlin Candy Bomber* (Bountiful, Utah: Horizon Publishers, 1997), 24–27, 97–128. See also Harold Nufer, "Uncle Wiggly Wings," *Air Power History* 36 (Spring 1989): 27–29.

14. Interview with Ann Tunner, October 15, 2002; telephone interview with Earl Morrison, March 12, 2003; telephone interview with Gail Halvorsen, April 21, 2003; interview with T. Ross Milton, September 14, 2002.

15. Tunner, *Over the Hump,* 207–209; "Report on the Airlift," 53.

16. Telephone interview with Dorothy Towne, March 31, 2003; Dave Bettinger with Brigadier General Sterling Bettinger, "Year 2000 Emergency Management: A Parallel to the Berlin Airlift," http://www.year2000.com/archive/bettinger.html, 11, October 7, 2002; interview with T. Ross Milton, September 14, 2002.

17. This story is in Halvorsen, *The Berlin Candy Bomber,* 136–44.

18. "Narrative Report of the 60th Troop Carrier Wing from a Supply Standpoint," Roll 34927, AFHRA.

19. U.S. Air Force Oral History Interview with Lt. Gen. William H. Tunner, October 5–6, 1976, K239.0512-911, AFHRA, 98–99.

20. "Report on the Airlift," 55.

21. Ibid., 69; "Narrative Report of Traffic Section, June 29, 1949," Roll 34926, AFHRA.

22. "Report on the Airlift," 56; "Orion," "The Berlin Airlift," *Journal of the Royal United Services Institute for Defence Studies* (February 1949): 84; Miller, *To Save a City,* 146.

23. Miller, *To Save a City,* 146–50; "Report on the Airlift," 57; Tunner, *Over the Hump,* 181.

24. Roger Launius, "Berlin Airlift," *Air Power History* 36 (Spring 1989): 16; "Report on the Airlift," 31.

25. "Report on the Airlift," 58–59.

26. For a discussion on the problems with tie-downs, see Tusa and Tusa, *Airlift,* 261.

27. Interview with T. Ross Milton, September 14, 2002.

28. "Report on the Airlift," 73.

29. "Briefing by Maj. William L. Tudor," December 2, 1948, Roll 34922 AFHRA; Tunner interview, AFHRA, 95.

30. Bill Gilbert, *The Seasons: Ten Memorable Years in Baseball and in America* (New York: Citadel Press, 2003), 85.

31. "Special Report Upon the Effect of the Berlin Airlift On Activities at the Rhein/Main Terminal," Roll 34926, AFHRA; "Loving Couple, Alter Bound, Confused by Vittles Run-Around," Roll 34928, AFHRA.

32. "History Summary of the Billeting Section," Roll 34926, AFHRA; "Special Report," Roll 34926, AFHRA; American Women in Occupied Berlin, "Operation Vittles Cook Book," January 1949, 43.

33. Interview with Rollin Ashbaugh, AFHRA; Harry Moseley, "Medical History of the Berlin Airlift," *United States Armed Forces Medical Journal* 1 (November 1950): 1261; Michael Haydock, *City under Siege: The Berlin Blockade and Airlift* (Washington, D.C.: Brassey's, 1999), 250, 252.

34. "Narrative Report of the 60th Troop Carrier Wing and Subordinate Units From a Personnel and Administrative Standpoint," June 30, 1949, Roll 34927, AFHRA; "Narrative Report on Special Services," June 3, 1949, Roll 34926, AFHRA; Moseley, "Medical History," 1261; Lieutenant R. D. Nauman, "Medical Aspects of 'Operation Vittles,'" *Journal of Aviation Medicine* 22 (February 1951) 8; Harrington, *Deliver Anything,* 81.

35. *Task Force Times,* August 28 and September 3, 1948, January 11, 1949.

36. Ibid., September 18, 1948.

37. *Stars and Stripes,* August 14, 1948; *Task Force Times,* September 18, 1948, and January 12, 1949.

38. *Task Force Times,* August 23, 1948.

39. *Ibid.,* March 14 and 28, 1949.

40. Richard Malkin, *Boxcars in the Sky: The Thrilling Story of Flying Cargo* (New York: Import Publications, 1951), 272.

41. *Newsweek,* August 23, 1948, 10.

42. Halvorsen, *The Berlin Candy Bomber,* 96–97; Robert Jackson, *The Berlin Airlift* (Wellingborough: Patrick Stephens, 1988), 127.

43. *Task Force Times,* February 26, 1949.

44. Ibid., October 12, 13, 29, 1948.

45. John Schuffert, *Airlift Laffs,* interview with T. Ross Milton, September 14, 2002.

46. Raymond Towne, "Tunner and the Saga of Airlift," *Air University Review* 16 (November–December 1964): 96; John Schuffert, *Airlift Laffs.*

47. Jake Schuffert, *Fassberg Diary,* Roll 34927, AFHRA.

48. Historical Division Intelligence, T-2, Air Technical Service Command, Wright Field, "Development of Transport Airplanes and Air Transport Equipment, Part VI, Four-Engine Transports," *Journal of the American Aviation Historical Society* 46 (Fall 2001): 217–18.

49. Nicholas Williams, "Globemaster," *Journal of the American Aviation Historical Society* 25 (Summer 1980): 90, 94; Nicholas Williams, *Aircraft of the Unites States' Military Air Transport Service, 1948 to 1966* (Leicaster: Midland Publishing, 1999), 126.

50. Robert Rodrigo, *Berlin Airlift* (London: Cassell, 1960), 136; Williams, "Globemaster," 94.

51. *Task Force Times,* September 24, 1948, and May 5, 1949; *Washington Daily News,* August 24, 1948. There is a picture of officials in front of a C-74 in Arthur Pearcy, *Berlin Airlift* (Shrewsbury: Airlife, 1997), no pagination.

52. Jackson, *Berlin Airlift,* 74; U.S. Air Force Oral History Interview with Maj. Gen. Richard Bodycombe, May 28–29, 1985, and September 25, 1985, K239.0512-1691, AFHRA, 12–13; *Time,* July 4, 1949, 18.

53. *Task Force Times,* November 13, 1948; *Aviation Week,* July 25, 1949, 7, and May 2, 1949, 15; Tunner, *Over the Hump,* 202–203; United Aircraft Corporation, *The Bee-Hive,* October 1948, 2–3.

54. *Aviation Week,* January 17, 1949, 16–17; William Tunner to Muir Fairchild, April 4, 1049, Roll 34921, AFHRA.

55. "A Special Study of Operation 'Vittles,'" *Aviation Operations* 11 (April 1949): 5.

Chapter 11

1. Edwin Gere, *The Unheralded: Men and Women of the Berlin Blockade and Airlift* (Victoria, B.C.: Trafford Publishing, 2003), 113.

2. "Log of Tunner's Daily Activities," November 8, 1948, Roll 34920, Air Force Historical Research Agency, Maxwell AFB, Montgomery, Ala. (hereinafter referred to as AFHRA); D. M. Giangreco and Robert Griffin, *Airbridge to Berlin: The Berlin Crisis of 1948, Its Origins and Aftermath* (Novato, Calif.: Presidio Press, 1988), 127.

3. Roger G. Miller, *To Save a City: The Berlin Airlift, 1948–1949* (College Station: Texas A&M University Press, 2000), 131; William Tunner, *Over the Hump* (1964; repr., Washington, D.C.: Office of Air Force History, United States Air Force, 1985), 182; Stewart Powell, "Berlin Airlift," *Air Force Magazine,* June 1998, 61.

4. "Report on the Airlift," 61; John Christie, "Tunner Outlines 'Ideal' Cargo Plane," *Aviation Week & Space Technology* 50 (January 17, 1949): 17.

5. "A Special Study of Operation 'Vittles,'" *Aviation Operations* 11 (April 1949): 86–90; *Task Force Times,* January 6, 1949.

6. Combined Airlift Task Force, "A Report on the Airlift, Berlin Mission," 168.7158-293, AFHRA, 22.

7. The story of Tunner and Clay is recorded in Tunner, *Over the Hump,* 182–83.

8. Memo from William Tunner to Laurence Kuter, July 6, 1948, Box I, Folder 1, Berlin Airlift Files, History Office, Air Mobility Command, Scott AFB, Ill.; memo from William Tunner to Laurence Kuter, August 3, 1948, Box IV, Folder 31, Berlin Airlift Files, History Office, Air Mobility Command, Scott AFB, Ill.

9. Memo from William Tunner to Laurence Kuter, August 3, 1948; memo from Laurence Kuter to William Tunner, September 2, 1948. All in Box IV, Folder 31, Berlin Airlift Files, History Office, Air Mobility Command, Scott AFB, Ill.

10. "Report of the Deputy for Operations and Training on Operation Vittles at Rhein-Main Air Force Base, III-Intelligence Section," Roll 34926, AFHRA; and Louis W. Conroy Jr. to Commanding Officer, 61st Air Base Group, May 25, 1949, Roll 34926, AFHRA; U.S. Air Force Oral History Interview with Lt. Gen. William H. Tunner, October 5–6, 1976, K239.0512-911, AFHRA, 93; memo from Warren Chase to Theodore Hadraba, August 6, 1947, Records Group 260, Entry 1153 (A1), Box 31, Suspicious Jokers Folder, National Archives, College Park, Md.

11. W. Tunner interview, AFHRA, 94.

12. Tunner, *Over the Hump,* 183; W. Tunner interview, AFHRA, 93.

13. "Conroy to Commanding Officer," 2; Frank Donovan, *Bridge in the Sky* (New York: David McKay, 1968), 117; Interview with Major Jack Payne, Head of Maintenance, Oberpfaffenhoven Air Force Depot, Oberpfaffenhoven, Germany, 24 September 1948, 2-5234-1, AFHRA, 3; Tunner, *Over the Hump,* 183.

14. Telephone interview with Dorothy Towne, March 31, 2003, interview with Ann Tunner, October 15, 2002.

15. Tunner, *Over the Hump,* 180; telephone interview with Betty Foreman Churchman, May 20, 2003.

16. *Time,* September 27, 1948, 25.

17. Biographical Data on General John Kenneth Cannon, K110.7004-68, AFHRA.

18. Interview with Ann Tunner, October 15, 2002.

19. Thomas Parrish, *Berlin in the Balance, 1945–1949: The Blockade, the Airlift, the First Major Battle of the Cold War* (Reading, Mass.: Perseus Books, 1998), 292.

20. T. Ross Milton, "Inside the Berlin Airlift," *Air Force Magazine,* October 1998, 63; interview with T. Ross Milton, September 14, 2002.

21. H. H. Arnold to Lt. General John K. Cannon, September 25, 1945, 519.9701-16, AFHRA; John K. Cannon to General H. H. Arnold, October 17, 1945, 519.9701-16, AFHRA; interview with Ann Tunner, October 15, 2002; W. Tunner interview, AFHRA, 101.

22. E-mail from Daniel Harrington to Robert Slayton, May 6, 2005.

23. Parrish, *Berlin in the Balance,* 289.

24. The account of Tunner's early interactions with Cannon comes from Tunner, *Over the Hump,* 188–90.

25. Ibid., 190–91; W. Tunner interview, AFHRA, 102.

26. Parrish, *Berlin in the Balance,* 293.

27. Daniel Harrington, *The Air Force Can Deliver Anything! A History of the Berlin Airlift* (Ramstein Air Base, Germany: USAFE Office of History, 1998), 59.

28. Miller, *To Save a City,* 136.

29. Parrish, *Berlin in the Balance,* 268.

30. Miller, *To Save a City,* 137; Parrish, *Berlin in the Balance,* 268; "Vittles," 90.

31. Miller, *To Save a City,* 138; Michael Haydock, *City under Siege: The Berlin Blockade and Airlift* (Washington, D.C.: Brassey's, 1999), 233.

32. Haydock, *City under Siege,* 233.

33. Telephone interview with Dorothy Towne, March 31, 2003; Tunner, *Over the Hump,* 190.

34. Tunner, *Over the Hump,* 193; "Vittles," 81; interview with Ann Tunner, October 15, 2002.

35. Operational Difficulties Statements, December 14, 1948, Box II, Folder 8, Berlin Airlift Files, History Office, Air Mobility Command, Scott AFB, Ill.

36. Tunner, *Over the Hump,* 193–94.

37. "Report of the Deputy for Operations and Training of Operation Vittles at Rhein/Main Air Force Base," Roll 34926, AFHRA; Major Edward Wittel, "Interview: Mr. Airlift, Lieutenant General William H. Tunner," *Airlift Operations Review* 3 (April–June 1981): 5.

38. The story of Tunner, Hope, and Symington is drawn from Tunner, *Over the Hump,* 194–97.

39. William Tunner to Laurence Kuter, August 16, 1948, Box IV, Folder 31, Berlin Airlift Files, History Office, Air Mobility Command, Scott AFB, Ill.

40. Memo from Captain Hogg to General Tunner, December 23, 1948, Box I, Folder 1, Berlin Airlift Files, History Office, Air Mobility Command, Scott AFB, Ill.

41. Raymond Towne, "Tunner and the Saga of Airlift," *Air University Review* 16 (November–December 1964): 97; interview with T. Ross Milton, September 14, 2002.

42. "Narrative of Air Installations Difficulties During Period of 26 June to Date," May 21, 1949, and handwritten letter to General Tunner, signature illegible, September 13, 1949. All in Roll 34921, AFHRA.

43. Interview with T. Ross Milton, September 14, 2002.

44. Muir Fairchild to William Tunner, April 8, 1949, Container 4, Military Air Transport Service Folder, Muir Fairchild Papers, Library of Congress, Washington, D.C.

45. Laurence Kuter to Hoyt Vandenberg, Container 46, Command-Transport Folder, Hoyt Vandenberg Papers, Library of Congress, Washington, D.C.

46. Gere, *Unheralded,* 54.

47. Material on Nathan Twining is from "Nathan Farragut Twining," http://www.arlingtoncemetray.net/ntwining.htm, November 24, 2004. Problems with Tunner's later career can be found in Phillip Meilinger, *Hoyt Vandenberg* (imprint by Air Force History and Museums Program, 1980), 235 n. 64.

Chapter 12

1. Arthur Pearcy, *Berlin Airlift* (Shrewsbury: Airlife, 1997), no pagination; Thomas Parrish, *Berlin in the Balance, 1945–1949: The Blockade, the Airlift, the First Major Battle of the Cold War* (Reading, Mass.: Perseus Books, 1998), 237; Daniel Harrington, *The Air Force Can Deliver Anything! A History of the Berlin Airlift* (Ramstein Air Base, Germany: USAFE Office of History, 1998), 14.

2. Mark Magnan, "The Berlin Blockade" (M.A. thesis, George Washington University, 1956), 89; Percy Winner, "Berlin Dreads the Winter," *New Republic,* October 11, 1948, 14; Collie Small, "Berlin's Winter of Fear," *Collier's,* February 21, 1948, 17; Ruth Andreas-Friedrich, *Battleground Berlin: Diaries 1945–1948* (New York: Paragon House, 1990), 247; *Christian Century,* December 4, 1948, 1334.

3. Parrish, *Berlin in the Balance,* 279.

4. William Tunner, "A Case of Identity," *Aerospace Historian* 16 (Summer 1969): 31; *Newsweek,* July 12, 1948, 28; Combined Airlift Task Force, "A Report on the Airlift, Berlin Mission," 168.7158-293, Air Force Historical Research Agency, Maxwell AFB, Montgomery, Ala. (hereinafter referred to as AFHRA), 61; W. Phillips Davison, *The Berlin Blockade* (Princeton, N.J.: Princeton University Press, 1958), 196–97.

5. *Newsweek,* October 4, 1948.

6. Michael Haydock, *City under Siege: The Berlin Blockade and Airlift* (Washington, D.C.: Brassey's, 1999), 243–44; Ann and John Tusa, *The Berlin Airlift* (New York: Atheneum, 1948), 307; D. M. Giangreco and Robert Griffin, *Airbridge to Berlin: The Berlin Crisis of 1948, Its Origins and Aftermath* (Novato, Calif.: Presidio Press, 1988), 157–58; Parrish, *Berlin in the Balance,* 202; "Ruined Berlin," *New Republic,* December 13, 1948, 13.

7. Eric Morris, *Blockade: Berlin and the Cold War* (New York: Stein and Day, 1973), 102; Roger G. Miller, *To Save a City: The Berlin Airlift, 1948–1949* (College Station: Texas A&M University Press, 2000), 168; *Aviation Week,* November 15, 1948, 14; Harrington, *Deliver Anything,* 74; memo from William Tunner to William McKee, December 1, 1948, Box II, Folder 15, Berlin Airlift Files, history Office, Air Mobility Command, Scott AFB, Ill.; Anfrei Cherny, *The Candy Bombers: The Untold Story of the Berlin Airlift and America's Finest Hour* (New York: G. P. Putnam's Sons, 2008), 452. The story of Howard Myers is in Stewart Powell, "Berlin Airlift," *Air Force Magazine,* June 1998, 57–58.

8. Office of Military Government, U.S. Sector, Berlin, *A Four Year Report,* 1949, 31; Pearcy, *Airlift;* Robert Jackson, *The Berlin Airlift* (Wellingborough: Patrick Stephens, 1988), 92; Andreas-Friedrich, *Battleground,* 251; Harrington, *Deliver Anything,* 75.

9. Roger Launius and Coy Cross, II, *MAC and the Legacy of the Berlin Airlift,* K300.04-61, AFHRA, 46–47; Henry Holden, *The Legacy of the DC-3* (Brawley, Calif.: Wind Canyon Books, 2002), 181.

10. Miller, *To Save a City,* 61.

11. Harrington, *Deliver Anything,* 77; Interview with Major Walter G. Wilson, USAF, Deputy Communications Officer, USAFE, August 30, 1948, 2-5234-1, AFHRA, 4; Pearcy, *Airlift,* no pagination; "Report on the Airlift," 37.

12. William Adams, "Transport Air Power in Action," *Aviation Week,* February 28, 1949; Parrish, *Berlin in the Balance,* second picture section; Robert Sterling, *When the Airlines Went to War* (New York: Kensington Books, 1997), 266.

13. Parrish, *Berlin in the Balance,* 281; Miller, *To Save a City,* 125; Roger Launius, "Berlin Airlift," *Air Power History* 36 (Spring 1989): 16; Wilson interview, 3.

14. "Launius, "Berlin Airlift," 17; "A Special Study of Operation 'Vittles,'" *Aviation Operations* 11 (April 1949): 34–35; Ardy Friedberg, "The Berlin Airlift," *The Gazette* (Colorado Springs), June 22, 1998.

15. Henrik Bering, *Outpost Berlin: The History of the American Military Forces in Berlin, 1945–1994* (Chicago: Edition Q, 1995), 104; Robert Jackson, *The Berlin Airlift* (Wellingborough: Patrick Stephens, 1988), 83; J. B. McLaughlin, "Berlin Airlift," *IFR,* June 1998, 8, 9.

16. *Aviation Week,* January 31, 1949, "Vittles," 43; Frank Donovan, *Bridge in the Sky* (New York: David McKay, 1968), 122; Jackson, *Berlin,* 82; United Aircraft Corporation, *The Bee-Hive,* October 1948, 26.

17. Harrington, *Deliver Anything,* 77; Mark Arnold-Foster, *The Siege of Berlin* (London: Collins, 1979), 61; telephone interview with Gail Halvorsen, April 21, 2003; interview with T. Ross Milton, September 14, 2002.

18. Aubrey Cookman Jr., "Life Line to Berlin," *Popular Mechanics,* February 1949, 286; Miller, *To Save a City,* 121.

19. "Vittles," 66; Max Charles, *Berlin Blockade* (London: Allen and Unwin, 1959), 114.

20. "Report on the Airlift," 39.

21. Miller, *To Save a City,* 126–27; Roger Launius, "The Berlin Airlift," *Airlift* (Summer 1988): 15; Nicholas Williams, *Aircraft of the United States' Military Air Transport Service, 1948 to 1966* (Leicester: Midland Publishing, 1999), 24.

22. Miller, *To Save a City,* 140–43; "Vittles," 116; Parrish, *Berlin in the Balance,* 280; Haydock, *City under Siege,* 226–27.

23. Figures on tonnage and flights come from Miller, *To Save a City,* 201, and from *Operation Vittles Briefing,* Roll 34922, AFHRA.

24. Charles, *Berlin Blockade,* 121.

25. *Time,* March 7, 1949, 30; "Summary of the Berlin Airlift," May 13, 1949, Roll 34921, AFHRA; Charles, *Berlin Blockade,* 119–20.

26. Telephone interview with Earl Morrison, March 12, 2003; interview with Ann Tunner, October 15, 2002; *New York Herald-Tribune,* November 18, 1948; interview with T. Ross Milton, September 14, 2002; telephone interview with Dorothy Towne, March 31, 2003.

27. Interview with Ann Tunner, October 15, 2002; interview with T. Ross Milton, September 14, 2002; Maj. William McKinney, "Lieutenant General William H. Tunner, Father of the Military Airlift Command," Air Command and Staff College, Air University, Maxwell AFB, Montgomery, Ala., Report Number 87-1700, 17.

28. "Log of Tunner's Daily Activities," Roll 34920, AFHRA.

29. This account is drawn from my interview with T. Ross Milton, September 14, 2002.

30. The trip to Spain is mentioned in William Tunner, *Over the Hump* (1964; repr., Washington, D.C.: Office of Air Force History, United States Air Force, 1985), 215, and was also confirmed by Earl Morrison in a phone interview with him on March 12, 2003. See also "Log of Tunner's Daily Activities," Roll 34920, AFHRA; interview with T. Ross Milton, September 14, 2002.

31. Tunner, *Over the Hump*, 218–19; Dave Bettinger with Brigadier General Sterling Bettinger, "Year 2000 Emergency Management: A Parallel to the Berlin Airlift," http://www.year2000.com/archive/bettinger.html, 8, October 7, 2002.

32. Miller, *To Save a City*, 174; U.S. Air Force Oral History Interview with Lt. Gen. William H. Tunner, October 5–6, 1976, K239.0512-911, AFHRA, 128.

33. Tunner, *Over the Hump*, 221; W. Tunner interview, AFHRA, 130.

34. Telephone interview with Earl Morrison, March 12, 2003.

35. Tunner, *Over the Hump*, 221–22; Office of Military Government, U.S. Sector, Berlin, *A Four Year Report*, 1949, 32; Pearcy, *Airlift*, no pagination.

36. Interview with T. Ross Milton, September 14, 2002; W. Tunner interview, AFHRA, 128–29.

37. Letter from Sterling Bettinger to William Tunner, October 10, 1960, Roll 34938, AFHRA; Miller, *To Save a City*, 174–75.

38. Pearcy, *Airlift*, no pagination; Parrish, *Berlin in the Balance*, 323–24.

39. Miller, *To Save a City*, 183; *Aviation Week*, June 20, 1949, 16; Pearcy, *Airlift*, no pagination.

40. Jackson, *Berlin Airlift*, 9; Miller, *To Save a City*, 184–85; Richard Collier, *Bridge Across the Sky: The Berlin Blockade and Airlift* (New York: McGraw-Hill, 1978), 158.

41. *Time*, April 25, 1949, 27; Clayton Knight, *Lifeline in the Sky: The Story of the US Military Air Transport Service* (New York: William Morrow, 1957), 65.

42. Deane and David Heller, *The Berlin Crisis: Prelude to World War III?* (Derby, Conn.: Monarch Books, 1961), 98–99; Tunner, *Over the Hump*, 223; Haydock, *City under Siege*, 276.

43. Miller, *To Save a City*, 201–202; Tusa and Tusa, *Berlin*, 256; *Aviation Week*, February 28, 1949, 77; Harrington, *Deliver Anything*, 103.

44. "The Airlift Safety Record," Box I, Folder 1, Berlin Airlift Files, History Office, Air Mobility Command, Scott AFB, Ill.

45. Jon Sutherland and Dianne Canwell, *The Berlin Airlift: The Salvation of a City* (Gretna, La.: Pelican Publishing, 2008), 178; Cherny, *Candy Bombers*, 510–11.

46. Roger Launius, "Lessons Learned, Berlin Airlift," *Air Power History* 36 (Spring 1989): 23; Charles Murphy, "The Berlin Airlift," *Fortune*, November 1948, 89.

47. *Aviation Week*, February 28, 1949, 78.

48. *Task Force Times*, May 7, 1949.

49. *Time*, October 18, 1948, 30; Murphy, "Airlift," 90; Richard Malkin, *Boxcars in the Sky: The Thrilling Story of Flying Cargo* (New York: Import Publications, 1951), 259–60.

50. Interview with T. Ross Milton, September 14, 2002; telephone interview with Dorothy Towne, March 31, 2003; interview with Ann Tunner, October 15, 2002.

Chapter 13

1. "History of Military Air Transport Service, January–June 1950," 300.01 V. 1, Air Force Historical Research Agency, Maxwell AFB, Montgomery, Ala. (hereinafter referred to as AFHRA); Robert Owen, "Creating Global Airlift in the United States Air Force, 1945–1977" (Ph.D. diss., Duke University, 1992), 82–83.

2. Troop Carrier was separate from ATC and MATS, so Tunner was never in charge of those operations. Nevertheless, as Roger G. Miller observed in a private communication, "Tunner would say 'airlift is airlift.'"

3. Interview with T. Ross Milton, September 14, 2002.

4. Richard Malkin, *Boxcars in the Sky: The Thrilling Story of Flying Cargo* (New York: Import Publications, 1951), 248.

5. "Owen, "Airlift," 85; David Wragg, *Airlift* (Novato, Calif.: Presidio Press, 1986), 83; Warren Thompson, "Haulin' Buns," *Airpower,* January 2004, 30; William Leary, *Anything, Anywhere, Anytime: Combat Cargo in the Korean War* (Washington, D.C.: Air Force History and Museums Program, 2000), 2–3; Major Edward Wittel, "Interview: Mr. Airlift, Lieutenant General William H. Tunner," *Airlift Operations Review* 3 (April–June 1981): 6.

6. U.S. Air Force Oral History Interview with Lt. Gen. William H. Tunner, October 5–6, 1976, K239.0512-911, AFHRA, 113.

7. Nicholas Williams, *Aircraft of the United States' Military Air Transport Service, 1948 to 1966* (Leicester: Midland Publishing, 1999), 29; Malkin, *Boxcars,* 242.

8. Owen, "Airlift," 95; W. Tunner interview, AFHRA, 113–15; William Tunner, *Over the Hump* (1964; repr., Washington, D.C.: Office of Air Force History, United States Air Force, 1985), 228; Leary, *Anywhere,* 3.

9. Tunner, *Over the Hump,* 231; Leary, *Anywhere,* 5.

10. Tunner, *Over the Hump,* 231; Owen, "Airlift," 98–99.

11. Maj. William McKinney, "Lieutenant General William H. Tunner, Father of the Military Airlift Command," Air Command and Staff College, Air University, Maxwell AFB, Montgomery, Ala., Report Number 87-1700, 20.

12. Leary, *Anywhere,* 12–13, 34; Tunner, *Over the Hump,* 246–48.

13. The account of Operation Chromite comes from Leary, *Anywhere,* 7–9; McKinney, "Lieutenant General William H. Tunner," 20–21; Clay Blair, *The Forgotten War: America in Korea, 1950–1953* (New York: Doubleday, 1987, 358–61.

14. Leary, *Anywhere,* 5–6; Charles Miller, *Airlift Doctrine* (Montgomery, Ala.: Air University Press, 1988), 197.

15. For material on the Chosin Reservoir campaign, I relied on Martin Russ, *Breakout: The Chosin Reservoir Campaign, Korea 1950* (New York: Fromm International, 1999); Jim Wilson, *Retreat, Hell!: The Epic Story of the 1st Marines in Korea* (New York: Pocket Books, 1988); Eric Hammel, *Chosin: Heroic Ordeal of the Korean War* (Novato, Calif.: Presidio Press, 1981). On the airlift, see Leary, *Anywhere,* 15–26; Tunner, *Over the Hump,* 254–58. The figure on casualty evacuation is in Russ, *Breakout,* 376.

16. Wilson, *Retreat,* 298; Russ, *Breakout,* 357.

17. Russ, *Breakout,* 358.

18. *Time,* December 18, 1950.

19. Leary, *Anywhere,* 26–27.

20. This incident is in W. Tunner interview, AFHRA, 118–21.

21. For the fight with Cannon, see Miller, *Airlift Doctrine,* 212–16.

22. Major General William Tunner, "Global Air Transportation," Roll 34920, AFHRA.

Chapter 14

1. Robert Owen, "Creating Global Airlift in the United States Air Force, 1945–1977" (Ph.D. diss., Duke University, 1992), 110–14.

2. U.S. Air Force Oral History Interview with Lt. Gen. William H. Tunner, October 5–6, 1976, K239.0512-911, Air Force Historical Research Agency, Maxwell AFB, Montgomery, Ala. (hereinafter referred to as AFHRA), 124–27.

3. Raymond Towne, "Tunner and the Saga of Airlift," *Air University Review* 16 (November–December 1964): 97.

4. *Washington Daily News,* June 9, 1952, Roll 3492, AFHRA, 1; Major General William H. Tunner, "Technology or Manpower," Roll 34938, AFHRA, 1.

5. Tunner, "Technology or Manpower," 3.

6. W. Tunner interview, AFHRA, 127; William Tunner, *Over the Hump* (1964; repr., Washington, D.C.: Office of Air Force History, United States Air Force, 1985), 281.

7. Tunner, *Over the Hump,* 281.

8. Telephone interview with Robin Olds, September 1, 2004.

9. Nicholas Williams, *Aircraft of the United States' Military Air Transport Service, 1948 to 1966* (Leicaster: Midland Publishing, 1999), 43.

10. *Belleville News-Democrat,* July 1, 1958, Roll 34936, AFHRA; Interview of Major General Russell L. Waldron, February 6, 1987, AFHRA, 10.

11. Owen, "Airlift," 188.

12. Tunner, *Over the Hump,* 298.

13. Discussion of the defense intellectuals is drawn from Owen, "Airlift," 206–207.

14. Stanley Ulanoff, *MATS: The Story Of the Military Air Transport Service* (New York: Franklin Watts, 1964), 89–90; John Mills to William Tunner, March 3, 1959, Roll 34909, AFHRA.

15. Frederick Thayer Jr., "National Airlift Policy" (Ph.D. diss., University of Denver, 1963), 421–22; Claude Witze, "The Gap In Our Military Air Transport," *Air Force and Space Digest,* May 1960, 47–50.

16. Clay Blair Jr., "Uncle Sam's Orphan Airline," *Saturday Evening Post,* June 4, 1960, 31, 77–79; "MATS' Wings Still Clipped," *Business Week,* May 28, 1960, 153–56; telephone interview with Dorothy Towne, March 31, 2003.

17. Rebecca Noel, "Exercise Big Slam/Puerto Pine," K300.04-13, AFHRA, 8–9.

18. Special Subcommittee on National Military Airlift of the House Committee on Armed Services, *Hearings,* 86th Congress, 2nd Session, March 8–April 22, 1960, 4166,

4177; Lieutenant General William Tunner, "Strategic Airlift," *Air University Quarterly Review* 12 (Winter–Spring 1960–1961): 112; Charles Miller, *Airlift Doctrine* (Montgomery, Ala.: Air University Press, 1988), 265; Witze, "Gap," 47; Noel, "Big Slam," 28, 38; Major General W. P. Fisher to MATS, April 8, 1960, K303.01.v.5, AFHRA; Ulanoff, *MATS,* 13.

19. Owen, "Airlift," 241; clippings can be found in Roll 34936, AFHRA.

20. Subcommittee Hearings, 4793; Duane Cassidy, "MAC's Moment of Truth," *Air Force Magazine,* September 1986, 116; Miller, *Airlift Doctrine,* 265–66; Noell, "Big Slam," 41–42.

21. Miller, *Airlift Doctrine,* 251–52.

22. Owen, "Airlift," 234; interview with Ann Tunner, October 15, 2002.

23. Clippings in Roll 34936, AFHRA; Subcommittee Hearings, 4156, 4815–16; Miller, *Airlift Doctrine,* 262–63.

24. Owen, "Airlift," 250; Maj. William McKinney, "Lieutenant General William H. Tunner, Father of the Military Airlift Command," Air Command and Staff College, Air University, Maxwell AFB, Montgomery, Ala., Report Number 87-1700, 25–26; Special Subcommittee on National Military Airlift of the House Committee on Armed Services, *Report,* 86th Congress, 2nd Session, March 8–April 22, 1960, 4051–55.

25. Clippings in Roll 34936, AFHRA.

26. Ibid.

27. Miller, *Airlift Doctrine,* 276.

28. Harold Martin, *Starlifter: The C-141, Lockheed's High-Speed Flying Truck* (Brattleboro, Vt.: Stephen Greene Press, 1972), 26, 36–37.

29. Ulanoff, *MATS,* 95; Phyllis Emert, *Transports and Bombers* (New York: Julian Messner, 1990), 46–49; Owen, "Airlift," 270; "C-141 Starlifter—The First Jet-powered Airlifter," http://wwwlmaeronautics.com/products/airmobility/c-141, July 8, 2003.

30. Martin, *Starlifter,* xi, 57; Ulanoff, *MATS,* 106.

31. Martin, *Starlifter,* 21, 61.

32. Press Release, "Thirty Years of Airlift," Roll 34936, AFHRA.

33. Brian Ditcham, "Of Air Transport—Reply," H-WAR, September 21, 2003; *New York Times* Business Day, April 10, 2004; Major Brian Maddox, "'Checkmate on the Northern Front,'" *Armor* (September–October 2003): 7; Lieutenant Colonel Patrick Warren, "Yes, TF-163 Armor was the First Unit to Air Insert M1A1s," *Armor* (March–April 2004): 46.

34. James Dunnigan, *The Perfect Soldier: Special Operations, Commandos, and the Future of U.S. Warfare* (New York: Citadel Press/Kensington, 2003), 238.

Epilogue

1. William Tunner to Timothy Seldes, July 15, 1959, Roll 34938, Air Force Historical Research Agency, Maxwell AFB, Montgomery, Ala. (hereinafter referred to as AFHRA); interview with Ann Tunner, October 15, 2002; Ann Tunner interview, October 6, 1976, U.S. Air Force Oral History, K239.0512-912, AFHRA, 34–35; Special

Subcommittee on National Military Airlift of the House Committee on Armed Services, *Hearings,* 86th Congress, 2nd Session, March 8–April 22, 1960, 4845.

2. Clippings in Roll 34936, AFHRA; Michael Haydock, *City under Siege: The Berlin Blockade and Airlift* (Washington, D.C.: Brassey's, 1999), 29; material from the Tunner Personnel File provided by the National Personnel Records Center, St. Louis, Mo.

3. Robert Owen, "Creating Global Airlift in the United States Air Force, 1945–1977" (Ph.D. diss., Duke University, 1992), 254.

4. *Life,* August 19, 1961, 40.

5. William Tunner, "Strategic Airlift," *Air University Quarterly Review* 12 (Winter–Spring 1960–61): 104–19 and "Do We Want a Supersonic Transport Or An $89 Trip to Europe," *Air University Review* 16 (March–April 1965): 18–21.

6. Booton Herndon to William Tunner, November 4, 1963; Erwin Christlieb and Warner Stichnote to William Tunner, May 7, 1963; William Tunner to Booton Herndon, handwritten note, October 20. All in Roll 34938, AFHRA.

7. Raymond Towne, "Tunner and the Saga of Airlift," *Air University Review* 16 (November–December 1964): 96; "Characters who were on my staff at various times," Roll 34938, AFHRA.

8. Letters to William Tunner from Sterling Bettinger, October 10, 1960; T. R. Milton, September 20, 1960; and Charles Murphy, April 28, 1960. All in Roll 34938, AFHRA.

9. Ann Tunner interview, October 6, 1976, U.S. Air Force Oral History, K239.0512-912, AFHRA, 35; Towne, "Tunner," 97; C. V. Glines, "Berlin Airlift Commander," *American Heritage* 20 (October 1969): 96; telephone interview with Ann Tunner, July 16, 2003.

10. For an interesting article with some parallels to Tunner's life, see William O'Neil's piece on Billy Mitchell, "Transformation," in *U.S. Naval Institute Proceedings* (March 2002): 100–104.

11. William Hallahan, *Misfire* (New York: Charles Scribner's Sons, 1994), 298–305, 317.

12. On how the U.S. Air Force changed in response to problems over Vietnam, see C. R. Anderegg, *Sierra Hotel: Flying Air Force Fighters in the Decade after Vietnam* (Washington, D.C.: Air Force History and Museums Program, 2001).

13. Telephone interview with Ann Tunner, July 16, 2003; *Airlift/Tanker Quarterly* (Fall 1995): 7.

Index